LIBERAL THOUGHT IN MODERN AMERICA

Dwight D. Murphey

Wichita State University

With a Foreword by

Otto Scott

Author and Lecturer

UNIVERSITY
PRESS OF
AMERICA

LANHAM • NEW YORK • LONDON

University Press of America,® Inc.

4720 Boston Way
Lanham, MD 20706

3 Henrietta Street
London WC2E 8LU England

British Cataloging in Publication Information Available

Library of Congress Cataloging in Publication Data

Murphey, Dwight D.
   Liberal thought in modern America.

   Bibliography: p.
   Includes index.
   1. Liberalism—United States—History.   I. Title.
JA84.U5M87   1987   320.5'1'0973   86-26659
ISBN 0-8191-5756-2 (alk. paper)
ISBN 0-8191-5757-0 (pbk. : alk. paper)

All University Press of America books are produced on acid-free
paper which exceeds the minimum standards set by the National
Historical Publication and Records Commission.

ACKNOWLEDGMENTS

For years, I have worked alone, separated from extreme isolation only by the knowledge that my ideas would join eventually the continuing "dialogue over the ages" that links thoughtful writers of all generations. It is for this reason that I am especially gratified to have found two distinguished conservative scholars ready to write Forewords for the final two volumes of this series. Their good will, support and critical evaluation provide me a window to what I hope will be a growing circle of friends in the world of thought. Again, I thank Arthur Shenfield for his fine contribution to <u>Socialist Thought</u>. And now I wish to thank, also, Otto Scott for his remarks here. I am aware that they may be excessively generous, especially in the comparison to Jose Ortega y Gasset; but if my work comes to be mentioned at all there will be enough undeserved slanders to more than offset the praise he gives me. I appreciate, too, the mildness with which he has voiced his reservations about my religious perspective. He is right, I think, in saying that my work has value even to those who feel themselves a cosmos apart from me on religion.

In preparing the notes that underlie this book, I received a great many hours of help from a sparkling young man of remarkable energy, ability and future potential--Dan Walker, who served as my graduate assistant during the 1985-6 academic year. Thanks, Dan, for all that wonderful help.

CONTENTS

FOREWORD

This is the final book in a quartet that began with a historical examination of what Dwight Murphey terms man's immaturity--an immaturity that leads him into discontent no matter what his circumstances or position.

The first volume of the quartet takes us through a marvelous sweep of the centuries, and constitutes an overview of the past, concluding with the present. It ends, unforgettably, with an objective description of our society, which has lost the allegiance of our intellectuals, who no longer defend us against totalitarianism.

This is a strong message; almost too strong for a single volume. Therefore Dr. Murphey wisely decided to examine, in depth, the major social and political philosophies that constitute contemporary, contradictory trends. These examinations occupy the remainder of the quartet.

In the course of this great undertaking, Dr. Murphey has persistently quoted from the writings of those he has examined. He has not followed the usual academic fashion of subsuming, or paraphrasing these views into his text and relegating their spokesmen to footnotes or to appendices. He has attached names to views. He has avoided the abstract and stuck to the particular as much as is possible in discussing ideas.

Dr. Murphey has followed this course in examining Socialism, Burkean Conservativism, Classical Liberalism and Modern Liberalism. He has not only traced the development of these philosophies, but their impact on the world through his particulars regarding their spokesmen and leaders.

This is an important approach, though persons caught in the passageways of political structures may not fully appreciate it, because ideas are what rule the world. Men move along the rails of

their ideas, however random their movements may
appear.

To understand movements, therefore, we must
understand ideas. But at the same time, we cannot
divorce ideas from the men they motivate. In
"Liberal Thought in Modern America," Dr. Murphey
has identified the modern liberal intellectual
community as promoting diverse and even contradictory programs in order to create influential power
blocs.

In order to accomplish this, Dr. Murphey
provides a mountain of evidence indicating that
modern liberal leaders have sedulously avoided
terming themselves Socialists, failed to create a
Socialist Party as such, but chose instead to
conceal their Socialism under the protective
coloration of the liberal label. In comparing
Socialist programs and principles with those advanced, defended or protected by modern liberals,
Dr. Murphey has proven that the difference is
almost entirely semantic.

On at least two occasions, Dr. Murphey
believes, the American liberal community "has come
very close to embracing totalitarian societies.
These were," he says, "the early 1930s and the
late 1960s...."

There was nothing in the least "liberal"
about these slips, any more than there is any
evidence of classical liberalism in the modern
liberal tendency to shout down opposition, to
engage in _ad_ _hominem_ methods of argument, or to
engage in blacklisting and censorship: all tactics
regularly employed by self-styled liberal cadres.

In uncovering the disguises of modern American liberalism, therefore, Dr. Murphey has made a
major contribution. He has clarified, in the most
scholarly manner, person after person and a stream
of events that reveal a consistent pattern of
dissimulation.

In the course of this searching examination, such figures as Herbert Croly, Theodore Roosevelt, Christopher Jencks, John Rawls, Robert Heilbroner, Robert Lekachman, Irving Howe and others appear in a new--and not a notably admirable--light.

For dissemblers should not be honored in any society. What Dr. Murphey has done has stripped the masks from many influential dissemblers.

In undertaking this task he has, as we all know, placed himself in a position of peril. It is a notorious fact of American life that anyone who takes issue with our liberal intellectuals can expect to encounter withering silence and private efforts to damage his career, or a torrent of abuse and public efforts to destroy his career.

In such a climate, it requires considerable moral courage to step forward even once. To do so in a major work that spans four volumes is extraordinary. I am proud to contribute a Foreword to such an eminent analysis, although I do not agree with all of Dr. Murphey's positions.

Not too long ago Dr. Robert Nisbet observed that he knew of no society that survived secularization. I tend to agree with that. I believe that the West, by breaking with its Christian heritage, at least on the top reaches of government, by that break began a terrible decline. Its dynamism began to ebb with its spiritual certainty.

Dr. Murphey sees this in part, and has made some very pertinent observations about the loss of a religion for which men are willing to die. On the other hand, we are witnesses to the fact that men will die even for religious substitutes, such as National Socialism, or Communism. Therefore this aspect of our situation may require more thought, more examination, more study.

But no such thought, examination or study will, or in my opinion can, negate or diminish what Dr. Murphey has produced. His analysis of immaturity and alienation carries the observations of Ortega y Gasset, whom he credits with his original inspiration, several steps beyond "The Revolt of the Masses."

These are steps that needed to be taken; an examination long overdue. All credit, then, to the scholar who has undertaken that task, and published his results.

Otto Scott
Murphys, California
15 August 1986

A NOTE TO THE READER

The project that I am now completing was begun in 1965, twenty-one years ago. When I started, I certainly did not anticipate that the subject would carry me into four volumes--of which this is the last.

The first book was <u>Understanding the Modern Predicament</u>. It presented an overview of certain themes in the history of Western civilization. The beginning chapter discussed the nature of what I have called "the modern predicament" and pointed to three factors that I would examine in detail.

The first of these picked up upon the analysis that was made by the Spanish philosopher Jose Ortega y Gasset in <u>The Revolt of the Masses</u>. At the same time it reflected some uneasiness that I felt about his thesis. In common with several authors, Ortega had pointed to an important fact about advanced civilization: that the average person has come to occupy all spaces, displacing the earlier aristocracies. Even though he pointed out that people exist at a higher level than ever before, he observed that the spiritual characteristics of this average humanity are mediocre.

Unfortunately, my own experience had confirmed Ortega's thesis. The mediocrity affects profoundly both our daily relations and the larger events of our society. Just the same, I felt the uneasiness that I have mentioned. In historical perspective, it was necessary to see this mediocrity not as a decline from a less fallible earlier condition, but as simply another manifestation of the fact that mankind has come only part of the way on the long journey from barbarism. A review of the earlier periods of Western civilization in Greece, Rome and the Middle Ages would show that periods of advanced civilization have been relatively brief. Mankind is in its infancy. My review of the immaturity occupied the first third of <u>Understanding the Modern Predicament</u>.

1

This historical review had the added advantage of showing the extent to which the modern age has been existentially open-ended. Modern Western society inherited a rich heritage but few, if any, satisfactory solutions. Because of this, it is not surprising that modern man has cast about in a crisis of consensus.

It has seemed to me that the second factor in the modern predicament has been the most important element in modern intellectual history: the alienation of the intellectual subculture from the predominant "bourgeois" culture. No other fact has been so central to the divisions and neuroses of the modern age. It would be impossible to understand the past two centuries without appreciating the role of alienation. An analysis of this alienation filled the middle third of <u>Understanding the Modern Predicament</u>. I then devoted the final third to a discussion of several episodes of modern history in light of the immaturity and alienation.

The first book could only point ahead to the third factor, which has been so extensive that it has been the subject of the next three volumes. It is that the divisions within the modern West have given rise to opposing "systems of interpretation," comprehensive ideologies by which people have sought to understand complex social reality. These ideas have then served as the atmosphere in which we live, guiding our understanding of ourselves and of the world.

Despite each ideology's conviction to the contrary, these mental systems are not themselves Truth, directly understood. They are devices developed by human beings to mediate social reality. The systems are profoundly affected by forces at work in the society. They are also powerful causal instruments in their own right. People act in the world as they perceive it. This means that their perceptions and those of others are part of the social reality, intermeshed with all other factors.

The second volume discussed two of these interpretive systems, Burkean conservatism and classical liberalism. The third examined socialist thought, and now the final volume will explore modern liberal thought in the United States. This will also discuss the New Left, the variation that emerged in the late 1950's and existed with explosive force in the Sixties before withering in the Seventies. Residuals of the New Left still strongly affect American life.

At the beginning of each book I have mentioned that the reader can take the book by itself with little difficulty but that the most serious readers should consider the series as a whole. It is the tension of the ideologies in a setting framed by the other factors that makes a deeper understanding possible.

. . . . .

This prefatory note is the best place for me to mention a peculiarity of modern liberal thought that has a bearing on one of my main themes.

In reviewing the other ideologies I have stressed the role of ideas, even though I have at the same time emphasized the importance of certain other forces which have provided the basis for something of a sociology of modern thought.

The history of American liberal thought, however, shows that ideas are sometimes the pawns of stubborn fact, not necessarily ultimate masters. Ideas have without question been important. Twentieth century Americans know the omnipresent "atmosphere" of liberal ideas. The stream of political action has largely reflected liberal attitudes. But during the past four years I have read extensively in the literature of liberalism: the almost 200 volumes of the The New Republic since it began publication in 1914, approximately 100 volumes of The Nation, and the books and articles of a good many liberal authors. A consequence of this reading is that it has become obvious to me

3

that American liberal thought has been essentially reactive. Liberal thought (which must be distinguished from liberalism's much more limited political agenda) has been buffeted about unmercifully. The result has been that the thinking has been literally pulled through several phases. Instead of an inexorable leading, there has been a pathetic following. The intellectual content has tagged along behind much larger forces than itself. Modern liberalism is the best example I know of of how an ideology can be, to a relatively high degree, impotent in the face of other forces.

The impression I received from its literature was one of pathos. It is likely that there has never been an ideology so unsure of itself and fragmented in its intellectual content while putting on so bold and monolithic a front. To conservatives, liberalism has, at least until recent years, seemed insurmountable. Even now it continues to command institutional action and public opinion with its fads and fancies. Nevertheless, liberal thinkers have shown an almost constant awareness of the thinness of their position and of how tentative a hold it has had vis-a-vis both the main culture and the intellectual world of the further-Left, which is the world that has counted most to them.

This thinness has been inherent in modern liberalism. Rather than representing a pure ideological model, this liberalism has constituted a tactical compromise within an ever-changing historical setting. It has rested uneasily in that compromise. There have been perpetual tendencies to slip off in either direction, toward the open field of the Left or toward a more accepting accommodation of the main culture. This is a situation that would have been shaky enough in any case; it has not helped that both the Left and the main culture have themselves been in constant change.

Liberalism thus runs counter to the notion that ideas are in all situations controlling. It is a mistake to hold to a naive version of the "lag theory" that "if an idea is accepted by the leading thinkers, society is bound to follow after a few years." While that is often true, a society is more complex than that suggests. Thus, I am not to be understood as saying that ideas are <u>exclusively</u> important. I am among those who say that the comprehensive mental systems for mediating social reality are <u>very</u> important, which is not the same thing. And yet, I have not been moved to point this out quite so emphatically earlier. The ideas of the Left have during much of my lifetime seemed to be sweeping the world. But the loss of elan within socialism and American liberalism has been so profound that the impression of the supreme power of those ideas no longer remains.

INTERPRETIVE ESSAY

Use of the term "liberal"

American conservatives have often objected to the way the word "liberal" has been used in the twentieth century. Those who are today called conservatives have placed quotation marks around "liberal" to indicate their belief that the word has in effect been misappropriated from the liberalism of the 19th century, which supported a very different set of values.

Although I agree with their concerns, I will not use the quotation marks. To do so would detract from the objective spirit that I hope readers have come to expect in my writing as I have reviewed the competing social philosophies.

My agreement with the point that my fellow conservatives make stems from my assessment of the differences between liberalism in its classical sense and the ideology that in twentieth century America has been known as liberalism. As I will make clear in this essay, I do not hold to the view that contemporary liberalism arose out of classical liberalism and merely added new dimensions to it. Rather, I see the two as having historically been enemies. The new liberalism was instantly and necessarily an adversary of the old.

Classical liberalism has been the philosophy of limited government and a free market; it has championed middle-class values; and it has been adamantly anti-socialist and anti-Communist. Its intellectual content is largely the product of the writing of the classical and neo-classical economists--such thinkers as Adam Smith, Frederic Bastiat, Ludwig von Mises and Friedrich Hayek. This sort of liberalism is today a part of what Americans call conservatism, which includes classical liberals, Burkean conservatives, and millions of

people who identify with capitalism and traditional American values without perhaps having a
distinctly formulated philosophical rationale for
doing so. (This is the sense in which I will use
the word "conservative" in this book unless I
indicate otherwise.)

The body of thought that during my lifetime
has commonly been called liberal, however, has
been a mixture of diverse tendencies, as we shall
see. Perhaps more than anything else, however, it
has represented the thinking of the world Left to
the extent that American intellectuals who have
wanted to stay on speaking terms with the American
mainstream have been able to embody it. It has
been the American socialism that has not seen its
way clear to call itself socialist.

Most of the time its thinking has coincided
with that of democratic socialism. This led me at
one point to consider defining it as "'social
democracy' applied in a politic way to the American context." But on at least two occasions it
has revealed a darker side; in the early 1930's
and the late 1960's its thinking has embraced, or
has come very close to embracing, totalitarian
socialism. This must necessarily give us second
thoughts about how precisely to classify it. At
other times it has amounted to little more than
the watered-down welfare statism and social-market
thinking that has been forced upon European
socialism by the failures (which many on the Left
have so acutely perceived) of the various attempts
at socialism.

Readers will understand, then, why I agree
with conservatives that the word "liberal," which
is the same word that was applied in the 19th
century to advocates of the free market, is suspect in its 20th century usage. It is a label
taken from one philosophy and applied to another
that is fundamentally antagonistic to it. Nevertheless, I shall use it in its currently accepted
sense, although frequently adding the adjective
"modern" to call to mind the difference from clas-

sical liberalism.

Relationship to socialism

It will be necessary for me to ask modern
liberal readers to hear me out. I realize that
what I have just said about the socialist content
of this liberalism is anathema to them. While
modern liberals have often admitted the relationship to socialism in the writing they have addressed to each other, it has been characteristic of
this liberalism to obscure this connection so far
as the American public is concerned. One of the
defining characteristics of a liberal in this
sense, as distinguished from those members of the
Left who have declared themselves socialists per
se, has been that he has been sensitive to the
fact that most Americans would not accept anything
directly labelled "socialist."

What I have just said is also anathema to
members of the far Left, who in their own frame of
reference see this accommodationist-style state
activism in either of three ways: as too much of a
cop-out to merit the socialist label; as a reformism that runs counter to the things-must-get-
worse-before-they-can-get-better school of revolutionary thinking; or as a shoring-up of capitalism
by those members of the bourgeoisie who are, from
the far Left's point of view, smart enough to see
that cooptation is the best defense against a full
on-rush of socialism. From the purity of their
own position, they are not prepared to acknowledge
how much socialist thinking really exists in
modern liberal thought.

We are reminded of how most, if not all,
anthologies of socialist thought omit the German
Historical School, apparently because the antholo-
gists' attention is drawn to the late-19th century
argument between the followers of Marx and Lassalle for supremacy in the German Social Democratic party.

9

When I suggest that modern American liberalism has been a product of the socialist worldview,
I realize that this is true only in major part. I
do not wish to obscure the other dimensions of
modern liberalism. A more complete definition
will have to reflect the ideology's relation to
the main culture, which it has both detested and
sought to exist within and to lead. Several
factors that are not themselves socialist will be
considered in the final part of this essay. Some
that we should note at least briefly at this time
are:

. That there has at all times, even in the
absence of socialist influence, been a movement
within American history that has wanted a more
active federal government. Much of what we think
of as liberal measures would probably have come
about, although perhaps in a somewhat more market-
oriented form, even if no socialist movement had
developed in Europe.

. That a number of secular tendencies
within American life, which have themselves had
nothing to do with socialist ideas, have created a
demand for a more politicized and centralized
life. Local loyalties, once quite strong, have,
for example, given way to a national identification because of mobility and communication.

. That classical liberal thinking, under
pressure since the early 19th century to defend
the main society from unremitting attack, lost its
critical and reformist posture. This has long
made it deficient in its formulation of the theory
of a market economy and, more broadly, of a free
society. This weakness has included ignoring the
problem of imperfect markets and giving too little
attention to the institutional framework that a
well-functioning market requires. Some of the
concerns that modern liberalism has voiced have
pertained to things that a more complete classical
liberalism would have addressed.

That most of the measures that are

called liberal are only a shadow of what liberal thought has called for. They are more the product of interest-group pressures and of the efforts of liberal politicians. (Virtually none of the politicians ever admit to a socialist rationale and, somewhat surprisingly, virtually all have been attacked as unworthy by liberal intellectuals.) These interest groups and politicians act within the concrete reality of the American political scene, although they are clearly influenced by liberal ideology.

Modern liberalism has been, then, a mixture that has existed, often in varying forms, within a specific and changing historical setting. I doubt whether any ideology has ever been rooted more relativistically in its own time and place. No ideology perhaps has been less candid about its aspirations or quite so opportunistic in its quest for approval by blocs that have often not fully sensed or shared those aspirations. Because of this, it would be a mistake to say that all who have called themselves modern liberals have either consciously or subconsciously been socialists.

Many no doubt have been socialists; but others have come to the ideology by routes that have had little to do with a socialist worldview. This acknowledges a fact that will be important later when we seek to explain the fragmentation and loss of elan that have plagued modern liberalism since the beginning and especially since World War II.

It is worth considering whether I have not overstressed the role of socialist thinking by ignoring the possibility that modern liberalism is a "middle way" between capitalism and socialism, influenced by both but actually amounting to a separate form.

Such a view seems plausible and has been seriously asserted. But it is contradicted by the facts of liberal history. We need to distinguish between liberal _thought_ and the popular version of

11

liberalism that has been preoccupied with the agenda of specific measures that liberal politicians have kept before the country at any given time. The halfway measures that have made up the agenda have made it difficult for conservatives to convince others that there is a socialist content to the liberal program. It has only been in the intellectual dimension that the socialist content has appeared consistently and clearly.

We will review the extent of the liberal intellectual identification with socialist models. This identification includes the enthusiasm for worker-controlled "industrial democracy" during and immediately after World War I; the infatuation with Soviet Russia's centralized planning during the 1920's, '30's and '40's; the great number of openly socialist authors within liberalism prior to World War II; and the fact that even since that war the main liberal thinkers have been men who, sometimes after the fact, have declared themselves socialists. I am thinking especially of Michael Harrington, Gunnar Myrdal, John Kenneth Galbraith, Christopher Jencks, Irving Howe and John Rawls, but secondarily of a great many others.

Liberal thought has never identified itself wholeheartedly with the "mixed society" model. The mixed society has been forced upon its intellectual community by circumstances.

<u>An historical review:</u>
<u>The condition of conservatism and liberalism</u>
<u>in early America</u>

Later chapters will discuss in detail many of the points I am about to make, but it is important in an overview to understand these points in their historical development and in the relationship that they bear to one another.

The generation of the Founding Fathers in the late 18th century was influenced by both of the main streams of social and political thought that

12

struggled for supremacy in that era. One of these was the vibrant classical liberalism that championed the Enlightenment and that was finding its best expression in the writings of Adam Smith and Jeremy Bentham. The other was Burkean conservatism. This conservatism gave philosophical form to the value-system of tradition, faith and hierarchy that had held sway in various forms in Europe during the Middle Ages and even during the Roman Republic.

In The Conservative Mind, Russell Kirk told of the extent to which that sort of conservative ethos informed early American thinking. Its influence was extensive. That is why it is a mistake to say, as Louis Hartz has, that the United States has been clearly liberal from the beginning. New England in particular, and eventually the South as it felt the pressure to defend slavery, kept a tie with this conservatism.

Nevertheless, the main spirit of the late 18th century was formed by the Enlightenment, which for quite a long time had been the onrushing opponent of that conservatism. Tolerant and deistic in religion, republican and constitutionalist in politics, free-market in its economic thinking under the influence of the Physiocrats and (as he became known) of Adam Smith, rationalist and increasingly empiricist in intellect, supportive of the individualism of the rising bourgeoisie, this spirit was liberal in the classical sense.

This liberal conception has formed an underlay that has constituted the American ideal for the two centuries that have followed. Despite the attack it has undergone from so many sides intellectually, this individualistic liberalism has been at the heart of the predominant commercial and middle class culture. The tremendous staying power and force of its view of the world is one of the main facts of American history. It has been against this underlay of ideas and aspirations that all other forces have had to contend, usually with considerable frustration.

Without diminishing that fact, it is important to appreciate that the intellectual foundations of this liberalism had only partially taken form in the 18th century.

Although its worldview had been developing for several centuries, it enjoyed no comprehensive philosophical statement. John Locke had expressed some of its elements, the Physiocrats others. Then in 1776 Adam Smith stated a rationale for the market system. He argued that a market system does in fact work. In this, he opposed the Mercantilists, who insisted it does not.

The work of the later classical and neoclassical economists, however, remained to be done in the 19th and 20th centuries. But even an economic rationale such as they supplied was not fully adequate, since there are spiritual, ethical, aesthetic, jurisprudential and other dimensions that a complete philosophical system must address.

One of the most damaging intellectual shortcomings, at least as we look back on classical liberalism from the 20th century, was that the 18th century's preoccupation with Natural Rights was intellectually related more to a deductive and somewhat fanciful rationalism than to empiricism. This means that it was not fully appropriate to the later development of the social sciences. To say this is not to blame the thinkers of the 18th century, but merely to point to something that explains why they have become increasingly irrelevant to modern intellectual culture.

Another problem was that this early liberalism lacked self-consciousness as an ideology. Classical economics was coming into its own in Europe, but liberals seemed to feel no need to formulate a complete and systematic theory of society and to see it as an integrated philosophy. They were practical men dealing with the specific problems of their day.

It is a shame that Franklin, Madison or Jefferson did not lay this sort of intellectual foundation in a form that future generations could look back to as a guiding text for the premises of a liberal society. (This is not surprising for a social system. The medieval value-system did not receive the Burkean intellectual statement until it had existed for many centuries and was so heavily under attack that it was about to expire.)

This remained true even as classical economics did its immensely productive work in the 19th century. When classical economics got into full swing with Ricardo, Senior, Say, James Mill and the others, its thinkers did not see themselves as stating a complete theory of society that included a good many value preferences and the reasons for them, but as laying a foundation for a deductive science of economics, which in fact was a much more limited project. I will hold off on commenting about John Stuart Mill, since he occupied the stage somewhat later and is important to the next phase of the history I am tracing.

Nor did classical liberalism enjoy a monopoly even in its unelaborated and un-self-conscious condition. In the late 18th century an articulate cadre of intellectuals rose to support hierarchy, faith, tradition and a hostile critique of the Industrial Revolution and of the rising individualism. Edmund Burke and Samuel Johnson come most immediately to mind. They supplied an intellectual defense of values that had long been implicit in medievalism.

Revulsion against the Enlightenment

What happened next was one of the most significant occurrences to affect the intellectual development of the modern world. It happened in Europe but was quickly reflected in the United States, which for most of its history has been an intellectual colony of Europe, as has most of the rest of the world.

I am referring to the revulsion against the Enlightenment that occurred when the French Revolution and the ensuing Napoleonic episode turned sour.

This revulsion skewered the Enlightenment on the lance of the Romantic reaction. A major part of European thought turned sharply against rationalism, empiricism, tolerance, individualism, the bourgeoisie, and classical liberalism. In Germany this gave rise to the thinking of such men as Novalis, Schlegel, Schleiermacher, de Maistre--and, mostly importantly, of Hegel. In England, Carlyle, Coleridge, Arnold, Ruskin and Southey were leaders in a somewhat tamer version. These men nevertheless expressed an intense alienation from the burgeoning bourgeois culture.

This revulsion both manifested and stimulated the "alienation of the intellectual," a force that has ranked among the most powerful causal agents during the 19th and 20th centuries.

Almost immediately Europe saw the rise of socialist ideology as intellectuals repudiated the bourgeoisie and commercial civilization and sought to gain numerical strength by an ideological alliance with all unassimilated and disaffected groups. By the 1830's and 1840's, socialist thought was coming into its own in Europe.

Outwardly it has seemed that these years were the high point of classical liberalism, which in a sense they were, but there is enormous significance in the fact that the classical liberal economist Frederic Bastiat in France felt almost totally isolated, and hungered for contact with the Manchester School of Cobden and Bright in England for at least some intellectual kinship.

The ideological thrust of a still-incomplete classical liberalism began to fail as the intellectual culture moved sharply to the left. This is evident in the life of John Stuart Mill, a leading classical economist who became quite dis-

16

affected with the commercial middle class's lack of attention to ideas, took an active interest in the conservative thinking of such a Romantic as Coleridge, and ultimately moved into the socialist camp at the end of his life.

The drying up of classical liberal intellectuality very largely deprived the middle class culture of Europe and America of the head and heart that it has so vitally needed. The intellectuals who remained behind within classical liberalism during the ensuing century and a half have done valiant work, but they have been far outnumbered and their tone has often been that of doctrinaire apologists rather than of original thinkers and reformers.

In the United States the victory of the Jeffersonians in the election of 1800 should have paved the way for a long period of classical liberal ascendancy. It did play a major role in establishing the "underlay" of classical liberal values that I have mentioned; and the Jeffersonian-Jacksonian liberalism did hold sway politically until 1861. But beginning in the early 19th century, its intellectual base was eroding. This was well before it had received a full philosophical exposition.

In his lecture "The New England Reformers" in 1844, Ralph Waldo Emerson looked back upon a quarter of a century of the strangest sort of intellectual dissatisfaction (in which he had shared). There had been "a fertility of projects for the salvation of the world," all expressing "the soul of the soldiery of dissent." At a time when most Americans were developing their reverence for the Constitution and when classical liberal concepts were guiding the majority political party, the literary culture, influenced profoundly by the thinking that was going on in Europe, declared the society sick.

If today we look back at that time with the expectation that a new republic, founded upon the

ideals of the Enlightenment, would have been full
of enthusiasm and hope, we are bound to be greatly
surprised. The intellectual tone was instead one
of despair and alienation.

It was still too early for an ideological
consensus to have formed around the alienation.
Nor was there yet a homogeneous subculture of
alienated intellectuality. During the years immediately preceding the Civil War, there were signs
of a growing socialist critique, as became evident
in the enthusiasm for Fourier that inspired a good
many utopian communities. And yet it was taking
at least a brief time for socialist philosophy to
germinate in Europe and to bridge the Atlantic.

After Jefferson's death in 1826, the divisions within American society between the North
and the South over tariffs and slavery increasingly turned the South away from its earlier classical liberalism and into a defense, largely on
Burkean-type grounds, of slavery.

After the Civil War

The Civil War consolidated the power of the
newly-formed Republican Party. This marked the
end of the supremacy of the Democratic Party, with
its Jeffersonian-Jacksonian commitment to the
limitation of the powers of the national government. The Republican Party was heir to the tradition of the Federalists and the Whigs, who had
favored a much more active national government.

Classical liberal insights that had once been
common ceased to be mentioned in presidential
messages to Congress, appearing again only briefly
when in the late 19th century Grover Cleveland, a
Democrat, vetoed aid to drought-stricken Texas
farmers. For the most part, the main culture went
through a period of little philosophical reflection, absorbed in its own expansion and activity.
After the Civil War, classical liberalism found
its principal expression in the legal profession,

18

where Constitutional thought was honed into a deductive science based on classical liberal desiderata.

In the academic and literary communities, classical liberalism continued to lack a self-conscious ideology. William Graham Sumner was a leading figure, drawing deeply from Herbert Spencer's defense of classical liberalism in England. But the tide was turning. Indeed, there was no movement as such calling itself "liberal" and prepared to fight for even so much as the retention of the name.

The decades following the Civil War saw the gradual coalescence of the American academic community into an ideologically homogeneous subculture. I say this advisedly, since anyone who has studied intellectual history knows how much real variety exists within any overall pattern. But there was a yearning for coalescence, as is evidenced by the letter that Henry Adams wrote to his brother Charles in 1862 expressing both alienation and a desire for "a national school of our own generation." And there was the continuing development of a socialist critique in place of the earlier "fertility of projects."

Influence of the German Historical School

The development of a homogeneous intellectual community with a common ideology was facilitated enormously by the migration of thousands of American graduate students to German universities, where they studied under the professors of the German Historical School. This migration was heaviest in the final quarter of the 19th century. The Historical School repudiated the "scientific pretensions" of classical economics and of the neo-classical Austrian School, and attacked the theoretical foundations of a market economy on relativistic grounds as being merely an analysis of relationships within a transitory historical period of bourgeois ascendancy. Its opposition to

19

classical economics was part of an overall animus toward a liberalism that was denounced as Philistine by so much of the European intellectual community.

The professors of the Historical School were known among themselves as "socialists of the professorial chair"--_katheder sozialisten_. They stood in close relationship to the Junker aristocracy as it installed the Bismarckian program of social welfare legislation. There has been considerable debate over whether theirs was a true socialism as distinct from a conservative cooptation of socialism. This same ambiguity has continued with regard to American liberalism itself.

The ambiguity is perhaps best resolved by the life story of Werner Sombart, who successively moved from being a leading member of the fourth generation of the Historical School to being a Marxist and then an enthusiastic adherent of Hitler. The thread that tied together all of these enthusiasms was his alienation against the bourgeoisie and his detestation of classical liberalism. His writing contains some of the more lucid explanations of socialist ideas.

The Historical School did not itself adopt the Marxism that was struggling for ascendancy among German socialists. Thus it did not support revolution or the theory of class struggle. The fact that it did not is important to its impact on the Americans who studied under it. These men returned to America as gradualists, not as revolutionaries.

Although it is not directly relevant to the ideological history I am relating, it is worthwhile to point out that the Historical School originated the empirical-statistical methodology, with its emphasis on monographs and the piling of fact upon fact often to the exclusion of theoretical connection among the facts, that has been so powerful a force within the American academic community throughout the 20th century. This methodological sway has formed a powerful intellectual orthodoxy. When combined with the self-absorbed credentialism that it has insisted upon, it has constituted a modern Scholasticism within American university life. I am no enemy to an intelligent empiricism, but during my years as a professor I have been in constant revolt against the trivialization and pseudo-scientific pretension that this orthodoxy has entailed. Needless to say, it carries within it not only its methodology but also a set of ideological suppositions that are far from scientifically neutral. What we know as the "social sciences" came into existence in their current form during this period and have to a very large extent reflected the Historical School.

What is important for us to grasp for the history of liberalism is that the experience with the Historical School represents the phase in which a common intellectual experience resulted in a shared ideology.

Taking on a style of dissimulation

During the same period, those who came to call themselves "liberal" in the new sense were making a fateful personal decision. Intellectuals who felt the alienation and drank deeply at the well of the European socialist philosophies sometimes chose, at considerable social and professional risk, to declare themselves openly as socialists, and sometimes as revolutionaries. Jack London is a prime example, although he managed to be accepted as one of America's most popular authors. A socialist movement flourished during the opening years of the 20th century.

But what typified the modern liberal as such, and has been his defining characteristic as distinct from these socialists, was his unwillingness to make so open a break with the main society. For this liberal there was a circumspection born out of a number of ingredients, which almost cer-

21

tainly included a less daring personal psychology and a sharper appreciation for both the individual and ideological benefits of not putting oneself too openly in jeopardy.

The individual who perhaps best exemplified the circumspection was Herbert Croly. Croly's book The Promise of American Life, published in 1909, is one of the monuments of American liberalism. This is so not so much for its content as for the fact that it is a masterpiece of dissimulation. He spoke of the book as "socialistic," but nowhere in it was there a direct endorsement of socialism. Croly continued this circumspection in his book Progressive Democracy, published in 1915, even though its content was clearly in line with the "industrial democracy" that was so much in vogue among British socialists at the time.

In late 1914 Croly was the leader among the group that founded The New Republic. Even though the other founders, Walter Weyl and Walter Lippmann, considered themselves socialists at the time, The New Republic was careful not to call itself socialist. This did not change until the early 1930's, when its editors were moved to throw caution to the winds.

Liberal orientation in Teens and Twenties

This refusal to make a clear ideological commitment led into the phases that followed. During the late teens and early 1920's, liberal thought centered around "industrial democracy."

This represented an infatuation with what was popular at the time among British socialists during the heyday of the Guild Socialist movement. The emphasis was on decentralization, which was consistent with the direction of much of 19th century socialist thought. Workers were ultimately to control industry from the bottom up. There was at the same time considerable enthusiasm for cooperatives—either of producers or consumers

22

and, with some thinkers, of both types. The pro-
fit-seeking entrepreneur and individual consumer
would be replaced by a grass-roots collectivism.

This was, of course, one of the clearly
socialist phases of modern liberal thought, even
though The New Republic avoided the socialist
label.

The decentralist approach of the Guild
Socialist movement lost favor among liberal intellectuals in the early 1920's when it was replaced
by enthusiasm for the Bolshevik Revolution and for
Soviet Russia's centralized model. The great light
that seemed to be shining during the 1920's was
from Soviet Russia, which was portrayed in idealistic hues by the many liberals who made the
pilgrimage.

Apparently, though, Soviet Russia's example
was too removed from what seemed possible here to
offer much real hope. Liberal thought slipped
into a funk. The 1920's was the decade of the
"Lost Generation" of literary expatriates and of a
counter-culture of Beatnik-like alienates in
Greenwich Village. Liberal thought lost focus on
social and political issues. Politically, the
Progressive movement made a final effort in the
1924 presidential election and then died out.

As editor the The New Republic, Herbert Croly
continued to personify the liberal mood, this time
by turning inward during the 1920's. The journal
called upon liberals to devote themselves to inner
self-examination. In contrast to the earlier
period, its editors and writers saw little worth
in theorizing about how to reform the existing
society, which they saw as steeped in Mammon.

This illustrates an important dynamic that
has been at work from the beginning as part of the
psychology of liberalism and of its associated
radicalisms: a cycle passing from a period of
despair, fatigue and withdrawal to one of yearning
for activity and from that to one of marked mili-

23

tancy and social action, all followed eventually by another period of exhaustion and withdrawal. This alternation reflects the psychology of the alienated intellectual. In Emerson's lecture "The New England Reformers" he spoke of the withdrawal of the "man of tender conscience," followed by that man's reentry into the world with "a ferment of activity 'for the salvation of the world.'"

The 1930's

After the Depression began in 1929 the mood changed again. The dissimulation that had masked the socialist worldview was no longer felt necessary. Overt socialism and enthusiasm toward the "Soviet experiment" filled the liberal journals.

By March, 1932, The New Republic went so far as to editorialize that "we are not liberals" and added that "the planning we have recommended is not designed to preserve the capitalist system." Liberal intellectuals had little enthusiasm for Franklin Delano Roosevelt during the 1932 campaign. In fact, The New Republic urged its readers to vote for Norman Thomas, the Socialist candidate. Under a committee of editors from 1933 to 1936, The Nation, the other major liberal journal, was avowedly socialist.

And yet the liberal intellectual community did manage, consistently with its long-standing preference for doing so, to keep at least one foot in the American political context. It warmed to Franklin Roosevelt during his first months in office. Those who favored the "New Nationalist" approach of fashioning corporate capitalism into a wing of government were hopeful about the National Recovery Administration, but it wasn't long before the N.R.A.'s industry-wide codes were seen not to reflect liberal social policy so much as the interests of the corporations themselves.

The Nation expressed sympathy for the New Deal, but also was able to say in 1934 that the

New Deal amounted to "a half-baked capitalism with so-called liberal trimmings."

The main fact about the intellectual history of the 1930's is that the liberal intellectual culture was far to the left of the New Deal, heavily preoccupied with the Soviet Union's 5-year plan and collectivization of agriculture. It defended the New Deal against attacks from the Right, but at the same time excoriated the administration bitterly. The New Deal was declared "sadly deficient" so far as a "thorough renovation of our society" was concerned.

This mood continued for _The New Republic_ until September, 1937. The Soviet Union had by that time stopped denouncing democratic socialists and liberals as "social fascists" and had called for a "United Front" against Hitler. The Communists lavished praise upon Roosevelt and the New Deal in direct opposition to their earlier denunciations. Whether consciously or unconsciously, the American liberal intellectual community, deeply absorbed in the color and texture of the Communist movement and its many front organizations, went along. In a sharp about-face, _The New Republic_ praised the New Deal, saying that "we have made more progress toward a socialized economy in the past four and a half years than in the two previous decades."

It is ironic that the New Deal had finally been accepted by the intellectual community just shortly before it began to lose whatever impetus Roosevelt's many inconsistencies had allowed it. _The New Republic_ had supported F.D.R. in his "court packing plan" in 1937 while still essentially sour toward him, and backed him in 1938 in his effort to purge certain conservative Democratic senators. But this was all quite late, since Republican gains in the congressional elections in 1938 made possible the coalition of conservative Democrats and Republicans that has possessed a veto in Congress ever since. (Only briefly after the election of 1964 did liberalism

25

again enjoy the combination of a liberal Congress and a liberal president.) In addition, the late 1930's saw the on-rushing international crisis further deflect Roosevelt from domestic reform.

Events in the Soviet Union were at the same time providing major shocks to American liberalism's love affair with Communism.

The liberal intellectual community had been willing to accept the enormities of Soviet brutality so long as whatever was done was in pursuit of "a good cause." It had turned a blind eye during Stalin's holocaust against the kulaks in 1932-33. A variously estimated three to seven million peasants were deliberately starved to overcome their resistance to the collectivization of their land. Fifty years later, in December, 1984, The New Republic's editors looked back and admitted frankly that "the scandal in the history of this journal is that in the '30's and '40's it accommodated to the zeitgeist (with occasional and important dissents) by downplaying at best and justifying at worst the crimes of Stalinism."

This acceptance of Communist atrocities started to erode when in 1934 Stalin began his purges of the other leaders among the Bolsheviks, many of whom were people known personally by American liberals. One thing followed another over a six year span. The two main liberal journals vacillated between justifying the purges and pleading agnosticism about them, but liberals were beginning to see the horror, slowly at first and then in larger numbers, as one atrocity was laid on top of another.

The crowning blow, after years of the United Front against Nazism, was the Hitler-Stalin Pact in August, 1939, especially when it was followed quickly by the invasion of Poland, first by the Nazi forces and then by those of the Soviets. The Soviet Union received the larger share of Poland's territory and by the end of 1939 had invaded Finland. In 1940 it attacked Estonia, Latvia and

Lithuania, absorbing them into the Soviet Union.

Nor was this all. Bitter divisions were spawned within America's liberal intellectual community by Stalin's purge of Leon Trotsky, who had been second only to Lenin as a leader of the Bolshevik Revolution. Trotsky was sent into exile after Lenin's death and was later charged with crimes against the Soviet Union. The preeminent American liberal philosopher John Dewey headed the American subcommission of an international body that inquired, over the objections of the Stalinists, into the facts concerning Trotsky. This was all capped by Stalin's having Trotsky murdered in Mexico in 1940. Each step of the way, liberals (and radicals of all shades on the Left) chose sides, bitterly attacking those on the other.

In the midst of this fragmentation, a cause that seemed to unite them was the Spanish Civil War. Socialists, anarchists and Communists fought together against the forces of General Franco. But this proved a mirage when the Communists proved the totalitarian bully on the block, seeking control by executing the others. John Dos Passos left the fold, gravitating eventually into conservatism, after he lost a friend in this way.

There would be reason to expect that these events would have seared an abiding hatred toward Communism into the thinking of American liberals. With some, they did. But the scene shifted again in June, 1941, when Hitler broke his Pact with Stalin by invading the Soviet Union. With some exceptions, the mood shifted back to enthusiastic acceptance of the Soviet Union. And when the United States became an ally of the Soviet Union after Pearl Harbor in December, 1941, the long-standing inclination of so many American liberals to favor the Soviet Union even became respectable and patriotic from the general American society's point of view.

It is important for us today to realize how much our perceptions are warped by the legacy of this bias. It continues to affect our view of the world. An example is that we continue to hear so many reminders about the Nazi's Holocaust, which is something the world should never forget, but almost none about the Gulags of the Soviets or the mass executions under Mao.

After World War II

After the war, the divisions that had come into being led to the formation of the Americans for Democratic Action by liberals who did not want to collaborate with Communists. Those further to the left formed the Progressive Citizens of America and in 1948 supported Henry Wallace in his third-party bid for the presidency.

An intensely alienated radicalism remained on the leftward fringe and laid the foundation for the later New Left and for the counter-culture of the 1960's and 1970's. Under the stimulus of the militancy of the civil rights, anti-poverty and anti-Vietnam War movements in the 1960's, much of American liberal intellectuality again flirted with the extremes of the Left and, as in the early 1930's, denounced liberalism per se. It is ironic that this undercutting of liberalism has been one of the more important causes of the success of American conservatism in the 1980's.

Since World War II, the principal fact about American liberalism has been its loss of thrust toward a comprehensive socialist vision, despite most of its leading thinkers considering themselves socialists. The coalition of conservative Democrats and Republicans in Congress, combined with the success of the Republican Party in electing a president much of the time, has made it seem remote and naive, as in the 1920's, to propose an overall program for the restructuring of American society. For the most part, liberal intellectuals have given up the attempt, although it would be a mistake to think that their attitudes have not been constantly at work in countless smaller ways within the bureaucracy, the media and academia.

Liberal presidents, when there has been one, have continued to offer the marginal, foot-in-the-door programs that have had to pass for liberal activism in the absence of a constituency for a thorough-going transformation of society. But even here they have mostly been stymied, as Truman was in his domestic program following the outbreak of the Korean War and as Kennedy and Carter were by the lack of a homogeneous and fully supportive liberal foundation. (We know how tenuous Carter's support was; Kennedy's weakness only becomes apparent to an outsider by a week-to-week reading of the liberal journals.)

After the 1964 election, Lyndon Johnson came closest to making a quantum leap, but it wasn't long before his Great Society lost its impetus. This resulted from a combination of factors: the sheer cost of the Vietnam War, along with the absorption of attention that the war entailed; the political and ideological cost of the anti-war movement, with the splitting of his base; and the quickly perceived failure, especially within liberalism, of his War on Poverty programs.

Although for liberalism the 1950's, 1970's and 1980's must be counted as periods of frustration and drift, the second half of the 1950's was typical of that phase of the liberal cycle that consists of an increased yearning for activity. Thus the late 1950's constituted a threshold period that was followed by the feverish activity of the 1960's.

During the 1970's, despite the political windfall that the Watergate scandal provided, the frustration, withdrawal and drift were again present. The Carter presidency was no exception to this. Carter combined qualities of a liberal technocrat with those of a Bible-belt fundamentalist that would have made the literati of the Harold Stearns generation early in the century blanch with horror. His nomination was a demon-

29

stration of the impotence of the intellectual elite.

This is an impotence that has always been present, since at no time in the history of liberalism have the literati been able to dictate the Democratic candidate. An awareness of this impotence has been a recurrent theme in liberal thought. But, of course, there are relative degrees of it, and the selection of Carter in the Democratic primaries of 1976 was one of its more evident manifestations.

Finally, after the defeat of Walter Mondale by President Reagan in 1984, there was much talk among liberals themselves about the death of liberalism and even of Europe's "social democracy." Whether the obituary notices are premature can only be known with time.

Much of this is bound to be surprising to the average American conservative, to whom liberalism has often seemed, at least until the mid-1970's, an irresistible juggernaut. Conservatives in general have not been aware of the fragmentation and self-conscious impotence that have so long been part of both liberal thought and the liberal political movement.

If the inherent weaknesses within liberalism result ultimately in its demise, this will only in small measure have been a result of the strengths of American conservatism. This is so because conservatism, when seen apart from the weight of an overwhelmingly non-reflective general society, has been almost as impotent and fragmented as liberalism itself.

Causes of the failure

The factors that have been most important to American liberalism's failure have been:

. The constant fact of blockage, imposed by an

electorate that has been basically content with the society as it is in the post-New Deal era, giving neither liberal nor conservative an unobstructed mandate. When many years ago Werner Sombart observed that socialism in America would founder on shoals of apple pie and ice cream, he understood the essentially middle class aspirations of the average American.

. The crumbling of the socialist faith in Europe in light of the enormities committed by the Communist regimes and of the disillusionment that experience has caused socialists to feel toward their own earlier visions.

. The loss of self-confidence within liberalism as a result of the bitter denunciation of it by the New Left. This criticism in effect amounted to a repudiation of the dissimulation and gradualism that have typified liberalism from the beginning. Further, the New Left marked a revival of the decentralist ethos of 19th century socialist thought, an ethos that saw little worthwhile in the gigantic structure of bureaucratic state capitalism and interest-group welfarism that liberalism had been so instrumental in creating.

. The perceived failure of liberal programs in light of the intractability of many of the problems they sought to address. When the zeitgeist no longer accepted the premise that had been at the heart of the liberal political agenda for so long that "all problems can be politicized and then solved by spending government money on them," there seemed nowhere for liberalism to go.

. The inability of a coalition-based ideology and politics to maintain their cohesion. We see how difficult it has been to hold the coalition together when we think of the components of "the Roosevelt coalition": the intellectuals (to the extent they chose to be affiliated), the South, the racial and ethnic minorities, organized labor, farm laborites and the big-city political machines. It is no wonder that there has been a

31

constant call since the late 1960's for "a new coalition." Through most of the post-World War II era the constituent groups have been at odds with one another, coming together mostly on election day, and not always then.

. The movement of several prominent liberals into "neo-conservatism" during the 1970's and 1980's. The New Left brought the alienation to a head, causing many to decide just where their loyalties lay. Some of those who were not primarily motivated by alienation moved to the right and, with Irving Kristol, began to speak in terms of, at least, "two cheers for capitalism." This is potentially one of the most important ideological shifts of our time. If an intellectual base that is both critically intelligent and yet lacking in alienation can come into being, it will tend to reorient the entire direction of modern intellectual culture.

A major diversion: Civil Rights

Despite all that I have said about the condition of liberalism since World War II, there has been an issue that has provided it enormous sustenance during those years. At times this issue has swept all else before it on behalf of what the American public has regarded as an unquestionable moral principle. I am referring, of course, to the issue of racial, ethnic and sexual equality.

Liberalism's relation to this form of equality is different than is commonly supposed. The relationship did not arise out of a spontaneous moral conviction in favor of such equality on the part of the liberal.

On the world scene, socialists generally have been neither more nor less given to such equality than have people holding other ideologies. In fact, Proudhon in the 19th century called for the extermination of the Jews. Collectivists of several types have been rabid in their intolerance.

Liberals in the United States did not provide conspicuous leadership to a movement for racial and ethnic equality until the issue came to life during and after World War II. Most Americans will be surprised to hear that it was the Progressives who were most instrumental in establishing the Jim Crow system in the South; they did so after the Populist movement created a fear of the potentially corrupting effects of a movement that would combine blacks and poor whites. Theodore Roosevelt is reputed to have made an embarrassingly bigoted comment about Negroes at the time of the Brownsville Affair. Woodrow Wilson originally wanted to include blacks in his administration, but backed off when this led to criticism from his Southern supporters. Franklin Roosevelt did not make civil rights legislation for blacks a significant part of the New Deal.

During all those years the many liberals connected with the liberal journals as editors and writers, while favorable to Negroes and horrified by lynchings, made no move to make "civil rights" a priority issue. As we look back from the moral ethos of the 1980's, we tend to think that racial, ethnic and sexual equality have held a place in the pantheon of liberal philosophy from the beginning. But that just is not so.

The migration of Negroes to northern cities and their improving economic condition, among other factors, led the blacks themselves to a much-increased activism at the time of World War II. Liberals tagged along. Their ideas did not lead the events. Rather, the Negro agitation slowly awakened liberalism to the issue. Among the intellectuals, only the Communists had been active in significant numbers for very long.

Certain of the elements that make liberalism what it is lend themselves strongly to this issue. Accordingly, modern liberalism, emerging from World War II and searching for a post-war program, had several reasons to consider it appealing. After a slow start, it became the central moral focus after World War II.

One reason for this has been that the Left in general, and liberalism as a form of the Left, has been involved from the beginning in a search for coalitions. For a century and a half in Europe the alienated intellectual subculture has sought an alliance successively with every unassimilated or disaffected group. Political success has depended upon what coalitions have been possible and how well they have been able to stay together. Ideologically, the rationale for any coalition has been readily supplied.

Ideally, of course, all such groups would be brought together in one grand coalition. But selective coalition-making has been forced upon the Left and liberalism by the fact that the groups have often been at odds with one another, and with the intellectual subculture. This is why the experience of liberalism with the various civil rights movements--of blacks, of Chicanos, of women, of homosexuals--has proved so checkered.

Another reason liberalism has been the natural champion of this sort of equality has been that liberalism has been willing to use "direct action" methods that the groups themselves have supported, but that have been unacceptable to conservatives.

To the classical liberal philosophy of individualism that lies at the heart of American conservatism, nothing is more abhorrent than for people to judge each other by the color of their skin rather than by their merits or what they produce. But the classical liberal also (1) wants the police power of the state to remain limited, (2) identifies with the main society without alienation toward it, and (3) sees the processes of change within an open society to be sufficient without techniques of confrontation. The result is that the classical liberal believes that the growth of racial tolerance must mainly be accomplished through ethics and education.

34

The idea of using the police power to command an absence of discrimination among hundreds of millions of people in their daily relationships has seemed preposterous to conservatives. Such a state-sponsored assimilation has subordinated the values of freedom of association, freedom of contract and property rights. It has threatened an unprecedented expansion of the police function. That this expansion has not come about has been due to the willingness of Americans to match their moral sanctimony with an hypocrisy that has kept enforcement to a minimum.

The method of social change through direct actionist confrontation, even as used by the proponents of "non-violence," seemed offensive and inappropriate to conservatives, who saw a society in which the condition of blacks had been rapidly improving. From the point of view of someone who was not alienated against the main society, it made no sense to engage in a rhetoric of condemnation that could only be consistent with abandoning historical perspective, forgetting all the good and remembering only the bad.

Such concerns did not weigh heavily with the groups themselves or with liberal spokesmen. In fact, they dismissed them as excuses for inaction.

So far as ordinary Americans have been concerned, they have been preoccupied, as they normally are, with the day-to-day concerns of their own lives. They have not thought deeply about classical liberal values or historical perspective. This lack of interest in ideas makes Americans incredibly receptive to fashionable ideology, at least so long as it does not inconvenience them too severely and seems consistent with their good-hearted natures. Because of this, nothing has seemed more irresistible than the egalitarian moral thrust of the post-World War II era.

Even a near-total intellectual and moral dominance, however, has not been enough to make the egalitarian issue sufficient for the political

35

success of liberalism, as events since the mid-1960's have shown. In one national election after another, liberals have sought a "new coalition," each time revealing the extent to which they have been unable to keep the old one together. The process has pushed the Democratic Party to embrace the fringes. But radical feminism and homosexual rights are not issues calculated to engage the majority of the American electorate.

It is especially important for us to understand that the entire minority-rights emphasis since World War II, regardless of its merits, has been a deflection of liberalism from its original impulses, which were heavily socialist. Seen from the point of view of liberalism's intellectual spokesmen, their "creeping socialism" has hardly seemed to creep at all. Their literature has been one of frustration and ennui.

This does not mean, of course, that a program of state activism, perhaps of socialism, may not be revived in America. Nor can the possibility be ruled out that the Left may emerge again in the form of social disintegration and heightened alienation. The experience with the New Left must certainly have educated us to the fact that the Left does not act solely through a growth of governmental functions. Those who think so will have learned little since the early 1960's.

One of the most important facts in the mid-1980's is that the predominant culture has not capitalized on the Reagan presidency. Despite Reagan's strongly conservative philosophy, neither presidential election in which he was elected was made a vehicle for a philosophical articulation of conservatism. During his presidency there has been no intellectual ferment marking a revival of classical liberalism. The bourgeoisie has simply kept on doing what it has always done, which is to pursue the daily round without having a strong interest in intellect or aesthetics and without seeing the need to create an intellectual subculture that is appropriate to a free society.

This means not only that "capitalism" continues to lack an ingredient essential to its own
sufficiency, but that an ideological void is present which leaves us in a condition of almost
total existential indeterminacy. We are in a
period of profound drift.

Despite Reagan's own personification of conservative values, America has to a large extent
lost its memory, which is to say, its meaning.
Both forms of liberalism lie exhausted within a
culture that, at least for the present, operates
upon the underlay that each has provided.

Indigenous factors in American history that have reenforced liberalism while adding other dimensions to it.

This overview of modern liberalism would be
incomplete if several other aspects of American
history were not given attention.

These factors have mostly augmented the call
for a more powerful federal government. At the
same time, however, they have given liberalism a
diversity that makes it unsound to define liberalism in terms of any one component. Liberalism has
been historically complex.

When the United States was founded in the
late 18th century, the situation was ideal from
the classical liberal point of view. (An enormous
exception was the presence of slavery within an
otherwise liberal republic.) Free institutions
had been established on the principles of the
Enlightenment, and the thirteen states were so
heterogeneous that they had little inclination to
surrender their power to the central government.

By the beginning of the 20th century, however, many tendencies existed that would have lent
themselves to state activism and centralization
even if the intellectual community had not veered
sharply to the left.

1.   There had been a steady erosion of the
intense loyalty that had originally been given to
state and local units. A more national perspective came into being.

In part this was due to the transciency
created by the frontier's movement westward. It
was also caused by the constant improvements in
transportation and communication. The victory of
the national government first in the Nullification
Crisis and much more significantly in the Civil
War put an end to centripetal tendencies. Thereafter, it was clear both politically and psychologically that the states were simply parts of a
whole.

2.   A Hamiltonian neo-Mercantilism inspired
first the Federalists and then the Whigs. At all
times, at least one of the major parties favored a
federal government that would play an active role
in the economy. The Republican Party continued
this tradition after the Civil War with the high
protective tariff, which was seen throughout the
19th century as the primary form of governmental
intervention. Toward the end of the 19th century,
The Nation, still strongly classical liberal,
commented that the tariff had accustomed people to
look to the government for economic intervention
on their behalf.

3.   The Jeffersonian tradition, even though
it was articulately classical liberal, contributed
two ingredients to the mix that was to be important at the end of the century. They were:

. Support for participation by more and
more people in a broader democratic base.

. an opposition to corruption and governmental favoritism.

These were both compatible with classical
liberalism, but they were also important to the
Populist and Progressive movements, which had
other ingredients that were incompatible with it.

4. During the 19th century the standard of living rose in the most successful economic expansion, democratically distributed, the world has ever known. It is ironic that this relates to the later welfare liberalism, but the connection becomes clear when we consider that the average person had always been so close to poverty that he had never been able to think seriously about insurance, about doing away with child labor, and about a steadily assured income. Only affluence made all of that possible.

The 20th century's "safety net" could have been attained with less anti-capitalist rhetoric and more reliance upon market mechanisms within a classical liberal context. The fact that it was not, and that it came in upon the wave of a very different ideology, should not keep us from realizing that the essential preconditions were laid by science, the Industrial Revolution, abundant resources and a remarkably productive capitalism. Marxism has been aware of this, and has long held that capitalism is a precondition to socialism.

5. Despite this affluence, the continuing existence of poverty has caused a number of governmental measures.

This poverty has largely been the result of a world-wide phenomenon that I call "peasant pressure." In England during the early Industrial Revolution the factory towns teemed with the poor who came from the countryside and from Ireland seeking the wages that the factories could pay. In Russia at the end of the 19th century, the textile mills of the beginning industrialization were flooded with serfs who swarmed into the cities.

One of the very real perversities of socialist thought has been to blame the squalor of the factory towns on the factories themselves and on their owners. In fact the presence of rural millions, mired in poverty but eager to move to jobs in the cities, has been both the creator and the constant replenisher of urban slums.

In the United States, the rural population has steadily declined, with migration to the cities; immigrants from all over the world have come first to hardship and then to a more complete enjoyment of our higher standard of living; Negroes have migrated from the rural South into the cities of the north and the west, and then partially back again. The sociologist Edward Banfield has pointed out that successive waves of poverty have been overcome, with new poverty taking their place.

The "peasant pressure" continues to this day. It comes in part from our still-shrinking agricultural population, but mostly from the immigration of the poor from Mexico, Latin America, Asia and the Middle East. (We also obtain many of their best minds.) Our affluence and freedom have continued to call into existence the very "problem" that has in turn provided the discontent and the votes to serve as the base for anti-capitalistic rhetoric and remedial governmental programs.

6. War and the need to stay prepared for war have played an important role in the long decline of classical liberal values.

Jacksonian classical liberalism understood the dangers, and therefore opposed a standing army. But the Civil War brought centralization and a shattering of the Jacksonian ideology. The great wars and threat of totalitarian expansionism in the 20th century have made necessary governmental powers that would otherwise have stayed dormant. Just as significantly, they have contributed to the erosion of the social, moral and aesthetic base of middle-class culture, an erosion that has led to some of the most visible characteristics of our national life in the late 20th century.

Ronald Reagan, a president with the most articulately classical liberal values in our history, has been handicapped since the beginning of his administration by the need for vast defense expenditures to match the Soviet build-up. It is largely because to this that he has been unable to implement his desire simultaneously to reduce taxation, the federal deficit, and the size of the federal government.

At the same time, this factor has produced a counter-effect. War and the heavy cost of national defense have done much to frustrate the goals of modern liberal presidents. The New Deal effectively ended when Franklin Roosevelt turned his attention to international issues. The North Korean attack in June, 1950, put an end to President Truman's domestic program. And the Vietnam War overshadowed Lyndon Johnson's Great Society program.

7. Immigration has been a factor. It has played a major role in the "peasant pressure." It has also contributed to the shift in the country's ideological orientation. We have undergone successive waves of immigration since the middle of the 19th century from parts of the world that have known little about classical liberalism. An example of this appears in Nathan Glazer's account of the all-absorbing socialist presuppositions of the Jews who immigrated to this country from eastern Europe.

The liberalism since World War II has been an "interest-group liberalism." The teeming multiplicity of the new ethnic culture has no doubt been a major contributor. The groups have come with ideologically conditioned expectations about the role of government. They have constituted voting blocs, and this voting power has lent itself to the coalition-seeking imperative within liberal politics and ideology.

8. The booms and busts of the trade cycle have several times undermined important preconditions of a market system.

Classical liberalism calls upon individuals and families to rely upon their own active role within a market system. This presupposes an adequately functioning market.

As we have seen, however, classical liberalism has long been on the defensive and drained of intellectual manpower. This has caused it to give too little attention to the institutional framework that is essential for a market. Its thinking has, of course, been relegated to the sidelines in any case. While technically the solutions making possible an acceptably stable market system have been known, there has been no coordinated thrust toward their implementation. An excellent example is found in the policies followed after the Crash in 1929, when the money supply was allowed to deflate by a third and the Smoot-Hawley Tariff and other protectionist measures throughout the world strangled the revival of international trade.

9. There is a less tangible but still quite real factor that has long seemed to me to be essential to an understanding of contemporary life. It is the fact I discussed at length in Understanding the Modern Predicament: the fundamental immaturity of mankind, even in advanced civilization, at our current level of development. Emerson was quite right when he said that humanity is only at the cockcrowing and the morning star.

As a classical liberal, I see the Enlightenment as having been humanity's most significant advance toward a liberal and humane civilization. It is impossible, however, for someone with my values to look back upon the past two centuries without profound regret. Even in Europe and America people have been mentally and spiritually unable and unwilling to grasp and then to meet those aspirations. The important exceptions have reflected the extent to which the cultural capital of the Enlightenment, which we are still consuming, has remained present.

All of the factors I have discussed have been

important, but the failure has also been due to the nature of people themselves. If we ask why we are plagued by mediocrity in personal and ethical relations, why performance is so often shoddy, why our public is the vehicle for so many thoughtless ideological fancies, why the aesthetic atmosphere is so poor, why so few genuinely well-founded ideas are brought forward, why the aesthetic tone of our civilization is so shrill, why the level of participation in our political process is so low, why massive educational facilities accomplish so little by way of true literacy and learning, why our families cannot stay together, why there is even a loss of the ethic of family obligation, we can see many parts of the answer in the intellectual and social factors I am analyzing. But ultimate responsibility lies with the average person. It remains true, as it has from the beginning of history, that the ordinary person is too preoccupied, as Thoreau said, with "the factitious cares and superfluously coarse labors of life" to be very much concerned about qualitative issues.

The disappointment that this engenders in idealists has shaken socialists since the mid-1930's and has sapped the elan of modern liberalism. But it is also the case that many of the characteristics of this weakness make up the substance of what is considered liberalism in contemporary America. The average person's intellectual and spiritual mediocrity complements the intellectual culture's long-standing attack upon personal responsibility, the "bourgeois ethic," and the institutions and acculturations of a classical liberal society.

Conclusion

This opening chapter has had both the advantages and disadvantages of an interpretive overview. The reader is aware, of course, that in this chapter I have not sought to document anything I have said. The remaining chapters will examine the specifics in much greater detail and

should provide ample documentation. They will
also examine a number of additional aspects of
liberalism that, though quite important, I have
not been able to include here.

2

PHASES IN AMERICAN LIBERALISM:
1800-1920

In <u>Rendezvous With Destiny</u>, Eric Goldman began his history of liberalism with the end of the Civil War. This was appropriate to his analysis, since he considered liberalism essentially a movement of "modern American reform" that has responded to the needs created by the urban, industrial, corporate environment that came into being in the second half of the 19th century.

My analysis differs significantly from Goldman's. I believe that by starting as late as he did he missed three factors that were crucial in the United States before the Civil War: the growing alienation of the intellectual in Western civilization against the middle class culture; the resulting drain of intellectual resources away from classical liberal thought; and the continuing role of traditionalist conservative forces that stood at odds with the secular, rationalist, open society that had come into being. If these earlier developments are missed, the role of alienation is deemphasized and the historian is unable to see the continuity that has existed within the intellectual culture both in this country and in its relation to European thought.

The developments that we will trace before the Civil War are important for still another reason. Their presence at the earlier time, a time that was agrarian and given only to small-shop capitalism, shows how the core impulse behind liberalism was in fact <u>not</u> a reaction to industrialization, urbanization, or the rise of the large corporation, as Goldman believed it was. The alienation preceded rather than followed the advent of large-scale capitalism. We have seen in my book on socialist thought that this fact is also highly significant in the analysis of socialism for precisely the same reason.

45

From Jefferson's election in 1800 to the
beginning of the Civil War in 1861, most Americans
shared the ethos of the Jeffersonian-Jacksonian
party, an ethos that was articulately classical
liberal. On the main economic question of the
19th century, it strongly favored free trade,
wanting a tariff for revenue only, not for "protection." In a running debate that lasted over
the entire 60-year period, it opposed the construction of internal improvements by the national
government. Consistently with its focus on liberty, it saw dangers in Henry Clay's call for a
standing army. And it was firmly democratic, in
keeping with the contemporaneous views of John
Bright of the Manchester School in England. It
saw value in democratic simplicity and strongly
opposed aristocratic privilege. Andrew Jackson's
fight against the rechartering of the second
United States Bank must be understood in this
light, since it reflected a belief that the Bank
enjoyed a privileged position resulting from a
marriage of government and finance. The Jacksonian opposition to privilege resulted from the
premises of classical liberal individualism rather
than from any animus against capitalism.

When the anti-slavery agitation began, the
Jacksonians urged moderation. In his Farewell
Address in 1837, Jackson criticized incendiaries
on both sides. This reflected the priorities of
the Jacksonian ethos, since to it the newly
created republic was the thing of paramount importance. Because the Jacksonian majority felt no
alienation, its adherents saw enormous value in
the main society, which they wanted to preserve.

It was during those years that the Constitution took on the reverential glow that it has
possessed within the American myth. (Here I use
"myth" in a favorable, not a pejorative, sense. I
refer, of course, to the need within society--even
within a secular, rationalistic one--to impute

meaning to objects and events.)

It was a time of extraordinary expansion. A country that a few years before had hugged the eastern seashore came rapidly to extend to the Pacific, and in one of the greatest migrations of all time its exploding population spread across thousands of miles. The telegraph, railroad and steam engine typify many developments in the advance of science, technology and capital.

Oddly, these achievements contrasted sharply with the profoundly pessimistic mood of the intellectual minority. The intellectual culture saw little value in the achievements of the main society (which were, however, revolutionary in the truest sense). It reflected, instead, a number of other influences.

Beginning in the early 19th century, the Romantic movement in Europe reacted violently against the Enlightenment, changing the direction of the world intellectual community. This caused a drain of intellectual resources away from classical liberalism, which thereafter received relatively little work outside of economics. It is of the utmost significance that there was no major classical liberal philosopher in the United States after Jefferson. Ralph Waldo Emerson might, in a different climate, have been that thinker, but he felt no calling to serve as a philosopher for individualistic liberalism. Instead, his great talent, as well as that of Henry David Thoreau, turned to the other-worldliness of Transcendentalism, a philosophy that Alice Felt Tyler says included a theory of an oversoul in "mystical union with God." It is possible that John Calhoun would have filled the role if the sectional differences developing in the country had not taken control of his life. However, it is a mistake to think mainly in terms of the failure of any given thinker. There is a larger responsibility for the philosophical void, which is shared. It lies with the intellectual culture in its faithlessness to the Enlightenment. It also lies with the bourgeoisie, which throughout history has rarely given enough attention to general ideas to germinate an intellectual culture appropriate to the free society with which it is identified and in which it thrives.[1]

All sorts of streams then fed a current that flowed into the void created by the intellectual movement away from classical liberalism. One of them was aristocratic, neo-Mercantilist conservatism in New England. Another was the Burkean-style Southern conservatism that sprang up after 1830 in defense of slavery. In George Fitzhugh's eyes the South came to represent a cultured, hierarchical civilization superior to what he saw as a money-grubbing, vulgar Northern society.

A third stream was resurgent Protestant religion. In the Second Great Awakening which began shortly after 1800, the evangelical spirit reached a fever pitch. It possessed a puritanical temper that had a lot to do with myopic self-righteousness and very little to do with how to build a truly liberal society. Protestantism no doubt played an historic role in establishing the foundations for individual freedom, but much of its worldview has also been at odds with precisely such a society. This provides one of the themes of modern history, since there has been a direct connection between other-worldly religious values and a loss of balance by the nihilist and by many reformers. Both 19th century Russia and pre-Civil War America experienced this connection. In varying degrees it has continued as a factor throughout American history.

Yet another element was a naive sentimentality, formed out of a combination of good intentions and foreshortened perspective. This was a mentality that emoted over all perceived abuses while ignoring the enormous progress that had been made. In England during the same period, the historian Thomas Babington Macaulay lamented how much this contributed to a generalized dissatisfaction. Despite conditions having improved at an historically unprecedented rate over those of earlier periods, the existing society was denounced as depraved. This lack of perspective, characteristic of the entire modern period, is a product of both the shallowness of a semi-educated public and the predispositions ideologically of the intellectual culture. Much of the neurotic tone of modern life is established by it.

Of greatest significance, however, was the Romantic movement itself. Most of the other factors had existed before. The Romantic revulsion against the Enlightenment brought them to a head, stifled the development of classical liberalism, and led to the alienation of the literary culture. In Europe, mystical, anti-rational, anti-bourgeois, anti-liberal thought became predominant. It was the spirit of a resurgent medievalism.

Those who absorbed this atmosphere came to think the main society diseased. Abuses were seen everywhere, remedies of all kinds suggested. Emerson spoke of "a fertility of projects for the salvation of the world." C. S. Griffin writes of movements that together "attacked every American institution, every idea, every conceivable sin, evil, or burden of suffering."2

Intellectually, the United States passed through a period similar to those seen in the Muckraker era of the early 20th century and in the intense alienation of the late 1960's and early 1970's. A characteristic of such periods has been a generalized disgust, in which everyone other than the speaker and his immediate audience is blamed, and only the vaguest rationale is presented for what is wrong.

We know, of course, that the abolitionist movement was building to a white heat against slavery. Although it was on the Enlightenment's side with regard to an extremely important moral issue, abolitionism reflected the hierarchy of values that is inherent in alienation. It subordinated the very existence of the United States, with all that it meant, to the slavery question. The Northern victory in the Civil War, both keeping the Union together and abolishing slavery, necessarily obscures this fact for us today. But before the Civil War there could have been no certainty that a drumbeat of hatred toward the South would produce anything but a fracturing of the Union, the assured continuation of slavery in one section, and incessant warfare between the two resulting countries (especially over westward expansion). Slavery was an anachronism in the modern age. All that was needed for its eventual disappearance was a modicum of patience and the general society's continued adherence to classical liberal values. (It is no coincidence that serfdom was abolished in Russia in 1861 without a civil war.)

The abolitionists were, however, just one of several movements. Some reformers threw themselves into Prohibition, seeing alcohol as the principal evil; there was a crusade against prostitution; pacifism was the focus for others. The religious revival called for a return to the Bible and to an emphasis on the Sabbath. There was an active anti-Catholic movement, since the vast immigration of Catholics, many of them the poor of Ireland and other places, was seen as a cause of the other problems. There were fads of phrenology, diet, free love, spiritualism, mesmerism, and hydropathy. Although the reformers ignored the plight of the Indians, there were movements to redeem criminals, to help the mentally incompetent and the insane, to reform the prisons. The feminist movement got underway with the first Women's Rights Convention, organized by Lucretia Mott, in 1848. In his 1844 lecture "The New England Reformers," after speaking of the "fertility of projects for the salvation of the world," Emerson said that "one apostle thought all men should go to farming, and another that no man should buy or sell, that the use of money was the cardinal evil." He said that "others attacked the system of agriculture, the use of animal manures in farming," while "others attacked the institution of marriage as the fountain of social evils."[3]

One of the ideologically more significant movements had to do with the creation of utopian socialist communities. The Oneida community was established by John Humphrey Noyes, embracing "Bible Communism" and "complex marriage." It was one of the more successful, continuing into the 1880's. Most of them were short-lived, and in historical perspective all have been considered failures. Robert Owen, a leader of early British socialism, set up New Harmony, which failed within two years. The Hopedale Community was created in 1841 to attempt a Christian socialism. Brook Farm began with Transcendentalism and shifted to the communism of the French socialist Charles Fourier. Fourier's thinking received considerable attention in the 1840's under the sponsorship of Horace Greeley and Albert Brisbane, when dozens of Fourierist communities were started. Anarchism found expression in Modern Times, a community established by Stephen Pearl Andrews and Josiah Warren in 1851. Speaking more generally, Walter Hugins says that "European socialists...formed only a small part of the European migration to the United States after 1815, but they contributed immeasurably to the reform agitation."[4]

The "fertility of projects" did not reflect a consensus favoring a socialist critique (just as it did not during the Progressive period almost a century later). As the different movements indicate, there were widely divergent diagnoses of the disease that they all claimed to see in society. Some of the movements, indeed, represented the antipathy of the middle class itself to deviations from its values. It is noteworthy that the writings of both Emerson and Thoreau contain many comments that differ sharply from attitudes taken later by the Left. This reflects the fact that the intellectual culture had not yet begun to seek alliances with the have-nots. Nevertheless, socialist thinking was important to the coalescence of ideology that came later in the century, at which time a distinctly anti-capitalist intel-

51

lectual rationale became widespread.

After the Civil War: alienation, yearning and coalescence

The ferment was largely stilled during the first few years after the Civil War. We understand from The Education of Henry Adams that there was a rush of excitement among intellectuals when Ulysses S. Grant was elected president, but that disillusionment set in quickly when his administration failed to meet their expectations.

A letter that Adams sent to his brother Charles in 1862 is significant. It shows that this period remained within the paradigm of the psychology of the alienated intellectual. There had been years of intense activity, capped by the exhausting experience of the Civil War. Now there was a period of quiescence, during which the alienation continued and nurtured a yearning for the renewal of activity. Adams showed the yearning when he wrote that "what we want is a school ...a national set of young men like ourselves or better, to start new influences...throughout the whole social organism of the country...." He then illustrated both his alienation and the historic failure of the bourgeoisie when he continued by saying that "that is what America has no power to create...It's all random, insulated work, for special and temporary and personal purposes."[5]

The reform movements after the Civil War were of two types. One involved reform from the top, led by such liberals (in the classical sense) as Edwin Lawrence Godkin and Samuel Tilden. These movements included the Liberal Republicans in 1872, a similar movement in the Democratic Party in 1876, and the Mugwumps in the 1880's. Tilden, raised in the Jacksonian school, has been called the father of the modern anti-boss reform spirit. Although these movements sought reform, primarily through Civil Service, they did not have an underlay of cultural alienation.

The other type of reform movement was agrarian. The agrarian crusades voiced the dissatisfaction of farmers with what they perceived as exploitation by lenders, railroads and storage elevators. Accordingly, they lent themselves to the growing rhetoric of anti-capitalism. They were especially susceptible to crank-money schemes, such as during the Greenback movement of the 1870's. As a debtor class, the farmers of that time saw real advantages in easy credit and inflation.

Depressions, the rise of labor, and the influx of immigrants (many of them influenced by the growing socialist movement in Europe after the revolutionary fervor in 1848) all contributed to a rising turbulence. Labor-management relations became violent. The Molly Maguires, dynamiting and murdering in the coal mines of Pennsylvania, were put down only when ten of their members were hanged. Anarchism, an import from southern Europe, flourished until public opinion turned sharply against it after the Haymarket Square bombing in 1886. (Subsequent terrorist acts attest to the fact that it didn't disappear totally.)

Later in the century, books appeared with a socialist critique. The most popular was Edward Bellamy's Looking Backward, published in 1888. It soon sold 10,000 copies a week. In part, it was a novel, telling the story of a man who sleeps until the year 2,000 and then wakes up in a socialist utopia; in the main, however, it was a bitingly alienated description of capitalism and a glowing description of a model socialist society.

During the 1880's and 1890's Lester Ward published a series of books and articles advocating what he called "Sociocracy," and looking forward to the day when "all the important public operations of society shall come more or less directly under the power of State regulation." His writing during that period is characteristic of much 20th century liberal thought.

Most importantly, however, the alienation coalesced, finally, into an ideology. Thereafter, there would still be "a fertility of projects," but the intellectual culture would at least share a common worldview, which it did not in the pre-Civil War period. It is probable that this coalescence would have occurred in any case, since European thought had arrived at that point, but the specific influence that most directly brought it about was the migration of several thousand American graduate students to German universities, mostly in the last quarter of the 19th century, where they studied under the German Historical School. I described this in Chapter 10 of Understanding the Modern Predicament. The details I gave there are of the greatest significance to the development of American liberal ideology. Rather than to repeat them here, however, it will be sufficient to highlight the following influences:

. The Historical School stood in close relation to the Junker aristocracy and to the government of Bismarck, which was enacting the first welfare state program in Europe.

. In common with so much European thought during the 19th century, the members of the School were intensely anti-bourgeois, and liberalism in its individualistic meaning was anathema.

. Its "historical method" stressed empirical scholarship, extensive use of surveys, specialization, publication of monographs, and the like. It thus created the paradigm to which American higher education adheres to this day.

. At the same time, the historical method adopted a relativism that attacked the scientific pretensions of classical and neo-classical economics. The School argued that that economic theory generalized from patterns that exist only in a bourgeois phase of history, and that therefore its conclusions had no permanent validity. This attack on classical and neo-classical economics was important in its own right both for the

54

methodological point it was making and because of
its assault on the main body of work within classical liberalism; it was also important because
such a relativism has been one of the main weapons
used by the Left and by modern liberalism to
undercut foundations of bourgeois society.

In its stress on relativism, the Historical
School reflected two very different aspects of
modern intellectuality. One was its anti-middle
class, anti-capitalist, anti-classical liberal
ideology. The other was the emphasis that secular
intellectuals have placed upon empirical science.
The ideology stemmed from the phenomenon of the
alienation of the intellectual, based on several
causes. One of these causes was the Romantic
movement's restimulation of medieval values (which
of course have never been fully defeated), with
their stress on hierarchy, religion, subordination
of the individual, and a strong state. At the
same time, the empirical aspect was in line with
the thoroughly secular nature of modern science.

. The members of the School were gradualists, not revolutionaries. This was important to
the decision by modern liberals, distinct from
that made by avowed socialists, to stay within
their culture, not putting themselves them beyond
its pale. In the United States, a gradualistic
program based on a socialistic worldview would
require dissimulation. This need led directly to
"liberalism" as we have known it.

. It is relevant to the later Progressive
movement and to modern liberalism in general that
the members of the German Historical School
believed in leadership from the top through a
statesman who would embody the aspirations of the
whole people. They also wanted the intellectual
culture to stand in close relation to that leader.

The influence of these ideas was not simply a
direct one. The rising British Left, which in
turn had a major impact in the United States, had
itself been under the sway of the German thinking.

In 1915, Randolph Bourne wrote that "British thought for forty years has come straight from German sources. What is the new social politics of liberalism," he asked, "but a German collectivism, half-heartedly grafted on a raw stock of individualist 'liberty'?" [6]

The direct influence, however, came through a number of American thinkers and universities. Simon Patten observed in 1914 that the "Wisconsin Idea," under which the University of Wisconsin became the intellectual center for state activism, was based on the German example. Lincoln Steffens was educated in Germany; W. E. B. DuBois graduated from both Harvard and Heidelberg; Edward Alsworth Ross attended the University of Berlin. Richard T. Ely studied under the Historical School and later became a teacher to both Thorstein Veblen and John R. Commons. Ely was an important member of the faculty at both Johns Hopkins and the University of Wisconsin. John Bates Clark studied in Germany, came to advocate Christian socialism, and was one of Veblen's teachers at Carleton College. George S. Morris became an Hegelian while studying in Germany, and later taught John Dewey. Louis Brandeis studied at Dresden in 1873-5. Eric Goldman says that five American universities became the principal repositories of these ideas: Johns Hopkins, Columbia, Chicago, Wisconsin and Washington. At the same time, newly forming academic associations reflected the rise of modern American social science. Lewis Gould tells us that "in 1885, a group of young men just back from German universities founded the American Economic Association." He refers specifically to Ely, Commons, Clark and Edward W. Bemis. [7]

The Populist episode

Twentieth century historical literature has fiercely debated the nature of Populism. (The same is true of Progressivism.) Because of the diverse nature of their subject, historians of each period have been akin to the blind men feeling the different parts of an elephant and thus arriving at very different descriptions.[8]

Lawrence Goodwyn is one who has emphasized a particular component. He argues persuasively that the central fact about Populism is that a "movement culture" arose among farmers, primarily in the South, reflecting first their discontent over the "crop-lien system" and then the efforts of the Farmers' Alliance. To Goodwyn, Populism's other factions were appendages. He accordingly considers the Free Silver component a "shadow movement." Fusion with the other factions, and especially with Free Silver, led to dissimulation and to an acceptance by reformers of the "hierarchical culture" that he says has dominated America ever since. Accordingly, he considers the election of 1896 the fateful turning point in modern American history, since it was to him the last desperate effort for real democracy. He criticizes John Hicks, Richard Hofstadter and Norman Pollack as historians who have not understood that the Alliance movement was the "core experience" of Populism.

The debate among historians is partly definitional and partly the staking out of territory for a given author's assertion of preferred values. We are not obliged to resolve it here. With any complex historical phenomenon, different authors will select and emphasize different things for different reasons. It will be sufficient for our purposes simply to notice the nature of the factions and of the ensuing programs.

In addition to the agrarian movement that is central to Goodwyn's analysis, Populism included several other elements:

• The economic radicalism that had shown itself earlier in Kelloggism and the Greenback movement. This called for monetary inflation, divided the economic world conceptually into producers and non-producers, and advocated extensive govern-

57

mental intervention.

. The socialist followers of Bellamy, who formed the "Eastern wing" of Populism. Compared to some of the other components, however, this wing was not a major contributor either of votes or of leadership.

. The enthusiasts for Henry George's "Single Tax." Despite the radical sweep of George's proposal to tax away the unearned increment in land values, his overall views were not socialistic.

. Labor, to the limited extent it chose to become affiliated. Major efforts were made to bring labor into the movement in Wisconsin, Illinois and Ohio after the panic of 1893. The Populists were split, however, over "Plank 10" of the American Federation of Labor program. This called for socialism, advocating the collective ownership of the means of production and distribution. Samuel Gompers favored a go-it-alone policy for labor, and opposed an alliance with Populism.

. The Free Silver movement, headed by William Jennings Bryan. To advocates of the gold standard, this represented a call away from "hard money" and toward inflation; to enthusiasts for fiat money, though, it was insufficient, since to them it appeared simply to add another metal to what was essentially a hard-money policy.

Formed of these elements, the Populist coalition necessarily had a difficult time staying together. We have seen that Populists split over Plank 10 and that Gompers opposed labor's affiliation. Henry George opposed governmental intervention, which was at the heart of what most Populists wanted. Poor whites in the South were hostile toward participation by blacks. Socialists wanted a more radical program. As a result, the movement flew apart, fading away after the defeat of William Jennings Bryan in the presidential election of 1896 and with the improvement in farm prices. The difficulty of cementing a coalition,

58

in light of diverse interests and theoretical rationales, has continued in the 20th century as one of liberalism's central problems.

The Omaha platform in 1892 summed up the positions taken by Populism: There was a call for the federal ownership and operation of the railroads, telegraph and telephone; for Free Silver; for the eight-hour work day; for Government to regulate all corporations and to break up monopolies. Democratizing measures were favored such as the secret ballot, the direct election of Senators, initiative and referendum. At the same time, unrestricted immigration was condemned as injurious to the workers and farmers who were already here. Little interest was shown in Civil Service or in the reduction of the tariff.

The Progressive episode

Another surge of reformist energy occurred in the Progressive movement in the early 20th century. Although historians of the epoch generally say it ended with the advent of World War I, there was political activity under the Progressive label until LaFollette was defeated as a third party presidential candidate in 1924.

"Progressivism," too, is subject to varied interpretations as a product of a loose coalition of divergent streams. But its coalition was not identical to Populism's, and the issues it stressed were somewhat, although by no means entirely, different.

So diverse were its factions that The New Republic could say in 1924 that "American progressivism is nourished almost exclusively by the grievances and the demands of special regions and groups. There is no one idea, program or leader." John D. Buenker said much the same when he observed that "there was no single progressive movement at work during the period, but rather many separate groups interacting and coalescing."[9]

Progressivism's emphasis was urban, replacing Populism's agrarian focus. Farmers had receded from their radicalism at the same time the new urban middle class of business and the professions in America's rapidly developing cities was coming into its own. This middle class, urban base was reflected in many of the issues that Progressivism championed, such as the opposition to corruption, the promotion of the city-manager system of city administration, and the control of franchise monopolies. It is significant that a study by L. Otis Graham, Jr., found that a clear majority of Progressives who lived into the 1930's were sufficiently conservative that they opposed the New Deal as too radical. This sheds considerable light on the ideological complexion of Progressivism. Since we will see that there was a substantial socialist influence within the intellectual culture of Progressivism, the presence of middle class "conservatives" shows once again how diverse the movements were that we are reviewing. Much of what Progressivism crusaded for would quite naturally have been the platform of a classical liberal reformist party if developments within the preceding century had not deflected that possibility.[10]

A second element was evangelical Protestant reformism. Robert M. Crunden has said that this "provided the chief thrust...of the original progressive ethos." We see again the continuing role played by what has been called "pietistic Protestantism." This time it threw itself into the Prohibition movement, obtaining the eventual passage of the 18th amendment to the Constitution, while an influential portion expounded the "Social Gospel." Ralph Henry Gabriel says the work of Sheldon, Grinnell, Munger and Gladden had "borne fruit in an increased social consciousness on the part of the churches." The Social Gospel led to the publication in 1907 of Walter Rauschenbusch's Christianity and the Social Crisis and the formation in 1908 of the Federal Council of Churches. In this and two later books, Rauschenbusch argued that "God is against capitalism" and called for

60

socialism.[11]

Two historians of the period, J. Joseph Huth-macher and his student John D. Buenker, have stressed the role of "urban new stock Democrats." They point to the millions of immigrants who crowded the cities, coming first from Ireland and, in the New Immigration after 1880, from southern and eastern Europe. These millions provided the base for the city political machines, which served their needs. Buenker says that the legislation that was enacted in the industrial states during the Progressive era with the active assistance of the city machines laid the foundation for the New Deal and the welfare state. Thus, there were two "urban liberalisms": one of middle class reformers, and another on behalf of the millions of first and second generation Americans.

In an analysis of liberal thought, we should never overlook, however, the role of the intellectual culture. Malcolm Cowley later wrote of "the bustle and hopefulness that filled the early years from 1911 to 1916. Everywhere new writers were...marching forward arm in arm against the old standards of life and culture." Joseph Featherstone has added that "between 1913 and 1922, ...anybody who was anybody wrote for Masses." The counter-culture of bohemian radicalism was at its height in Greenwich Village. According to Lewis Coser, "the young men and women who began flocking to Greenwich Village about 1910 were in revolt against small-town philistinism...For a few years the Village embodied the full flowering of an intellectual, artistic, political, and emotional counterculture." As with all such phenomena since the early 19th century, a central theme was alienation from the middle class. The counterculture was enthusiastically socialist. Although The Masses under the editorship of Max Eastman was most influential, this was the period of the "little magazines" that appeared in great profusion, vibrant with the intellectual, artistic vitality of that period.[12]

61

Although the deeper origins of the Greenwich Village counterculture lay in the Romantic movement and in the intellectual developments within Europe during the preceding century, the counterculture was more immediately stimulated by the sensationalist exposure and condemnation of a great many facets of American life during the Muckraker movement between 1902 and 1911. Louis Filler says that Henry Demarest Lloyd's Wealth Against Commonwealth in 1894 had been "the first Muckraking book," but that Muckraking did not become a movement as such until McClure's publication in October, 1902, of Lincoln Steffens' "Tweed Days in St. Louis." The serialization of Ida Tarbell's The History of the Standard Oil Company began in the following month's issue. For the next nine years exposes appeared in rapid succession not just in the popular magazines, but in books and in newspapers noted for their "yellow journalism."

The ice, sugar, coal, patent-medicine, beef and other trusts were attacked. The stockyards and meat packing industry were investigated, and this led in 1906 to Upton Sinclair's famous book The Jungle. There was a Post Office scandal. Senators were identified as part of land frauds. Bribery was exposed in state legislatures. Organized finance was challenged, becoming the focus of Louis Brandeis' early career and of his book Other People's Money. A crusade was begun against railroad accidents. Life insurance frauds were brought to light. Child labor was bitterly assailed. Political bossism was attacked and a movement for municipal reform begun. There was a campaign against the power of the Speaker in the House of Representatives (and ironically this resulted in the power of committee chairmen under the seniority system, which in turn became an issue half a century later). It is no wonder, then, that Theodore Roosevelt, although essentially friendly toward the Muckraker movement, made his reference to "the man with a muckrake" in Bunyon's Pilgrim's Progress, thereby giving the epoch its name. This was the second of three major episodes in American history during which everything (except, as I have indicated, the speaker and his immediate audience) has been denounced as corrupt.

Within the intellectual culture, certain issues were of course more important than others. The one that stands out most prominently, and that divided the intellectuals themselves, both during the Progressive movement and at all times since, had to do with big business.

Herbert Croly's book The Promise of American Life made him the intellectual mentor of the "New Nationalism." Edward Bellamy's utopian socialism had been known as "Nationalism." Bellamy had predicted that socialism would come through corporations growing ever larger and merging together until finally there would be one giant trust, which would then blend with government to undertake all social and economic functions. Croly likewise envisioned corporations becoming larger, and favored their coming more and more under the wing of government. In contrast to Bellamy, however, Croly masked the socialist content with a fog of dissimulation. There was hence a "new" Nationalism. It welcomed bigness as industrially efficient and wanted government to make that bigness an instrument of national policy.

Despite his reputation as a "trust buster," Theodore Roosevelt became the political champion of the New Nationalism. (It is worth noticing, however, that liberal authors have mainly remembered him as opportunistic and inconsistent.) There is an interesting, although minor, dispute in the literature about who influenced whom. Learned Hard sent Croly's book to Theodore Roosevelt in Africa. According to John Chamberlain, Roosevelt read it with "a leaping brain." Roosevelt thereupon had Croly to lunch at Oyster Bay. But Arthur Schlesinger, Jr., argues that Croly's "influence on Roosevelt has been considerably exaggerated" and says that "it was certainly less than Roosevelt's upon him." He points out that

63

much of the programmatic content of Croly's book seemed based on Roosevelt's January 31, 1908, message to Congress.[13]

At the same time, Louis Brandeis was the intellectual mentor of an opposing view called "the New Freedom," which was championed by Woodrow Wilson in the campaign of 1912. This advocated a "regulated competition" in which government would be the guarantor of a truly competitive market. Instead of encouraging the growth of business and then absorbing it into government, the New Freedom envisioned what Charles Beard, one of its critics, called "a democracy of small business." [14]

Again, however, the political leader fell short of the aspiration. Even during the campaign of 1912, Wilson couched his advocacy in platitudes. There was little follow-through by him as president, except to the extent that lowering the tariff helped remove one of the major causes of bigness. His other pre-World War I measures, such as the creation of the Federal Reserve System and the passage of the Clayton and Federal Trade Commission Acts, did not involve breaking up big business. After 1916 the war in Europe deflected Wilson from domestic reform, and in fact augmented quite significantly the forces leading toward concentration. Years later, Max Lerner looked back and said that Wilson "never made any efforts to smash the trusts." [15]

Intellectually the difference between the New Nationalism and the New Freedom paralleled the argument that was going on within socialist thought, both in the United States and England, about the relative advantages of a centralized or a decentralized collectivism. The Guild Socialist movement, which was strong in England until it was eclipsed by the allure of the Soviet system that followed the Bolshevik Revolution, opposed "state socialism" and wanted a decentralized socialism based on worker control.

In the United States, the intellectuals among

the New Nationalists wanted an absorption of large-scale corporate capitalism by the federal government--really a state socialism, masked by dissimulation. So far as the New Freedomites in general were concerned, they cannot be said to have wanted a decentralized socialism, since they were not on the whole socialists. Certainly Woodrow Wilson was no socialist. But in this book we are concerned about liberal <u>thought</u>, and it is of no small significance that Louis Brandeis, the New Freedom's principal intellectual mentor, embraced the Guild Socialist model in his private letters when he said that he looked forward to an ultimate worker control. In a letter in 1922 he spoke of workers' "participation in, and eventual control of, industry." So far as liberal thought in either school was concerned, the socialist models were never very far out of mind.[16]

I have brought up the Guild Socialist influence in connection with the New Freedom. This influence was much more pronounced, however, in the intellectual vogue, during the 'Teens and early 1920's, of what was called "industrial democracy." Herbert Croly's book <u>Progressive Democracy</u> in 1915 reflected this vogue, and looked forward to eventual worker control, speaking of the need for "the deliberate education of the wage-earners for the position, which they must eventually assume, of being responsible as a group of self-governing communities for the proper organization and execution of the productive work of society." (He didn't foresake his habitual elitism, however; he saw the need for "a body of expert administrative officials" to carry out the public will, which, in common with Rousseau, he perceived as not being the same thing as the wishes of any given electorate.)[17]

When <u>The New Republic</u> began publication under Herbert Croly, Walter Weyl and Walter Lippmann in November, 1914, it repeatedly called for the two sides of industrial democracy: worker control and the extensive organization of consumer cooperatives. British socialist authors were for several years prominent in its pages. This continued as the journal's emphasis until the early 1920's and is one of the threads that has reappeared from time to time. In the 1980's the idea of worker control is again popular within the American Left.

The broad themes that I have discussed were important to the theory. In the politics of Progressivism, however, a number of specific proposals, each backed by its own special constituency, provided the momentum for the movement.

Many of the proposals were democratizing, notwithstanding Croly's elitism: the campaigns for the short ballot, the city-manager system of city governance combined with proportional representation, the abolition of the electoral college, a uniform system of presidential primaries, the direct election of Senators, initiative, referendum, recall, the recall of judicial decisions, and women's suffrage. In significant contrast to the post-World War II emphasis on ethnic rights, however, there was little interest in enhancing the position of Negroes. The democratizing measures related closely to the fierce opposition to corruption (except that recent authors have shown that the city political machines, catering to the votes of immigrants, also played a major role, even though this runs counter to the anti-corruption theme of the middle class supporters of Progressivism).

Social measures such as support for minimum wage laws, social insurance, the Settlement House movement to aid the poor, and the Income Tax amendment to the Constitution gave substance to the program. One of the more important issues, Prohibition, reflected a moral emphasis.

Historians, looking back, have identified certain concepts that they consider typical of Progressivism. (These are often belittled in the literature as naive.) One was the thrust toward openness in politics (a thrust that reached its culmination a half a century later after the

Watergate episode). Another was the focus on national politics. This related to a third, the faith in a strong popular leader. Together, these shifted power to the presidency. They also reflected the influence of German attitudes, which emphasized the leadership-principle long before Hitler came onto the scene. Associated with this was the faith in management by experts.

A fifth concept had to do with the mixture of reform and moralism. (Liberals would later criticize the moralism as inconsistent with a "scientific" attitude toward social control. Progressivism was itself ambivalent, as liberalism has continued to be, in its combination of moralism and the expert.)

The combination of all these things has led historians into a running debate over just what Progressivism really was. The debate is largely an argument over what social groups should be considered most representative of it. It has been common to think of Progressivism as a middle-class movement, but Huthmacher and Buenker have shown the importance of the city political machines and the ethnic-immigrant vote. The reader is aware, too, that I would never have us lose sight of what was happening in the intellectual culture.

Most certainly the Progressive period was an age of ferment. In light of the diversity within the movement, however, I see some merit in the conclusion by Peter G. Filene, as paraphrased by Link and McCormick, that "what has been called the progressive movement never existed as a historical phenomenon."[18]

Progressivism is said to have gone into eclipse by the time the United States became involved in World War I, but major activity actually continued until the defeat of Robert LaFollette as a third-party presidential candidate under a Progressive Party label in 1924.

Why did the ferment die away? A New Republic

article in 1926 said that "the 'new freedom' was buried during the War in the same grave with the 'new nationalism,'" thus ascribing the demise to the war, which absorbed national attention. Otis Graham, Jr., speaks of the disheartening effect of both the war and the disappointing peace that followed it; of the frustration that idealists felt in light of public apathy and the perseverance of special interests; of the "high personal costs of attention to public affairs"; of "the persistent leadership crisis"; and of the "minimal effect" of Progressive measures "upon the visible ills of America." We must add the fragmentation that inevitably occurs among the various groups within so diverse a movement and the fatigue that follows a period of high ferment.[19]

NOTES

1. Alice Felt Tyler, Freedom's Ferment (New York: Harper Torchbooks, 1944), p. 48.

2. C. S. Griffin, The Ferment of Reform, 1830–1860 (New York: Thomas Y. Crowell Company, 1967), p. 2.

3. For books dealing with the movements during the half-century before the Civil War, see Tyler, Freedom's Ferment; Griffin, Ferment of Reform; and Walter Hugins (ed.), The Reform Impulse, 1825–1850 (New York: Harper Paperbacks, 1972).

4. Hugins, Reform Impulse, p. 6.

5. Henry Adams' letter is quoted in Henry May, The Discontent of the Intellectuals: A Problem of the Twenties (Chicago: Rand McNally & Company, 1963), p. 42.

6. New Republic, September 4, 1915, p. 117.

7. New Republic, November 14, 1914, p. 22; see also Charles McCarthy, Wisconsin Idea, published in 1912; Eric F. Goldman, Rendezvous With Destiny

(New York: Vintage Books, 1977), pp. 80-1; Lewis L. Gould, The Progressive Era (Syracuse: Syracuse University Press, 1974), p. 16.

8. Lawrence Goodwyn, The Populist Movement (New York: Oxford University Press, 1978).

9. New Republic, May 14, 1924, p. 297, editorial; John D. Buenker, Liberalism and Progressive Reform (New York: Charles Scribner's Sons, 1973), p. 40.

10. L. Otis Graham, Jr., An Encore for Reform: The Old Progressives and the New Deal (New York: Oxford University Press, 1967), p. 50.

11. New Republic, March 7, 1983, p. 36; Ralph Henry Gabriel, The Course of American Democratic Thought (New York: Ronald Press Company, 2nd Ed., 1956), pp. 274, 276-7.

12. New Republic, March 3, 1937, p. 102; New Republic, January 16, 1965, p. 19; Lewis A. Coser, Men of Ideas, A Sociologist's View (New York: The Free Press, 1965), pp. 111, 118.

13. New Republic, November 8, 1939, p. 34; New Republic, May 8, 1965, p. 17; New Republic, April 8, 1972, p. 22.

14. New Republic, November 14, 1914, p. 18.

15. New Republic, October 11, 1933, p. 251.

16. The Brandeis letter referred to is quoted at length in Alpheus Thomas Mason, Brandeis: A Free Man's Life (New York: The Viking Press, 1946), p. 585.

17. Herbert Croly, Progressive Democracy (New York: The Macmillan Company, 1915), pp. 390, 356, 227.

18. Arthur S. Link and Richard L. McCormick, Progressivism (Arlington Heights, Ill.: Harlan Davidson, Inc., 1983), p. 2.

19. New Republic, June 9, 1926, p. 73; Graham, _Encore for Reform_, pp. 162-3.

3

PHASES IN AMERICAN LIBERALISM:
1920-1953

The 1920's: a period of drift and yearning

Several themes were important to liberalism during the 1920's, but the overriding tone was one of disillusionment and withdrawal.

This corresponds to the psychology of the intellectual. As an individual, an intellectual passes through a series of alternations. He is acutely sensitive to the imperfections of the world, which run counter to what he sees as possible. The weight of these things causes him to withdraw. But eventually he reenters the world, led by his fervent concerns and by his tendency, after a period of withdrawal, to forget the reasons for it. He then throws himself into passionate activity, believing that people can be brought to see things as he does and to reform themselves accordingly. But it is not long before he sees through to their essential apathy and self-interest, and before they themselves react hostilely to the inconveniences of his idealism. This sends him flying back into withdrawal, partly of his own accord, partly because that is where the world wants him.

This is the pattern described by Emerson; it is the pattern shown by the withdrawals of the 1920's, of the late 1940's, of the 1970's. Although I have described the pyschology of the individual intellectual, the intellectual culture as a whole tends to reflect the cycle. At the same time, a counterculture of withdrawal seems at at least a certain level to be a permanent institution. There were the Beatniks in the 1950's and the Hippies in the 1960's before the mass movement into mysticism in the 1970's.

As always, Herbert Croly was paradigmatic of

71

the liberal mood. Beginning in 1922, <u>The</u> <u>New</u> <u>Republic</u> under his editorship began to urge an inner cultivation in place of politics. Arthur Schlesinger, Jr., says that "Croly himself lost faith in political solutions after the First World War and grew increasingly absorbed in psychology and mysticism." Eric Goldman reports how Croly "began bringing to <u>New</u> <u>Republic</u> luncheons a bearded Englishman named Orage, who explained that what the world needed was the self-discipline of yoga."[1]

This found its counterpart in the broader literary world. Gertrude Stein referred to Ernest Hemingway as "the Lost Generation," but it was a label that stuck for the entire literary generation. Malcolm Cowley's book <u>Exile's</u> <u>Return</u> tells of the "flight" of "American writers...from hometown to Greenwich Village--from the Village to Paris--from Paris to New England farms." The period of withdrawal lasted roughly until 1930. Cowley told his readers in 1935 that "it was during the second year of the depression that everyone began talking about a new phenomenon. The intelligentsia was 'going left'; it was becoming friendly with the Communists; it was discussing the need for a new American revolution." The withdrawal was over and a new period of ferment had begun.

One of the manifestations of the withdrawal had been the student counterculture of the early 1920's. "The students of the early twenties," William Harlan Hale wrote in 1931, "were the last word in radicalism and smart progressivism... Everyone remembers...the baggy trousers, the collegiate semi-bohemianism." In 1923, H. M. Kallen wrote of "rebellious youth," whose hero was Randolph Bourne. The youth culture's "spirit," he said, "is discontent; its cry: There is no good in the institutions of modern life." George Soule reported in 1931 that "the more intelligent escaped to Europe, to sexual experiment, to egocentric psychological fads, to religion, to esoteric literary and esthetic expression or to an

72

irresponsible Menckenian cynicism."[2]

Alienation burned intensely within the intellectual culture. Its focus came to rest primarily in two _cause celebre_'s: the Mooney-Billings case and the more famous Sacco-Vanzetti case.

The Mooney-Billings case stemmed from a bomb explosion at the Preparedness Day parade in San Francisco on July 22, 1916. Thomas J. Mooney and Warren K. Billings were convicted of complicity in the explosion and sentenced to life imprisonment. For many years The New Republic crusaded for their release, arguing that they had been given an unfair trial because they were "radicals."

The case that brought liberal fury to a white heat, however, was the conviction and eventual execution of Nicola Sacco and Bartolomeo Vanzetti for the murder of a paymaster and a guard during a robbery in South Braintree, Massachusetts, on April 15, 1920. Each anniversary of their execution on August 23, 1927, was for several years commemorated bitterly by The New Republic, which at first claimed only that they had not received a fair trial (again for the reason that they were radicals) but later that they were innocent. The years prior to their execution were filled with a rising crescendo of alienation--the proclamations of defense committees, demonstrations, fund-raising appeals, seemingly endless editorials. Sacco and Vanzetti became as a result martyred folk heroes of the Left. (We recall that during the revolutionary fervor of the late 1960's a folk song by Joan Baez recalled their memory.) To the Left, the case symbolizes "Red hysteria" at its worst.

I have of course not been able to make a detailed study of the case to comment upon its merits, but it is worth pointing out that there were many such episodes, including labor violence and a number of terrorist attacks, each with its aftermath of prosecution and punishment, during the late 19th century and the first half of the

73

20th. During that period the Left rarely, if ever, admitted the guilt of anyone who was prosecuted. It was always as though the wrong men had been apprehended, and frequently the Left pointed to the possibility of <u>agent</u> <u>provocateurs</u> to explain the violence. The main society was always painted as venal in its response to the crimes. Because of that pattern, the protests of the Left carry little <u>prima</u> <u>facie</u> credibility. It is worth noting that the Sacco-Vanzetti convictions underwent years of review by the courts and by the governor of Massachusetts before the executions were carried out.

During these years of withdrawal and alienation, the primary intellectual focus was on Soviet Russia, newly emerged after the October Revolution in 1917. We will later discuss the 1930's as "the Red Decade," which is a label often attached to it, but even though that label is appropriate, we should not lose sight of the fact that the infatuation of the intellectual culture with the Soviets began much earlier, and that it continued through much of the 1940's.

My examples from <u>The</u> <u>New</u> <u>Republic</u> are, of course, simply illustrative of a much broader phenomenon. In 1923, Robert Dunn wrote an article "Seven Lies About Russia." In 1924, the first advertisement for the <u>Daily</u> <u>Worker</u> appeared, thus initiating what was to become the texture of the journal for the next fifteen years, during which advertisements for trips to the Soviet Union, for Communist books and journals, and for front-group meetings and proclamations were liberally distributed through its pages. In 1926, an article by Jerome Davis called "Russia Today" justified the secret police: "...every country has its G.P.U., especially in a period of war and revolution." In 1927, H. N. Brailsford wrote that "society in Russia is spontaneously evolving its own appropriate organs of democracy." Albert Rhys Williams added an article making a Pioneer (young Communist) meeting seem like a Boy Scout outing (can we imagine such an article about the Hitler Youth?).

Also in 1927, H. M. Kallen wrote in an article about religion in Soviet Russia that "dictatorship though it be, [the Soviet regime] has liberated their energies, animated them with an altogether unprecedented sense of personal dignity and inward worth."[3]

In 1928, the premier liberal philosopher John Dewey contributed a series of six articles about his trip to Russia. His tone: "In spite of secret police, inquisitions, arrests and deportations of Nepmen and Kulaks...life for the masses goes on with regularity...There is an enormous constructive effort taking place in the creation of a new collective mentality." The American Federation of Labor thereupon voted to expunge a tribute to Dewey because he had "aligned himself with Bolshevist propaganda," to which The New Republic editorially responded that the A.F. of L.'s action was a "stupid thing."[4]

Domestically, liberalism suffered the blahs. Leaders were scarce; there was little interest, even by The New Republic, in formulating a program. In 1925 a New Republic editorial said that "liberalism is at present paralyzed politically by its lack of a program." Senator Nye's "Platform for Progressives" in 1927 set forth twelve remarkably mundane planks. In 1929, TRB surveyed the existing leaders--and found each lacking. At the end of the period, in 1930, John Dewey wrote that "liberalism today is hardly more than a temper of mind, vaguely called forward-looking, but quite uncertain as to where to look and what to look forward to...."[5]

The result was, as John Buenker has written, that "until the publication of Arthur Link's article in 1959, the prevailing view had always been that the 1920's was a decade of unrelieved reaction, an arid valley between two peaks of social progress." But Link and Buenker argue that something was going on, that the focus of progressive domestic legislation had simply shifted back to the states. "Despite the decade's reputation

75

for reaction," Buenker writes, "it saw great ad-
vances in most states in the realm of welfare
legislation." He cites "rent controls, public
housing, regulation of the milk industry, expanded
public health facilities," and the like. [6]

The 1930's: the New Deal

There are two sides to the intellectual history that I wish to relate about the 1930's. The
first will pertain to the intellectuals' response
to the New Deal of Franklin Delano Roosevelt. The
second will have to do with the extreme leftwing
infatuation of the intellectual culture that has
caused the period to be labelled "The Red Decade."
I shall leave this second aspect to the next section.

It will be worthwhile to review a number of
the New Deal's specific programs, noticing the
continuity that links them with the liberal thinking that preceded and has followed them. We will
leave some of the main issues, however, for more
detailed discussion later in this section.

1. The Tennessee Valley Authority reflected
in part an aspiration for large federal reclama-
tion projects that had been voiced in The New
Republic in 1915. [7]

In the socialist thinking that surfaced repeatedly in liberal writing, regional "valley
authorities" were seen as one of the alternative
routes to socialism, especially when combined with
the nationalization of natural resources, transportation, communication and banking that was so
often proposed. Indeed, this was the original
thinking behind the T.V.A., as The New Republic's
readers were told by Jonathan Mitchell in October,
1933. He said that "the Tennessee Valley Authority was designed consciously to be the first
large-scale experiment in economic and social
planning ever undertaken outside Soviet Russia.
It was expected to produce, as rapidly as poss-

ible, a sort of baby Gosplan which later, perhaps, might serve as a model for the nation."[8]

An article by John T. Moutoux in January, 1934, described the extent of intended governmental activity: "The town of Norris, Tennessee,...will be the first example in the United States of what genuine, coordinated planning can accomplish...The sole landlord, the sole builder, will be the T.V.A. itself...The land and buildings at Norris will be for rent only...At one end of the common will be the town center, which will include...a hotel, a restaurant, a drug store, a barber shop and beauty parlor, a general store and a post office. All these will be built and owned by the T.V.A. It has not yet been decided whether the T.V.A. will operate them itself or lease them...."[9]

Perhaps most significantly, the aspiration among liberal theorists was eventually to establish such an authority in every feasible river valley in the United States. In 1936, The New Republic "warmly approved" when Senator George Norris proposed a valley authority for the entire Mississippi Valley except for the Ohio River area. Rexford Tugwell was reported by TRB to have "had great plans" in 1933-4, "such things as rehousing industrial workers in greenbelt cities and organizing farmers in collective farms." I cite this not because it related to a valley authority, but because it was in the same spirit as the Town of Norris conception. In 1943, the members of President Roosevelt's National Resources Planning Board had, according to a New Republic special section, "the vision and courage to demand that there should be a similar enterprise [to T.V.A.] wherever in America the geographical conditions make it possible." In 1949, President Harry Truman's program included a Columbia Valley Authority.[10]

It is a part of the ultimate disillusionment of liberalism that very few of these objectives were met. As we shall see, the American electorate has at almost all times since 1937 created

77

what has essentially been a political deadlock between liberals and conservatives, with neither being able to enact anything approximating its full program.

2. The Securities Act of 1933 and Securities Exchange Act of 1934 established a national framework for the full disclosure of information in securities transactions. This was consistent with the article by Professor William Z. Ripley in Atlantic Monthly in 1926 that urged the Federal Trade Commission to become the vehicle for such a disclosure system.

In terms of intellectual history, however, it is significant that in 1934 Bruce Bliven, the leading editor of The New Republic after Croly's death, was critical of the "truth-in-securities" approach. He wanted much more--a determination by government of the allocation of capital. His preference was consistent with The New Republic's advocacy in 1933 of complete government ownership and operation of banking. [11]

3. England had created an unemployment insurance system in 1911. Germany patterned its system after England's in 1927.

In the United States in 1910, New York established the first unemployment compensation system. Forty-four states had such laws by the time the federal government came into the picture in 1935. Liberals debated among themselves about the most desirable sort of system. Wisconsin created one in 1932 that placed substantial financial incentives on employers to stabilize their own hiring. But in an article in The New Republic in 1934 Abraham Epstein opposed such a system based on individual company reserves, arguing that help for the unemployed was more important than the prevention of unemployment. [12]

The unemployment insurance system established by the Social Security Act in 1935 has, in common with the Social Security system in general, been criticized by liberals for having made a meagre beginning. Paul Conkin says it "delegated most responsibility to the states and invited chaotic variations in always inadequate payments." During the ensuing half-century the system's scope and benefits have been substantially enlarged.[13]

4. Conkin says that "the Social Security Act of 1935 became the supreme symbol of a welfare state." But he adds that "it hardly deserved the honor or opprobrium," since it covered only half the population, included a tax upon the workers themselves, did not cover accident and illness during the working years, had no medical insurance feature, and "paid benefits on the basis of past earnings instead of present needs."

It, too, has been expanded over the years, but it has frustrated liberals that the United States has never adopted a system of national health insurance.

Almost a half-century after the Social Security system was established, it ran into deep financial trouble. Despite the impression it creates of being an insurance system, it is not based on a fund that is actuarially determined. Essentially it is a system of benefits paid for by taxes. The tax has risen to an astonishing level that for many taxpayers exceeds that of the income tax. With the increasing number of elderly Americans, more and more of the burden is placed on the correspondingly few who are currently employed.[14]

5. The New Deal is closely associated in the public mind with large public works projects to provide employment. For the intellectual history of such programs, we know what H. N. Brailsford told readers of The New Republic in 1929: "The broad idea--that public works should be used as a regulator to counteract the vagaries of the trade cycle...--is as old as the famous minority report on the Poor Law which the Webbs drafted twenty years ago...It has always been a Fabian doctrine." Most classical liberal opponents of expanded

government have been unfavorable to such programs, since they believe that the trade cycle is preventable through sound monetary policy. Herbert Hoover, however, had supported the concept since at least 1922.[15]

The actual spending on public works during the New Deal was spotty. Roosevelt was, until his conversion to Keynesianism was completed in 1938, ambivalent between the opposing philosophies of budget-balancing and countercyclical spending.

6. With Section 7(a) of the National Industrial Recovery Act and the Wagner Act of 1935, the federal government placed its imprimatur on collective bargaining. The union movement grew enormously during the 1930's.

This would be a major fact within the history of liberalism if the union movement had not flagged and if the "New Deal coalition" had been able to stay together better than it has during the years since World War II. Since the New Deal, the movement has been, as it was before the 1930's, one of the anchors that has rooted liberalism in the actualities of American life. Its increasing weakness relative to other forces was well illustrated in 1976, when neither organized labor nor the intellectual culture was able to determine the Democratic presidential candidate.

7. There were many programs that I will not be able to discuss, but a final one that I will mention because of its prominence as a liberal concept after World War II is the idea of "yardstick industries." This involved having government corporations compete in private industries, thus establishing a "yardstick" to evaluate capitalism's performance. In 1974, Melville Ulmer said the idea was "one of the seminal ideas introduced in the New Deal, though its initial formulation appeared in an article by Walter Durand in The New Republic...[in] 1926."[16]

I have left certain additional issues for

more extended discussion. The first of these is the split that occurred within the New Deal over the New Nationalist and New Freedom approaches to the regulation of business (thus continuing the liberal debate of 1912).

The New Nationalist policy suffered from a multiple personality. First, its business supporters wanted a legal and institutional framework for a "more rational" conduct of industry that would avoid the rigors of competition. This was intended to be consistent with the profit motive and the businessmen's own control of their industries. Second, the intellectuals who supported it saw it as perhaps the best vehicle for a centralist socialism, albeit one that integrated businessmen into its administrative structure. And, third, similar integrations of business and government had for several years been popular within the totalitarian ideologies.

A business proposal for the "stabilization of industry" through trade associations under federal supervision that could "stabilize prices" came from Gerard Swope, president of the General Electric Company, in 1931. In the same year, the United States Chamber of Commerce wanted the antitrust laws amended to allow competitors to allocate production with government oversight.[17]

Those liberal intellectuals who were inclined toward a centralized socialism wanted industry organized under government with an eye primarily to social goals. In May, 1933, TRB reported Franklin Roosevelt's call for a "partnership" of government and business. "Actually, I think, control is a more accurate word," TRB said. "That this trend is distinctly towards socialization of industry is not denied. Private operation and ownership will be retained, but there will be federal planning and control." The next week, The New Republic's editors responded to the bill to establish the National Recovery Administration by saying that "conceivably, it may mark the beginning not merely of recovery but of a collectiviza-

81

tion of the economic system...We are now about to
be committed to national economic planning and
control."[18]

A proposal that Lenin had made shortly before
the Bolshevik Revolution was actually preferred by
the editors of The New Republic. "Lenin's proposal went much further than Mr. Roosevelt's does in
two significant directions--control by organized
labor and organization of consumers," the editors
said. "Unless the partnership is extended to
these important functions, monopolistic capital
will almost certainly attempt to sequester too
large a share."[19]

In Italy, Mussolini had in 1925 announced a
plan for a similar organization of the economy,
but he did not actually institute it until he
established his 22 "corporazioni" in 1934. In
1936, an article by Paul H. Douglas said that
"these are roughly comparable to the code authorities under the N.R.A., except that the workers'
syndicates have nominally equal representation
with the employers." A New Republic editorial had
commented on the Swope plan by saying that "this
type of control is exactly what Mussolini means by
'the corporate state'--though with a considerably
larger formal place both for labor and for the
government...."[20]

In Germany, according to Malcolm Cowley in
1941, "Hermann Rauschning and his conservative
friends were planning to use the Nazis for their
own ends...They believed that in each industry or
trade, the employers, the salaried employees and
the workers should together form a corporation
legally authorized to fix prices and wages and to
limit production; it would be a permanent N.R.A."
Nor was this simply a futile dream by Rauschning.
Hitler placed industry under centralized direction, integrating its constituent elements. He,
too, included a substantial ingredient of ideological cohesion.[21]

The New Nationalism was instituted in the

United States through the National Industrial
Recovery Act's establishment of the National Recovery Administration (the N.R.A.).   There was a
corresponding program for agriculture through the
Agricultural Adjustment Act (the A.A.A.).

Under the N.R.A., industry-wide codes were
drawn up in virtually every field. These codes
put limits on production, raised prices, forbade
"unfair competition," and set out wage-and-hour
provisions, collective bargaining rights, and
stipulations against child labor.   Under the
A.A.A., farmers were induced to cut production in
exchange for government payments.

The personalities whose names are associated
with one or another of the variants of the New
Nationalist phase of the New Deal are Raymond
Moley, Hugh Johnson, Adolf Berle, Gardiner Means,
Donald Richberg, Rexford Tugwell, Jerome Frank and
Charles Beard.

Almost immediately after N.R.A. was established, liberal intellectuals who were predis-
posed in its favor became soured. A New Republic
editorial in August, 1933, referred to "a heart-
breaking record two and a half months after the
Recovery Act came into effect" and said that "the
nation's great fundamental industries...are fighting the government." In early September another
editorial said that "the industrial aspect..., as
it stands today, is a failure." By December, John
T. Flynn, then quite prominent among The New
Republic's writers, made what was to become the
standard liberal complaint against the N.R.A.:
that both the content and the enforcement of the
codes served the purposes of business itself and
not of governmentally-established social policy.[22]

In April, 1935, TRB said that the N.R.A. "and
to a less degree the A.A.A." were "in a state of
collapse." An editorial two weeks earlier urged
new legislation for the direct regulation of business in place of the "partnership" represented by
N.R.A., although the editors said dolefully that

"the whole effort is likely to fail unless industry is socialized." Within a short time thereafter, the United States Supreme Court declared
the N.R.A. and parts of the A.A.A. unconstitutional. [23]

This marked the demise of the New Nationalist
phase of the New Deal, and led into what is considered the New Freedom phase. The phasing should,
however, be considered mainly a classification for
convenience. It must be taken with both caution
and reservations. After the passing of the N.R.A.
the administration had no clear commitment to the
breaking up of big business; nor did Franklin
Roosevelt forsake entirely the effort to adopt an
integrationist approach.

The new phase, such as it was, was backed by
Felix Frankfurter, Thomas Corcoran, Benjamin
Cohen, James Landis, Marriner Eccles, William O.
Douglas, Leon Henderson and Lauchlin Curry, among
others. [24]

Public actions during the phase included
President Roosevelt's call in 1935 for a "tax on
bigness" that would place high progressive tax
rates on corporations and would eventually use
taxation to eliminate holding companies. (The New
Republic, still preferring the New Nationalist
approach if properly applied from its point of
view, ran an article by Jonathan Mitchell attacking "the primitive economic system of the so-
called 'Brandeis group'...which was illustrated by
the 'tax on bigness'....") [25]

In 1936, Roosevelt made his famous attack on
"economic royalists" in his speech accepting the
Democratic nomination. In 1937 he strongly trum-
peted the antitrust laws. Thurman Arnold was put
in charge of the antitrust division of the Justice
Department in 1938 and began vigorous enforcement.
This was muted, however, by the onrush of World
War II and by inconsistency within the administration, so that Barton Bernstein has concluded that
"there was no effort to atomize business, no real

84

threat to concentration." The administration's version of the Public Utilities Holding Company Act would have empowered the S.E.C. to give a "death sentence" to any utility holding company that it found to be without economic justification, but this was softened by Congress.[26]

Roosevelt made no clear philosophical commitment, however. Even after the "New Freedom phase" was supposedly underway, the administration obtained passage of the Guffey Act, which The New Republic said "created "a 'little N.R.A.' for coal." The Federal Trade Commission established N.R.A.-type rules for the wholesale tobacco industry. In February, 1937, TRB reported that Roosevelt wanted to revamp the Supreme Court so that he could recreate the N.R.A. and the A.A.A. Donald Richberg had proposed a new N.R.A. to be run by the Federal Trade Commission.[27]

Roosevelt was a master politician and philosophically indeterminate. These combined to create an almost legendary inconsistency. He played all sides and made frequent use of deception, especially before elections. During the 1932 campaign, The New Republic reported "the philosophical opportunism at the base of the candidate's thought." In January, 1934, the journal said that the New Deal was going partly right, partly left, following the line of least resistance. That October, Lewis Mumford spoke disparagingly of the New Deal's "pragmatism," which he called "aimless experiment, sporadic patchwork."[28]

Although this pragmatism was praised after the Left, including the Communist Party, shifted its support dramatically behind Roosevelt as a result of the United Front, the ultimate verdict by the intellectual culture was expressed by Paul Conkin when he wrote that "the story of the New Deal is a sad story, the ever recurring story of what might have been." He said that "the New Deal failed to fulfill even the minimal dream of most reformers." [29]

This inconsistency causes some difficulty for those who have broken the period into a "First" and a "Second New Deal" (a classification that differs somewhat from the distinction, also foggy, between the New Nationalist and New Freedom phases).

Basil Rauch's The History of the New Deal in 1944 is said to have been the first commentary to speak in terms of two New Deals. The first phase was that of the N.R.A.; the second was from 1935 to 1938, consisting of "reforms intended to raise mass purchasing power and security." Walter Lippmann later spoke of the first New Deal as continuing until Roosevelt's court-packing debacle in 1937, followed by a second New Deal consisting of "the compensated economy." [30]

Arthur Schlesinger, Jr., has distinguished between a first New Deal of 1933-4 and a second New Deal, starting in 1935-6, that mixed the New Freedomite tendencies of Brandeis and the counter-cyclical spending theories of Keynes. [31]

Needless to say, all such classifications have had their critics because of the complexity of the subject-matter and the ambivalence of the administration. Huthmacher represents a sizeable body of thought when he writes that "the attempt to define a Second New Deal may be as misleading as the attempt to depict the so-called First New Deal of 1933 in terms of a coherent, prearranged plan of action." He says that "the Brandeis-Frankfurter faction failed to win a clear-cut victory during the Second Hundred Days." The New Deal in general, he says, was characterized by a "bewildering pattern of conflicts."

In the preceding discussion, the reader will have noticed the references to Keynes and to the theory of countercyclical spending. The victory of the Keynesians, so to speak, in 1938 established one of the main features of liberalism as it emerged into the post-World War II period.

We have already seen that H. N. Brailsford in 1929 referred to the idea of government spending to counteract the trade cycle as "as old as the famous minority report on the Poor Law which the Webbs drafted twenty years ago," and that he added that "it has always been a Fabian doctrine." In 1931, Gordon Hayes wrote that "for more than a hundred years, socialists have been fond of attributing depressions to the inability of the masses to buy the products...However, it is only recently that the idea has been accepted in...respectable circles." [32]

John Maynard Keynes, then, was not the formulator of the policy. He was, however, its chief twentieth century theoretician and popularizer, especially through his General Theory of Employment, Interest and Money, published in February, 1936. He also played an important role in the dissimulative dynamic of American liberalism, since he provided a more current source for the ideas, which have not then been attributed generally to socialist thought. A similar role has been played by Berle and Means with regard to the Marxist concept of the separation between ownership and control in corporations.

According to Dean May, the concepts of the "multiplier," of the "propensity to consume" and of "liquidity preference" which are at the heart of the Keynesian system all existed independently of Keynes. [33]

George Soule has given what he calls a "brief and oversimplified" summary of "the essentials of the theory of a compensatory fiscal policy." These include the idea that "there is a tendency for people to save money faster than money is invested in new production. This means that there occurs, from time to time, a net reduction in... purchasing power...The result is depression...The government can compensate for this shrinkage by spending more than it collects in taxes." [34]

Before he became converted to Keynesianism in

1938, Franklin Roosevelt was torn between balancing the budget and countercyclical spending. The administration spent freely in late 1933, but curtailed spending in early 1934. TRB later said that Keynes' influence was "enormous" among New Dealers in 1934-5. In 1935, there was the $4.8 billion work-relief program, but the P.W.A. was dismantled in the same year and Henry F. Morgenthau, Jr., a devout advocate of a balanced budget, rose in prominence. In December, 1937, Roosevelt vowed to veto any new spending. But then in April, 1938, he responded to the downturn of 1937-8 by embracing the Keynesian system.[35]

The New Republic said that Leon Henderson had been "one of the first and sternest evangelists of the consumer-purchasing-power theory." But it was Marriner Eccles, with the assistance of Harry Hopkins, who won both Morgenthau and Roosevelt over to the Keynesian view in early 1938.[36]

Keynesian-type fiscal policy has played a central role since World War II, although not without increasing difficulty due to the dilemma of "stagflation" (which, contrary to the Keynesian expectation, combines inflation and unemployment). Liberal thinkers have often urged going beyond it, seeing social goals beyond mere stabilization. Dean May is correct, though, when he says that "the eventual widespread diffusion of the idea that budgetary policy is really social policy was one of the significant consequences of the New Deal response to the events of 1937-38."[37]

This is not to say, however, that the New Deal ever really solved the problem of the depression. There is much to support the conclusion that Herbert Hoover stated in his memoirs that the New Deal strung the depression out. In March, 1935, two years after Roosevelt was inaugurated, 22 million people were on relief. The downturn in 1937-8 was as sharp as in 1929-30. As late as 1940 eight million people were unemployed, constituting 14.6 percent of the workforce.[38]

The New Deal's political support arose in large part, of course, from Franklin Roosevelt's popularity and from the Depression, but political theorists speak also of what has become known as the "New Deal coalition." This was a diverse combination: organized labor, ethnic and religious minorities, the Solid South, the big-city political machines, farm laborites, liberal Republicans and the intellectuals (when, especially after the United Front began, they chose to lend support).

The coalition had been a long time in coming. Woodrow Wilson had tried to put it together in 1912, hoping to combine Catholics, Jews, labor, immigrants and the South. The Al Smith candidacy in 1928 had, according to TRB in 1968, "opened the doors" to millions of newcomers; there had been 20 million immigrants between 1880 and 1910. Smith's candidacy "made it possible for FDR to put together his 1932 coalition."[39]

The coalition has provided the political base for liberalism, but also committed it to the "interest group politics" that came under such fire from the New Left purists in the 1960's. Perhaps, too, the most remarkable thing about the coalition has been its diversity and fragility. It is no wonder that liberals have been searching for a "new coalition" since at least 1968.

As I read The New Republic for the New Deal period, I was surprised by the extent of the intellectuals' hostility toward various parts of the coalition. In 1935, an editorial referred to "reactionaries of the South" and to "sordid political machines." The next year, the editors criticized James Farley and "machine politics." Bruce Bliven was talking in 1939 about the "ladling out of federal patronage to crooked politicians." In 1943, Bliven said that Southern Democrats and corrupt city machines "never were convinced in their hearts that the New Deal was a good thing." And in 1947, James Loeb, Jr., lamented that "there never existed an authentic liberal coalition which could survive the loss of

Roosevelt." Henry Wallace looked back and said that even during the New Deal Roosevelt had "no unified labor movement and no coherent liberal movement with which to work."[40]

The deadlock that has existed in American politics became evident in about 1937. According to Leon Keyserling, "FDR lost his power to put through domestic legislation circa 1937, when the Southerners in Congress withdrew their support." Since then, with the exception of the brief period following the election of 1964, there has been no time when there has been both a liberal president and a clearly liberal Congress. Roosevelt lost momentum in the late 1930's as a result of the fight over his court-packing proposal, his effort to purge certain conservative Democratic senators, and the Republican victory in the 1938 congressional elections. He sought no significant legislation after 1938.[41]

So far as the intellectual culture was concerned, it remained far to the left of the New Deal until, as I have said, the United Front, seeking a unified opposition to Hitler, caused it to be much more favorable. The New Republic repeatedly called for a new labor party in 1931 and 1932; it urged its readers to vote for Norman Thomas, the Socialist candidate, and not for Roosevelt, in 1932. Despite its brief interest in the N.R.A., it set down a drumbeat of criticism of Roosevelt: as he came in as president it said that he did not understand "the fundamental malady" and was offering a patch-up job; after he had been in office a year, the editors spoke of his "dismal" record; after another year, John T. Flynn opined that the New Deal was "crumbling" and was "a grand bust"; in June, 1936, the editors said the New Deal was "sadly deficient" compared to their socialist aspirations.[42]

But then in late 1937 the journal's mood changed dramatically. The editors exulted that "we have made more progress toward a socialized economy in the past four and a half years than in

the two previous decades." And the next June an
article by John Chamberlain was able to make the
change appear a thing of the distant past: "Only a
few short years ago [sic.] it was a favorite
ideological sport of radicals, whether Communist,
Socialist, Brandeisian or free-lance, to pour
scorn upon Franklin Delano Roosevelt's 'confused'
[efforts]...to make the American economic system
work." "I must," he said, "plead guilty with the
rest." Granville Hicks, long on the extreme Left,
was even able to write a book entitled I Like
America. It was a time when the Communist Party
was declaring Communism the very pillar of free
enterprise. 43

I will close my discussion of the New Deal by
telling of an issue that throughout the 1930's was
one of the intellectual culture's major themes:
the call for "planning." In January, 1931, The
New Republic editorialized for a national structure to "allot new capital according to plan,
regulate prices, profits and incomes." Rexford
Tugwell said in 1932 that "...the interest of the
liberals among us in the institutions of the new
Russia of the Soviets...has created wide popular
interest in 'planning'...."44

Oddly, in light of the fact that there was so
much open support for socialism, "planning" served
as a euphemism that continued a certain amount of
dissimulation. Many liberals, however, were at
that time willing to be as forthright as Edmund
Wilson was when he wrote that "we have always
talked about the desirability of a planned society...But if this means anything, does it not mean
socialism? And should we not do well to make this
perfectly plain?"

Beginning in March, 1931, George Soule became
one of the leading advocates of planning: "We
shall have to have a textile plan, a coal plan, a
housing plan. Indeed, there ought to be a general
staff for every industrial group, heading into the
General Staff...Private investment will have to be
planned...." This remained his theme for several

91

years. His book <u>A Planned Society</u> appeared in 1932; in 1939 he set out extensive details for a structure of "scientific planning." That same year, W. Jett Lauck called for a "National Planning Board," with "Industry Councils" consisting of "equal representation of industry, labor and the public." There would be a "Capital Issues Banking Board" to determine the direction of investment. [45]

An interesting twist is that John T. Flynn, who had written prolifically for <u>The New Republic</u> during the '30's, eventually became a crusader against the dissimulative introduction of socialism through "planning." In <u>The Road Ahead</u> he warned that "planning" was a euphemism for socialism and that, although George Soule and Stuart Chase had supported it for several years, it became "respectable" as the program of a broad movement in about 1938. His warnings came after his falling out with <u>The New Republic</u>. By that time, he had moved toward conservatism. He had earlier associated himself with the journal during years in which it was far to the left.

The 1930's: the Red Decade

Although the intellectual culture kept one foot in the domestic political scene, the other was squarely planted in far-Left ideology. We have already seen the infatuation with Soviet Russia in the 1920's. By the late '20's, this had become a passionate theme.

In my earlier discussion of the 1920's, I cited examples of the intense interest in Soviet Russia that appeared in <u>The New Republic</u>.

This continued at an even higher intensity during the 1930's. The excitement was reflected in <u>The New Republic</u> by advertisements for Communist causes, manifestoes of front organizations, enthusiastic letters from readers, all combined with innumerable editorials, articles and book reviews. Although there is no substitute for reading the actual journals of that period, I hope that a few examples from The New Republic will give some idea of the tone:

Bruce Bliven, who spent many years with the journal and was the leading editor after Croly, wrote in 1931 that "even with all proper cautions..., I still find this graphic picture of Russia's material progress tremendously exciting." M. R. Werner said that Stalin emerged from a book he was reviewing "as a person for whose character one has a tremendous respect." The next year, Edmund Wilson wrote that "Communism...has for the first time brought humanity out into the great world of creative thought and work." In 1935, Waldo Frank, a frequent contributor, sent in a letter saying that "I wish to stress...my entire loyalty to the Soviet cause and my strict partisanship with its government in its struggles against a hostile world...The U.S.S.R. is the 'fatherland' of all true revolutionaries, the world over."[46]

In 1937 Andre Gide asked in The New Republic "Who shall say what the Soviet Union has been to us? More than a chosen land--an example, a guide. What we have dreamt of, what we have hardly dared to hope, but towards which we were straining all our will and all our strength, was coming into being over there."[47]

The Nation was just as far left. Its editor Oswald Garrison Villard wrote after a trip to Soviet Russia in 1929 that "it is all so new, so genuinely thrilling." In 1934, The Nation editorialized that the New Deal was just "a half-baked capitalism with so-called liberal trimmings"; and in 1937 that "the Soviet government...[is] the leadership of the anti-fascist forces in the world...the chief element of hope." [48]

So engrossing was this ideological partisanship that it led to what future generations will almost certainly consider an intellectual scandal

93

of unspeakable proportions. A major fact about the 1930's is that the world intellectual culture condoned and even justified the mass slaughter within the Soviet Union, just as it has been a major fact since World War II that Hitler's Holocaust has been made the justifiable subject of absolute moral condemnation while the Gulags under Stalin, the execution of many millions under Mao, the genocide in Cambodia, and countless other atrocities under Communist regimes have in the main been ignored by the intellectual culture when they have occurred and then have been given only passing attention.

We have seen that in 1926 Jerome Davis wrote a justification for the Soviet secret police in The New Republic when he said that "...every country has its G.P.U., especially in a period of war and revolution." In 1927, an article told of the execution of twenty-two counter-revolutionaries in Russia, and attributed it to Soviet fears caused by the West and by the assassination of the Soviet ambassador to Poland. In 1930, there was an article justifying the "rooting out" of the kulaks (the prosperous peasants). On the same page, Vera Micheles Dean was the author of a strangely non-judgmental article about the Soviet drive to "liquidate" the kulaks. Later that year, after the New York Times reported the execution of "scores of men" for shortcomings in carrying out the Soviet Five-Year Plan, the New Republic's editors wrote: "Well, in America we execute people for murder and for holding unorthodox political opinions; in Russia they execute people for abusing positions of high responsibility."[49]

In 1931, William Henry Chamberlain informed The New Republic's readers (and editors) of the "ruthless smashing of the kulaks...[who are] banished to concentration camps and places of remote exile." But later that year Herman Simpson reviewed Anna Louise Strong's book The Soviets Conquer Wheat and argued that "the violence which has marked the agrarian revolution seems...to be an inevitable accompaniment of so profound and

far-reaching a transformation...." In the issue
of October 11, 1933, Maxwell S. Stewart spoke of
"the bountiful harvest of 1933," and said that "in
view of the truly remarkable advance made during
the past year, it is difficult to explain the
large number of reports in the American press
depicting famine conditions in Russia...." 50

In 1934, Joshua Kunitz reported that "with
the exception of a relatively few kulaks and anti-
Bolshevik die-hards, the Soviet population stands
solidly behind the government." In 1935, The New
Republic ran an article by Anna Louise Strong
(with an equivocal editorial note introducing it)
which said that "there are 'labor camps' in many
parts of the country, as part of the Soviet method
of reclaiming anti-social elements by useful,
collective work...Men in the labor camps draw
wages, have vacations...." 51

In 1937, a book review by Corliss Lamont
praised the Soviet Union for building production
with "less suffering than capitalism at any time."
That same year, Maurice Hindus looked back and
praised the collectivization of agriculture and
"...the brilliance with which this leadership has
converted the most disastrous calamity, which
collectivization was in its early years, into the
most consummate triumph of the Revolution, if not
of all history." 52

But slowly the terrible reality began to
seep through. Eugene Lyons wrote a letter to The
New Republic in 1937 saying that "Mr. Josephson is
egregiously in error in asserting that in 1932
American intellectuals were 'misinformed' about
Soviet blunders of that period. Not misinformed,
but uninformed. The 1932 equivalent of today's
Josephson's prevented knowledge from reaching
their breathren by shouting down every unpleasant
truth...." In 1939, John Chamberlain wrote of
"...the great 1932-33 famine, in which three or
four million peasants died as a result of the
inept handling of the drive for agrarian collectivization." [Notice that even then he attributed

95

the famine to "ineptness," and that he went on to
blame the famine primarily on the West's refusal
to give Russia capital.][53]

Two months later, Vincent Sheean wrote that
"a program of collectivization in agriculture was
enforced from 1931 onwards by means of the most
ghastly sacrifices, in which six or seven million
peasants are believed to have died of starvation
in the Ukraine alone." The intellectual tragedy
of the period is encapsulated in his admission
that "this is the first criticism I have ever made
of the Soviet Union."[54]

Eugene Lyons, whom I quoted above, became
staunchly anti-Communist after being editor of the
Soviet Russia Pictorial and working for four years
for Tass, the Soviet news agency. After he broke
with Communism, he wrote The Red Decade, in which
he revealed that "in the winter of 1932-33 a
famine greater than any in Russia's history devas-
tated...the Ukraine, North Caucasis and Central
Asia. What made it unspeakably sadistic was that
it was...a planned famine...." He said that "we
all saw it coming. We all knew that the government could head it off by spending a few million
dollars for Canadian or South American grain. But
these little men in the Kremlin....decided to
'punish' a population of forty or fifty million
for their sullen passive resistance against the
state's seizure of their land, tools and live-
stock...How many millions died? Maurice Hindus,
while still among the leading apologists for
Soviet horrors, 'admitted' three million corpses.
Soviet officials and journalists in private conversation put it at seven millions——mentioning the
figure, sometimes, even a little boastfully."[55]

Adam B. Ulam has cited a figure of "four or
five million." He mentions that during the famine
"the state exported a million and a half tons of
grain to secure foreign currency for industrialization."[56]

From what we have seen, it is little wonder

96

that in December, 1984, a later generation of the New Republic's editors would look back and say that "the scandal in the history of this journal is that in the '30's and '40's it accommodated to the zeitgeist (with occasional and important dissents...) by downplaying at best and justifying at worst the crimes of Stalinism." [57]

The intellectual scandal was, however, much broader than simply within the The New Republic. In 1963, Malcolm Muggeridge wrote about "the monstrous cruelties which accompanied the collectivization of agriculture" that had occurred while he had been a correspondent in Moscow, and how both "the flower of the English intelligentsia" and prominent Englishmen had ignored the horror. Frank A. Warren III has told how in the United States Louis Fischer, Maurice Hindus and Walter Duranty (each of them a prolific liberal author) had all justified the slaughter on the basis that "the end justifies the means." [58]

Although the largest part of the intellectual culture turned a blind eye to the starvation of the kulaks (and additionally to the imprisonment of many millions in the Gulags over more than a thirty-year span), it watched Stalin's purges with intense interest. The purges bitterly divided the Left as the 1930's went on and as the slaughter, often of Bolshevik leaders whom the liberals knew personally, mounted. The purges were one of several "shocks" that eventually led many intellectuals to oppose Communism.

Again, it is a history that can be illustrated graphically through the pages of The New Republic:

There was an ironic optimism in a 1933 editorial which forecast that "there will be a new 'purging' of the [Soviet] Communist party...to weed out incompetents, traitors and the indolent." Then its reports of the actual purges began. Its issue of December 19, 1934, reported that "since the assassination of Sergei Kirov, member of the all-powerful Political Committee..., 127 men and women have been arrested. Of these,...sixty-six were executed within twenty-four hours." The editors were non-judgmental. A month later they argued that "fairness demands a suspension of judgment until all the facts are available." [59]

The issue of August 26, 1936, spoke of the trial of Zinoviev and Kamenev, and reported that they and 14 others had been executed for allegedly participating in a plot in which Trotsky collaborated with the Nazis. "The evidence points," the editors said, "to the genuineness of the plot." [60]

In January, 1937, Edmund Wilson and Malcolm Cowley wrote opposing articles about Stalinism. Wilson attacked, Cowley defended. In February, the editors professed their agnosticism toward the treason trials. In April, they reported that John Dewey had become chairman of the American subcommission of the "commission of inquiry into the guilt or innocence of Trotsky." By June, their mood had become one of bewilderment: "The world was puzzled and disturbed by news from the Soviet Union of further convictions and executions for treason, including eight prominent generals." Finally, they shed their neutrality, at least temporarily, saying that "the events...carry their own implications." [61]

The New Republic did not, however, swing decisively to the anti-Stalinist camp. It continued to reflect the competing views. In July it carried an article by Walter Duranty defending Stalin. Duranty said of "the Kremlin's enemies" that "their Trojan horse is broken and its occupants destroyed." In October an article by John Stevens upheld Stalin: "The trials and arrests definitely strengthened the Soviet Union." [62]

On the other side, the editors reported in December that "Dr. Dewey said the members of the committee 'are appalled by the utterly discreditable character of the whole Moscow trial proceedings, at once flimsy and vicious.'" The editors wrote in January, 1938, that "nearly every member of the group that made the Russian Revolution is gone"--and called it "a major disaster." Nevertheless, they reiterated their inability to make a judgment. This was followed by a long interval during which the purges were hardly mentioned. Then in June, 1939, the editors said that "we have seen no evidence conclusive to us that the political trials were 'frame-ups'...."[63]

A startling accumulation of events, which included the purge trials, laid the foundation for a reevaluation of Communism and the Soviet Union. The purges had created doubt and bitter division. Then the brutality of Communist power-seeking against the other leftist factions during the Spanish Civil War precipitated the breaking away of others, most notably John Dos Passos. Finally, the Hitler-Stalin Pact, followed almost immediately by the invasion and partition of Poland by Germany and the Soviet Union, and then within a short time by the Soviet invasion of Finland and of Latvia, Lithuania and Estonia, shook the intellectual culture to its core.

Unfortunately much of the old affinity was reestablished after Hitler invaded the Soviet Union in June, 1941, and after England and the United States became allies of the Soviet Union in World War II. But things were never totally the same, and the "shocks" that rocked the Communist world after World War II (such things as the Lysenko affair, the Hungarian Revolution, Krushchev's revelations about Stalin, the "Polish October," and the crushing of the Dubcek regime in Czechoslovakia) continued to erode the position of the Soviets within the world intellectual community.[64]

The announcement of the Hitler-Stalin Pact, entered into on August 23, 1939, stunned the intellectual culture. The New Republic called it "paralyzing." The Nation said "the disillusion which will follow among the left forces here and abroad will be bitter."

99

The shock was compounded by embarrassment. On August 10, less than two weeks before the Pact was declared, a group of America's most prominent liberal writers, calling itself "the Committee of 400," had issued its famous letter stating their collective faith that political dictatorship was only a transitional phase in the Soviet Union and that "the Soviet Union continues as always to be a bulwark against war and aggression." The signers included many of the names best known to readers of the liberal journals: Waldo Frank, Granville Hicks, Matthew Josephson, Max Lerner, Robert Morss Lovett, Frederick L. Schuman, Vincent Sheean, Maxwell Stewart, I. F. Stone, and James Thurber.

The shock was not enough, however, to keep a tenacious New Republic from rationalizing the Pact: "The Russian explanation of why the treaty was signed seems to make good sense...it frees her from having to fight on two fronts at once in case of a major conflict with Japan."[65]

In late September the journal reported the Soviet armistice with Japan and invasion of Poland. The next week, a letter from Granville Hicks told why he was resigning from the Communist Party, but pledged to continue to defend the party and not to denounce the Soviet Union. Then in early November Vincent Sheean's description of the Soviet Union as a "fascist state" appeared. In mid-December the editors finally came forward: "There never has been a clearer case of...aggression...than the invasion of Finland by the Soviet Union."[66]

This eventual candor was followed by surprisingly little comment in The New Republic during the next year and a half. There was no introspection into the role it had played. Even after reporting the assassination of Trotsky in Mexico in 1940, the journal chose not to mention it again for several months.

This insouciance lasted until Hitler attacked the U.S.S.R. on June 22, 1941. The New Republic

immediately urged aid to the Soviet Union (a policy favored, as well, by Winston Churchill). In
November, Roger Baldwin wrote hopefully that there
would now be a way to influence the Soviets toward
"socialist democracy." In the same issue, A.
Jugow glowingly praised the social justice that
existed within the Soviet Union, and Maurice Hindus argued that Stalin's ruthlessness had had the
advantage of hardening the Soviet Union for its
contest with Germany. The new mood, which for
many was a renewal of the old, was captured by
Vice President Henry Wallace in a speech in early
1942: "Russia...was changed from an illiterate to
a literate nation within one generation and, in
the process, Russia's appreciation of freedom was
enormously enhanced." 67

During World War II

Everyone knows, of course, that the Allies
won militarily in World War II, defeating Germany,
Japan and Italy. But it is equally significant
that the non-Communist world lost the peace.
Within slightly more than four years after the war
ended, the Soviet Union had taken the eastern half
of Europe and the Communists under Mao had con-
quered China. This set the stage for the Cold War
and for the Korean and Vietnam wars.

I will leave a more complete discussion of
this to my chapter on liberalism's international
worldview and policies. For the present, it will
be sufficient simply to have referred ahead to the
subject and to have observed that the major cause
of the disastrous aftermath of the war lay in the
illusions that the Left and liberalism fostered
about Communism.

The tone of the intellectual culture during
the war is well illustrated by The Nation's having
run a number of articles by Anna Louise Strong,
for many years prior to her own fall from grace
one of the most unquestioning apologists for the
Soviet Union. One of these was her 1944 article

"With the Red Army." [68]

While Winston Churchill saw the war in realistic geopolitical terms and sought a strategy
that would minimize the post-war position of the
Soviet Union, Roosevelt overrode him. This was
due to a blindness born out of the illusion
spawned by the ideological context that I have
been tracing. In vitally important ways, although
not entirely, Harry Truman continued to act under
this illusion after he became president. Although
liberalism has been ambivalent, the illusion has
remained as a vitally important part of the liberal worldview ever since. An understanding of its
presence and of the consequences that have flowed
from it is essential to a comprehension of the
second half of the 20th century.

On the domestic front, Roosevelt in 1943 proposed his "American Charter" for the post-war
period. This included his "Economic Bill of
Rights," with its explicit politicization of the
problem of individual economic well-being, and a
number of interventionist measures. A T.V.A.-type
project was proposed for all feasible river val-
leys. Roosevelt's 1944 State of the Union address
expounded on his "Second Bill of Rights."[69]

The issue of racial segregation began to
appear in liberal writing. In April, 1943, The
New Republic declared that "segregation has made
possible the greatest injuries to the Negro
people."[70]

In May, 1944, The New Republic published "A
Platform for Progressives" that corresponded to
Roosevelt's proposals. Although it wanted "more
T.V.A.'s," it did not otherwise call for socialism. Rather, there was to be a strengthening of
what the journal referred to as "the social service state." The editors included a forceful call
for a fight against racial discrimination.[71]

A conservative coalition controlled both
houses of Congress. There was, in addition, dis-

102

sension among the factions of the "New Deal coalition." It infuriated the intellectual culture, for example, when William Green, the president of the American Federation of Labor, endorsed Martin Dies, the chairman of the House Committee on Un-American Activities, for reelection. In another matter, The New Republic denounced "corrupt big-city machines" and "Southern Tories" for having forced Henry Wallace out as Roosevelt's running mate in 1944.[72]

Truman's "Fair Deal"

Domestically, the years of the Truman administration between 1945 and 1953 were marked by the scaling down of liberal aspirations from those of socialism to those of a "welfare state," which Michael Straight, then the editor of The New Republic, described in 1949 as "a cooperative, state-aided capitalism dedicated to human welfare."[73]

Throughout the post-World War II period, the most prominent liberal authors have retained their aspiration for socialism, but this has been relegated to the background because there has seemed to be no route to attain it. Indeed, a number of historic factors have brought European socialism to embrace a combination of the market economy and the welfare state. The British socialist G. D. H. Cole told The New Republic's readers in 1952 that the social democratic variant of Marxism in Western Europe "has accepted the idea of using the parliamentary instrument for advancing in the direction of the Welfare State." Ben Seligman said about a book by Harry K. Girvetz that "the positive program for today's liberals that he offers is a compound of Beveridge, Keynes and Hansen, with Britain and Scandinavia set up as suitable models."[74]

This was the beginning of the type of liberalism that we have known since World War II, a liberalism that has consisted of a "liberal agenda" before the Congress for measures leading to a piecemeal expansion of federal power.

Since many of the proposals have been of the "foot-in-the-door" variety, with liberals intending further growth of the function once government has begun to exercise it, conservatives have labelled it "creeping socialism."

The New Republic praised Truman's State of the Union message in early 1946, which Henry Wallace later said "contained a magnificent New Deal program." The speech proposed federal aid to education, a national public works program, a federal health system, a permanent Fair Employment Practices Commission, an increased minimum wage and a federal scientific research agency.[75]

Keynesian economics was institutionalized by the Employment Act of 1946. After his conversion to conservatism, one of The New Republic's writers Garet Garrett described the Act as "a law of revolutionary purport" that "delivered into the hands of government ultimate control of the American economy." The Act committed the federal government to maintain full employment.[76]

In the 1948 presidential election campaign, Truman went to the country with what TRB described as "the most radical platform in presidential history." Among other things, the platform, he said, "advocates government ownership and operation of transmission lines from government dams right up to the consumers' electric stoves." A New Republic editorial reported that Truman "has chosen to fight on principles of militant liberalism."[77]

Then in his 1949 State of the Union message in which he set forth his "Fair Deal," Truman proposed what TRB called "a social-welfare state [that] amounts to the most leftward-leaning program ever sent by an American president to Congress." Truman urged creation of a Columbia Valley Authority for the Northwest. To TRB, the

Brannan Plan for agriculture was "breath-taking." He wrote that "the basic theory's simple and revolutionary: We give a particular class economic security in return for quite heavy regimentation." The administration called for public housing, the extension of Social Security, more progressive rates for the income tax. [78]

From all of this it may seem that those were exuberant years for a liberalism willing to content itself at least temporarily with the incremental techniques of a welfare state. But such an impression would seriously miss the mark.

Although Truman's program and rhetoric were applauded by liberal intellectuals, the actual direction of his administration was not to their liking. In 1946, a New Republic editorial reported that progressives no longer had a major spokesman within the administration. In 1948, Henry Wallace wrote that "no significant part" of the "magnificent New Deal program" that Truman had submitted two years before had been enacted. In May of that year, the editors complained that Truman's actions had been quite different from his speeches, and that the New Dealers in the administration had been replaced by men from the military and from Wall Street. [79]

The New Republic endorsed Truman for election later that fall after he stepped up his militant rhetoric and after Henry Wallace was replaced by Michael Straight as editor. But in 1949 TRB was observing again that there was "a basic paradox" in "the difference between the President's almost radical words and the men advising him." James Wechsler's verdict years later was that Truman "was something less than a resolute, adventurous liberal crusader...[He] could gruffly pay his rhetorical respects to progressive legislation but he was neither creative nor original in this realm." [80]

Even if Truman had had the qualities that a man like Wechsler would have wanted, there were

three obstacles standing in the way of the Fair
Deal program: the presence of the Republican 80th
Congress in 1947 and 1948, the Republican-Southern
Democrat coalition in Congress the rest of the
time, and the Korean War that began in June, 1950,
and drained away the possibility of domestic inno-
vation.

During all of this, there was a struggle
within the liberal intellectual culture over the
movement's relation to Communism. The far-left
Progressive Citizens of America (P.C.A.) was
formed in December, 1946. This stimulated the
formation of the Americans for Democratic Action
(A.D.A.) in early 1947, which Chilton Williamson,
Jr., says "adamantly opposed...working with Communists and fellow-travelers." According to
Wechsler, the A.D.A. became "a leading factor in
the rout of the U.S. Communist movement in the
1948 campaign" when the Communist-run Progressive
Party failed to attract widespread liberal
support.[81]

Thus, the main body of American liberals had
broken with the Communist Left. Instead, in
Wechsler's words, "the A.D.A. has provided the
stimulus of a sort of American Fabian Society."
It is interesting how this was seen by the differing points of view: to the Left it meant a major
movement of American liberalism to the right; to
conservatives the Fabian tactic of piecemeal
socialism seemed just as threatening as before.[82]

It will be best for me to leave my discussion
of liberalism's relationship to international
affairs during this period to my later chapter on
that subject, since it cannot adequately be
discussed without giving it detailed attention.
The capsule summary that follows is necessarily
oversimplified:

American liberals slowly struggled toward the
doctrine of containment vis a vis Communist expansion, proposed by George Kennan in 1947. Nevertheless, American policy was heavily, and disas-

trously, influenced by the continuing illusion about Communism, which unfortunately was not fully dispelled by the split between the P.C.A. and the A.D.A.

Over Churchill's objections, Eastern Europe was allowed to fall into the hands of the Red Army and become consolidated as part of the Soviet empire; the Soviet Union was encouraged to come into the war against Japan despite the United States' possession of the atom bomb, and this gave the Communists great strategic advantages in their fight to conquer China; illusions were vigorously advanced about the nature of the Maoist movement in China, and the anti-Communist government of Chiang Kai-shek was vilified unmercifully, leading to policies that resulted in the Communist victory in late 1949; and policies were pursued and statements made that encouraged the North Korean Communists to invade South Korea, which they did in June, 1950.

On the other side of the ledger, Western Europe was maintained and strengthened as part of the non-Communist world. Once the idea of having the Soviet Union join in the Marshall Plan was out of the way, the Marshall Plan became a major instrument on behalf of the free world. In Greece, the Truman Doctrine was successful in defeating the Communist insurgency. This prevented a shift in the balance of power to the Soviet Union in the eastern Mediterranean. It is worth observing, however, that the Truman Doctrine was strenuously opposed editorially by both The New Republic and The Nation.[83]

NOTES

1. New Republic, June 7, 1922, p. 34; New Republic, April 8, 1972, p. 23; Eric F. Goldman, Rendezvous With Destiny (New York: Vintage Books, 1977), p. 223.

2. New Republic, May 13, 1931, p. 348; New Repub-

lic, January 10, 1923, p. 168; New Republic, January 31, 1931.

3. New Republic, June 6, 1923, p. 42; New Republic, April 9, 1924, p. 187III; New Republic, October 13, 1926, p. 211; New Republic, June 1, 1927, p. 36; New Republic, September 21, 1927, p. 112; New Republic, November 2, 1927, p. 279.

4. New Republic, November 21, 1928, p. 12; New Republic, December 12, 1928, p. 79.

5. New Republic, December 23, 1925, p. 123; New Republic, September 28, 1927, p. 133; New Republic, February 20, 1929, p. 15; New Republic, February 5, 1930, p. 295.

6. John D. Buenker, Liberalism and Progressive Reform (New York: Charles Scribner's Sons, 1973), pp. 230, 231, 51.

7. New Republic, April 10, 1915, p. 250.

8. New Republic, October 18, 1933, p. 272.

9. New Republic, January 31, 1934, p. 330.

10. New Republic, April 22, 1936, p. 302; New Republic, March 1, 1939, p. 100; New Republic, April 11, 1949, p. 14; New Republic, April 19, 1943, p. 536.

11. New Republic, May 16, 1934, p. 13; New Republic, March 15, 1933, p. 118.

12. New Republic, November 30, 1927, p. 42; New Republic, November 21, 1934, p. 38.

13. Paul K. Conkin, The New Deal (New York: Thomas Y. Crowell Company, 1967), p. 61.

14. Conkin, The New Deal, p. 61.

15. New Republic, May 15, 1929, p. 355; New Republic, November 28, 1928, p. 27.

16. New Republic, January 5, 1974, p. 14.

17. New Republic, September 23, 1931, p. 137; New Republic, October 14, 1931, p. 217.

18. New Republic, May 24, 1933, p. 44; New Republic, May 31, 1933, p. 57.

19. New Republic, May 17, 1933, p. 4.

20. New Republic, March 4, 1936, p. 105; New Republic, November 15, 1933, p. 4.

21. New Republic, August 25, 1941, p. 260.

22. New Republic, August 23, 1933, p. 33; New Republic, September 6, 1933, p. 87; New Republic, December 6, 1933, p. 100.

23. New Republic, April 3, 1935, p. 21; New Republic, March 20, 1935, p. 146.

24. Arthur M. Schlesinger, Jr., The Age of Roosevelt: The Politics of Upheaval (Boston: Houghton Mifflin Company, 1960), p. 387.

25. New Republic, July 3, 1935, p. 205.

26. New Republic, January 29, 1936, p. 334; Richard S. Kirkendall (ed.), The New Deal: The Historical Debate (New York: John Wiley & Sons, Inc., 1973), p. 131; Conkin, The New Deal, p. 66.

27. New Republic, September 4, 1935, p. 87; New Republic, February 24, 1937, p. 72.

28. New Republic, September 28, 1932, p. 164; New Republic, January 17, 1934, p. 263; New Republic, October 3, 1934, p. 223.

29. Conkin, The New Deal, p. 73.

30. Bernard Sternsher, Rexford Tugwell and the New Deal (New Brunswick: Rutgers University Press, 1964), p. 122; New Republic, December 25, 1944, p.

877; New Republic, July 25, 1960, p. 21.

31. New Republic, September 26, 1960, p. 23.

32. New Republic, June 3, 1931, p. 67.

33. Dean L. May, From New Deal to New Economics (New York: Garland Publishing, Inc., 1981), p. 59.

34. New Republic, January 28, 1944, p. 268.

35. New Republic, July 5, 1939, p. 250.

36. New Republic, May 10, 1939, p. 3; May, From New Deal, p. x.

37. May, From New Deal, p. 26.

38. Sternsher, Rexford Tugwell, p. 76 (re Hoover); New Republic, March 20, 1935, p. 141; May, From New Deal, p. 4; Louis A. Zurcher, Jr., and Charles M. Bonjean (ed.s), Planned Social Intervention (London: Chandler Publishing Company, 1970), p. 213.

39. Lewis L. Gould, The Progressive Era (New York: Syracuse University Press, 1974), p. 97; New Republic, September 7, 1968, p. 6.

40. New Republic, May 22, 1935, p. 33; New Republic, January 1, 1936, p. 211; New Republic, February 8, 1939, p. 12; New Republic, May 17, 1943, p. 660; New Republic, January 27, 1947, p. 3; New Republic, December 16, 1946, p. 785.

41. New Republic, October 27, 1958, p. 13.

42. New Republic, March 8, 1933, p. 89; New Republic, March 14, 1934, p. 116; New Republic, January 9, 1935, p. 245; New Republic, January 30, 1935, p. 332; New Republic, June 10, 1936, p. 157.

43. New Republic, September 29, 1937, p. 201; New Republic, June 15, 1938, p. 163.

44. New Republic, January 21, 1931, p. 259; Howard Zinn (ed.), New Deal Thought (Indianapolis: Bobbs-Merrill Company, 1966), p. 14.

45. New Republic, January 14, 1931, p. 234; New Republic, March 11, 1931, p. 89; New Republic, November 8, 1939, p. 29; New Republic, July 5, 1939, pp. 244, 245.

46. New Republic, May 27, 1931, p. 42; New Republic, June 10, 1931, p. 102; New Republic, May 11, 1932, p. 349; New Republic, February 27, 1935, p. 77.

47. New Republic, March 31, 1937, p. 231.

48. The Nation, Vol. 129, p. 515; The Nation, October 31, 1934, p. 498; The Nation, Vol. 145, p. 521.

49. New Republic, October 13, 1926, p. 211; New Republic, June 29, 1927, p. 137; New Republic, March 5, 1930, p. 59; New Republic, December 3, 1930, p. 57.

50. New Republic, February 25, 1931, p. 42; New Republic, December 16, 1931, p. 142; New Republic, October 11, 1933, p. 230.

51. New Republic, January 17, 1934, p. 277; New Republic, August 7, 1935, p. 358.

52. New Republic, January 20, 1937, p. 363; New Republic, August 18, 1937, p. 35.

53. New Republic, December 29, 1937, p. 229; New Republic, September 6, 1939, p. 112.

54. New Republic, November 8, 1939, p. 7.

55. Eugene Lyons, The Red Decade (Indianapolis: Bobbs-Merrill Company, 1941), p. 97.

56. New Republic, March 27, 1976, p. 13.

57. New Republic, December 10, 1984, p. 10.

58. New Republic, November 9, 1963, p. 47; Frank
A. Warren III, Liberals and Communism: The 'Red
Decade' Revisited (Bloomington: Indiana University
Press, 1966), pp. 71, 72.

59. New Republic, January 4, 1933, p. 198; New
Republic, December 19, 1934, p. 151; New Republic,
January 23, 1935, p. 293.

60. New Republic, August 26, 1936, pp. 58, 88.

61. New Republic, January 20, 1937, pp. 345, 348;
New Republic, February 10, 1937, p. 33; New
Republic, April 28, 1937, p. 343; New Republic,
June 23, 1937, pp. 169, 174.

62. New Republic, July 14, 1937, p. 272; New
Republic, October 20, 1937, p. 296.

63. New Republic, December 22, 1937, p. 182; New
Republic, January 5, 1938, p. 240; New Republic,
June 28, 1939, p. 202.

64. New Republic, August 30, 1939, p. 85; The
Nation, August 26, 1939, pp. 212, 228.

65. New Republic, September 6, 1939, p. 118.

66. New Republic, October 4, 1939, p. 244; New
Republic, November 8, 1939, p. 7; New Republic,
December 13, 1939, p. 219.

67. New Republic, June 30, 1941, p. 871; New
Republic, November 17, 1941, pp. 651, 654, 665;
New Republic, May 25, 1942, p. 725.

68. The Nation, Vol. 159, p. 121.

69. New Republic, April 19, 1943, p. 523.

70. New Republic, April 19, 1943, p. 492.

71. New Republic, May 8, 1944, p. 644; New

Republic, October 22, 1945, p. 515.

72. New Republic, March 6, 1944, p. 301; New Republic, July 31, 1944, p. 115.

73. New Republic, August 15, 1949, p. 2.

74. New Republic, March 24, 1952, p. 10; New Republic, March 12, 1951, p. 20.

75. New Republic, January 28, 1946, p. 108; New Republic, January 5, 1948, p. 9.

76. Garet Garrett, The American Story (Chicago: Henry Regnery Company, 1955), p. 387.

77. New Republic, November 15, 1948, p. 3; New Republic, September 27, 1948, p. 32.

78. New Republic, January 31, 1949, p. 3; New Republic, May 9, 1949, p. 3.

79. New Republic, September 30, 1946, p. 396; New Republic, January 5, 1948, p. 9; New Republic, May 17, 1948, pp. 14, 18.

80. New Republic, August 8, 1949, p. 3; James A. Wechsler, The Crucial Decade: America, 1945-1955 (New York: Alfred A. Knopf, Inc., 1956), p. 47.

81. New Republic, February 9, 1974, p. 23; Wechsler, The Crucial Decade, p. 55.

82. Wechsler, The Crucial Decade, p. 56.

83. New Republic, March 24, 1947, p. 6; The Nation, Vol. 166, p. 342.

4

PHASES IN AMERICAN LIBERALISM:
1953-1985

Four postwar decades: all one period

The analysis I am about to make of the phases of liberalism since the Truman administration is a different analysis than I would have made before I read as extensively as I did in the liberal literature of the period.

My impression had been that there were distinct phases—the 1950's, the tumultuous '60's, and the uncertainties and drift of the 1970's and '80's.

I am persuaded now that the entire span (in which we could just as well include the eight years under Truman) has involved a continuous trend. If we do not treat it as the same period, we are likely to lose sight of that continuity. Surprisingly enough, the 1960's are best considered an interlude of frenetic activity in what has otherwise been a steady liberal decline.

I am aware, of course, that this perspective may not hold up. If liberalism regains its vitality and renews its vision, it will then seem that the '60's are the most representative. Only time will tell.

A capsule summary

Variations will appear as we look into the detail, but a summary of the trends within liberalism since World War II will include the following characteristics that have been common to the period as a whole:

    . Even though most of the principal liberal authors have retained their allegiance to socialism, they have done so in a world in which many socialists, especially in Europe, have long been at loose ends. Within both European "social democracy" and American liberalism there has for many years been a more or less constant feeling of drift, of loss of vision, of futility.

. This has been accompanied by a general puncturing, within the public at large and the intellectual culture, of the liberal myths that were powerful for so long. This has included a loss of implicit faith in the ability of government, given an application of reason and enough money, to solve every problem. This deflation is only in small measure a result of conservative efforts. It has come more from the Left's own acceptance of the biting attacks upon "interest group liberalism" and "the Establishment" made by the New Left in the 1960's. It has also come from the seeming intractability of certain realities for a Keynesian-social service society: of inflation, of unemployment even during inflation, of the infinite expandability of social spending without seeming effect, of the decline of productivity, of the failure of the Soviet lion to lie down with the American lamb.

. American voters have continued the deadlock between liberals and conservatives, giving neither of them enough power to carry out new initiatives. Although there is some tinkering and much fidgeting, the country has long-since settled into a post-New Deal consensus following what was in effect the consolidation of the New Deal under Eisenhower. Even the Reagan administration has had little power to carry out its conservative agenda.

. The New Deal coalition has had some staying power, or else liberalism would have passed from existence long ago, but it has also been engaged in a constant process of bickering and division. This has led to a long and thusfar futile search by liberals for a "new coalition."

116

• The Civil Rights movement, on the cutting edge of liberalism during the 1950's and the first half of the '60's, has lost much of its moral force. Pathetically, it has deteriorated into a collection of narrowly self-interested groups, some of which are on a politically unappealing fringe of American society.

• New movements have struggled for vision and may (or may not) point the way to the future: neo-conservatism, with its dispelling of illusion, its anti-Communism and its "two cheers for capitalism"; neo-liberalism, thusfar calling uncertainly for a new Mercantilism that will place government activism behind selected forces within the market; and academic Marxism, which for fifteen years has kept an anti-capitalist critique and the emotions of radicalism simmering within an intellectual culture that has otherwise made its peace, more than ever before, with the society at large.

• It is a fact of the greatest significance that I cannot include in the list an emergent neo-classical liberalism. On the Right, the popularity of Ronald Reagan as president should by all reasonable expectation have stimulated a great intellectual resurgence. Nevertheless, the administration has not seen the importance of being midwife to a new intellectual culture, and one is not developing spontaneously among the country's young people (or otherwise). This suggests that the Reagan years may only be an interregnum. By this failure, the predominant middle class culture retains the flaw that has plagued civilization in virtually all earlier periods of history. This includes the same void that has dominated Western society since the Enlightenment. Such a vacuum, if it continues, will make future ideological neuroses inescapable.

• During all this, both American society and the world have been undergoing changes at an unprecedented rate that will produce existential effects that even the best futurist cannot possibly foretell.

American cultural and moral standards have continued their long decline. The Space and Computer Ages offer hopeful new worlds. Women have left home for business and the professions. Our society has become increasingly heterogeneous ethnically and racially, for whatever revitalization or division that may produce.

Europe has since the world wars shrunk from its preeminence. Its hegemony has been replaced in the "Third World" by a tragic contradiction in which the potential for emergence into modernity is pitted against an insistent tendency on the part of powerful prehistoric forces to pull whole peoples back down into poverty and degradation. Islamic fundamentalism haunts the world with its militant medievalism. The Soviets hold fast to their totalitarian state, but the Chinese now want more of Athens, less of Sparta. It's a world at sea with "lots of sail and little anchor."

A socialist intellectual core

As we have seen, American liberal intellectuality was something of an eclectic hodge-podge of leftist fashions prior to 1945. As I describe its "decline," I do not wish to suggest that it was ever very solid or sure of itself. But it did at least know what it liked and what it disliked, and this knowledge kept it consistently identified with the various fashions of the Left.

Since World War II, liberal thought's socialist core has been almost equally apparent to anyone who has read the literature extensively.

Many of post-World War II liberalism's most prominent writers have been socialists. Michael Harrington and Gunnar Myrdal, both socialists, laid the foundation for the War on Poverty that John F. Kennedy was about to launch when he was assassinated and that was central to Lyndon Johnson's "Great Society." Harrington and Myrdal have, in addition, been prolific authors of books and contributors to the liberal journals.

John Kenneth Galbraith, after many years as a leading liberal spokesman, finally declared himself a socialist--and added that he had been one for many years. This revelation was, of course, no particular surprise; what was surprising was his willingness to breach the usual dissimulation on the subject. Readers of his books had known their actual content for years. It is significant that similar content appears in the writings of many others who have not discovered such candor.[1]

Others who have written prominently within post-World War II liberalism and who have at the same time identified themselves with socialism have included Christopher Jencks, John Rawls, Robert Heilbroner, Robert Lekachman, Irving Howe, Sidney Hook and Christopher Lasch. Irving Kristol was among them until he moved into neo-conservatism.

There are other authors, of course, who have not made the identification, or who even deny that liberalism has such a connection.

One of the more prominent of these has been Eric Goldman, whose book Rendezvous With Destiny is an immensely readable history of "modern American reform." Goldman argues that liberalism is quite distinct from socialism, even though it has been influenced by it and has adopted some of its measures. But to me his argument is puzzling unless we limit it to liberal politics and exclude liberal thought. During my reading of The New Republic, the first article I noticed by Eric Goldman was in November, 1944. He thus began his writing for that journal just shortly after it participated so effulgently in the excesses of the Red Decade. In 1944 the editors were still actively justifying the Soviet system, and had launched a major campaign in favor of the Communists in China.

119

Goldman presented his interpretation of liberalism in a <u>New Republic</u> article co-authored with Mary Paull in July, 1946. I remember how incongruous it seemed among the other articles. (As if deliberately to defrock Goldman's argument, for example, the next week's issue contained a book review by Heinz Eulau entitled "Liberal Manifesto" about a book by a "liberal socialist" that contained "a good deal of Marxist thinking.") Goldman's thesis would seem more plausible today, but made no sense at the time. [2]

<u>Liberalism's loss of vision</u>

Despite the continuation of a generalized socialist faith, liberal intellectuals since World War II have had a problem that didn't exist during the preceding half-century. No longer has it been so easy for them to root their enthusiasms in up-and-coming European movements. The role models have dissolved in the disrepute of the Soviet Union and the quandary of European social democracy.

As early as 1948 George Mayberry was writing in <u>The New Republic</u> that "the hope for international socialism seems more remote today than in many generations." During the 1950's reports repeatedly came in of disillusionment with British socialism. By 1958, Carl Kaysen wrote that "we are all Jeffersonians, now that belief in socialism is dead." In 1960, Daniel Friedenberg wrote that the "failure of American Fabianism" was due to the watering down of German and English socialism. Friedenberg himself was critical of that dilution, concluding that "whores cannot be Fabians." As part of the soul-searching after Walter Mondale's defeat in 1984, <u>The New Republic</u> ran an article speculating on "the death of social democracy" in Europe. Clearly, European socialism since World War II has not seemed the wave of the future. Without a model to go by, only vague aspirations have remained. [3]

During the entire four-decade span since 1945, subject to less of a respite in the 1960's than may be imagined, liberal writing has bemoaned the loss of clear vision, of a long-term aspiration.

In 1946, _The New Republic_'s editors wrote that "there is no clear way beyond the New Deal." Two years later, the Americans for Democratic Action tried to draft Eisenhower to run for president. Since they had no hint of his philosophy or positions on issues, they were as opportunistic and ideologically bankrupt in that attempt as Eisenhower's pre-convention Republican supporters were four years later.[4]

In 1953, John Kenneth Galbraith wrote that "it would be hard at the moment to say what the Democratic Party is for...We are still trading on the imagination and intellectual vigor of the Roosevelt era and that capital is running thin." The columnist TRB in 1956 saw no improvement: "The Democrats' chief obstacle is...their own bankruptcy. [They lack] any clear-cut issue of principle...." In a book in 1960, James Wechsler said that "liberalism admittedly seems defensive, sluggish, apologetic...."[5]

It would be reasonable to think that this ennui was soon replaced by excitement during the Kennedy years and the feverish first two years under Johnson. But to think so is again to confuse the liberal intellectual culture with the effusions of liberal pop culture. In the issue of _The New Republic_ that was written immediately before John F. Kennedy's assassination, Victor Lange spoke of the prevailing sense of futility. He wrote of "the dilemma in which the contemporary intellectual finds himself: unable to accept the reality of his time but being far from any prospect of changing it by a social revolution, he has made up his mind that he must acquiesce in it."[6]

This emptiness at a time when the liberal media were enthusiastically mythologizing the

Camelot-like qualities of the Kennedy presidency shows us something that we have not previously had occasion to notice--that Lange's "contemporary intellectual" was someone quite different from the popular image of a liberal. The great orthodoxy of the liberal media, which had by that time become such an aggressive national institution, has actively projected what we might appropriately call a "pop liberalism." This is a simplistic liberalism that is fashioned at almost a comic-book level. Emotional and non-introspective, it reflects the media's manipulation of the general public's extreme shallowness. Accordingly, the public sees very little of the self-doubt and fragmentation that has been so characteristic of the liberal intellectual culture.

As Richard Nixon's fortunes crumbled in mid-1974, The New Republic observed that "the Democratic party is rich in possible presidential candidates," but that rank-and-file Democrats "are not sure where they wish to be led." In 1975, at a time when the prospects for electing a Democratic president the next year were excellent because of the Watergate scandal, Kalman Silver wrote that "ideas about how to achieve social change and the good society are in disarray almost everywhere." Curtis Gans at the same time reported that "when 125 liberal Democrats gathered...to plot 1976 presidential campaign strategy...they departed without a candidate, a program or a strategy." He surmised that "perhaps underlying the lack of agreement was the feeling that the people gathered here shared in common only the past but not a common vision of the future...[One participant said] 'Some of us are populists; others of us are socialists.'"[7]

A month after Jimmy Carter was inaugurated in 1977, Alan Tonelson wrote that "there is no constituency for reform in this country" and that "Jimmy Carter has stepped into the moral vacuum left by Democratic liberals." In late 1982, a year and a half after Carter left office, a New Republic book review said that Robert Lekachman was observing that "New Deal and Great Society liberalism" had "run out not only of policy ideas, but of inspiring symbols." Lekachman was said to be calling for "a new and more comprehensive 'agenda for the left,' which would fill the intellectual void." Then after Walter Mondale's landslide loss to Ronald Reagan in 1984, The New Republic editorialized that "American liberalism is in crisis...The old liberal confidences...now lie shattered...."[8]

This review since 1945 shows us that the loss of vision, the shattering of confidence, has been a continuing theme within American liberalism since World War II, not just a reaction to a particular electoral defeat. Its roots lie in the diminished vitality of the world Left.

This general disillusionment has had certain specific counterparts. One of these has been a perception by liberals that their own programs haven't worked. In 1969, Norman S. Care reported "the rethinking of liberalism prompted by the failure of organized political attempts to realize liberal aims." TRB said in 1972 that there was "an undercurrent of disassociation, a feeling almost of despair," consisting of a "terrifying ...lack of confidence in the capacity of govern- ment to solve problems...." In early 1980 Henry Fairlie wrote that "there seems at last to be an end to the belief in the ability of quick if not deep or penetrating minds--seducible or purchas- able or both--to identify real problems and their possible political resolution."[9]

A century ago, Herbert Spencer wrote that in England until the middle of the 19th century it was considered progressive to remove governmental interventions into people's lives, but that the tone had then shifted to a clamor for more and more political solutions. The latter mood, re- flecting the influence of the Left, lasted in the United States until recently. During most of my lifetime, the call for the politicization of all identifiable problems, followed by the formation of interest-group constituencies around each issue and by programs of governmental expenditure to solve the problems has seemed irresistible. The move away from that fixation, if it proves more than a temporary fashion, will be of the utmost significance.

This has been accompanied by and has reflected a diminished trust in government and the presidency. In October, 1967, Hans J. Morgenthau spoke of "this withering away of the public's trust in the government." A year later James MacGregor Burns said that "for the first time in decades the power of the Presidency is undergoing critical reevaluation by American liberals." In 1976, a New Republic review spoke of "the hundreds of books and monographs assessing Great Society undertakings [that are] mostly expressive of a 'new realism' mood--a perspective sobered by the short-comings of positive government in its encounters with social complexity."[10]

Liberals have also for many years been becoming more sceptical about the value of governmental regulation. The old Progressive faith in the rationality and objectivity of independent experts has given way to a "realistic" awareness that the agencies become the captives of the very processes they regulate.

This awareness was not a new insight to the period we are discussing, since there were various references to it earlier. In 1934, for example, a New Republic editorial said that "the effort of the speculative community, knowing that it was to be regulated" by the Securities Act of 1933, "has been to control the regulators." But it is a view that has grown within liberalism since World War II. In 1949, the editors referred to the I.C.C., F.T.C., C.A.B., S.E.C., F.C.C. and F.P.C., and said that "the regulatory agencies created during reform waves soon pass into industry's hands." The scepticism gained momentum later when consumer advocate Ralph Nader levelled his criticisms. By the mid-1970's, Irving Kristol was able to say that "everyone suddenly seems to be in favor of 'deregulation.'" Many liberals and conservatives came to share the view that in a number of areas a return to the market would be preferable to regulation. This "odd coalition," as Kristol called it, ironically came about during an enormous expansion of regulatory activity in the 1970's, in which "vertical agencies" regulating a particular industry were complemented by vast "horizontal agencies" addressing a certain problem wherever it may exist in the country.[11]

From what I have said earlier, it would have been surprising if psychologically the alienated intellectual culture had ceased during this long period of disillusionment to go through the cycle in which yearning-for-action led to energetic activity and then to frustration, fatigue and withdrawal. Such a cycle has, in fact, been an important part of the history of the decades following World War II. In my chapters on the New Left I will discuss in detail how the yearning became apparent in the late 1950's, led into the passions of the '60's, and eventuated finally in withdrawal and religious faddism in the '70's.

Presidents and programs

As a result of the New Deal, there had been a vast shift of Constitutional jurisdiction and of activity to the federal government. The shift seemed meagre to those who wanted socialism, but to conservatives it amounted to a revolutionary break from the Constitutional limitations of the past.

The Eisenhower presidency resolved the question of whether the Republican Party, once it regained power, would seek to undo the New Deal. The issue was fought out inside the Republican Party at each national convention. When eventually the conservatives have been able to nominate the presidential candidate, their own initiatives have been blocked, first by the defeat of Barry Goldwater and later by the many constraints under which Ronald Reagan has found it necessary to work.

The consolidation of the New Deal under Eisenhower was commented upon by Reinhold Niebuhr in 1956 when he wrote that Eisenhower "reconciled the American business community to the social revolution, initiated by Roosevelt and resisted by the business community until Eisenhower swallowed the whole revolution with a minimum of polemics and no explicit recognition of the volte face." I would add, though, that the consolidation was fought over quite bitterly within the Republican Party. It certainly didn't creep up on the Republicans who chose Eisenhower over Taft in 1952.[12]

The consolidation continued under Presidents Nixon and Ford. Melville J. Ulmer commented, for example, that Nixon's wage and price controls in 1971 "went farther to the left than the proposals of most Democrats." The Ford administration stayed within the flow. Lyndon Johnson's "Great Society" had expanded the concept of "entitlements," by which all citizens were considered to have a legal right to the benefits provided by a broad substratum of governmental action, and Theodore H. White says that "no succeeding Congresses, from Nixon, through Ford, through Carter, dared deviate from the path of the Great Society." Social spending and horizontal regulation continued their upward spiral until the public's thinking began to shift in the late 1970's.[13]

This growth of entitlements and regulation had been consistent with the main programmatic thrust of post-World War II liberalism, which was always to have a "liberal agenda" of incremental increases before the country. It was clearly a Fabian program of "blowing air into the balloon." In 1950, J. Roland Pennock wrote in his book Liberal Democracy that "there is not the slightest suggestion of any point beyond which this process may not go if its indefinite continuation proves acceptable to the majority of Americans."[14]

126

This process was accelerated from 1961 through 1965 under Presidents Kennedy and Johnson. John Kenneth Galbraith's book The Affluent Society was highly popular among liberals in the late 1950's. It argued that the public sector is starved while the private sector is surfeited. (Leon Keyserling soon interjected, however, that growth should be the source of increased public spending, so that a liberal program should not emphasize only "a change in 'priorities.'") In 1959 TRB reported that "the demand for activist government is arising" and added that "the country [is] waiting for an FDR." Galbraith called, among other things, for a "final attack on poverty," even though he acknowledged that "there has been much progress in the reduction of privation and want." This stress on poverty was something new. It was soon augmented by Michael Harrington's book The Other America. Post World War II liberalism had found a constituency and a cause.[15]

In the late '50's, there were two types of yearnings within liberalism: one was for governmental activism, a "new New Deal"; the other, composed of those further to the left, was for more "movement-type" activism, as we shall see in the chapters on the New Left.

Liberals began to express disappointment, however, almost immediately after John F. Kennedy took office. In September, 1961, TRB complained that "Kennedy has been a disappointment as a teacher...No rousing 'cause' has forced Kennedy to appeal to the nation over the heads of Congress." Kennedy moved to the center as Congress balked at his proposals. As it turned out, Kennedy did not fully accept Galbraith's position; with his tax cut proposal, Kennedy sought to bolster private purchasing power rather than to increase government spending. The long-standing liberal-conservative deadlock was continued, too, when the 1962 Congressional elections again left Kennedy without a majority that would enact his program.[16]

After Kennedy was assassinated on November

127

22, 1963, Lyndon Johnson took full advantage of one of the rare occasions when a liberal president has had full Congressional support. He benefitted from the national mood following the assassination. He was also able to capitalize on his landslide victory in the 1964 election for at least a year. Then, under pressure from a number of factors, things began to fall apart.

Johnson declared his "War on Poverty," in which the poor were engaged in the planning process within Community Action programs. He put through the tax cut and came forward with a rent subsidy program that TRB called "one of the boldest ever sent to Congress." When he secured passage of the Civil Rights Act of 1964, he signed into law one of the most comprehensive enactments in our history. The Voting Rights Act of 1965 laid the foundation for greatly expanded Negro participation in Southern politics in the years to come. In July, 1965, TRB exulted that "Johnson's...domestic record in this Congress will be historic." [17]

It is worthwhile to understand the relationship of all of this to liberal theory. I have already commented on the influence of the Galbraith and Harrington books. Galbraith's The Affluent Society had stressed essentially the same theme that had been raised early in the century by Simon Patten and Walter Weyl (a socialist and one of the three founding editors of The New Republic) when they talked about a "social surplus." Charles Forcey says that "by social surplus Weyl meant the increment of wealth the United States had produced over basic human needs. The surplus was social because it was the product of all society and not of particular individuals. Being surplus ...it could easily be directed toward social ends." He points out that "Weyl borrowed his notion of the social surplus largely from Simon Patten." [18]

Gunnar Myrdal contributed what Leon Keyserling called "a great book," Challenge to Affluence, in 1962, in which he argued that growth and social priorities must be bound together.[19]

The War on Poverty's stress on decentralization and on "maximum feasible participation" by the poor themselves on Community Action boards is discussed in the literature as having arisen more or less accidentally. It has a long history, though, in leftist thought. During the same period, the New Left talked about "participatory democracy," which was much the same. Nathan Glazer has written that "participatory democracy...is a concept derived from the Paris Commune [of 1870] in which, according to Marx's account, the people, permanently politicized, permanently in arms, met every day to settle their fate."[20]

Despite the rush of activity in 1964 and 1965, all was not well. The Civil Rights movement became more fragmented; in its militancy it took on an "anti-white liberal" tone. The movement in opposition to the war in Vietnam was heating up, and led to a bitter split among liberals and to Johnson's eventual withdrawal from the presidential race in 1968. The New Left was damning liberalism as the voice of an "establishment" that combined the military, big business, and politics. Inflation became rampant as the administration sought to sustain both the war and social spending at the same time. The congressional elections in 1966, in which the Democrats lost 47 seats, again gave conservatives a veto. And the War on Poverty programs were soon perceived by many liberals to be failures, eaten alive by the tussle of interest groups, the poor's own lack of interest, and the beginning of some realistic thinking about the poor.

The dissatisfaction with the War on Poverty was apparent as early as December, 1965, when James G. Patton, the President of the National Farmers Union, wrote that "sleazy politicians and self-serving private groups conduct a tug-of-war for poverty money." He said that "it appears that the poor are not to be served but to be perpetuated." Two months later, Andrew Kopkind wrote that "the War on Poverty...is more attentive to the politicians, the businessmen and the social workers than it is to the poor." Paul Marx reported in 1968 that "everyone is dissatisfied" with the Community Action programs.[21]

Heresy sprang up within liberalism questioning the whole theory of the civil rights movement. Ronald Berman has written that "the great event of the Sixties was, I think, the publication of the Moynihan Report [on the Negro family]." Daniel Moynihan, Nathan Glazer, Edward Banfield and others began to question whether the condition of the Negro was entirely the fault of white society and to suggest that such things as the matriarchal family structure and the lack of an adequate time-perspective were contributing factors. "The Negro Family, with its description of social pathology," Berman said, "was particularly demoralizing to those who gave their faith to political action."[22]

Even Keynesianism, which not long before had seemed to offer the ultimate solution to the trade cycle, was in trouble. As early as 1958, Leon Keyserling had recognized what later became known as "stagflation." This was the problem that unemployment and a sluggish economy, instead of disappearing in the face of inflation, would often co-exist with it. Prices were rising despite the 1958 recession. By the late 1970's and early '80's, experience had caused a major reevaluation of Keynesianism. In 1977, The New York Times complained of "the bankruptcy of modern theory." In 1980, Gar Alperovitz and Jeff Fox were speaking in The New Republic of "the bankruptcy of the basic assumption of American Keynesianism: that the upward trends of the immediate postwar period could be maintained by the simple manipulation of fiscal and monetary policy, and that the resulting economic growth would allow the nation to avoid politically sticky questions of income and wealth distribution."[23]

The poor performance of Keynesianism was

attributed to rigidities in the economy. Thomas
Balogh voiced a common theme when in 1980 he
faulted the increased concentration of business
and labor. He said that "the combination of oli-
gopoly in the goods markets and bilateral monopoly
in the labor market destroyed the basis of conventional economic analysis." What this translates
to, in part, is an admission that various deviations that liberalism itself has encouraged from a
competitive market were the cause of the economic
dilemma. Keynesianism had sought to use inflation
to out-strip the structural unemployment caused by
collective bargaining, minimum wage laws and a
fixation against downward adjustments in wages.
But even that wasn't working. In addition, the
inflation, which became rampant in the late
1970's, was among the factors destroying the basis
for liberal social policy. Theodore H. White
summed it up in 1982 when he wrote that "inflation
is the...leukemia of planning and hope." [24]

Important, but tangential, issues

The absence of an overriding liberal mission
was compensated for during the 1970's by other
issues. In long-term perspective these must be
understood as at best only tangential to liberalism's socialist aspiration.

The moral imperative of equality, in the
sense of everyone's participating without differentiation, provided the most burning issue, which
was feminism. But while the more radical feminists drew upon a century-and-a-half of socialist
denunciations of marriage to give feminism a
socialist meaning, the movement has hardly meant
that for most American women. To the majority, it
has meant the meeting of the practical needs posed
by their movement into careers.

A career orientation for women within a market economy is no doubt damaging to social values
that classical liberalism considers important to a
free society, but the career orientation does not

131

itself move the society closer to socialism. The movement into careers mainly results from a number of underlying economic and social causes that are not essentially ideological. Rather than causing those factors, the feminist movement has reflected them, at least so far as its mass support has been concerned.

The homosexual-rights movement has not had nearly the drawing-power for public acceptance, but has occupied much the same role. It, too, has been related to the thrust toward equality in the participative sense, and has thus been tangential to what liberals before World War II would have considered their main aspiration. This is not to say that certain aspects of leftist ideology do not play a part; it is no doubt much easier for liberalism to support the homosexual-rights movement than for conservatism to do so. Liberal ideology, in common with the Left in general, has long been alienated from many middle-class values, has stressed relativism as a cutting tool, and has sought alliances with unassimilated groups.

Another issue identified with liberalism in the 1970's was consumer protection. This issue reflected a combination of factors. One of these would be the continuing imperfections within the market system and its legal framework. These are imperfections that a vigorous classical liberalism would be just as inclined to root out. Another factor was the tendency of modern liberalism to fall back upon Muckraking esposes at times when liberalism is not occupied with a more systematic program. (I don't mean to suggest that the exposes, to the extent they are not exaggerated, are off the mark in pointing to abuses. But it is significant that liberals themselves have denigrated the Muckraking tendency when they have felt that they have had better things to do.) The criticism of abuses within the market system may reflect alienation, but is itself peripheral to a socialist program unless it can be made part of a general assault on capitalism.

132

An issue of the 1970's that received less public awareness was the call for "the social responsibility of business." This phrase is so ambiguous that it could mean almost anything, and indeed it has been used by most ideologies, including the Nazi; but to liberals it has meant making the large corporation a vehicle for a wide range of social policies, largely through exhortation and without systematic governmental oversight.

It should be apparent, in light of all that we have covered, how desperately this is a "fall-back" position. Although it is in the tradition of the New Nationalism, it is a pale substitute for what liberals have traditionally wanted. To most earlier liberals it would have seemed ludicrous to make an unsupervised corporate capitalism the executor of liberal policies.

The closest that contemporary liberals have been able to come to an ideological justification for the "social responsibility" emphasis has been the argument, which has time-honored origins in Marx and Bellamy and several others, that large corporations are composed of the members of a new technocratic professional class that is becoming more and more divorced from the traditional values of capitalism. Galbraith's next generation of writings after The Affluent Society was based on this theme. But at a time when liberal confidence is as low as it is, such a rationale, once a powerful tool in the effort to pull corporate capitalism into a collectivist orbit, seems too much like wishful thinking.

Still another peripheral issue was the post-Watergate call for "openness in government." This is reminiscent of the Progressive movement's early 20th century drive for "good government." In part it reflected the generalized distrust for all institutions that was fostered by the New Left.

There was a time when "environmentalism" was a burning issue. The New Left made it a vehicle for alienation in the late 1960's, giving it an hysterical revolutionary quality. But the issue was soon "coopted," as the Left would say, when federal and state legislation was enacted to deal with it. It has remained an issue on two levels: as a practical concern for the solution of remaining problems; and, on a very different plane, as part of the anti-industrial Romanticism of some groups that continue on the left.

The main product of domestic liberalism during these years was the vast increase in social spending. In 1980, Morton Kondracke spoke of "what actually has been accomplished in the United States in the past 20 years: a total reversal of federal priorities from defense spending to domestic concerns. In 1958 the U.S. budget allocated $43.7 billion to defense and $38.9 billion to non-defense programs. In 1980, non-defense outlays were more than three times the Pentagon budget." His comparison, of course, includes the '60's, but the process remained underway in the '70's. The shift provided the background for the Reagan administration's push in the '80's for holding the line on social spending and revitalizing military forces that had been allowed to deteriorate badly while the Soviet Union was engaged in a rapid build-up.[25]

The Carter presidency

The end of the 1970's was dominated, of course, by the presidency of Jimmy Carter. For liberalism, this meant another opportunity under a Democratic president; but above all it was a telling sign of liberalism's fragmentation and weakness. After one term as governor of Georgia, Carter was able to win the Democratic nomination by defeating the established Democratic leaders. The liberal intellectual component wasn't able to secure the victory of one of its own; nor was organized labor able to make up its mind and impose its will. A New Republic editorial pointed out that Carter was able to win the presidency "without establishing any strong base within his own party and often without committing himself on the party's main issues." 26

The Carter presidency then proved a debacle from almost everyone's perspective. Its story from a liberal point of view can be traced through the reports in The New Republic: In the issue that appeared two days after Carter's inauguration on January 20, 1977, Doris Kearns Goodwin reported "the widespread disappointment with the establishment nature of the Cabinet he has chosen." Michael Harrington said that "Mr. Carter rushed to the center ground as he prepared to assume power. It has turned into a swamp. Unless he finds some new place to stand, he will be sunk before 1980." A month later E. N. Luttwak asked whether the administration had a foreign policy. "All we have heard from it so far has been an unsorted collection of single-issue declarations, often contradictory." In October, an editorial said that "at just about the time a new administration should begin hitting its stride, Jimmy Carter's is slumping badly." It complained that "the Carter legislative programs amount to unrestrained activism, grounded in no ideology beyond the 111-page looseleaf book of campaign promises...." 27

In July, 1978, the editors spoke of Carter's "stern words...followed by weak deeds." The next month, they reported that his legislative program had bogged down; "the list of wrecks is impressive." In March of the next year they said that "Carter's poll rankings are nearly new lows, cartoonists are making him a laughing stock."

A year later, they declared the administration "incompetent and reckless in the conduct of foreign policy." Later that year they saw fit to endorse John Anderson, an independent, for president over Carter. Mark Green has written that after "beginning with enormous good will and popularity, Jimmy Carter managed to leave office with no close associates on Capitol Hill and no Democratic constituency he could call his own--for by November 1980, Jewish, Catholic, and labor voters

135

were unhappy with him." If I were quoting conservative commentaries, that would be one thing; but
these were observations made by liberals about the
only Democratic president between 1969 and the
writing of this book in 1986.[28]

Liberal thought's disdain for all of liberalism's political leaders

The Carter presidency no doubt deserved much
of the opprobrium it received, but it is significant to the history of liberalism that the intellectual culture has been to the left of working
liberal politicians generally and has been unen-
thused about virtually all of them. Certainly
that was true of Theodore Roosevelt, Woodrow Wilson, Franklin Roosevelt and Harry Truman.

Adlai Stevenson was an urbane, articulate
standard-bearer for the Democratic Party in two
presidential campaigns in the 1950's. He would
seem to have been, in the language of the day, an
"egghead's delight." But in fact the enthusiasm
for him was mitigated by considerable reservations
within the liberal journals. Edwin A. Lahey said
that Stevenson's nomination meant a defeat for the
left-wing of the Democratic Party and a victory
for organized labor. Stevenson, he wrote, was "a
middle-of-the-road candidate who is probably the
most conservative man to head the ticket since
John W. Davis." For its part, The Nation endorsed
Stevenson, since it considered Eisenhower "a cap-
tive of big business," but its editors criticized
Stevenson as "exaggerating both the dangers of
Communism and the measures required to deal with
it."[29]

There was a singular lack of enthusiasm in
1956. Michael Straight complained in late 1955 of
Stevenson's vagueness on issues, and in March,
1956, TRB spoke of the Democrats' overall "bankruptcy," which he said made a victory that fall
unlikely. The New Republic took little interest
in the fall campaign.[30]

136

The most withering denigration of Stevenson occurred later. According to Gilbert Harrison, Stevenson was an object of ridicule within the Kennedy group. In 1968, reflecting the atmosphere of the late '60's, Anthony Howard in The New Republic called Stevenson "a puzzling pouchy little figure who brought out the throngs of students and the middle-aged hosts." Howard spoke of Stevenson's "servile performance" as ambassador to the United Nations under Kennedy.[31]

For his part, John F. Kennedy was faintly praised in The Nation in 1960 in an editorial entitled "Two Cheers for Kennedy." The New Republic greeted his candidacy more favorably. Right before his election in 1960, James MacGregor Burns wrote that "I believe that Kennedy in his campaign has deliberately prepared the way for the most consistently and comprehensively liberal Administration in the history of the country." A year later, though, TRB was complaining, as we saw earlier, that "Kennedy has been a disappointment as a teacher." And in early 1962 TRB complained again to the effect that "the electrifying 'let's get going' slogan is almost forgotten." Later that year he reported "considerable irritation toward Kennedy from a lot of liberals."[32]

In 1971, Gerald Clarke wrote in The New Republic that "only lately have I put it all together and realized that the Administration of John F. Kennedy was a failure, by his standard as well as mine." He asked, "how could we have been thrilled by that pompous Inaugural Address?"[33]

It is significant that this perspective has survived the New Left period. In 1978, the mood was summed up by Henry Fairlie when he said that "the disaster wrought by the Kennedy's is that they did so little but in a way that we cannot forget them." A New Republic editorial referred to the Kennedy's as "that cohort of monomaniacal ideologues and whiz-kid technocrats" and spoke of "the haughty style...often mistaken for ability." In 1980, Wilfrid Sheed wrote in a book review that "by the time they're through digging and peering under skirts, it may turn out that none of the Kennedy's was fit for the presidency." All of this stands in stark contrast to the adulation given to Kennedy by the liberal press. Inside the intellectual culture, there have been few, if any, heroes. [34]

Hubert Humphrey was a favorite until he was tainted in liberals' eyes by his association with the Johnson administration and the Vietnam War. In August, 1964, TRB said "Mr. Humphrey is about our favorite man in Washington." This is to be compared with a New Republic editorial's observation in early 1968 that "Humphrey can count on the backing of George Meany and his allies in the labor movement," but that Humphrey had been "fatally compromised by his dutiful performance as number-one salesman for Johnson's Asian policy."[35]

Lyndon Johnson was looked upon with suspicion while he was Senate majority leader and then Vice President under Kennedy. There was enthusiasm for him in 1964 and early 1965 during the rush of Great Society legislation. But his period as a liberal hero was brief. In May, 1965, James Deakin wrote that "Mr. Johnson's alienation from the academic and intellectual communities over Vietnam and the Dominican Republic is now almost complete." His support having evaporated, Johnson took himself out of the race for reelection in 1968.[36]

Neither Eugene McCarthy nor Robert Kennedy, the two competing leaders of the stop-Johnson movement in 1968, have gone unscathed in liberal literature. Each comes across as flawed.

There was then a time when it seemed that Teddy Kennedy would be the natural heir to liberal leadership. This died at Chappaquidick in 1969. He made a bid for the presidency in late 1979, but was cut up unmercifully by liberals themselves. Theodore White says that when Kennedy was interviewed by Roger Mudd on television on November 4,

1979, "Mudd dissected Kennedy on the tube and left him shredded, as a man without any real purpose in his pursuit of the presidency." A New Republic editorial in 1980 said Kennedy's "elevated talk about national purpose masks a peculiarly impoverished and fragmented vision...He sees the country primarily as a patchwork of interests...."[37]

Splits in the coalition

This negative critique of all of their leaders has been symptomatic, of course, of the fragmentation and loss of vision within liberalism itself. The fragmentation has been most evident, however, in the splits that have occurred within the "coalition"--and in the inability of liberals, despite constant effort since 1968, to put together a "new coalition."

We have already seen that Southern congressmen began in 1937 to combine with conservative Republicans in a coalition that has held a veto during most of the ensuing half century. The Solid South's participation in the liberal coalition so far as presidential politics was concerned also began to crumble quite soon after World War II. Indications of Republican presidential vitality in the South were already apparent in 1924, when Calvin Coolidge received a large vote. The Dixiecrat split from the Democratic Party in 1948 marked a significant break. Frances Fox Piven and Richard A. Cloward have said that "the first overt signs that the North-South partnership was in danger of dissolving appeared during the presidential campaign of 1948." They added that "the South has not been 'solid' since."[38]

These authors foresaw an eventual liberal resurgence in the South from a coalition of the newly-enfranchised Negroes with white liberals. Although black voting has increased enormously in the South since the Voting Rights Act of 1965 and a large number of Negroes have been elected to office, Republican presidential candidates have continued to receive most of the electoral votes, with the exception of 1976 when the South went for Carter as a native son.

The labor movement would in most countries have been considered the traditional rock upon which the politics of the Left would be based. But from the point of view of the American intellectual culture, the labor movement has long been a disappointment. Until 1906, Samuel Gompers, distrusting the state, kept labor out of electoral politics. It entered politics only sporadically until 1933. Since then, of course, organized labor has given enormous support to Democratic and liberal candidates. But the main body of the labor movement has always been to the right of the intellectual culture. (We remember how The New Republic in 1928 considered it "stupid" for the A.F. of L. to expunge a tribute to John Dewey because of his articles praising Soviet Russia.) After World War II, liberal literature showed a growing split between organized labor, which has itself often been divided, and the intellectual culture.

Despite the merger of the A.F. of L. and the C.I.O., Tom Brooks reported in 1959 that "lethargy and constant bickering within the federation has paralyzed the will to act." In 1965, TRB complained that "the American labor movement is a disappointment to a lot of us. Its membership seems stuck on dead center. So far from being radical, it is to the right of the Chamber of Commerce in international affairs." Then in the bitterness of 1968, a New Republic editorial spoke of "the ossified trade union executives—men like George Meany, who have transformed the labor movement from an inspiring force for social justice into a baronial club."[39]

In 1972, George McGovern won the Democratic nomination despite the opposition of most unions. Labor's impotence in 1976 was apparent when it formed a coalition that supported almost all Democratic candidates successively, hoping simply

140

to "back a winner." The declining numerical strength of unions was commented upon in 1980 by James Ring Adams: "American unionism peaked in the 1950's, when it included some 35 percent of the country's non-farm work force. But...its share has fallen steadily to under 25 percent." Municipal unions had "grown explosively," but the change in the economy toward high-tech industry has continued to erode the basis for unionism.[40]

Big-city political machines were once a powerful part of the coalition. We have seen how Huthmacher and Buenker emphasize their role in the Progressive movement. The intellectual culture has from the beginning, however, felt liberalism's hands soiled by their presence. A New Republic editorial in 1930 praised Franklin Roosevelt as governor of New York, but said that "he can hold office only with the approval of Tammany Hall, an organization which...stands for corruption." In 1932, TRB criticized F.D.R. severely for not repudiating his Tammany support. In 1938, an editorial said Mayor Frank Hague of Jersey City had "one of the most brazenly corrupt political machines ever brought into existence."[41]

The machine system began to crumble after World War II. In 1948, The New Republic reported that "the basic supports of the machine system are rotting away," in part because the welfare state had done away with the machines' role in giving "doles and baskets." Despite this erosion, however, an editorial in early 1952 was able to say that the machine leaders had been "the powers in the last four Democratic conventions." Amid a bitter chorus of ridicule from the New Left, the liberal media and the intellectual culture, Mayor Daley of Chicago was a leading figure in securing the nomination for Hubert Humphrey at the 1968 Democratic convention.[42]

Religious and ethnic minorities were important parts of the New Deal coalition, and have continued to give major support since World War II. In 1964, the vote of Southern Negroes was more than 95 percent Democratic; in 1976, "Carter received over 90 percent of the black vote nationwide, and blacks provided his margin in at least 13 states," according to the The New Republic. Catholic participation in the coalition stemmed in part from Al Smith's candidacy in 1928. Smith was not only the first Catholic candidate; he also gave impetus to the process of bringing the heavily Catholic "immigrant" vote into the coalition. The Jewish vote, consisting largely of immigrants from eastern Europe, was related to this. The socialist orientation of these eastern European Jews is described in detail by Nathan Glazer in Remembering the Answers, where he concludes that "the Jews are people of the left." In 1980, Morton Kondracke said that "normally, Jews vote heavily Democratic...In 1968, Hubert Humphrey received close to 80 percent...."[43]

Although they remain important, the religious and ethnic components of the coalition have themselves been eroding. Many blacks demonstrated their independence of the Democratic party in 1984 by supporting Jesse Jackson's third-party candidacy. Over the years there has, for a number of reasons, been considerable friction between blacks and organized labor, the Jews and liberal intellectuals: with labor over the discrimination it has so often perpetuated; with Jews over "affirmative action" quotas, which many Jews have considered a threat to the rationale for an achievement-oriented equality within American life; and with intellectuals because of the widespread denunciation of "white liberals" within militant black groups starting in the early 1960's.

The Jews have declined in numbers and in devotion to the Democratic cause. Theodore White says that "they are a diminishing population group in the United States," and that "politically, they are still Democratic property, but much less so than formerly." The neo-conservative movement that began in the late 1960's has been primarily Jewish.[44]

142

Liberals at one time considered the media conservative, but since World War II it has been a highly partisan center for popular liberalism. The media have had a collective elan amounting to a herd quality that permeates the culture. This is created in large part by the imperative that every newspaper feature-story writer, every television special reporter, every free lance author, and every social science teacher assigning a project apparently feels to produce something that will fit in snugly with the prevailing enthusiasm. The swings of liberal bathos give the media an overwhelmingly propagandistic quality.

I have written elsewhere that even a classical liberal society will need myths, in the sense of commonly-held beliefs that mold values together with selected facts, as an essential social cement. All social systems are reenforced by them. We should notice that myth-making is precisely what the pop-liberalism has been doing, and that at least in part the effect is conservative.

On a recent trip to Nashville, I attended a stageshow for the tourists at Opryland that fashioned a patriotic review of 20th century American history out of such figures as Franklin Roosevelt and Elvis Presley. During the writing of this chapter, I have witnessed the torrent of media images that have attended the first national observance of the Martin Luther King, Jr., holiday. The far Left would say that this absorption merely proves that these personalities were part of the bourgeois society in the first place. The New Left would have called the process "cooptation." We should see, though, that it is the molding of popular myths. The figures are folded into the culture. This is "conservative" in its down-playing of the discordance that actually marked these men's lives and in its demand that everyone accept the same sanitized images.

I have already commented on the difference between the liberal intellectual culture, with its long-standing despair, and the pop-liberalism of

143

the media, which reflects little of the self-doubt and fragmentation. This means that liberalism has one face for itself, another for the culture at large.

Liberal domination of the media continues in 1986, but I indicated earlier that we have seen an important change since the early 1960's. The media no longer stand solidly behind liberal leaders. Since 1968, they have been about as willing to cannibalize these leaders as they have to devour conservatives. This has lessened the propagandistic effect and has both reflected, and contributed immeasurably to, the fragmentation.

Perhaps the most telling development in recent years has been the deterioration of the Civil Rights and welfarist movements into a collection of narrowly self-interested groups. Theodore White summed it up by saying that "one movement in the grand transformation slowly developed, year by year, into a monster...: the division of Americans by race and national origin into groups, each entitled to special privileges." This divides the country, but the division focuses most obviously within the Democratic party. It enhances the image of contemporary liberalism as lacking a high moral aspiration.[45]

There are several components of the liberal coalition that I have not discussed. These include the farm-laborites, consumer groups, the gay liberation movement, a significant part of big business, the radical and liberal clergy, the Hispanics, and the welfare constituency, among others. Each is a subject in itself, with its own complexity. No group is ever totally cohesive or passively a member of the coalition.

The search for a new coalition

There has been much talk since 1968 of a search for a "new coalition," which has sometimes also been referred to as a "new politics."

Strangely, the term "new politics" seems to have originated in a wildly chaotic effort in 1967 to create a Popular Front among the various groups on the far left. A tumultuous convention of the "National Conference of New Politics" was attended, according to James Ridgeway's report in The New Republic, by black nationalists, members of the W.E.B. DuBois Clubs, members of the Communist Party (who "were out in the open for the first time in years" and "were the most conservative element present"), peace advocates, some labor leaders, members of Students for a Democratic Society (SDS), a large group from the Vietnam Summer Project, and others. Martin Luther King, Jr., was the keynote speaker. [46]

In 1968, Senator Eugene McCarthy challenged Lyndon Johnson in the primaries and called his movement "the New Politics." A New Republic editorial spoke of a proposed coalition composed of "the students, the clergy, professional workers, teachers, suburbanites (many of them women)." In December, 1968, Paul R. Wieck said that "the most visible organization of the new politics is the New Democratic Coalition (NDC)...put together by leaders of the McCarthy-McGovern-Kennedy forces at Chicago." But fourteen months later Wieck reported that "NDC's national operation has been meagre...No sturdy new politics has been built. Why? Perhaps exhaustion...A lot of people left Chicago drained, disillusioned."[47]

Within what would have to be called (in the context of the times) the right wing of the Democratic party, two associates of Hubert Humphrey, Richard C. Scammon and Ben J. Wattenberg, called in 1970 for a different sort of effort. Leonard Ross summarized their book The Real Majority by saying that their "prescription is extremely simple...The real majority is neither young nor black nor poor. Rather it is middle-aged and middle-class, increasingly liberal on economic questions but ever more conservative on social issues such as race, crime and drugs." This sort of coalition was pursued in 1971 by Senator Henry Jackson, whom

145

Wieck said was seeking "a broad centrist national coalition" which would "isolate the Democratic left."[48]

Senator Fred Harris countered from the left with a call for a "New Populism." Then in 1972, Senator George McGovern tried unsuccessfully to draw a vast constituency from blacks, students, women, minorities and workers. Four years later, Jimmy Carter was able to call upon enough of the old New Deal coalition to defeat Gerald Ford in a close election. His status as a Southerner, combined with a special effort to appeal to blacks, gave him both the South and the black vote; and, consistently with the Democratic patterns of the past, he was able to win enough of the large industrial states to put him over the top. Nevertheless, a New Republic editorial after the election warned that "it would be misleading to conclude that Carter has actually revived FDR's New Deal coalition." The mercurial nature of Carter's support became apparent during the four years of his presidency. By 1981, Michael Kinsley could write that "good people everywhere view the future of the Democratic party with growing indifference...It represents a dwindling collection of special interest groups whose interests are less and less those of either the general populace or the tired and poor."[49]

In 1984, Thomas Ferguson and Joel Rogers in The Nation said that during Walter Mondale's campaign "almost every group in the party came to recognize how violently its interests clashed with those of the others." Nevertheless, the journal's editors again called for a new coalition—of the very same groups that have been proposed so many times since 1968. The New Republic, however, saw deeper: "The Democratic Party must find a way to represent a national interest that transcends the mere sum of these perfectly legitimate but still comparatively narrow group interests."[50]

146

Developments pointing to the future

Prominent members of the Left have been converting to one form or another of conservatism since the mid-'30's. Former Communists, for example, made up the bulk of the intellectual circle that founded the Burkean-conservative National Review.

The movement by various intellectuals, primarily Jewish, from the Left into "neo-conservatism" that began in the mid-'60's did not lead into Burkean thought. Generally speaking, neo-conservatives have not renounced liberalism as such, or even the welfare state, but still believe that there is much for government to do. Their thinking is touched, however, by a realism about the poor and about blacks; they no longer accept the ideas that have arisen from the Left's ideological, political coalition-seeking with such groups, ideas that have found it easy to lay exclusive blame on the predominant society and to command solutions by decree. The neo-conservatives have also abandoned liberalism's continuing illusions about Communism. No longer alienated from the main society, they unabashedly support America's role as the leader of the free world.

Although neo-conservatives are quick to point out how loosely defined a category it is, some of those whose names are most often associated with it are Irving Kristol, Norman Podhoretz, Nathan Glazer, Jeane Kirkpatrick, Daniel Patrick Moynihan and Edward Banfield.

"Neo-liberalism" has also received considerable attention since the late 1970's. Still only vaguely defined, and with no real consensus about specifics, it has stemmed from the efforts of Democratic congressmen and presidential candidates to develop a revitalized program in light of an increasingly competitive world market and the shift from heavy industry to "high tech."

Although he was not the first to speak in

these terms, Senator Paul Tsongas called for a "new liberalism" in a speech delivered to the Americans for Democratic Action in June, 1980. He wanted a liberal attitude on social issues such as homosexual rights, abortion, school busing to overcome de facto racial segregation, affirmative action programs to encourage the hiring of minorities, and opposition to capital punishment. On economic issues, Tsongas wanted what Robert M. Kaus in The New Republic later called "a modified 'Japan, Inc.' strategy...a broader labor role in management...government investment in research and education...export subsidies" and other governmental measures to stimulate keener American competition for world markets and to provide "shock absorbers" to alleviate any displacements caused.[51]

Along the same lines, Morton Kondracke reported in October, 1982, that Democrats were working out a program that would consist of several elements. One was "large-scale expenditures to restore America's 'infrastructure'--its decaying roads, bridges, sewers, and waterways." Another was "increased federal spending on 'human capital' programs" to develop skills. There would be an "industrial policy" involving government spending on research and on the sponsorship of "technological 'winners'." These things would be paid for out of a cut-back in the arms build-up.

Japan's success produced many other calls for a neo-Mercantilist imitation. In March, 1983, Bob Kuttner in The New Republic referred to "Japan's brilliantly successful mercantilism" that "doesn't try to pick winners blindfolded," but "creates them." Kuttner called for a system of "managed trade."

The defeat of Mondale in 1984 has left the debate over future liberal policy open. If the neo-liberals have their way, liberalism will become energetically state-capitalist, with a welfare-state floor under people's needs and an increasing role for labor in the ownership and management of industry. The similarity of such a liberalism to the "industrial democracy" that was so popular among British socialists and liberals in the 'Teens and early 1920's is apparent.

Despite this similarity, liberalism is not quite coming full circle. In late 1984, The New Republic found it both possible and necessary to say many things that earlier would have been unthinkable. The editors mixed a call for worker ownership and control, which is clearly socialist, with calls for more deregulation and lower tax rates. They admitted that "there may be some problems that can't be solved, even with...a hefty bit of cash." The editors urged that the United Nations be replaced by a "United Nations of the democracies" and David Bell added that the pullout from UNESCO was justified. Glenn C. Loury wanted black leaders to "have the courage to reexamine their ideas" and then to support more market-oriented solutions in the ghettos. These are ideas that are fundamentally at odds with the liberal worldview as we have known it.[52]

The Nation, however, continued to speak in traditional leftist categories. Sidney Lens praised Austria's socialism, but said it couldn't work in the United States because the bourgeoisie would simply make it a vehicle "for the suppression of the class struggle." David Gordon urged—"broader and stronger coalitions."[53]

NOTES

1. Irving Kristol, Two Cheers for Capitalism (New York: Mentor Book, 1978), p. 11.

2. New Republic, July 22, 1946, p. 70; New Republic, July 29, 1946, p. 106.

3. New Republic, November 1, 1948, p. 24; New Republic, March 17, 1958, p. 20; New Republic, February 29, 1960, pp. 17. 18.

4. New Republic, October 21, 1946, p. 500.

5. Mr. Galbraith is quoted in Mark Green, <u>Winning Back America</u> (Toronto: Bantam Books, 1982), p. 7; New Republic, March 12, 1956, p. 2; James A. Wechsler, <u>Reflections of an Angry Middle-Aged Editor</u> (New York: Random House, 1960), p. 33.

6. New Republic, November 23, 1963, p. 23.

7. New Republic, June 29, 1974, p. 5; New Republic, 3/22/75, p. 19; New Republic, April 5, 1975, p. 9.

8. New Republic, February 26, 1977, pp. 18, 19; New Republic, September 20, 1982, p. 32; New Republic, December 10, 1984, pp. 9, 12.

9. New Republic, November 11, 1969, p. 26; New Republic, January 1, 1972, p. 6; New Republic, May 31, 1980, p. 19.

10. New Republic, October 28, 1967, p. 20; New Republic, March 16, 1968, p. 25; New Republic, August 7, 1976, p. 29.

11. New Republic, June 6, 1934, p. 84; New Republic, October 17, 1949, p. 5; Kristol, <u>Two Cheers</u>, p. 100; for a discussion of the expansion of regulatory activity in the 1970's, see Theodore H. White, <u>America in Search of Itself</u> (New York: Harper & Row, 1982), pp. 128, 129.

12. New Republic, October 29, 1956, p. 11.

13. New Republic, December 11, 1971, p. 19; White, <u>America in Search</u>, p. 126.

14. J. Roland Pennock, <u>Liberal Democracy</u> (New York: Rinehart and Company, Inc., 1950), p. 267.

15. New Republic, October 27, 1958, p. 15; New Republic, January 5, 1959, p. 2; New Republic, February 9, 1959, p. 7.

16. New Republic, September 11, 1961, p. 2.

17. New Republic, July 3, 1965, p. 4; New Republic, July 10, 1965, p. 4.

18. Charles Forcey, The Crossroads of Liberalism (New York: Oxford University Press, 1961), pp. 80, 81.

19. New Republic, April 4, 1970, p. 35.

20. Nathan Glazer, Remembering the Answers: Essays on the American Student Revolt (New York: Basic Books, Inc., 1970), p. 182.

21. New Republic, December 11, 1965, p. 38; New Republic, February 5, 1966, p. 15; New Republic, July 6, 1968, p. 31.

22. Ronald Berman, America in the Sixties: An Intellectual History (New York: The Free Press, 1968), p. 73.

23. New Republic, October 27, 1958, p. 17; the New York Times is quoted in Green, Winning Back America, p. 38; New Republic, May 10, 1980, p. 28.

24. New Republic, June 7, 1980, p. 16; White, America in Search, p. 137.

25. New Republic, July 19, 1980, p. 11.

26. New Republic, January 29, 1977, p. 8.

27. New Republic, January 22, 1977, p. 34; New Republic, January 22, 1977, p. 60; New Republic, February 26, 1977, p. 13; New Republic, October 22, 1977, p. 5.

28. New Republic, July 29, 1978, p. 5; New Republic, August 5, 1978, p. 5; New Republic, March 3, 1979, p. 5; New Republic, March 15, 1980, p. 5; Green, Winning Back America, p. 4.

29. New Republic, August 25, 1952, p. 8; The Nation, Vol. 175, p. 341.

30. New Republic, November 21, 1955, p. 12; New Republic, March 12, 1956, p. 2.

31. New Republic, December 15, 1962, p. 8; New Republic, December 21, 1968, p. 35.

32. The Nation, Vol. 191, p. 237; New Republic, October 31, 1960, p. 14; New Republic, September 11, 1961, p. 2; New Republic, January 8, 1962, p. 2; New Republic, September 10, 1962, p. 2.

33. New Republic, January 15, 1971, p. 13.

34. New Republic, September 9, 1978, p. 34; New Republic, September 23, 1978, p. 5; New Republic, June 7, 1980, p. 28.

35. New Republic, September 5, 1964, p. 2; New Republic, April 13, 1968, p. 5.

36. New Republic, May 29, 1965, p. 11.

37. White, America in Search, p. 13; New Republic, January 19, 1980, p. 7.

38. New Republic, April 20, 1968, pp. 20, 22.

39. New Republic, September 7, 1959, p. 19; New Republic, May 15, 1965, p. 4; New Republic, July 27, 1968, p. 5.

40. New Republic, May 10, 1980, p. 19.

41. New Republic, October 15, 1930, p. 220; New Republic, May 4, 1932, p. 324; New Republic, February 2, 1938, p. 352.

42. New Republic, July 12, 1948, p. 15; New Republic, May 19, 1959, p. 5.

43. New Republic, November 28, 1964, p. 7; New Republic, September 17, 1977, p. 5; Glazer, Remembering the Answers, pp. 222, 231, 236, 242; New Republic, September 6, 1980, p. 10.

44. White, _America in Search_, p. 371.

45. White, _America in Search_, p. 129.

46. New Republic, September 16, 1967, pp. 9, 10.

47. New Republic, September 7, 1968, p. 8; New Republic, December 14, 1968, p. 21; New Republic, February 28, 1970, p. 12.

48. New Republic, October 24, 1970, p. 26; New Republic, September 18, 1971, p. 17.

49. New Republic, November 13, 1976, p. 7; New Republic, July 25, 1981, p. 14.

50. The Nation, October 6, 1984, p. 315; The Nation, November 17, 1984, p. 501; New Republic, November 26, 1984, p. 8.

51. New Republic, November 25, 1981, pp. 29, 30.

52. New Republic, December 3, 1984, p. 6; New Republic, November 26, 1984, p. 8; New Republic, December 31, 1984, p. 9.

53. The Nation, November 17, 1984, p. 301; The Nation, January 12, 1985, p. 15; The Nation, February 9, 1985.

5

THE NATION and THE NEW REPUBLIC

The Nation and The New Republic have been preeminent among the liberal journals of opinion. Their pages have conveyed the views of such a wide variety of authors over such a long period of time that anyone who wants to be familiar with the development of liberal thought will need to be conversant with the history of these journals.

The Nation existed as a classical liberal journal for almost a half-century before The New Republic was founded in 1914. Because it was first in chronological order, it will seem most natural to discuss it first.

The Nation

Edwin Lawrence Godkin was the commanding figure on The Nation from its founding in 1865 until shortly before his death in 1902. Born in Ireland to English parents, he was a correspondent in the Crimean War before coming to the United States from England in 1856. He was considered a follower of John Stuart Mill, although he had none of Mill's eventual affinity for socialism. The Nation itself contains conflicting information about who, as between Godkin and Wendell Phillips Garrison, was formally the first editor. It is clear, though, that Godkin was at least the de facto editor until as late as 1899. Godkin's name is thus synonymous with the early Nation.[1]

Wendell Phillips Garrison had worked closely with Godkin from the beginning, and after Godkin stepped down in 1899 continued the journal until his own death in 1907. He was the son of William Lloyd Garrison, whose The Liberator had been a fiery Abolitionist weekly in Boston for the thirty years preceding the Civil War.

155

Under both Godkin and Garrison, The Nation was independent, reformist--and steadfastly classical liberal. (It is, however, significant that its pages do not reflect the existence at that time of a coherent, self-conscious classical liberal movement.) The journal was at first associated with liberal Republicanism, but threw its support to Grover Cleveland in 1884. It broke with Cleveland a year later, considering him too jingoistic. As it looked back later, however, it gave him high praise.

The Nation's classical liberalism was apparent in the many positions it took on the issues of the late 19th and early 20th centuries:

It was strongly for free trade and against the protectionism that the Republican Party had imposed since the Civil War. It believed that free trade could solve the problem of business concentration, and so it was not in favor of antitrust legislation against bigness. It did, however, favor legislation against specific abuses, such as price discrimination.

The Nation's free trade, freedom-of-contract rationale caused it not only to oppose the protectionist tariff, but also to stand against such interventions as were proposed for the 8-hour day, minimum wages, the nationalization of coal (which Bellamy demanded), the municipal ownership of utilities, and usury laws. It favored collective bargaining, but not the closed shop. On the money question, it stood for the gold standard against bimetallism and the various inflationary schemes that were so much in the air.

Under Godkin and Garrison, The Nation supported the trend toward greater democracy and the struggle for cleaner government. They accordingly favored the proposal for the direct election of senators, encouraged the revolt against political bossism, opposed the spoils system, and urged every city to have a league for good government.

Although they blamed the tariff most specifically for the "venality of politics," they were acutely aware of a serious erosion of American values and classical liberal perspectives during the decades following the Civil War. They commented upon how "money-making eminence" had superseded "intellectual eminence," and how a "belief in paternalism" had grown out of the activities of government during and after the Civil War. They saw "the eclipse of Liberalism" both in the United States and Europe. In the United States, they said, "nationalism in the sense of national greed has supplanted Liberalism."[2]

The Nation was, during those years, strongly opposed to socialism. "Human nature," an editorial thundered in 1890, "will never agree to pass its life in a hugh boarding house with a lot of ranting orators regulating the diet and hours of sleep of the inmates." It gave respectful but critical attention to the writings of such socialists as Rodbertus and the Webbs, and concluded that "real Liberalism can never be socialistic."[3]

In foreign affairs, it favored a non-belligerent policy. When the Spanish-American War was about to break out, it condemned the hysteria over the sinking of the Maine, arguing perceptively that it was not known whether Spain had done the sinking. It opposed an American colonialism, and urged the government to set up a self-governing system in Cuba and then to get out. The editors protested the brutality of the subjugation of the Phillipines, and opposed any effort to "raise the Phillipines to a higher level of civilization." They compared Theodore Roosevelt to French militarists for what they considered his glorification of the army. And they called upon other nations to join with the United States in a confederation for the prevention of war.

The Nation was always interested in the well-being of blacks, although it is not surprising that the editors, consistently with their overall classical liberal orientation, agreed with Booker

T. Washington's position that the situation of blacks would best improve if they devoted themselves to gaining education and property. An editorial in 1890 criticized the notion that laws can correct the effects of discrimination. The editors continually drew attention to the barbarity of lynching, and argued that in part the lynching came from an exaggeration of the number of black rapes of white women. They pointed out that the best way to stop a lynch mob would be for the authorities to shoot the first person to act. And they opposed the South's move into segregation, such as when a proposed statute in Kentucky threatened to abolish Berea College by prohibiting the coeducation of whites and negroes.[4]

When the Muckraking movement began, The Nation welcomed the illumination of actual abuses, but opposed a nihilistic exaggeration. In 1894 the editors called Henry Demarest Lloyd's Wealth Against Commonwealth "the wildest rant," but in 1905 they were sympathetic to the early Muckraking articles and joined in a call for an investigation of the Equitable Life Assurance Society's affairs. By 1906, however, they were fed up, and said that the Muckraking "runs unceasingly through the daily and periodical press, spreading dark suspicion abroad without suggesting remedies." They pointed out that "the idea of reforming is quite subordinate to...creating a hatred." [5]

Their comments on an income tax were perspicacious. They said such a tax is just, but that because its collection would depend upon a self-reporting system "its burden [would] fall chiefly on those who are too honest to shirk it." [6]

And finally, the editors took a dim view of the "scientific pretensions" of the German-trained academics pouring in from the Historical School. Of the new sociologists, they said that "the great thing is to get their work called scientific, no matter whether it is useful or reasonable." "Scholarship," they added later, "suffers from an overproduction of monographs...stretching a thin substance to the cracking point."[7]

It was a fascinating period. Article after article presaged the issues of the 20th century, which were by that time far more than negligible clouds on the horizon. The Nation under Godkin and Garrison met those issues head on, speaking for classical liberal values that even then were sinking into the status of a gigantic underlay. There was no broad classical liberal movement it could champion, and intellectually the journal left much untouched that is vital to a sound classical liberalism. Nevertheless, the dust-covered volumes of The Nation for that period stand as monuments to American values.

Within eleven years after Garrison's death, The Nation passed through the hands of three editors, Hammond Lamont, Paul Elmer More and Harold deWolf Fuller. All three were described in the 100-year-centennary issue in 1965 as having been "conservatives." Both More and Fuller were said to have been breaking away from the Godkin-Garrison laissez-faire liberalism. Despite these descriptions, my own reading shows The Nation's content to have remained remarkably consistent with the earlier views until at least 1913. Only then do we begin to see legislation favored, and rationales expressed, that were at odds with the earlier philosophy. Just the same, no sharp break occurred. In 1914 and 1915, criticisms appeared of socialism and of Croly's book on industrial democracy.

All that I have traced so far has been looked upon later as "the 'pre-modern' Nation." The ideological watershed was in 1918 when Oswald Garrison Villard, a nephew of Wendell Phillips Garrison, became owner and editor. Villard was editor until 1933, and then stayed with the journal as a columnist until 1940 when he broke with it over his conviction that the United States should stay out of the storm in Europe.

Under Villard, The Nation during the late

'Teens and 1920's was virtually a twin of The New Republic, except for a few specifics. Garrison had considered closing down The Nation for want of an appropriate successor as editor, but had been persuaded to allow it to continue under Hammond Lamont. No doubt he would have let it die if he had been able to foresee the editorial in 1919 that said that "out of the soviet experiment, and out of the ideas of the Guild Socialists in England, is evolving what some sanguine optimists hope will prove to be the State-norm of the immediate future." The editorial spoke of "the freedom to prey upon others, which was really the essence of the old individualism...."[8]

The "modern" Nation threw itself wholeheartedly behind "industrial democracy," which it said "courageously undertakes to substitute service for profits as the motive force in industry." It published a speech by the French socialist Anatole France in which he said that "I wish with all my heart that a delegation of the teachers of all nations might soon join the Workers' Internationale...We shall see fulfilled the great socialist prophecy: 'The union of the workers will be the peace of the world.'" Louis Fischer was the journal's main correspondent in Soviet Russia--and sent glowing reports. Villard himself made a trip to Russia in 1929 and told the readers that "it is all so new, so genuinely thrilling."[9]

Villard did not parallel Croly's mystical withdrawal in the '20's, but much else was the same. There were calls for the extensive organization of cooperatives, for the public ownership of power, for the nationalization of the mines. The Nation joined in the impassioned defense of Sacco and Vanzetti. In 1932, it endorsed Norman Thomas, the Socialist candidate, for president.

Editorial control was under a board of editors between 1933 and 1936, with Freda Kirchwey a major figure. Under this leadership, The Nation considered the N.R.A. insufficient and called for "a socialist approach to the economic crisis,"

160

according to Richard Clark Sterne in the centenary issue. It published an article by Norman Thomas calling for the nationalization of banking. Some sympathy was shown toward Franklin Delano Roosevelt, but the New Deal itself was considered "a half-baked capitalism with so-called liberal trimmings."[10]

Between 1936 and 1938, Kirchwey and Max Lerner shared the editorship. Kirchwey then served as the sole editor for the long period between 1938 and 1955. The Nation enthusiastically supported the Left in the Spanish Civil War, again sending Louis Fischer as its correspondent. In 1937, there was lavish praise for the Soviet Union on the 20th anniversary of the Bolshevik Revolution, and elaborate justifications were made for Stalin's purges. The collectivization of agriculture was praised--with no mention of the mass starvation.

During this period there was at least one major difference between The Nation and The New Republic. Over Villard's objections, The Nation supported the idea of collective security against Hitler. The New Republic, on the other hand, remained pacifist until 1940.

The Nation softened its attitude toward the New Deal somewhat earlier than The New Republic. It was basically favorable to Roosevelt in 1936, while still being careful to maintain its connections with the far Left. (Villard, however, used his column to endorse Norman Thomas in 1936.) The Nation endorsed Roosevelt for third and fourth terms in 1940 and 1944.

The Hitler-Stalin Pact and the aggressions that followed it were shocks to those associated with The Nation just as they were to the men and women connected with The New Republic, but after Hitler attacked the Soviet Union it wasn't long before The Nation was filled with adulatory articles about the Soviet Union by Anna Louise Strong. The Nation joined, too, in the growing drumbeat of

criticism of Chiang Kai-shek and of praise for
Mao.

As Europe faced the post-war period, The
Nation under Kirchwey called for the creation of a
socialist "third force" in Britain and on the
continent. She criticized the Marshall Plan,
saying it was being used to stop Communism in
Western Europe more than to create such a third
force. She considered the Truman Doctrine in
Greece to have been a "failure" for having defeated the Communist insurgency by keeping a
"cruel, corrupt oligarchy" in power. In the meantime, Alexander Werth, the journal's Moscow correspondent, wrote still more glowing reports about
the Soviet Union. (We should remember that this
was the period during which the Gulags described
by Solzhenitsyn were at their worst.) The attacks
on Chiang Kai-shek were continued until China fell
to the Communists in 1949. Mao had no sooner won
than The Nation began urging the United States to
recognize his government.[11]

An editorial in 1948 held back from endorsing
Henry Wallace's Progressive Party candidacy. It
argued that the Progressive Party could not become
a viable labor party without organized labor's
support, which it did not have, and that a large
third-party vote would elect the Republicans.
The Nation thus adopted a stance very similar to
that taken by The New Republic after Wallace
ceased being its editor. In 1952, The Nation
endorsed Adlai Stevenson despite its criticism of
him as "exaggerating the dangers of Communism."

Carey McWilliams became editor in 1955 and by
continuing in that capacity until 1976 established
most of what has been the post-World War II posture of The Nation. During his tenure, The Nation
shared The New Republic's malaise about domestic
policy. Its position was nondescript, with one
foot placed tenuously in domestic liberal politics, the other in socialist yearnings. These
yearnings did not show up as a detailed program;
they were evidenced primarily by the presence

162

within The Nation's pages of such socialist
authors as Christopher Lasch, Theodore Roszak,
Erich Fromm, Theodore Lowi and Michael Harrington.
The journal was never in close privity with either
the New Frontier or the Great Society.

The clearest direction was on foreign policy.
Under McWilliams, The Nation continued to criticize the United States for adopting a "Cold War"
posture based on an "anti-Communist obsession"
toward the Soviet Union. Alexander Werth travelled to the Soviet Union again in 1960 to write
yet another favorable report. Castro's bloodbath
after gaining power was justified as unfortunate
but necessary. The American role in the Vietnam
War was denounced as "a dirty, shameful war in
which we are trying to put down an indigenous
revolutionary movement whose aim is to free the
country from foreign domination."[12]

As the New Left heated up in the second half
of the 1960's, The Nation reported its activities
and, with scatter-gun ambivalence, served as something of a platform for it. Mainly, though, it
held to a more orthodox line on the "moderate
Left." Examples of this would include Richard F.
Hamilton's call in 1965 for the formation of "a
socialist or labor party in this country" and
Michael Harrington's 1972 "Call to American
Socialists." In 1972, there were many editorials
mildly favorable to George McGovern's candidacy
against Richard Nixon, but there was no ringing
endorsement. [13]

Blair Clark was editor for the brief period
between 1976 and 1978, and then Victor Navasky
held that position through the end of my reading
in early 1985. The Nation remained to the left of
the Democratic Party. It was severely critical of
Walter Mondale as the candidate in 1984, and did
not associate itself with the mercantilist "neo-
liberalism" that was receiving so much attention.
In an article in February, 1985, entitled "Up From
the Ashes: Getting Our Act Together," David Gordon
called for long, patient work to create "permanent

163

networks" that would link labor, women, minorities, small farmers, church activists, homosexuals, environmentalists, middle class liberals, and senior citizens in a "broader and stronger coalition."[14]

The New Republic

It would be redundant for me to give a detailed chronological history of The New Republic, since my many references to that journal in the chapters on "the phases of liberalism" have in effect already provided that. It will be sufficient to add any significant details that have not already been covered.

Off and on during my reading of the almost-200 volumes of The New Republic for the period between 1914 and 1985, I have been surprised when liberal associates in the academic community have asked me querulously, "Why The New Republic?" They have not considered it sufficiently to the left to be truly representative of liberalism. When I have asked them to explain, they have made it clear that this is their impression based on the last few years rather than on the first sixty or so years of the journal's history. It is interesting that even though The New Republic has made no sharp swing to the right in recent years, they consider themselves sufficiently to the left of it that it is no longer representative of their thinking.

Their observation obscures the main truth that The New Republic has since 1914 served as a vast sounding-board for quite literally hundreds upon hundreds of authors, many of them famous as the intellectual and literary leaders of liberalism.

I have already quoted many of these authors, seeking to give the feel and texture of the thinking they represented. The reader should be aware, of course, that it would be possible to distort a

164

history by such a process; the ocean of material is so vast that differing emphases can easily be supported by quotation. The author of such a history as this must immerse himself so deeply in the reading that he can know what is representative and what is not. As I have selected my quotations, I have sought to be representative.

Nevertheless, the attempt to describe accurately the main thrust of liberal thought has had a certain distorting effect, since the main thrust is not the only thing that has appeared in The New Republic. I have been impressed from the beginning by the diversity of authors and views. The journal has served a broad literary and intellectual purpose and has at no time been narrowly sectarian, even during the Red Decade. The views have been within the range of the American Left, of course, and there has been no recognition of a conservative intellectual position of any respectability, but the views have not been restricted generally to any given slice of the Left. It is valid to say this even though there have no doubt been many instances in which some exclusion has been exercised.

I have already commented upon the distinction that I have come to feel between the intellectualized liberalism of The New Republic and the "pop-liberalism" of current fads generated primarily by the media.

The identity of the chief editor of The New Republic was not made entirely clear from the masthead of the journal until the mid-1940's. Herbert Croly was simply listed among several editors, but liberal literature is unanimous in designating him as the first editor. He served as such from the opening issue of November 7, 1914, until his death in 1930. For the next several years, a committee of editors was listed without differentiation. The literature does not point nearly so strongly to one individual as dominant. It seems justifiable to say, though, that Bruce Bliven, who joined The New Republic as one of its editors in 1923 and remained as chairman of the editorial board even during the 1950's while Michael Straight was editor, can be considered to have been "first among equals" on the editorial staff during those years.

Henry Wallace was made editor with much fanfare on December 16, 1946. Michael Straight commented years later, however, that Wallace was so preoccupied with other things that he paid little attention to his editorial duties. Certainly Wallace's tenure as editor was brief. He served only until January 12, 1948, although he retained a column for a short time thereafter. He was the Progressive Party candidate for president that year, but did not receive the indorsement of The New Republic under its new editor, Michael Straight, despite Straight's continued liking for him personally. In part, Wallace's leaving reflected the division that was becoming bitter within the American Left. The split between those, such as Wallace, who were "willing to work with Communists" and those, such as the A.D.A., who were not was being fought out in 1948.

Michael Straight was editor from 1948 until May, 1956. It was a period marked by the deepest hypocrisy. The public face of The New Republic was one thing; the secret harbored through all those years by its editor was something very different.

By far the most heated national issue during his editorship had to do with Communism. Although Straight liked Herbert Philbrick's book I Led Three Lives about Philbrick's years as an undercover agent within the Communist Party and there was a review critical of a book defending Alger Hiss, the main emphasis of The New Republic during these years was one of vehement denunciation of virtually all efforts by anti-Communists.

Congressman Thomas, the chairman of the House Committee on Un-American Activities, was denounced by Daniel Gillmor as "a master of loading a

166

phrase, at ripping a quotation out of context and at implying guilt without leveling an outright accusation." An editorial argued that Attorney General Tom Clark was arbitrary in listing certain organizations as "subversive." Jack Winocour wrote that the French were "obsessed with anti-Communist hysteria." An editorial denounced the New York City Board of Education as bigoted and hysterical for "attempting to bar from the teaching profession known Communists or suspected Communists." TRB wrote that Harry Dexter White was being "smeared by Miss Bentley." An editorial defended Owen Lattimore against the McCarran Committee's charge that he had been "a conscious articulate instrument" of Communism in his writing about China. Another editorial acknowledged the guilt of the Rosenberg's, but called for a reduction of their sentence to life imprisonment. And, most emphatically, the journal joined in liberalism's scathing denunciations of Senator Joseph McCarthy's crusade against suspected Communists in government. [15]

Many years later, in 1981, it became publicly known that Straight had joined a Communist cell at Cambridge in 1935 and had for several years been a part of the espionage ring that included Guy Burgess and Anthony Blunt. Straight has told the story of those years in his 1983 book After Long Silence. His book tells of his Communist activities and meetings with both Burgess and a Soviet agent acting under the pseudonym "Michael Green." One meeting with Burgess was as late as 1949. This was four years before Burgess and another agent, Donald Maclean, of whom Straight says he had no knowledge, fled to the Soviet Union. If Straight's book can be taken at face value, he was always a reluctant, peripheral member of the espionage cell, and never sought or conveyed information other than his own impressions of the American political scene. He says that he faked a break with Communism when he became part of the espionage cell, but held mixed feelings and was for several years plagued with fear and guilt.

167

These years included a time when he had easy access to President and Mrs. Roosevelt. He even worked with Eleanor Roosevelt "as she struggled to maintain the ties between the administration and the radicals in America." They included all of the years he was editor of The New Republic. He finally went to the F.B.I. and then to British intelligence in 1963 when President Kennedy's offer to appoint him chairman of the National Endowment for the Arts made an F.B.I. check of his background imminent. The public did not know the story until the London Daily Mail broke it in 1981.

The hypocrisy has been summarized by Straight himself: "My fear and sense of guilt were secret, shared by no one. At the same time, as editor of The New Republic, I had to share my thoughts and my feelings week after week on the allegations of espionage that were surfacing and on the larger issues that they raised."[16]

Debts incurred during the effort to build The New Republic's circulation at the time of the Wallace editorship finally forced Straight to sell the journal in 1956. This ended many years of financial association by the Straight family with The New Republic. Michael Straight's parents, Willard and Dorothy Straight, had been the first owners and financial benefactors, establishing the journal in 1914 with Herbert Croly as editor after they read his book The Promise of American Life. Willard Straight died of influenza at the end of World War I. It tells us a lot about Mrs. Straight, and provides some explanation of her son Michael's role, that she continued her financial support throughout the journal's most radical phase in the 1930's.

Gilbert A. Harrison became the editor after Michael Straight, serving during the tempestuous years from 1956 to early 1975. Martin Peretz purchased The New Republic in 1974 and took Harrison's place as editor the next year. This remained the situation when I completed my reading in preparation for this book in early 1985.

During most of The New Republic's existence, the column by "T.R.B." has been something of an institution. It was begun in 1925 with Frank Kent as the first of several anonymous authors. Kenneth Crawford and Jonathan Mitchell have also been mentioned as having contributed to it before Richard Strout began his 40-odd year tenure in March, 1943.

The New Republic has itself given varying explanations of what the initials mean. In 1946, an editorial broke silence, saying that "the idea of 'T.R.B.' was born during a ride on the old Brooklyn Rapid Transit subway...." The initials were simply reversed, and thus came to stand for "Transit R. Brooklyn." The explanation was disputed, however, by an editorial in 1983, which said that "there's no such line as the BRT." The editorial told of competing explanations. One was that the initials stand for the typeface Times Roman Bold. Another, offered by John Midgley of the Economist, "is a variation of the subway theory: the editor took the initials IRT (for Interboro Rapid Transit) and BMT (for Brooklyn Manhattan Transit), and crunched them together." 17

Fortunately, we can say about the T.R.B. mystery that it is as harmless as it is amusing.

NOTES

1.   During the "pre-modern" era, The Nation's editorial masthead did not indicate who the editors were. The conflicting commentary about the editorship appears in the issues of July 13, 1905, p. 30, where Garrison is said to have been editor since the beginning, and of July 8, 1915, p. 68, where Godkin is referred to as "the founder and first editor." The 100-year-anniversary article by Richard Clark Sterne on September 20, 1965, is obscure on the point.

2. The Nation, August 9, 1900, p. 105.

3. The Nation, May 8, 1890, p. 367; The Nation, December 5, 1897, p. 442.

4. The Nation, January 23, 1890, p. 61.

5. The Nation, November 8, 1894, p. 348; The Nation, March 22, 1906, p. 234.

6. The Nation, November 30, 1893, p. 404.

7. The Nation, May 24, 1894, p. 382; The Nation, October 11, 1894, p. 264; The Nation, April 25, 1901, p. 332.

8. The Nation, August 2, 1919, p. 137.

9. The Nation, September 16, 1919, pp. 327, 353; The Nation, Vol. 129, p. 515.

10. The Nation, October 31, 1934, p. 493.

11. The Nation, Vol. 166, pp. 117, 341.

12. The Nation, Vol. 190, p. 63; The Nation, Vol. 201, pp. 149, 317.

13. The Nation, Vol. 201, p. 384.

14. The Nation, February 9, 1985.

15. New Republic, May 31, 1948, p. 17; New Republic, June 7, 1948, p. 13; New Republic, June 28, 1948, p. 13; New Republic, July 12, 1948, p. 7; New Republic, December 6, 1948, p. 3; New Republic, July 14, 1952, p. 7; New Republic, January 19, 1953, p. 7.

16. Michael Straight, After Long Silence (New York: W. W. Norton Company, 1983), p. 231.

17. New Republic, March 18, 1946, p. 390; New Republic, April 18, 1983, p. 11.

6

DISSIMULATION

In various of its aspects, liberalism cannot be identified precisely with either socialism or alienation. The coalition that has made up the modern Democratic Party has been broader than liberalism and has included groups and individuals who have been neither socialist nor alienated. This is even true of a more narrowly defined "liberal coalition" and of liberalism in its popular manifestations as a mass phenomenon.

It is important to realize this if we are to avoid thinking of liberalism as more homogeneous than it actually is.

If, however, we inquire into the nature of liberal _thought_, we are talking about a body of ideas that has been intimately related to the intellectual culture. A completely honest analysis then requires a recognition that this thought has been fundamentally socialist. Liberal ideology has been one of the consequences of the alienation of the intellectual and of the intellectuals' search for alliances.

This is not to say that liberal and socialist thought have been identical. They have not been. The difference has lain in the willingness of socialists to accept the socialist label--indeed, to proclaim it loudly--and to stand up openly for their objectives. Subject to brief periods of overt radicalism, American liberal thinkers have generally done everything they can to avoid the socialist label and to obscure their ultimate objectives. This has been especially true with regard to the face they have presented to the American public, which has been something very different from what they have said in the writing they have addressed to each other.

Beginning in the late 19th century, modern liberal thinkers have precisely been those who for reasons of personality and tactics have chosen not to divorce themselves from the American mainstream. To embrace the socialist values of the West's intellectual culture (of which they have wanted very much to be a part) without seeming to do so, such men as Herbert Croly, Thorstein Veblen, John Dewey and John Kenneth Galbraith have woven into their ideology an elaborate fabric of dissimulation.

The other ideologies I have discussed in these volumes--Burkean conservatism, classical liberalism and the various forms of socialist thought--have all been straight-forward. They have said what they mean, directly and forcefully. But this has not been true with modern American liberalism. Much of its expression has been masked by euphemism and dissimulation.

This is an irritating subject for liberals themselves. They detest any suggestion of dissimulation when it is brought up by conservatives. It is noteworthy, however, that the dissimulation has been discussed at length within liberal literature. It is that discussion that I will be reviewing in this chapter.

1. Liberal literature has often admitted quite candidly the existence of the dissimulation.

Thus, Max Lerner wrote about Thorstein Veblen that "the Veblenian irony is a way of saying things and yet not saying them, the Veblenian mystification is a form of protective coloration." Lerner argued in 1935 that Veblen "no longer needed to hide his meaning" after he finally tore away the veil by publishing The Engineer and the Price System. In that book, Veblen had called for a seizure of power and the creation of a "technical soviet."[1]

In 1931, John Dewey called for a new political party. Here is his discussion of the dissimu-

172

lation he thought necessary for it: "I think a new
party will have to adopt many measures which are
now labelled socialistic...But while support for
such measures in the concrete, when they are
adapted to actual situations, will win support
from the American people, I cannot imagine the
American people supporting them on the ground of
Socialism...The prejudice against the name may be
a regrettable prejudice, but its influence is so
powerful." [2]

In 1970, Michael Harrington wrote of "a mass
social democracy in the United States." He said
that it "is invisible because, in typically
American fashion, its socialistic aims are phrased
in capitalistic rhetoric." [3]

Irving Kristol has spoken of the "paradoxi-
cal" use of labels in the United States, and has
said about liberals that "it would certainly help
to clarify matters if they were called, with
greater propriety and accuracy, 'socialists' or
'neo-socialists.' And yet we are reluctant to be
so candid. In part, this lack of candor is simply
the consequence of a great many 'liberals' being
demagogic or hypocritical about their political
intentions." He went on to say that "I find it
striking that the media...should consistently
refer to John Kenneth Galbraith as a 'liberal'
when he has actually taken the pains to write a
book explaining why he is a socialist."[4]

In 1939, Bernard Smith wrote a review of
Parrington's Main Currents in American Thought.
Of Parrington, Smith said that "his radicalism
wasn't altogether obvious. He was certainly not
so foolish as to flaunt it...I can state quite
dogmatically that he had some acquaintance with
Marxism, had been influenced by it, and knew that
his method was related to it. I have seen a
letter by him in which he said as much."[5]

Dissimulation has not only been acknowledged
generally, but also in connection with specific
liberal undertakings. In 1936, for example, the

173

British socialist Harold Laski, writing in The New Republic, wrote that "under the auspices of the American Historical Association a commission sat for the five years from 1929 to survey the educational position in the United States with special reference to social studies." He said that "stripped of its carefully neutral phrases, the report is an educational program for a socialist America." [6]

In 1939, a New Republic editorial reported that "Mr. Thomas R. Amlie, nominated to be Interstate Commerce Commissioner, admitted to a great skepticism about the future of capitalism. His senatorial listeners watched him with shocked faces. As experienced men, they themselves had precisely the same skepticism; what shocked them was the fact that Mr. Amlie had the courage and candor to say what was in him." [7]

Christopher Jencks said that the Elementary and Secondary Education Act of 1965 was "like all Johnson proposals,...being promoted with a highly traditional rhetoric." He added candidly that "nevertheless, anyone who looks carefully at the bill will see that it...proposes" what Jencks described as a major centralization of educational decision-making. [8]

Liberal literature has often referred to the compromise and opportunism inherent in the Fabian method. In 1914 in one of its first editorials The New Republic said that "anything so vast as a reconstruction of society can only be accomplished by an immense amount of little steps, a constant readjustment of theory, and a depressing amount of compromise." It called for people "who are loyal to their end and opportunist about their means." In 1930, an article by William Orton about England urged progressives to "avoid everything doctrinaire" and "to leave the particular means to be developed pragmatically." He added that "this is, no doubt, a plea for opportunism." In 1939, Bruce Bliven called for a Fabian emphasis on incremental steps: "New Dealers...need to stop talking in cliches which unnecessarily frighten the average citizen, and to appeal instead to the concrete opportunities for a nation."[9]

Liberals have often spoken among themselves of their "foot-in-the-door" strategy--or, as Senator Robert Wagner referred to it, of their tactic of "getting the camel's nose under the tent." In the context of Lyndon Johnson's Great Society agenda in 1965, TRB wrote that "many of these are toe-in-the-door programs for future amplification." A year later, he spoke of "the government's foot in the door with the rent subsidy program."[10]

2. The reasons for the dissimulation have also been commented upon extensively in liberal literature.

In 1931, Matthew Josephson spoke of the personal motives that often lie behind it. He told about "how in adolescence those of us who received their education more or less consciously became socialist at heart," but that "then, as prospective men of letters or of the professions, we foresaw the most meager stake for ourselves under the heedless capitalist arrangement; so that our interests, quite deterministically, lay behind our indifference and made us secretly or waitingly Marxian...Not all of us wished as yet to be uninvited 'martyrs': or, as successful, practising agitators, to pass a life resembling that of Jesuits."[11]

A fear of the adverse impact of candor on the political acceptability of liberalism has, of course, long been a major concern among liberal politicians. Charles Beard said that "Theodore Roosevelt praised [Croly's The Promise of American Life] but looked upon Mr. Croly as too radical for practical purposes." In a 1912 editorial about Robert LaFollette, The Nation observed that "radical public men...when they seek support for high office...minimize their radicalism." In 1936, Thurman Arnold, later Franklin Roosevelt's chief trust-buster, wrote that "I decline to support the Socialists until they become less perfectionist ...and show signs of becoming an effective political group with ability to use political techniques." In 1968, David Riesman revealed that "a senator from one of the Mountain States once said to me, if my constituents knew what I was really like (which in fact the right wing keeps telling them) they would throw me out."[12]

Not surprisingly, though, liberalism has been seen as an advantage for a faculty member's success in the academic world. Morton Cronin wrote in 1957 that "the adoption of a liberal orientation is an important method for getting on in the academic world." Personal motivations for success in a career are important in sustaining an ideology. Cronin added that "the world of academic liberals, in short, is saturated with careerism."[13]

3. Liberalism's dissimulation has been the counterpart of American conservatism's success in causing the American public to reject socialism and anything that the public understands to be socialist.

Benjamin Ginsburg pointed angrily but accurately at the practical underpinning of liberalism in The New Republic in 1931 when he paraphrased liberals as saying: "One must never mention the word socialism, inasmuch as the American people will not hear of socialism...."[14]

4. An extensive use of euphemism has been a stylistic by-product of the dissimulation. One of the earliest, best and most influential examples of this was Herbert Croly's book The Promise of American Life, published in 1909. The closest he came in hundreds of pages to announcing his socialist goals was a sentence such as this: "...the organization of labor like the organization of capital may gradually be fitted into a nationalized economic system." No one could quarrel with a suggestion that something may

176

happen; nor could anyone say absolutely that he had advocated it. Croly's style of suggestion rather than advocacy has remained typical of much liberal writing. Thus, we have become accustomed to seeing such statements as that made by Dow Votaw in his book _Modern Corporations_: "The great corporation may ultimately itself become a political or electoral unit in a vastly different governmental structure than we know today."[15]

After John T. Flynn broke with _The New Republic_, Flynn attacked the use of the term "planned economy" as a euphemistic substitute for socialism. In 1949, he wrote in _The Road Ahead_ that socialism "is being promoted in America by organizations that never pronounce in public the word socialism. They call their system the Planned Economy." He added that "that is a fraudulent brand name. It is used to sell socialism to an unsuspecting population." (Flynn was guilty of considerable dissimulation himself in that book, in which he did not wish to tell his conservative readers of his own earlier endorsement of the "planning" concept. He had been a leading columnist for _The New Republic_ during most of the 1930's. In 1936, he had declared that he would vote for Norman Thomas, and found it "disconcerting" that many on the Left were coming out for Roosevelt. "The great choice which confronts the peoples of every country today is--who is to control their economic societies? By control I mean conscious, deliberate, planned control.")[16]

5. Those further to the left, of course, have always looked upon the dissimulation with contempt; and during the brief periods when the liberal intellectual culture has itself been willing to endorse socialism more overtly, many have expressed disgust with the cravenness of the less forthright approach. On other occasions, individual liberals have from time to time become willing to declare their socialist affinity--and then have looked back scornfully.

The New Republic had no sooner started publication than Amos Pinchot wrote it complaining that "The New Republic...concentrates attention on symptoms and incidentals, and maintains silence in regard to the foundations upon which the whole fabric of social injustice rests."[17]

In 1931 Edmund Wilson penned an impassioned plea for liberals to give up Croly's "gradual and natural approximation to socialism" and to embrace socialism openly. "They must take Communism away from the Communists, and take it without ambiguities or reservations...." A letter from Lewis Mumford in 1935 congratulated The New Republic for "leaving behind the stale liberalism of capitalist compromise," and called for liberals to create a non-totalitarian communism.[18]

In 1956, Paul Goodman, one of those who laid the foundation for the New Left, made the same radical critique: "Throughout the nineteenth and twentieth centuries, the radical-liberal program was continually compromised, curtailed, sometimes realized in form without content." In 1957, Harvey Goldberg and William Appleman Williams wrote that "'radical' defines a nature different in quality from the temporizing 'liberal' spirit, so expert in weighing principle against expediency." They said that Heywood Broun had "made the point with characteristic directness: 'In the final count of reckoning I believe the angels will indulge in few long cheers for any liberal. With minor exceptions he's a trimmer.'"[19]

6. This tension between temporizing and radical assertiveness is what explains the phenomenon of "liberal 'guilt'" that is so often commented upon. Thus, Ronald Berman has spoken of "the guilt of liberalism--a guilt which exists because liberalism refuses to make the leap between what it is and what, given its doctrine, it might become."[20]

A pathetic passage in Arthur Schlesinger, Jr.'s, The Politics of Upheaval speaks to this issue: "Measured against the Bolshevik, with his infinite courage and his terrible calm, the American bourgeois [liberal] could only feel a sense of his own unworthiness." Referring to the time in 1934 when Lincoln Steffens had declined an offer to join the Communist Party, Schlesinger quoted him as having said: "I think I am not to be trusted in the party or in the front ranks of the struggle...We liberals must not have power, not ever; we must not be leaders, we must not be allowed to be parties in the leadership...We, who have fitted successfully into the old culture, are to the very degree of our education and adjustment,--we are corrupted and unfit for,--the kingdom of heaven.'" Schlesinger spoke of this as "liberal self-abasement." [21]

7. The dissimulation has allowed a great deal of socialist thought to be presented in disguised form.

In my chapter on "Liberalism and the Modern Corporation" I will discuss the "Berle and Means thesis." At that time, we will see that one of the major concepts of modern liberalism has had a long history in socialist thought and was even advanced in Marx's Das Capital. A reader would not know the idea's lineage, however, from reading liberal discussions of the concept. They talk as though it originated with the book by Adolf Berle, Jr., and Gardiner Means in 1932.

It has been surprising to me how much R. H. Tawney's thought is incorporated--without attribution--into liberal writing. Tawney, a British socialist, wrote The Acquisitive Society in which he made a distinction between "an acquisitive society," in which people pursue their own "rights" for their own advantage, and "a functional society," in which the performance of "functions" (public service) is paramount. He argued that commerce must give up its profit orientation and take on the characteristics of service-oriented professions. Tawney classified property into several types according to the degree of absentee ownership. In his book Religion and the

179

<u>Rise</u> <u>of</u> <u>Capitalism</u>, he was not wholeheartedly
favorable to the Middle Ages, but nevertheless
praised that period for its "functionalism," which
he said was undermined by the later victory of
bourgeois acquisitiveness.

The reader will recognize that this is pretty
much the standard critique made by socialists
generally. But we will also want to notice the
vocabulary. Tawney expressed socialist concepts
in an easily recognizable form.

A few years ago I used Joseph W. Towle's book
<u>Ethics</u> <u>and</u> <u>Standards</u> <u>in</u> <u>American</u> <u>Business</u> in a
course on business ethics. It contains a chapter
by Albert William Levi of Washington University.
No mention is made of Tawney either in the body of
the chapter or in footnotes. From the presenta-
tion, the students would think simply that the
ideas are those of a liberal professor in the
United States. But here are some of the things
the chapter says: "The aim of business is profit.
The aim of a profession is the performance of a
service...Modern capitalism is based upon a philosophy of individualism which, when spelled out,
implies that the basis of society is to be found
not in responsibilities but in rights...Medieval
economic structure entroned principles which were
just the reverse...A philosophy of individual
rights has gradually undermined the organic functionalism of medieval society. What has happened,
then, over the past five hundred years has been
the gradual development of a 'functional' into an
'acquisitive' society." This is pure Tawney. But
the students aren't told that.

A chapter in a business ethics textbook is
only a small example, but when multiplied by tens
of thousands of others it becomes one of the more
significant facts about liberal ideology. The
content is socialist, the style one of dissimulation.

180

NOTES

1. New Republic, May 15, 1935, pp. 8, 9.

2. New Republic, April 1, 1931, p. 178.

3. Michael Harrington, Socialism (New York: Saturday Review Press, 1970), p. 133.

4. Irving Kristol, Two Cheers for Capitalism (New York: Mentor Books, 1978), p. 127.

5. New Republic, February 15, 1939, p. 42.

6. New Republic, July 29, 1936, p. 342.

7. New Republic, March 1, 1939, p. 86.

8. New Republic, February 6, 1965, p. 17.

9. New Republic, December 26, 1914, p. 6; New Republic, January 29, 1930, p. 266; New Republic, June 21, 1939, p. 184.

10. Senator Wagner's tactic is discussed by J. Joseph Huthmacher in his Senator Robert F. Wagner and the Rise of Urban Liberalism (New York: Atheneum, 1968), at page 113 and again at page 214; New Republic July 10, 1965, p. 4; New Republic, May 14, 1966, p. 4.

11. New Republic, February 18, 1931.

12. New Republic, November 8, 1939, p. 78; The Nation, January 4, 1912, p. 4; New Republic, September 30, 1936, p. 223; New Republic, April 13, 1968, p. 21.

13. New Republic, January 7, 1957, p. 11.

14. New Republic, February 18, 1931, p. 17.

15. Herbert Croly, The Promise of American Life (New York: The Macmillan Company, 1914), p. 390; Dow Votaw, Modern Corporations (Englewood Cliffs,

N. J.: Prentice-Hall, 1965), p. 96.

16.   New Republic, November 4, 1936, pp. 17, 18.

17.   New Republic, May 29, 1915, p. 96.

18.   New Republic, January 14, 1931, p. 234; New Republic, February 6, 1935, p. 361.

19.   Paul Goodman, Growing Up Absurd (New York: Random House, 1956), p. 15; Harvey Goldberg (ed.), American Radicals (New York: Modern Reader Paperbacks, 1957), p. 1.

20.   Ronald Berman, America in the Sixties: An Intellectual History (New York: The Free Press, 1968), p. 108.

21.   Arthur M. Schlesinger, Jr., The Politics of Upheaval (Boston: Houghton Mifflin Company, 1960), p. 185.

7

LIBERALISM AND AMERICAN CULTURE

An important cultural dimension of American liberalism comes from the fact that the liberal intellectual culture has for the most part joined in the Left's century-and-a-half old assault upon the values and culture of the middle class (which is often referred to as the "bourgeoisie").

We have seen how before the Civil War the intellectual culture began quite early to view American life as sick. Henry David Thoreau spoke of "lives of quiet desperation" in which effluvia took the place of serious values. He complained that he could find no one in Concord who could discuss a good English classic with him. "Our reading, our conversation and thinking are all on a very low level, worthy only of pygmies and manikins," he said. "We are a race of tit-men, and soar but little higher in our intellectual flights than the columns of the daily paper."[1]

A comparable period of social criticism occurred in the early twentieth century. Liberals of Randolph Bourne and Harold Stearns' generation found fault with almost every facet of our national life. In this chapter, we will examine the main contours of that critique.

1. The social critics have often complained of the middle class's traditional commitment to the work ethic and to moral constraints. As Morris Cohen wrote under the pseudonym "Philonous" in 1919, "it is the Puritanic feeling of responsibility which has blighted our art and philosophy and has made us as a people unskilled in the art of enjoying life." Alfred Kuttner wrote in 1914 that "so long as we frown upon leisure as a yielding to the devil and an invitation to our competitor to overreach us, the finer issues of life must remain in abeyance."[2]

Randolph Bourne objected to the redemptive theme within American novels, which sought "the moral transformation" of the characters. Bourne praised Theodore Dreiser and urged all literature to "follow the pattern of life, sincere, wistful and unredeemed." An article in The New Republic in 1930 by another author spoke of "a country stifled by generations of Puritanism," and in the area of sexuality called for a "breaking down of the secrecy and hypocrisy."[3]

To classical liberalism, the culture's internalizing of moral values and discipline within its individuals is a vitally important part of the social cements that allow a free society to exist. This is precisely something that the Left, including such modern liberals as Cohen and Bourne, has attacked as part of its assault on individualistic liberalism.

Perhaps the most incredible statement of the Left's view has come from Jerry Rubin in his book Growing (Up) at 37. Using the typical Dadaistic shock method that became so popular a weapon with the New Left, he tells of a "psychic therapy" session in which the participants sought release from their "childhood deprivation." He says, "I started shouting at my mother for the specific messages she gave me. 'Thanks, Mommy. You white-skinned no-good sexless asshole cap-toothed cancerous venom of a snake who destroyed me from birth...You taught me to hate myself, to feel guilty, to drive myself crazy,...to hate my body, to hate women...I have your self-righteous right-wrong should-should-not programming...with that stupid JUDGE inside me that I got from you. I don't see people as they are, but as they fit my standards, my self-righteous beliefs ...Oh, it is so liberating for me to tell the truth. MOMMY I AM GLAD THAT YOU DIED. IF YOU HAD NOT DIED OF CANCER, I WOULD HAVE HAD TO KILL YOU...You taught me to compete and compare, to fear and outdo. I became a ferocious achievement-oriented, compulsive, obsessive live-in-my-head asshole...Well fuck you, Mommy, fuck you in the ass with a red-hot poker." (Rubin's capitalization.) When we compare this passage with those I have quoted from Cohen and Bourne, we see that the conceptual content is the same. Rubin's, though, gives us insight into the nihilistic extreme to which those concepts--when articulated through the shock tactic of totally disregarding so-called "middle class" standards of expression--have been carried by the more militant members of the Left.[4]

2. The attack on the work ethic and on "middle class" moral constraints has gone hand in hand with objections to our culture's emphasis on material success.

John Dewey complained that "a regime of pecuniary profit and loss still commands our allegiance." He urged that "we question the worth of a dominantly money-civilization." John Dos Passos added that there was an "imperial American procession towards more money, more varnish, more ritz, that obsesses all our lives." During the late 1960's, Henry Fairlie compared the counterculture with his own youth, and wrote that "the young today, on the whole, despise business for the same reason that the young of my own day despised it: that it _seems_ to be concerned only with making money by processes which _seem_ to be intellectually and emotionally unsatisfying."[5]

3. A commercial, middle class society involves a peaceable day-to-day existence that has long struck many thinkers as intolerably mundane. Largely oblivious to the human drama that that life encompasses, these authors have felt a longing spiritually for "something bigger, more absorbing than individual lives."

Such a perspective was felt deeply by the adherents of the Romantic movement in the early 19th century. Thomas Carlyle yearned for "heroes" and considered the tradesman thoroughly mediocre. These were attitudes that reflected a resurgence of medieval and aristocratic values.

185

As secular religions, the totalitarian ideologies have yearned for a sense of transcendent destiny. In <u>Mein Kampf</u> Adolf Hitler angrily raised the rhetorical question of why he had been born in "an age of shopkeepers" rather than during the Wars of Liberation "when a man, even without a business, was worth something." In Communist writing, the "Bolshevik heroes" and the Stakhanovite heroes of self-sacrificing labor typify this commitment of the individual to the larger entity.

It is not surprising, then, that modern liberals have also reflected this yearning for a secular religion. Thus, Martha Higley wrote in <u>The New Republic</u> in 1931 that "the life of a large portion of the population is meaningless, because there is no centralizing force in their lives, no feeling that they are part of a social system greater than the individual unit." TRB complained in 1961 that "our culture has a genius for demeaning greatness." 6

Although I believe that these complaints about the emptiness of bourgeois life miss a great deal of the meaning that is actually there, I have made the point that a free society <u>does</u> need, as much as any other, a transcendent sense of meaning. I agree with the other philosophies that a daily life based on small preoccupations is <u>not</u> enough in itself to satisfy humanity's basic psychic needs. The historic failure of bourgeois life in this dimension is a vitally important one. The blame for it, though, is only partly the bourgeoisie's. The social critics are blind to the fact that a significant cause of the failure is due precisely to the intellectual culture's own choices. That culture has for almost two centuries thrown itself into alienation when it could have served as a vitally important component of a liberal society (in the historic sense of "liberal") and have worked to provide such meaning.

4. An oft-repeated charge is that bourgeois society is "hypocritical." In his preface to

<u>Civilization</u> <u>in</u> <u>the</u> <u>United</u> <u>States</u> in 1921, Harold Stearns said that one of the themes appearing in most of the book's thirty essays was "that in almost every branch of American life there is a sharp dichotomy between preaching and practice." Anyone who lived through the New Left period of the late 1960's must certainly remember how often our society was charged with hypocrisy.[7]

It should be apparent, though, that hypocrisy, as a slippage between what is professed and what is actually done, is a universal human trait. It cannot be considered the exclusive possession of any particular culture. To stay on track, the discussion should debate the relative degree of hypocrisy.

I have not been able to find a detailed explanation of why modern liberalism feels that bourgeois society is more hypocritical than others. The absence of this explanation in the literature makes it a matter of conjecture.

My own analysis in the chapter on "Existential Problems in a Commercial Culture" in <u>Understanding</u> <u>the</u> <u>Modern</u> <u>Predicament</u> suggests that a special form of hypocrisy does exist within a commercial society. It arises out of the split that exists between the "extroverted outer flow" among people, which trivializes everything into what is pleasant, and the "radical solitude" of meaningful life to individuals. The very gregariousness that in so many ways makes our life pleasant also puts it under a veil of trivia. Real values are covered over and ignored. Anyone caring about those values will tend to think the resulting human relationships hypocritical.

The trivialization is a serious problem in the spiritual and intellectual life of our society. Whether, however, it creates a condition that justifies the contempt of intellectuals more than the hypocrisy within other cultures does is another question.

187

5. The social criticism has created a caricature of middle class individuals that is closely associated with the complaints I have mentioned. It pictures the typical bourgeois as uninspired, insipid and preoccupied with money and social status.

The classic stereotype along these lines was drawn by Sinclair Lewis in his 1922 book Babbitt. Lewis' theme has been summarized by Henry May: "George F. Babbitt was a realtor in Zenith, Ohio ...Essentially confused and timid, he joined in the town's scramble for social prestige, its false, gregarious jollity...." May says that "much the same picture of dulness and conformity was painted by other poets and novelists, by foreign lecturers like Andre Siegfried, and by sociologists like the authors of Middletown...."[8]

Because of the currency of this stereotype, it is no surprise that George Babbitt is virtually the same character as George Bernard Shaw's Mr. Burgess in Candida. According to Shaw's stage directions, Burgess is a man "made coarse and sordid by the compulsory selfishness of petty commerce...a vulgar ignorant guzzling man...."[9]

The stereotype appears again in Theodore Dreiser's An American Tragedy when Dreiser describes Roberta Alden's father and family: "Titus Alden was one of that vast company of individuals who are born, pass through and die out of the world without ever quite getting any one thing straight...A single, serious, intelligent or rightly informing book had never been read by any member of this family--not one. But they were nevertheless excellent, as conventions, morals and religions go--honest, upright, God-fearing and respectable."[10]

6. This caricature of the middle class has been accompanied by an equally slashing attack upon the rural American, who is often depicted as ignorant, provincial, vicious and narrowly limited by an anti-intellectual fundamentalist Christian-

ity. H. L. Mencken wrote of "rustic ignoramuses" and said of William Jennings Bryan that he "seemed only a poor clod like those around him, deluded by a childish theology, full of an almost pathological hatred of all learning, all human dignity, all beauty, all fine and noble things. He was a peasant come home to the barnyard." 11

This critique found its <u>cause</u> <u>celebre</u> in the Scopes trial in 1925 after John T. Scopes was charged with violating the Tennessee statute against the teaching of evolution. Clarence Darrow was the attorney for the defense, William Jennings Bryan for the prosecution. <u>The</u> <u>New</u> <u>Republic</u> editorialized that the statute had been "passed by the lunatic fringe--a broad one--in the Fundamentalist movement." 12

It is worth noting that the critique has usually focused on the South, although it is actually broader than that would suggest. Tennessee Williams and Carson McCullers are authors whose works are central to the alienated portrayal of the South.

The intellectual culture's hostility toward what it considers a "hick" America is important if we are to understand the depth of the reservations that liberal intellectuals felt toward both Lyndon Baines Johnson and Jimmy Carter. Given the literary history of the twentieth century in the United States, Johnson and Carter were inevitably outsiders, no matter how liberal their programs and rhetoric. To the intellectual culture they were essentially "peasants come home to the barnyard."

7. Actually, of course, the alienation has been a general one, not limited to either the middle class or the rural American. It is a mistake to break it down too sharply into specifics. The larger alienation has been visible in countless ways, and I have discussed it extensively in my writing. I will illustrate it here by a relatively small example: the inclination of

liberal authors to blame the nation as a whole for the assassinations of John F. Kennedy and Robert Kennedy. In December, 1963, right after the first assassination, TRB's alienation was apparent when he spoke of "this hapless situation, set off by a senseless horror in Dallas, where they breed such things. There is a crackpot hatred in America...." Then in June, 1968, after the murder of Robert Kennedy by Sirhan Sirhan, a _New_ _Republic_ editorial said that the killing "tells us once more that we nurture in our society a disposition to violence." These are emotional outpourings expressed without regard to the specifics of the assassinations. They would hardly come from anyone who did not already feel deep alienation.[13]

8. Elitism will inevitably be an important characteristic of an intellectual culture that feels itself so superior to its milieu.

If this is surprising about American liberalism, it is only because liberals have so long been the ideological champions of democracy, material equality and compassion. These values have been dictated by the political, ideological imperatives of their alliance with the have-nots. At first, it seems incongruous that such a democratically oriented intellectual culture can also have been profoundly elitist. But anyone who thinks the various elements incompatible does not fully grasp the "layered" nature of liberalism.

"Majority rule" is supported whenever it is thought to lend itself to social legislation and to the forms of equality that liberalism pursues. Although liberalism sees itself as consistently democratic in the truest sense, majority rule, as such, will be subordinated to liberalism's other values if they conflict. One of the best examples is the Warren Court's striking down Proposition 14 which was passed by an overwhelming majority in a referendum in California and that sought to repeal that state's open-housing law. Another is the Court's having invalidated various state referenda that sought to reinstate a geographical component in the make-up of state senates after the Court's reapportionment decisions. The fact that large majorities had voted a certain way was not seen to matter. Both "majority rule" and the doctrine so popular with liberals in the 1920's and '30's of "let the local majorities experiment" were subordinated by the liberal majority on the Court at that time. Although some justices continued to espouse the judicial restraint that they had preached while conservatives dominated the Court, the Warren Court's majority was given to judicial activism.

The alienation and elitism that I have illustrated in this chapter are also prepared to subordinate the values of democracy, equality and compassion to other values. There is no natural affinity of the intellectuals for the have-nots, whom they know to be even less given to intellectual values than the bourgeoisie. For a century and a half, the intellectuals and the have-nots have been ideological allies as the Left has sought coalitions against the predominant middle class culture. Because that is a long time so far as the perspective of any given person is concerned, the illusion is created that the connection is permanent. This illusion is the reason for the surprise and disillusionment that has followed in the wake of the actual behavior of Communist regimes, in which a brutal elitism soon becomes apparent. (Ironically, the elitism of the intellectuals is often replaced by that of a clique of political cronies, such as under Stalin. But if the analysis made by Konrad and Szelenyi is to be credited, there is later a tendency for an elite of at least technocratic intellectuals to assume power.) [14]

9. There is a striking similarity between the social critique and elitism of American liberalism (and of the Left in general) and that of Burkean conservatism, which sees modern life through the lens of a medieval worldview.

When John Dewey wrote that "the individual

191

has become lost through detachment from acknowledged social values" and that "individuals are
loosened from the ties which once gave order and
support to their lives," we could easily close our
eyes and imagine that the words were written by
Richard Weaver or Russell Kirk--or, going back
further, by Carlyle, Ruskin or Arnold in the 19th
century or by Samuel Johnson in the 18th. The
medievalist critique of bourgeois society has been
overtly on the side of elitism. Its criticisms
have been the same as the Left's, although it made
them well before the Left came into being. The
bourgeois has historically been seen as a vulgar-
ian by those who have championed a leisured aristocracy. The proletarian, of course, has been
thought of as even worse, although entitled to the
noblesse oblige of the aristocracy.[15]

A Burkean's rebuttal to this might well be to
point to liberalism and the Left's attack on
values, tradition and norms. That attack has
joined forces with the very vacuity of which
liberal social critics have complained and, increasingly as the 20th century goes on, with the
rhythms of black culture. The result has been
seriously to weaken the American social fabric in
the 20th century and to raise the neurotic hub-bub
to a pitch that is truly deafening. It is legitimate for the Burkean to argue that this is all
very much at odds with conservative values.

Such a response, however, would miss the
point about the layering. The Left's enthusiasm
for Dadaistic nihilism and for various art forms
such as that of the proletarian art of the 1930's
or the black rhythms that predominate in the late
20th century is directly related to its enthusiasm
for attacking what it sees as "bourgeois" values.
The roots of this aesthetic militancy, however,
lie in the same alienation from bourgeois culture
that the Burkean has felt. The difference is that
the Burkean, so long as he remains a Burkean, does
not see fit to ally himself with the have-nots
and with the more vulgar and hedonistic propensities of the middle class itself. The Left has

192

done so precisely because of its active immersement in the preoccupations of its allies and because such an immersement has been consistent with
its assault on the middle class's value system.

When in the preceding paragraph I pointed to
the Left's support for "the more vulgar and hedonistic propensities of the middle class itself," I
realized that I introduced an element that I have
not discussed before. What is important to realize is that modern liberalism and the Left's negative critique of the middle class is not primarily
an opposition to the middle class's weaknesses and
vices, but precisely to its strengths and virtues.
True, it dislikes the intellectual, aesthetic
mediocrity that arises out of the middle class's
preoccupation with daily life and competitive
success; but it also opposes the very value system
of competition, of the work ethic, of family discipline. It sees no incongruity, given its willingness to mold itself to its tactical needs, in
supporting and promoting (as our predominantly
liberal media do) the hedonistic and vulgar sides
of the middle class psyche. It is this combination of the intellectual culture with both black
culture and middle class hedonism that has given
rise to the predominant cultural tone in the
United States in the 20th century, especially
since World War II. [16]

We will see in a later chapter that many of
the leading intellectuals of the American Left
have moved to the right. Most have then embraced
Burkean conservatism, not classical liberalism.
This choice makes sense. It leaves intact certain
fundamental aspects of their orientation: their
elitism and their desire to stand outside the
bourgeoisie.

10. Throughout this discussion, I have
referred to the "defiance of convention" which has
often been one of the consequences of the assault
upon middle class values. The passage by Jerry
Rubin illustrated it starkly. Although liberalism
itself is given to dissimulation to avoid con-

frontation, there is a direct connection between liberalism's critique of the society and these more extreme expressions of the critique.

In 1927, The New Republic, speaking of the American theater, said that "in its defiance of convention it has been expressing a widely prevalent revolt against the manners and values of previous generations." This revolt is intellectually, artistically related to the revolutionary theater of the New Left sixty years later.[17]

In 1932, Malcolm Cowley looked back to the time when Dos Passos was a student at Harvard immediately before World War I. It was the time of the "Harvard esthetes," who believed that "society is hostile, stupid and unmanageable; it is the world of the philistines...That the poet... should, in fact, deliberately make himself misunderstandable...That art...is the poet's revenge on society." Cowley spoke of the poet's flight into mysticism "by any means in his power--alcohol, drugs...." This was the same period that the Dadaist school in Europe was proclaiming art as a weapon against the bourgeoisie and against art itself.[18]

In Exile's Return, Malcolm Cowley explained that the Dadaist impulse had actually gotten started in Europe in the early 19th century. (It is no coincidence, of course, that that would correspond with the Romantic movement, with its deep revulsion against modernity and bourgeois culture.) In the same book, Edmund Wilson told how the 19th century author Flaubert "with several of his friends once visited a brothel in Rouen. On a bet, before them all, he made love to a prostitute without removing his hat or taking the cigar from his mouth. The gesture was something more than an ugly boast. It announced a furious contempt for everything held sacred by society."[19]

Years later, Eldridge Cleaver explained that this concept of "revenge upon the culture," applied in a racial context, lay behind why "I became a rapist." He said that "it seemed to me that the act of rape was an insurrectionary act. It delighted me that I was defying and trampling upon the white man's law, upon his system of values."20

11. A final point is important in its own right but is sufficiently different that it will also illustrate how far-reaching the implications of the rejection of American cultural values can be.

Liberal thought has often said that it wishes to divorce "middle class" moral judgments from the social policies directed toward the poor.

In part it has wanted to do so in order to "become more scientific." In Comte's three-part classification of historical stages, the scientific "positivist" phase would supplant the "metaphysical" phase that preceded it. Individual morality has been identified with the metaphysical phase (or with the theological phase, which was even earlier). An excellent example of the attempt to get away from so-called metaphysics and theology by applying a deterministic analysis to the exclusion of values is B. F. Skinner's Beyond Freedom and Dignity.

In addition to wanting to become clinically scientific, liberalism has had motives dictated by the tactical needs of its ideology in its quest for alliances with the poor. By negating "middle class" moral values, liberal ideology has accomplished two things: First, it has made it possible for itself to be easily empathetic toward the poor by rejecting the need to make adverse judgments. Then, in an associated step, it has made itself "the enemy of their enemies." It has been able to oppose those who do have adverse moral judgments to make. These two aspects affect a number of practical issues.

We have seen, for example, an editorial such as the one in The New Republic in 1968 in which

195

the editors denounced specific policies that were based upon moral evaluations. One was a Louisiana statute that made it a crime for someone to parent a second illegitimate child. Another was the rule which many states had adopted that provided that Aid to Families With Dependent Children would not be payable if there were an able-bodied man living in the household. It is in the context of such issues that modern liberalism has established the web of "non-judgmental" programs that exist today. The result is that a humanitarian concern for the poor has been replaced by a paternalism that is extended as well to the irresponsible poor. For this and a number of other reasons, the problem of irresponsibility in its endless variety, of indwelling barbarism within civilization, is one of today's most intractable problems.

A lesser, but functionally very compelling, reason for the divorce from the so-called "middle class" principles of personal responsibility has been to make it possible for social workers and other professionals to establish a non-judgmental working relationship with the poor. If for no other reason than to encourage those who are irresponsible to seek counseling, and to continue with it once begun, a non-judgmental relationship is considered necessary between the counselor and the subject. This causes professionals in such fields constantly to seek ways to depersonalize (i.e., render deterministic) the explanation of the causes of the distressed condition of their subjects. (I recently attended a school meeting on the drug problem in which the audience was told over and over again that "neither the young person nor the parent is to blame" for the child's having become an addict. This was said in the abstract, as a general principle negating anyone's responsibility. The facts of any given case were abstracted away in favor of the moral neutrality.

Such a stance may or may not be conducive to effective counseling, but it clearly is predicated on the assumption that moral constraints, socially enforced, are no longer important to modern society. We can only hope that after a few years enough moral perspective will remain to allow our society to evaluate the effects of this assumption, and to adopt a different principle if it is found not to have worked.

NOTES

1. Henry David Thoreau, <u>Walden-Essay</u> <u>on</u> <u>Civil</u> <u>Disobedience</u> (New York: Airmont Publishing Company, Inc., 1965), p. 81.

2. Morris Cohen is quoted in Henry May, <u>The</u> <u>Discontent</u> <u>of</u> <u>the</u> <u>Intellectuals:</u> <u>A</u> <u>Problem</u> <u>of</u> <u>the</u> <u>Twenties</u> (Chicago: Rand McNally & Company, 1963), p. 23; New Republic, December 12, 1914, p. 21.

3. New Republic, April 17, 1915, p. 7 of the Literary Supplement; New Republic, June 4, 1930, p. 68.

4. Jerry Rubin, <u>Growing</u> <u>(Up)</u> <u>at</u> <u>37</u> (New York: Warner Books, 1976), pp. 140-142.

5. New Republic, April 24, 1929, p. 271; New Republic, April 16, 1930, p. 236; New Republic, April 8, 1967, p. 13.

6. New Republic, June 24, 1931, p. 152; New Republic, January 23, 1961, p. 2.

7. Harold E. Stearns (ed.), <u>Civilization</u> <u>in</u> <u>the</u> <u>United</u> <u>States</u> (New York: Harcourt, Brace and Company, 1922), p. vi.

8. May, <u>Discontent</u> <u>of</u> <u>the</u> <u>Intellectuals</u>, pp. 30, 31.

9. Another Babbitt-like characterization of American culture is summarized in the review of Sherwood Anderson's <u>Marching</u> <u>Man</u> in the September 29, 1917, issue of New Republic, p. 249.

10. Theodore Dreiser, <u>An</u> <u>American</u> <u>Tragedy</u> (New

York: The Heritage Press, 1962), p. 166.

11. Mencken is quoted by May in *Discontent of the Intellectuals*, p. 27.

12. *New Republic*, January 26, 1927, p. 260.

13. *New Republic*, December 7, 1963, p. 30.

14. George Konrad and Ivan Szelenyi, *The Intellectuals on the Road to Class Power* (New York: Harcourt, Brace, Jovanovich, Inc., 1979).

15. *New Republic*, February 5, 1930, p. 296.

16. Two qualifications should be voiced with regard to what I have said in this paragraph: That my reference to black culture is by no means intended to be a universal condemnation of it; and that many dedicated members of the Left oppose the marriage with hedonism, wanting a purer method.

17. *New Republic*, February 23, 1927, p. 6.

18. *New Republic*, April 27, 1932, p. 303.

19. Malcolm Cowley, *Exile's Return: A Narrative of Ideas* (New York: W. W. Norton & Company, Inc., 1934), pp. 148, 151.

20. Ronald Berman, *America in the Sixties: An Intellectual History* (New York: The Free Press, 1968), p. 281.

8

EMPHASIS ON SOCIAL CHANGE

Modern liberalism has focused on the desirability of social change. It has stressed the impermanence of values and institutions. On issues of method, such as those involving "civil liberties" and confrontational techniques, it has taken positions that facilitate change rather than impede it. It would not be off the mark to say that the emphasis on change has been as central to modern liberalism as the emphasis on stability has been to traditionalist conservatism.

The relationship of this focus to liberalism's tactical situation is apparent. Liberal thought has not relished the existing culture--has, in fact, been deeply alienated from it--and has been anxious to move to something else.

For most liberal thought, that "something else" has been, as we have seen, one form or another of socialism. Although this has not been nearly so true for the other components of the liberal coalition such as the South, organized labor and the ethnic minorities as it has been for the intellectual culture, most of those other components have at least wanted an active program calling for social and legislative changes.

At the same time that liberalism has desired to emphasize change, it has intuitively kept in mind its need for dissimulation. During most of modern liberalism's history, liberals have avoided a direct advocacy of socialism. What has been needed, instead, has been a philosophical formulation that would focus on change as a process rather than as a conflict between well defined alternative systems. This explains why "pragmatism," American liberalism's most distinctive version of relativism, has been so popular within liberal thought. By denying theory and insisting

199

that only the short-term and the concrete count, pragmatism has been consistent with the reluctance to reveal long-term aspirations.

This discussion of the liberal emphasis on change will involve an examination of four specific aspects of liberalism: the uses of pragmatism and of relativism; liberal educational theory; the role of "civil liberties"; and the liberal attitude toward confrontational techniques as catalysts of social change.

Relativism and Pragmatism

Chapter 10 of my book Socialist Thought was a discussion of the role that relativism has played in socialist thinking. That chapter is important as background for our present discussion, since most of what I said there would apply equally well in an analysis of liberalism.

One of the points that I made was that relativism arises in part out of the perspectives of science. Those who seek evidence and verification for their views are led to the "methodological individualism" of a Descartes and a Heisenberg. In addition, those who are primarily empirical come quickly to see that there is great variety within the world. Their studies constantly remind them that any particular set of values, institutions, laws or acculturations is simply one alternative among many.

This is illustrated by what John Chamberlain said about William Graham Sumner's sociological discussion in Folkways: "The one great idea that you take away from 'Folkways' is the idea of the relativity of cultures, the feeling that no custom or habit-pattern is right or wrong except in relation to a time and a place." Chamberlain's review was written as part of a New Republic series on the books that had most influenced liberal thought. Even though Sumner was a devout follower of Herbert Spencer's classical liberalism, his empirical relativism was congenial to liberal intellectuals, who have closely identified with the main trends of modern intellectuality.[1]

The rapid communication and travel that are available today constitute another major source of relativism. Local provincialisms become ever more difficult to sustain.

Because of these sources of relativism, it would be a mistake to attribute the modern relativistic philosophies exclusively to the tactical needs of the Left. Nevertheless, it would be an equally serious mistake to overlook the role played by those needs, which have served as a third great source of relativism.

Eric Goldman was commendably candid in his book Rendezvous With Destiny about liberalism's tactical use of relativism as a "social acid." He said that liberals in the late 19th and early 20th centuries found it necessary to attack the "steel chain of ideas" by which the American public was bound to classical liberalism. Goldman summarized this aspect of liberalism in the final sentence of his chapter called "Dissolving the Steel Chain of Ideas." He said that "between the depression of 1873 and the beginning of World War I, and especially during the early 1900's, these thinkers developed ideological acids capable of dissolving every link in conservatism's steel chain of ideas."[2]

Arthur Bestor discussed the same point in a New Republic article in 1955. He pointed out that "the alliance between pragmatism and liberalism was a fortuitous one, called forth by a particular historic situation...Pragmatism constituted, in essence, [a] sacred act of intellectual spoliation." Speaking from a liberal perspective, he said that "it was as a dissolvent of untenable dogmas and misapplied certitudes that pragmatism served the liberal cause" (emphasis added). (It is worth noticing that he was not himself enthused about the relativism. He observed that pragmatism "revealed its fundamental inadequacy" in the late 1930's when it became necessary to articulate definite convictions to oppose the totalitarian systems. But we should notice, too, that there has been no repudiation of relativism by liberals in general. It has been used extensively in liberal ideology during the four decades since World War II.)[3]

It should not confuse us that Bestor's article uses the term "pragmatism" instead of "relativism." Pragmatism is nothing other than the name given to the relativism that was put forward under that label by such thinkers as Charles Peirce, William James and John Dewey. Relativism without the label has continued to be used by liberalism as a "social acid" despite the reputed demise of pragmatism as such. When in the late 1960's we were told so often that "middle class values are just 'artificial structurings,'" we were being presented with a relativistic undercutting, even though nothing was said about pragmatism. In the 1970's we heard a similar argument, this time from feminists, that "the role assignments of 'masculinity' and 'femininity' are just artificial acculturations, with no inherent justification." Again, relativism was being used to dissolve people's attachment to existing norms. In both instances, it was quite successful. The relativistic undercutting has sufficient plausibility that most people, lacking a philosophical understanding of the values they have held, have no defense against it.

"Pragmatism," as such, is almost impossible to define, since, as F. C. S. Schiller said, there have been "as many pragmatisms as there were pragmatists." The entry by H. S. Thayer in The Encyclopedia of Philosophy traces the origin of pragmatism to the "Metaphysical Club" conducted in Cambridge in the 1870's by, among others, William James and Charles Peirce. Thayer says that James credited Peirce with having coined the name.

Readers who would like an introduction to the

technical philosophical dimensions of pragmatism will do well to read Thayer's entry and the one preceding it by Gertrude Ezorsky on the "Pragmatic Theory of Truth." Dewey best expressed the technical aspects in his book Logic: The Theory of Inquiry.

Our concern here will be with the application of pragmatism to social philosophy. This will center of John Dewey's version of pragmatism, since it was Dewey who used it to become perhaps the leading philosopher of liberalism. Peirce and James played no similar role.

As understood by liberal commentators, Dewey's pragmatism, which he preferred to call "instrumentalism," emphasized that knowledge is tentative and must come from an experimental attitude. Randolph Bourne praised Dewey for his "scientific method, with its hypothesis and bold experimentation." Morris Cohen saw its essence as being that Dewey used ideas as "instrumental for reforming the world" (my emphasis). Dewey was consistent with this when he spoke of "a conviction that consequences in human welfare are a test of the worth of beliefs."[4]

This amounted to a value-laden flexibility, with an emphasis on the particular rather than the general. The values were those of liberalism. Dewey's pragmatism was a rationale for Fabian gradualism. We see these same ingredients in Charles Forcey's discussion of the views of Herbert Croly and Walter Weyl when he said that "pragmatism did not mean for [them]...mere expediency and drift ...'The democracy, though compromising in action,' wrote Weyl, 'must be uncompromising in principle ...and realized as opportunities permit.'" We should remember that Weyl considered himself a socialist; his reference to "democracy" was to the "industrial democracy" that was so popular at that time among British socialists and American liberals.[5]

It is no secret, of course, that John Dewey

203

was also a socialist. The focus on experiment, on looking to social consequences, on judging ideas by their usefulness for social change, was ideal for an ideology that wanted to stress method, process and change while at the same time making its own standards of social value the largely unarticulated measure for judging validity.

As a social philosophy, there was little that was new or profound about Dewey's pragmatism. His popularity as a social philosopher was due to his ideas' usefulness for liberalism. The same homage that was extended to Dewey as a philosopher was afforded to Oliver Wendell Holmes, Jr., for having applied relativism to law. Both men's positions must be understood in the context of liberalism's tactical needs at that time.

Even though "pragmatism" as a movement may have died, references to the need to "be pragmatic" continued to be useful to liberalism after World War II. As we will see in the chapter on "the process of politicization," liberal thinking has seen virtually all human problems as appropriate subjects for governmental solution, preferably at the national level. The most direct way to address a problem was to establish an agency and to arm it with a few billion dollars. Whenever a conservative would object, he was implored to "forget that nonsense; be pragmatic." Direct action through government seemed much more immediate, "practical" and "compassionate" than to wait for people to work out their own problems or for the market to address them.

In this connection, it is worth noting that pragmatism is closely tied to at least three separate aspects of the modern mentality. It reflects the politicization that I have just mentioned. It relates, too, to the use of the state as a "direct action" tool, which is something that the Spanish philosopher Jose Ortega y Gasset considered in his book The Revolt of the Masses to be a major part of the primitive psychology of "the mass man." And it reflects the type of "ration-

204

alism" that has appealed to intellectuals of the Left, who have not thought in terms of simply creating frameworks for otherwise unplanned human interaction.

A word of warning is in order, however. Many practical-minded people in American life have prided themselves on their "pragmatic" willingness to "solve problems." When a politician or a businessman calls himself "pragmatic," he usually means nothing more by it than that he is practical. He does not understand himself to be part of Dewey's movement, and he would certainly deny that he has any Fabian intentions. There is no particular ideological significance to the word "pragmatic" when it is used in that manner.

Although what I have just said is true in its own way, I believe that this popular usage does nevertheless have a dimension that is quite significant to our discussion of the ideologies. I made the point in my book about classical liberalism that individualistic liberalism was forced onto the defensive more than a century ago, and that that posture has kept it from being as reformist and as critical as it otherwise would have been. The theory of a free society in the classical liberal sense has accordingly not been developed in a fully adequate way. I am thinking especially of its failure to deal with the problems raised by market imperfections, although there are other issues that are equally affected.

If we understand this, it becomes evident that politicians and businessmen within our society have often felt a need not to adhere strictly to the too-narrow rationale that has been spelled out by free-market theorists. They have felt the insufficiency of that rationale. Without an alternative theory of their own, they have justified their departure from the rationale by saying that they are "simply being pragmatic." It is likely that most such people have little, if any, socialist affinity; their common sense just tells them that they need to be free to act independently of

205

a theory that most Americans have continued to embrace in general but have intuitively felt to be insufficient. Pragmatism's focus on the concrete allows a downplaying of theory. For liberals like Dewey, it has been a vehicle for bypassing conservative theory and for not having to articulate their own. For the average American, it has allowed a commonsense adaptation of inadequate theory to felt needs.

Another point about relativism that we should notice is that "true believers" within the American Left have often rejected relativism, just as they have rejected dissimulation. Such people have wanted to make a forthright statement of their values and social preferences. They have had a sense of the timidity and essential dishonesty of liberal dissimulation.

Thus it is that in 1932, during the period when liberal intellectuals were most moved to repudiate the dissimulation, Waldo Frank wrote with disgust about "that flabby relativism which goes by the name of liberalism in the West and which is so often nothing but a want of conviction...." Lewis Mumford, another who chafed in the same way, added in 1934 that the New Deal "is pragmatism in action: aimless experiment, sporadic patchwork, a total indifference to guiding principles or definitive goals." John Dewey, of course, would have denied that pragmatism as he favored it lacked goals, since he fully intended it to embody socialist values; but Mumford's statement is a good illustration of the irritation that some felt.[6]

In the context of this debate, I should point out that it is entirely possible to be both a relativist and a devotee of theory, principles and long-term values--and to combine them without using relativism as a mask for unarticulated theories. I myself see real truth in the methodological individualism of science and in the cross-cultural awareness of empiricism. And yet I am attached to classical liberal values and to a

206

modified form of classical liberal theory. My quarrel with relativism as it has been used by the Left in the past century is that it is intellectually insufficient when used as a debunking mechanism. This is because it is not enough to point out to somebody that "your values and institutions are just one cultural alternative among many"--and to let it go at that. It is incumbent upon a serious analysis to go further. It must examine the comparative utility of the various cultural alternatives for the service of a number of values that most human beings would agree are important to civilized life. Unless we are to assume that all alternatives are equally serviceable, this step is essential. But it is almost invariably omitted when relativism is used as a debunking tool.

A final point that I will mention has to do with the relativism that Eric Goldman refers to as "Reform Darwinism." He says that in the late 19th century liberalism countered the popularity of Herbert Spencer's individualistic "Social Darwinism" by advancing an opposing form of evolutionary theory. Spencer theorized in terms of the struggle of individuals, with the most fit surviving. Reform Darwinism spoke of the evolution of societies as a whole, moving from one phase to another.

It was the vogue at the time to express most things in an "evolutionary" context. What Reform Darwinism did was to restate the historicist thesis of the German Historical School in Darwinian terms. The content was the same. The German Historical School was arguing that cultures pass through phases, and that any given phase--such as the bourgeois period of the 19th century--had no rightful claim to permanence. Among other things, this provided the basis for an attack upon the claims of classical economics, which saw permanent validity in its descriptions of how a market economy works.

When John Dewey said that conservatism talked "as if the only individualism were the local episode of the last two centuries," he was simply repeating the critique made by the German Historical School. Lester Ward had made the same point in 1881 when he wrote that "all truth is relative. Doctrines that were true for one age cease to be true for a later one; principles which really worked the salvation of the last century cannot be utilized in the present one."7

Eric Goldman describes Reform Darwinism's emphasis upon the evolution of institutions and cultures: "Why not insist on thoroughgoing evolution and argue that contemporary institutions could and should change rapidly?...Why not, in short, work out a Reform Darwinism that would dissolve away conservatism's steel chain of ideas ...?" The result would be a philosophy that would "replace dreary inevitabilities with a philosophy of flux that justified experiment and change." From this, we can see that, despite the application of different labels over the past century in keeping with whatever was most in vogue, there is no significant difference between the German Historical School, Reform Darwinism, Dewey's Pragmatism, and the tactic of gradualism advocated by the British Fabian socialists.8

John Dewey's educational theory

In addition to being a philosopher of pragmatism, John Dewey was the leading theorist for "progressive education." There is a great deal of similarity between the two. They are much the same thing, applied to different areas.

Just as with pragmatism, the emphasis within progressive education was upon flexibility, experiment, openness, a getting-away from the discipline and forms of the past. As with pragmatism, there was a socialist content, since the experimentation was not intended to be value-free. A third similarity was that the state would be a vehicle to accomplish these purposes; Dewey was quite clear about his willingness to use education for ideological indoctrination.

We see these elements in what Dewey himself had to say about the type of education he desired. That he wished to dissolve the connection between education and the existing social system appears from his comment in 1914 that "every ground of public policy protests against any use of the public school system which takes for granted the perpetuity of the existing industrial system...." That he wanted education to serve socialist values appears in such statements as the one in 1930 about the need to create "a new psychological and moral type." He desired "the creation of a type of individual whose pattern of thought and desire is enduringly marked by consensus with others, and in whom sociability is one with cooperation in all regular human associations." He called for "a new individuality...that is social."9

Morton White has described the thesis of Dewey's book The School and Society (1899), which White says was Dewey's "most widely read book and the earliest exposition of his theory of progressive education." White says that "Dewey's school was to be socially minded, imbued with the values of community life, rather than with the values of individual acquisitiveness." (We should notice that community values and "individual acquisitiveness" are seen as opposing values. Classical liberal individualism differs from socialist thought in considering them complementary. It thinks both important.)10

That Dewey was anxious to use education for ideological indoctrination is apparent from his statement that schooling should involve "indoctrination, or, if one prefer, teaching, with respect to preparation for a different social order."11

It was in 1928 that John Dewey wrote his series of six articles for The New Republic about Soviet education, reporting on his trip to Soviet Russia. A passage in his second article not only typifies the series in its mixture of caution and enthusiasm, but also shows how much he thought the

Soviets were carrying out his educational goals: "In spite of secret police, inquisitions, arrests and deportations of Nepmen and Kulaks, exiling of party opponents,...life for the masses goes on with regularity, safety and decorum...<u>There</u> <u>is</u> <u>an</u> <u>enormous</u> <u>constructive</u> <u>effort</u> <u>taking</u> <u>place</u> <u>in</u> <u>the</u> <u>creation</u> <u>of</u> <u>a</u> <u>new</u> <u>collective</u> <u>mentality</u>...." (emphasis added) This is precisely the goal that he made central to progressive education.[12]

What are we to think of this? All cultures use their educational systems for the transmission of values. Children nowhere enjoy existential freedom. Although the New Left, reflecting anarchist thought, argued for such freedom, it is a "freedom" that would be inconsistent with the maintenance of advanced civilization and even of a free society. A middle class society rooted in classical liberal values uses family, church, school and other mechanisms to transmit its heritage. It does this every bit as much as Dewey or the Soviets would inculcate socialist norms. An objection to the indoctrination of children must be directed to the content of the indoctrination rather than to the fact that it occurs. But this does not mean that Dewey's proposed indoctrination should be accepted by us. It comes down to this: if we are socialists, we will welcome it; otherwise, we should very emphatically reject it.

Given a clear choice, most Americans would have rejected Dewey's educational theory, while the main intellectual culture would have embraced it. Consistently with liberal dissimulation in general, the socialist purpose was rarely revealed. Dissimulation has befogged liberal educational philosophy with the same ambiguity that has befuddled so many other issues. Nevertheless, despite the obfuscation and the pressures that the intellectual culture has been able to bring to bear upon people to accept liberal thinking under threat of otherwise not appearing sophisticated, a great many Americans <u>have</u> opposed progressive education.

A different set of issues is raised by the fact that liberalism has often sanctioned the use of the state and of the mass media for the ideological indoctrination of the <u>adult</u> public. At the height of the the anti-Vietnam War movement, for example, the editors of <u>The New Republic</u> justified the politicization of the universities on the ground that, after all, "the times are abnormal." In 1977 the federal government sponsored a series of women's conferences leading to a large national conference. Gloria Steinem argued for the exclusion of conservative women: "The legal purpose of these conferences is to further the status of women and, therefore, there is no legal obligation to include representatives of groups who want to retard the status of women."[13]

Individual examples of this sort are insignificant, however, in comparison to the willingness of the intellectual culture to use television and film quite egregiously as propaganda vehicles for the Left. During my lifetime, the propagandistic content has been so blatant that I cannot help but feel that it demonstrates an almost complete lack of respect for the intelligence of the American public. This is an attitude that would be consistent with the cultural critique that liberalism makes and that I reviewed in the preceding chapter. Unfortunately, the critique seems in large measure an accurate one, since, despite the many conservative voices raised for many years against the propaganda, most people accept it without a second thought. (Those in the future who want to view examples of what I am talking about would do well to find an archive copy of the excellently made movie <u>Reds</u>—or, on a lower level, of the films <u>Poltergeist</u>, <u>Shampoo</u> or <u>Prophecy</u>.)

It would be utopian and perhaps not even sound to expect government as an institution (as distinct from the political leaders, who necessarily express views on controversial subjects) always to be strictly neutral with respect to the ideas that are currently under debate within a society, or to expect the intellectual culture wholly to eschew propaganda. Nevertheless, a free society should always to be concerned about the health of its processes of debate and discussion. There is basic inequity, as well as grave danger, in government's using tax money and its vast organizational strength to institutionalize a certain position that does not already enjoy a substantial consensus. And for the intellectual culture to approach the public forum with a partisanship that is so overwhelming that it colors and selectively censors all discussion, as the liberal media has during my lifetime, and especially during the 1960's and early '70's, is not consistent with a healthy marketplace of ideas.

It is appropriate to comment upon these aspects, despite (or even especially because of) liberalism's oft-repeated devotion to free speech. The actual performance of liberalism does not show its advocates to be more tolerant than are people who support most other points of view. It is worth remembering that there is a totalitarian Left which explicitly urges the repression of all non-socialist points of view. This was a position that was advocated prominently by the New Left philosopher Herbert Marcuse in his <u>Essay on Liberation</u>. And it is the spirit reflected in the statement I have quoted from Steinem.

The <u>role</u> of "civil liberties"

American liberals have prided themselves on their support for "civil liberties." This is a term that they define differently than classical liberals define "liberty" in general. In common with democratic socialists, modern liberals intend the term to denote the freedoms associated with free speech and political participation as distinguished from property rights and freedom of contract.

It is a serious mistake to believe that most of the proponents of an ideology are not sincerely committed to the values they espouse. This is

212

certainly true with regard to modern liberalism's championing of civil liberties. Just the same, a complete understanding requires an awareness of additional aspects:

1. The liberties of speech and political participation are not simply values within a model of society that liberals favor; they also have an instrumental value. They are directly serviceable to the liberal desire for social change. Since they play a tactical role, it becomes important to examine the permanence of liberalism's attachment to them.

2. The enthusiasm that so many liberals felt toward the totalitarian Left during the 1930's, and again during the late 1960's, suggests that, at least to a good many liberals, socialist values, when they appear within grasp, take priority over civil liberties and what have come to be called "human rights."

I recall an article by Joshua Kunitz in The New Republic in 1933 justifying the Soviet execution of six people for stealing and selling food. "That the decree is terribly drastic there can be little doubt. The Communists, however, believe it to be supremely just." Kunitz also justified a decree punishing "a single unexplained absence from work" by discharge, loss of living quarters and loss of ration card. "They had to be broken in, educated to a realization of their duties as Soviet citizens." In 1935, Anna Louise Strong, a frequent contributor to both of the main liberal journals, wrote about the Soviet concentration camps that "there are 'labor camps' in many parts of the country, as part of the Soviet method of reclaiming anti-social elements by useful, collective work."14

This gives us pause. Such passages directly contradict the liberal emphasis on civil and human rights. In my opinion, it would be a mistake to consider them mere aberrations. They are, instead, meaningful glimpses into the hierarchy of

213

values that exists within liberal ideology.

3. The tactical usefulness of these liberties almost certainly explains why liberals are willing to carry them beyond the limits that classical liberals, who are also devotees of the same liberties, think desirable.

The Warren Court declared in the Yates decision that the abstract advocacy of revolution is protected by the principle of free speech. Only when this advocacy is followed with some form of action can it be considered illegal.

This is a principle that will appeal primarily to those who ignore important other values. It overlooks entirely the type of world in which this "abstract advocacy" is to exist. The 20th century world is one in which terrorist killings and kidnappings are rampant and in which totalitarian states with great military power seek on ideological grounds to expand their power. Any group founded upon the "abstract advocacy" of violence stands as a ready reserve for terrorism and aggression. In case of war, it is an existing reservoir for espionage and sabotage. Under such circumstances, it is impossible to say that it does not at each moment constitute a "clear and present danger." (Sometimes I think that those who speak of "abstract advocacy" forget that it is assassination, destruction of property and the overthrow of free institutions that is being talked about. The word "abstract" seems to make it bloodless to them.)

In other connections, liberals have had little hesitation to affirm the need of a free society to protect itself. After Hitler gained power in Germany, a 1933 New Republic editorial asked appropriately: "Was not the ultra-liberal tolerance of this [Weimar] Republic largely to blame, which respected the right of association so scrupulously that it allowed the formation of party-armies?" A New Republic article by Stetson Kennedy in 1946 favored the mandatory registration

214

of any group, such as the Ku Klux Klan, "having more than 20 members and requiring an oath as a condition of membership." Liberals acknowledge the right of a society, such as West Germany, to outlaw Nazi organizations. In stark contrast is Morris Ernst's 1949 argument that "I believe Communists have the right publicly to advocate the overthrow of the United States."[15]

Attitudes toward confrontational techniques

Classical liberal theory has long seen coercion as the central problem among people. It seeks a society in which coercion is reduced as much as possible, with voluntary interactions accentuated. When a society actually exists that approximates these objectives, classical liberals identify with it, as distinguished from those who stand in an alienated relationship to it. They also think of its processes as sufficient to allow the expression of freedom.

Modern liberalism, on the other hand, has been ready to endorse methods of social change that are either coercive or confrontational. This posture is consistent with (a) their theoretical frame of reference, which does not see coercion as the central problem; (b) their alienation from the predominant society; (c) their impatience for more rapid social change than would come about without such techniques; and (d) their belief that there is a significant flaw in the communication that goes on in the absence of confrontation, since those wanting change do not otherwise seem to be able to "get the public's attention."

When I speak of coercive techniques, I do not mean that liberals have favored violence, at least directly. (My reason for qualifying the disclaimer will soon become apparent.) Coercion is a category that includes but is much larger than violence.

Labor conflict has been one of the areas in

215

which this has been important. Classical liberalism was historically favorable to "friendly societies," associations of workers who joined together for mutual support and improvement. It was opposed, however, to the "right to strike," seeing a strike as coercive in the same way that a concerted boycott by suppliers is coercive. Modern liberalism, on the other hand, has been strongly influenced by the Left's perspective that workers are exploited by their employers--and has accordingly thought in terms of industrial conflict. It has sanctioned a number of coercive devices.

A passage from Herbert Croly's Progressive Democracy (1915), in which he described how workers could bring about a socialist "industrial democracy," is illustrative: "[Workers must engage in] warfare appropriate for the purpose. Their 'Constitution of Freedom' must be gradually extorted from their employers by a series of conflicts in which the ground is skilfully chosen and permanent defeat is never admitted. In that way only can the wage-earning class win effective power...Practically all of the wage-earners as a group should be unionized as the result of this warfare...." [16]

In 1936, the CIO's United Automobile Workers Union used the sit-down strike for the first time in the United States. Its members seized the General Motors plant in Flint, Michigan, for six weeks. Writing in The New Republic, Robert Morss Lovett justified this weapon: "...the sitdown strike [is] a weapon of industrial conflict. The right of non-working employees to occupy the plant...is one of the industrial liberties which are on the way to becoming legally recognized." [17]

The liberal call for class consciousness among workers and for coercive techniques failed to result in the great social divisions after World War II that it might have. This is due to the fact that instead of increasing in power, the union movement came to occupy a proportionally lesser place in American life. The intellectual

216

culture came to view it with contempt precisely because it did not on the whole continue a militant posture expressing alienation and a desire for socialism. The liberal imagination has been captured by such things as Cesar Chavez's angry "grape boycott," but this has been on the periphery of the labor movement rather than central to it.

In the 1960's, the Civil Rights and anti-Vietnam War movements involved mass techniques of coercion and confrontation. Until they had escalated into the burning of cities and an underground terroristic movement of bombings and kidnappings, these techniques received widespread liberal support. As the methods became more extreme, much of the liberal sympathy withered away. But this withering took a long time in coming. It should not be forgotten how much the intellectual culture and the media supported the behavior of the "Yippies" in Chicago at the time of the Democratic convention in 1968. It was not the revolutionary Left, but the Chicago authorities who responded to it, who were the objects of the overwhelming opprobrium of the intellectual culture.

Probably the main residual of that period within liberal thought is the conviction that "non-violent direct action" is a legitimate means for provoking social change. This is inherent in the recent elevation of Martin Luther King, Jr., to the status of one of America's great heroes.

To place "non-violent direct action" in perspective, it will be well for us to recall the conservative viewpoint on Civil Rights: that, despite all imperfections, the main society was one that deserved fundamental support; that the condition of blacks had been improving dramatically, not worsening as the rhetoric of the Civil Rights movement had us believe; and that the most constructive and surest way for blacks to continue to make progress was for them to continue to improve themselves and to gain the respect of the white majority.

217

From that perspective, a great national agitation was precisely <u>not</u> the best way to seek change. Conservatives stood in horror at the violence that resulted from the frustrations and hatreds that the "non-violent" mass demonstrations brought into play. And conservatives thoroughly opposed the legislation that sought omnipresently to command non-discriminatory human relationships. Fortunately, the vast federal police power of surveillance and prosecution that this legislation calls for has not, for the most part, come into use. This is due, as I pointed out in Chapter 1, to our willingness to be hypocritical. The laws are on the books, but only partly enforced. This has made possible a <u>modus</u> <u>vivendi</u> that is tolerable precisely because of the softening effect of its hypocrisy.

In contrast to the conservative perspective I have just described, modern liberalism welcomed both the legislation and a mass movement of confrontational "non-violent" demonstrations.

To assess the philosophy of "non-violence," it is necessary to realize that it goes in two directions at once. Its proponents genuinely wish, consistently with theories going back to Gandhi and Thoreau, to avoid committing any violence themselves. Their appeal is to moral strength through suffering. At the same time, however, they endeavor in every way possible to build passions to a pitch at which violence by others is virtually inevitable. This violence is something they can hardly hope to control. The proponents of non-violence are quite conscious of the fact that they are playing with fire. And although they fear the resulting violence, they often seek to use it to their advantage. Despite their protestations that they are divorced from it, their posture toward the violence is profoundly irresponsible.

All of these elements are apparent in Martin Luther King, Jr.'s, utterances. His genuine dislike for violence was evident when he said that

218

"resistance and non-violence are not in themselves good. There is another element in our struggle that then makes [them] truly meaningful. That element is reconciliation." [18]

At the same time, though, his awareness of the violence that his methods could unleash was apparent when he added that "the tactics of non-violence without the spirit of non-violence may become a new kind of violence." He had to be potently aware of the violence that agitation could produce, since he was still alive when one riot after another led to the burning of substantial parts of major American cities.[19]

Finally, it appears that he was often willing to use warnings of violence that might be committed by others as a weapon. Nat Hentoff wrote that King and others "warn of violence [that may be committed] if those victories are not large enough and do not come soon enough. The warning is partly in itself a tactic to frighten the white folks...." Such warnings should also be understood as essentially hypocritical. They were as much goads to and justifications for violence as they were genuine warnings. Edward Banfield pointed this out when he wrote that "one who said that if drastic measures were not taken to end injustice riots could be expected might be correct, but correct or not his words would help form an impression in the public mind that rioting is a natural and perhaps even laudable response to the continuance of an injustice."[20]

If the predominant culture were in fact despicable, as so much of the rhetoric of the 1960's described it as being; if blacks had not benefitted immeasurably from their presence in American society; and if their condition had not been improving rapidly for several years prior to the stirring of the mass movement, the argument that a vast confrontational agitation was necessary would be much more compelling than it is. The support that modern liberalism gives to such methods is deeply at odds with classical liberalism. The difference is not a superficial one, but instead reflects their widely divergent world-views.

One part of this divergence consists of the willingness by the Left, including modern liberalism, to drop the temporal context whenever it is expedient to do so. They then talk without reference to historical progression. Their historical relativity is totally abandoned in favor of utopian absolutes when that is useful in creating the critique that is so basic to the moral posture of one of the egalitarian movements. At such times, all perspective is lost, and there is no recognition given to the fact that conditions for the group in question have actually been improving. The result is in large measure ideological fakery. It consists of a storm of cliches and emotions that are based on partial truths and on an intolerance toward any recognition of the unspoken truths. It is this process that has, perhaps more than any other, given a neurotic, dreamlike quality to modern social philosophy and to the "pop liberalism" that periodically dominates our national mentality with one or another of its issues.

I should not close this discussion without observing that there has been dissent, some of it quite significant, within liberalism itself.

Supreme Court Justice Abe Fortas wrote a short book, for example, that sought to delineate strictly the appropriate bounds of civil disobedience. He argued that only the laws that are thought to be unjust should be disobeyed, and not others. He also believed that the activist must be willing to accept the penalties for violating the existing laws, however unjust.[21]

Much more significant dissent came from the "realism" injected, beginning in the mid-1960's, by those who eventually became known as the "neo-conservatives." These thinkers simply refused to accept the illusions that had been built up as the ideological foundation for the civil rights movement. The main society was not the entire cause of the plight of the Negro, but rather there was much that Negroes themselves could do to improve their own situation. Indeed, that situation would stay mired in difficulty until Negroes made that effort. This, of course, was a perspective that was totally at odds with the rationale for alienation and militancy. Instead, it called for constructive building.

NOTES

1. New Republic, May 31, 1939, p. 93.

2. Eric F. Goldman, Rendezvous With Destiny (New York: Vintage Books, 1977), p. 81.

3. New Republic, August 29, 1955, p. 18.

4. New Republic, March 13, 1915, p. 155; New Republic, March 17, 1920, pp. 82-6.

5. Charles Forcey, The Crossroads of Liberalism (New York: Oxford University Press, 1961), pp. 77, 78.

6. New Republic, July 20, 1932, p. 256; New Republic, October 3, 1934, p. 223.

7. New Republic, February 19, 1930, p. 14; Henry Steele Commager (ed.), Lester Ward and the Welfare State (Indianapolis: The Bobbs-Merrill Company, Inc., 1967), p. 23.

8. Goldman, Rendezvous With Destiny, pp. 72-3.

9. New Republic, December 19, 1914, p. 12; New Republic, February 19, 1930, pp. 14-15.

10. Morton White, Social Thought in America: The Revolt Against Formalism (Boston: Beacon Press, 1957), p. 94.

11. John Dewey, _Problems of Men_ (New York: Philosophical Library, 1946), p. 50.

12. New Republic, November 21, 1928, p. 12; the other articles appear in the issues of November 14, November 28, December 5, December 12, and December 19, 1928.

13. New Republic, September 20, 1969, p. 12; Steinem was quoted in a Wichita Eagle-Beacon article in July, 1977, about the Kansas Women's Weekend.

14. New Republic, May 24, 1933, pp. 42-3; New Republic, August 3, 1935, p. 358.

15. New Republic, May 31, 1933, p. 61; New Republic, July 1, 1946, p. 929; New Republic, January 31, 1949, p. 7.

16. Herbert Croly, _Progressive Democracy_ (New York: The Macmillan Company, 1915), pp. 390-1.

17. Howard Zinn, _New Deal Thought_ (Indianapolis: The Bobbs-Merrill Company, Inc., 1966), p. 215.

18. New Republic, May 2, 1960, p. 16.

19. New Republic, May 2, 1960, p. 16.

20. Nat Hentoff, _The New Equality_ (New York: Viking Press, 1964), p. 210; Edward C. Banfield, _The Unheavenly City, The Nature and Future of Our Urban Crisis_ (Boston: Little, Brown and Company, 1970), p. 201.

21. Abe Fortas, _Concerning Dissent and Civil Disobedience_ (New York: Signet Books, 1968).

9

LEGAL PHILOSOPHY

The analysis that legal philosophers have made of the law over thousands of years has been formulated within a wide variety of cultural and ideological contexts. Jurisprudence accordingly includes a great deal that can be considered apart from any particular ideology. Most jurisprudence is discussed as though it stands on its own.

For many of the more important issues, however, this separateness amounts to a sterilization that is, in effect, a serious intellectual mistake. This is so because much of what is most meaningful about legal philosophy <u>does</u> relate intimately to the "ideologies," i.e., to the great systems of thought about politics and society. "Ideology," in a non-pejorative sense, plays a vitally important role. Each of the major world-views necessarily has its own preferences about government and law. These preferences in part reflect the philosophy's vision of an ideal society and legal system. They incorporate the values, and the means to the attainment of those values, that the worldview considers desirable. In addition, they necessarily take tactical considerations into account, since each worldview must exist within a certain time and place in competition with other forces and ideas.

The classical liberalism that formed the main American <u>ethos</u> during the nineteenth century had, as we will see, a distinct legal philosophy of its own. This was drawn from sources thousands of years old and was favored precisely because it would protect the system of limited government that classical liberalism favored. This legal philosophy was by no means a thing apart from classical liberalism's overall social philosophy. In this chapter, it will be important to gain an understanding of this "conservative" legal philo-

223

sophy so that we can fully understand the attack
that modern liberalism has made upon it.

The legal philosophy that modern liberalism
has espoused has also been one that has been
responsive to its larger philosophy's overall
position and to certain tactical imperatives.
This liberalism has needed an approach to law that
would simulataneously (a) serve the active state
that modern liberalism has favored, and (b) constitute an effective instrument for bringing about
the substantial Constitutional and legal changes
that were necessary if the United States were to
make the transition from limited government to an
active state.

Not surprisingly, it has been relativism,
applied to legal philosophy, that has served both
of these needs. Relativism has accordingly been
the main thrust of modern liberal legal thinking
(although mixed from time to time with the absolutes to which liberals are wont to hold). This
is the reason I have thought it most appropriate
to place this chapter immediately after the chapter in which I discussed liberalism's extensive
use of relativism as a method of social change.

The classical liberal Constitutional myth: a major barrier to modern liberalism

When I refer to the classical liberal Constitutional "myth," I am not using the word to
undermine that position, but to point to the fact
that classical liberalism invested the Constitution, and the American nation at large, with a
system of values, meanings and ideals, all based
upon classical liberalism's own worldview. Every
philosophy seeks a similar investiture of meaning
to events and institutions that, without such an
imputation, would lack symbolic content. The
struggle over legal philosophy between classical
and modern liberalism has been a struggle between
such systems. Modern liberalism has had its own
myth to offer--its own perception of history, of

what law ought to seek to accomplish, of where it wants America to go. An interesting thing about such a struggle is that neither side is prepared to see that that is what the struggle is all about; each claims to have unmediated Truth on its side attesting to the self-evident validity of what it is asserting, and sees only the other as a product of human will.

When I say that classical liberalism clothed the Constitution with a certain meaning, I am referring to an extremely broad phenomenon rather than to the thinking of any particular group of men. What I have in mind is the "spirit of the age" of the late 18th and early 19th centuries, a time when the ideals of the Enlightenment burned brightest (although by the early 19th century they were coming under attack by the Romantic reaction in Europe). It will be impossible for anyone in the future to understand American history without appreciating the extent to which this spirit became immanent within the American people. As I have indicated before, this outlook and value system has continued as a major "underlay" throughout the 20th century.

By no means was its acceptance unmixed or uncontested. The Burkeans are no doubt right when they point to a number of traditionalist values that have inhered in American life; the intellectual culture has stood outside for a century and a half thoroughly detesting the potency of classical liberal values; many issues have been argued out, and have been the subject of violent political controversy, without reference to larger principles; and hundreds of millions of people have gone about practical life without deep reflection concerning the milieu in which they have lived. Nevertheless, the liberal impulse, in the classical sense, has been a major part of American life. Modern liberals sensed this a century ago when they launched their attack upon the many links in what Eric Goldman has called "conservatism's steel chain of ideas."

225

The link that related to legal philosophy was especially important. Classical liberalism embraced the concept of the "Rule of Law" that went back as far as Pericles' "Funeral Oration" in Athens and that had received strong reiteration in the philosophy of John Locke. This was the conception of "law" as ideally meeting certain criteria: it would be a dependable framework of known rules, impartially administered and applying equally and more-or-less permanently as guideposts to action. These guideposts would bind both private citizens and the government, all of whom must "act within the law." Thus, the law would serve its normal functions of adjudicating disputes, militating against crime, providing principles of conduct, recognizing property and carving out a protected sphere for the individual. At the same time, it would provide a major check against arbitrary action by government. The state, according to this ideal, would itself be subject to the established rules. And if it wished to change the rules, it could do so only by enacting rules that were declared in advance and that possessed the other characteristics required by the "Rule of Law."

Friedrich Hayek's book The Constitution of Liberty is an excellent discussion of the history of the Rule of Law ideal. For our purposes, we should note that he considered the distinctive American contribution to be the introduction of a written Constitution. When augmented by the doctrine of judicial review as proclaimed by Chief Justice John Marshall in Marbury v. Madison, the Constitution became far more than a mere grant of power to government; its contours channelized government, separated its functions, divided its powers, and limited it.

To the Jeffersonians in particular, the government that was created under the Constitution was limited to the "enumerated powers" (the functions spelled out by a list of specific responsibilities in Article I). There was also explicit recognition that individuals were to enjoy a

226

general "liberty" that government could not validly abrogate. When the objection was made in the ratifying conventions that there was no "bill of rights," James Madison, whose name comes down to us as the "father of the Constitution," was reluctant to add one. He is said to have feared that the listing of certain rights would give rise to an inference that there were no others. (His concern was no doubt founded upon his awareness of the usual legal rule for interpreting documents, the legal doctrine of *ejusdem generis*, that says that general concepts are to be understood in light of any specifics that are mentioned.)

Accordingly, when eventually he undertook to draft the Bill of Rights as we know it today, Madison was careful to include the Ninth Amendment. From a classical liberal point of view, what the Ninth Amendment says is fundamental to the American Constitutional scheme: it provides that "the enumeration in the Constitution of certain rights shall not be construed to deny or disparage others retained by the people."

This explicitly recognizes the existence of a reservoir of unspoken liberties. In turn, this gives rise to the question of what content that reservoir is to have.

The Supreme Court first began to address this question in the *Dred Scott* case in 1857. The specific facts of the case (relating to the return of a runaway slave) were such, of course, as to make it notorious as an affirmation of slavery and as a forerunner of the Civil War. But it had another side to it, one that is very important to a free society in the classical liberal sense. Chief Justice Roger Brooke Taney, a leading figure in the Jacksonian party who had been appointed to the Chief Justiceship by Andrew Jackson in 1836, based the Court's opinion on the principle that the right to property is a part of the reservoir of Constitutionally protected liberties.

The Constitutional provision upon which Taney

227

predicated this holding was the "due process clause" of the Fifth Amendment. Thereafter, the reservoir has been thought of as finding expression in that clause and in a similar one, applicable to the states, that is part of the Fourteenth Amendment. Thousands of court decisions refer to the due process clauses, and virtually none mention the Ninth Amendment. Although this seems odd, the reason for it is simple: that if a reservoir of liberties is taken to exist, as it must be in light of the Ninth Amendment, it is appropriate to consider it within the purview of clauses that prohibit any deprivation of life, liberty or property without due process of law. The due process clauses are consistent with, and presuppose, the thinking that underlay the Ninth Amendment. After the Fourteenth Amendment was approved, there was an additional reason to use the due process clauses, since the two of them together apply to both the federal government and the states.

The articulation of classical liberal principles, at least by presidents, went into eclipse when the Civil War ended the ascendancy of the Jeffersonian-Jacksonian Democratic Party. Nevertheless, the legal profession and the Supreme Court continued to develop the Constitutional implications of classical liberalism. Christopher G. Tiedeman's book Constitutional Limitations, published in 1886, is a excellent example. He saw law as, in effect, a science of liberty within a natural law context.

On the Supreme Court, there was, for a time, a struggle between Justice Samuel F. Miller, who wrote the decision in the Slaughter House cases and held to an expansive view of governmental power, and Justice Stephen J. Field, who wrote a dissent. Though Field was in the minority in those cases, his views soon became those of a majority, and the Supreme Court enunciated the principle of "freedom of contract" as a major economic liberty that was Constitutionally protected.

228

When the Court under Taney and Field gave judicial cognizance to the rights of property and of freedom of contract, what it was doing was to include within the reservoir of unstated liberties the economic freedom that is so vital a part of classical liberalism. This could not have been surprising. Far from breathing "Herbert Spencer's _Social Statics_" into the Constitution in any narrow way, they informed it with the central core of liberalism in the classic sense. Freedom within a market has been as important to classical liberals as is freedom of speech or of religion. Indeed, the philosophy does not see freedom as a series of separate liberties, but rather as a unified system of personal freedom.

This libertarian construction of the Constitution similarly embraced the other concepts that have been central to the Rule of Law and to classical liberalism.

• "Due process" was held to invalidate statutes that are vague, thus giving voice to the Rule of Law principle that the law must be knowable.

• "Procedural due process" was held to require an impartial hearing of disputes in a way that would give each party an adequate opportunity to present argument and evidence.

• The doctrine of "the separation of powers" split governmental functions among the three branches, thereby minimizing the likelihood of unchecked abuse.

• The "division of powers" split the functions another way, decentralizing a substantial number of them in the states.

• The "interstate commerce clause" was interpreted to grant power to the national government only over goods during transit, commencing at the time they were put in their "original package" for shipment and terminating when they were removed from that package. This meant that the great commercial and industrial processes preparatory to shipment--such as manufacture, mining, agriculture, horticulture and fishing--were outside the jurisdiction of the national government.

. Finally, decisions were handed down judging the "equality" of the rules of law by whether they made only "reasonable classifications." There have been thousands of court decisions on this issue, which relates directly to one of the Rule of Law criteria.

The presence of slavery and its aftermath in American history would seem to contradict the adherence to legal equality, but it is important to understand that these constituted an historically implanted exception that was in basic contradiction to the liberal principles that guided the society. Even though the United States had tremendous difficulty dealing with these problems, their presence does not render the liberal principles meaningless. Nor would it be correct to say that they were held to hypocritically. American law was quite consciously attached to the ideal of "equality under the law."

None of this is to say that American law in the 19th century formulated a perfect application of classical liberal principles. What I said earlier is pertinent here: that classical liberalism was itself insufficiently developed. It did not, and has not to this day, addressed all of the subtleties of social and economic questions. By the second half of the 19th century, classical liberalism had gone on the defensive and had lost its reformist eye. Its defensiveness caused it to give inadequate attention to the framework of law and institutions that is needed precisely as a part of a classically liberal society to facilitate the free interaction of individuals. A good deal of what free-market enthusiasts have considered "interventionism" has been at least in part a reaction to the absence of a thoroughly satisfactory framework. Certainly in the 19th century much work remained to be done.

In this section, I have described the 19th century classical liberal Constitutional position --a position that I believe was very much in keeping with the principles of a free society. If, however, we do not wish to lose sight of the mixed nature of the concrete realities of the late 19th century, we should notice that the classical liberal construction was not shared by all members of the Supreme Court. Looking back in 1940, Max Lerner considered Justice Miller very much a modern liberal hero for having opposed Justice Field's direction during the 1870's and 1880's. In 1915, The New Republic commented that the Court had been moving away from the classical liberal position, only to return to it with its decision in Coppage v. Kansas. Then in 1931, the editors commented again on how a "liberalization" had been underway but had stalled. John Marshall Harlan, who served from 1877 to 1911, and Oliver Wendell Holmes, Jr., who was on the Court from 1902 to 1932, were articulate opponents of the classical liberal interpretation. Because of this, it would not be correct to think that the entire Court moved from one ideology to another in 1937 when finally it began upholding the legislation of the New Deal. Modern liberalism had long been represented on the Court, and had had occasional majorities.[1]

The legal, Constitutional needs of modern liberalism

Since the rise of the Left in the early 19th century, there has always been significant support for a decentralized, non-statist socialism based upon cooperatives, communes, labor organizations, or the like. Modern liberalism has shown an affinity for this type of socialism during its "industrial democracy" phase and during the years of the New Leftist counterculture in the late 1960's. For the most part, however, modern liberalism has pursued a program of state intervention. It has

231

seen the federal government as the prime instrument for social and economic progress.

Virtually all programs of state intervention in Europe and America during the 19th and 20th centuries have embraced a legal philosophy attacking the Rule of Law and arguing for administrative and judicial flexibility. The opposition to pre-established rules to which government must itself conform has been the central characteristic of legal positivism, legal historicism, the free law school, and legal realism. The Rule of Law criteria are exceedingly functional if the purposes are the classical liberal ones of establishing guideposts for individual conduct and of delimiting government. They are usually thought to get in the way if the desire is to vest free-wheeling power in government to address a vast range of matters within a society.

It is not surprising, then, that in 1915 an article in The New Republic exulted that "this is fast becoming a government not of laws, but of men, perhaps really a government, after all, no longer a pious treasury of past generalizations." Rexford Tugwell was able to argue for "a rule of men, not laws, if the right men are called to govern." In these statements there is a striking reversal of the classical liberal preference for "a Rule of Law, not of men." The body of American law is perceived as obstructive, and it is precisely the "rule of men" that is welcomed.[2]

Probably even more important than the need to free the state for flexible administration was modern liberalism's tactical need for a legal philosophy that would allow the existing corpus of law, and most especially of Constitutional law, to be circumvented without the necessity of formal amendment.

Under the Constitution, the most expeditious method for an amendment to take effect is for it to be proposed by a two-thirds vote of both houses of Congress and then approved by the legislatures

232

of three-fourths of the states. This is a proce-
dure that is calculated to require a substantial
national consensus before an amendment can be
enacted.

Since the Civil War, the process has been
pursued successfully primarily for the "democratizing" amendments, which have had a moral appeal
that has received wide public support: the post-
Civil War amendments dealing with slavery, the
direct election of senators, the right of women to
vote, the limitation of a president to two terms.
The income tax amendment was passed, but without
the public having any idea at the time that the
tax would soon be raised to confiscatory levels.
The Prohibition movement against alcohol, which
was part of the Progressive thrust, was able to
secure passage of the 19th Amendment, but this was
repealed within a few years.

For the most part, the idea of revamping
American government from its classical liberal
Constitutional base into a European-style social
democratic state by Constitutional amendment has
not seemed feasible to liberals, who have fully
sensed the lack of a sufficient consensus to
obtain passage of the necessary amendments.

Even during the Great Depression in the
1930's, only passing attention was given to the
possibility of validating New Deal-type legislation by Constitutional amendment. In 1915, The
New Republic had recognized the difficulty when it
called for making the process of amendment easier.
In 1918, Lewis Mayers wrote that "we encounter a
constitutional obstacle, the extremely obstructive
machinery of amendment." After World War II, TRB
complained that "an honest rewriting of the Constitution is probably impossible."3

At the same time that he commented upon liberalism's inability to obtain amendments, TRB
pointed openly to the implication for liberalism's
tactical position. He said about the Constitution
that "the sooner we circumvent it (i.e., 'stop

233

standing on the letter') the better."

In saying this, TRB expressed the essence of modern liberal legal philosophy. The overriding tactical need has been to justify a loose construction. It has been to remove the Constitutional constraints upon governmental power without waiting for formal amendment.

The result has been a philosophy that has (a) raised flexibility and legal change to the highest value and has (b) simultaneously denied the validity of the classical liberal interpretation of the Constitution.

Content of liberal legal philosophy

As I discuss the specific points made by liberal legal philosophy, I will quote extensively from what liberals themselves have said so that the texture of their point of view can be felt.

1. A liberal justice such as Felix Frankfurter was so acclimated to the liberal call for "judicial restraint" (which prior to 1937 implored the conservative justices not to invalidate social legislation) that he continued throughout his years on the bench to believe that judicial restraint was the hallmark of liberal jurisprudence. It would seem, however, that Frankfurter's views reflected more an absorption of a tactical position than an expression of the main liberal preference about the role of the Court. That preference has been for a political, activist Court. The "activist" majority on the Warren Court was more in line with this.

Liberal writing had long favored a politicized Court. In 1921, The New Republic said that "the radical view is that the Supreme Court is and ought to be a political body." It went on to say that this should involve "interpreting the Constitution and the law according to the spirit of the age, subject, of course, to certain elastic

234

limits of legal plausibility." The next year, the editors wrote that law should be considered "an instrument of progressive social engineering." In 1930, they argued that "the truth is that the Supreme Court is a supreme policy-making body."[4]

All of this was consistent with Jerome Frank's later praise of the thesis expressed by Charles Curtis in Lions Under the Throne. Here is Frank's commentary on Curtis' position: "With respect to constitutional questions, the Supreme Court, he says, is not a court. Its power to nullify legislation compels it, he asserts, to be primarily a peculiar kind of political agency, although legal tradition requires it to talk as if it were a judicial tribunal. Thanks to Mr. Justice Holmes, this approach to constitutional decisions is now openly accepted by the Supreme Court justices...."[5]

As with most other aspects of liberalism, the open radicalism of the 1930's offers a window into the ultimate preference. A New Republic editorial in 1935 called for replacing the Supreme Court with a "Supreme Planning Council." "This policy-making body...must differ from the Supreme Court in essential respects. It should act before the event, not after...It should consist, not of precedent-minded logicians, but of experts in social and economic management...In other words, instead of a Supreme Court we ought to have a Supreme Planning Council." The reason, they said, is that "there is no hope of gradual evolution towards an effective socialism within the existing framework of the United States...To have a socialist society we must have a new Constitution."[6]

The preference enunciated in 1935 is the same one voiced by William Beaney and Alpheus Mason, two writers who have been prominent on behalf of liberal legal philosophy, in their 1968 book The Supreme Court in a Free Society. They said that by the early 1940's, under a liberal majority, "the Court had apparently accepted the collectivist theory of government. Social democracy could be achieved...."[7]

2. Constant stress has been given to the changeability of law and to the power of judges to disregard precedents.

In The New Republic in 1918, Lewis Mayers spoke of "the time-honored method of gradually wearing down constitutional restrictions--the President and Congress taking the initiative with unconstitutional legislation and the Supreme Court reluctantly 'distinguishing' out of existence the constitutional obstacle." It is in this spirit that liberal writing has so often quoted Chief Justice Charles Evans Hughes' dictum that "the Constitution is what the judges say it is." In Equal Justice Under Law, published under the auspices of the Foundation of the Federal Bar Association, the authors quoted Holmes to the effect that the "Constitution is an experiment" and praised him as having "inspired generations of lawyers to shun classic attitudes of jurisprudence and recognize that law changes with society's needs."[8]

The stress upon change and upon arbitrary judicial power is what makes Oliver Wendell Holmes, Jr.'s, definition of law so popular in liberal legal writing. He said that "the prophecies of what the courts will do in fact, and nothing more pretentious, are what I mean by law." We can imagine that to legal thinkers in the future this definition will seem to have been deliberately reductionist. It is utterly banal in its over-simplification of the legal process. But its serviceability to liberal ideology is that by centering upon the empirical question of "what judges do in fact," it treats as irrelevant the Rule of Law definition of law. This is that law is the body of statute and precedent--i.e., the rules that have been set down in advance--to which lawyers and judges recur when they ask each other "what does the law say?" with regard to a point at issue.[9]

3. I mentioned earlier that an important element of liberal thinking has been the denial of the validity of the classical liberal construction of the Constitution.

As with so many of these points, Justice Holmes made the leading statement. Holmes denied the core of classical liberal doctrine--that economic freedom is an essential part of Madison's reservoir of liberties--when he wrote that "a constitution is not intended to embody a particular economic theory" and that the Constitution "is made for people of fundamentally differing views." He said essentially the same thing, although in a more clever and sophistical fashion, in his famous statement that "the Fourteenth Amendment does not enact Mr. Herbert Spencer's Social Statics." Chief Justice Harlan Fiske Stone made a similar argument when he wrote that "the Fourteenth Amendment has no more embodied in the Constitution our preference for some particular set of economic beliefs than it has adopted, in the name of liberty, the system of theology which we may happen to approve." (The analogy to religion is only superficially plausible. A classical liberal would agree that the Constitution does not dictate a specific economy; but he would say that it dictates a system of economic freedom, just as it commands a system of religious freedom.) [10]

4. A corollary to this denial has been the charge that classical liberal jurists were "activists" when they construed the Constitution as they did.

Thus, Mason and Beaney charge that these judges made themselves "virtually a superlegislature." Justice Holmes wrote that "the dogma, Liberty of Contract,...is merely an example of doing what you want to do, embodied in the word liberty." Justice Frankfurter said that "between the presidencies of Grant and the first Roosevelt, laissez faire...was imported into the Constitution." And, speaking of the judges who in the 1930's considered much of the New Deal's legislation unconstitutional, Arthur Schlesinger, Jr., commented that "far from being engaged, as they supposed, in a process of immaculate interpretation, the conservative four, like the liberal three, were reading their own notions of social wisdom into a designedly ambiguous charter of government."[11]

5. In the passage I have just quoted from Schlesinger he acknowledges that the liberal judges were "activists." It is curious that generally the literature damns conservatives for what it considers their activism, while praising modern liberal judges for theirs. There is quite obviously a double standard applied about the validity of activism, even assuming the correctness of the liberal charge that a classical liberal construction of the Constitution amounts to judicial activism.

The double standard is accounted for, of course, by the fact that modern liberals _like_ the purposes for which the liberal justices have been activists, while they dislike those of the conservatives.

For the most part, such a double standard merely reflects the common human tendency to employ whatever arguments are handy, regardless of consistency. Mason and Beaney have offered the only attempt I have seen to rationalize it: "The thought of the so-called [liberal] activists... seems to be that though the Constitution does not embody, as Holmes said, any particular _economic_ philosophy, it does incorporate a particular political theory...Judicial self-restraint does not mean that the Court is paralyzed. 'It simply conserves its strength,' as Attorney-General Jackson put it, 'to strike more telling blows in the cause of a working democracy.'...The 'self-restraint' banner raised in 1937 has not blinded Chief Justice Warren's Court to certain positive responsibilities." The upshot is that these justices think the Constitution _does_ embody some theory--but just not the central principles of classical liberalism.[12]

6. An important part of the attack upon the classical liberal interpretation of the Constitution was the economic determinist argument that the Founding Fathers, in writing the Constitution, were motivated not by a sincere idealism, but by their own economic self-interest.

J. Allen Smith launched the attack in 1907 with his book The Spirit of American Government. Eric Goldman writes that Smith "brought down upon the Framers...the onus of greed." Smith's thesis, he says, was that "the Framers were profit-minded and little else." Arthur A. Ekirch, Jr., says that Smith's book "influenced among other progressives both Theodore Roosevelt and Robert M. LaFollette." He observes that "the book...weakened the case for conservatives' devotion to the sanctity of the Constitution."[13]

The name that is most famous in connection with this debunking is that of Charles Beard, whose An Economic Interpretation of the Constitution was published in 1913. Beard argued that "the members of the Philadelphia Convention... were, with a few exceptions, immediately, directly, and personally interested in, and desired economic advantages from, the establishment of the new system. The Constitution was essentially an economic document...A large propertyless mass was, under the prevailing suffrage qualifications, excluded at the outset from participation...." Writing in The New Republic in 1944, Goldman said that "it reduced the abstractions of conservatism to the special pleading of a special economic group. Little wonder that the Beardian economic interpretation became the bulldozer of liberalism...."[14]

It is no accident that the books by Smith and Beard appeared in close proximity to the Muckraker era. After World War I, liberal thought began to reflect some awareness of the over-simplication inherent in such debunking. In 1922, Zechariah

Chafee penned an intelligent piece for <u>The New Republic</u> that was critical of the reductionism that was inherent in applying a purely economic determinism to judges' decisions (which was the specific issue his article was addressing).[15]

7. Unfortunately, it is rare for the advocates of any one philosophy really to understand another philosophy's point of view. In general, modern liberal thinkers have had no empathetic understanding of why American conservatives have held the beliefs and values they have, any more than conservatives have put themselves into the thinking of liberals.

Modern liberal legal commentators have shown almost no awareness of the idealism that supports the Rule of Law and its embodiment in the written Constitution of the United States. Certainly such an awareness has not been evident in any of the passages I have quoted in this chapter so far.

Probably the most egregious example of imputing every motive to an opposing philosophy except a sincere adherence to a set of perceptions and values is Jerome Frank's book <u>Law and the Modern Mind</u>. Frank excoriated the Rule of Law criteria as "mechanical jurisprudence." Without being a psychiatrist, he reflected upon every conceivable psychoanalytical explanation for why lawyers, judges and the public value certainty in the law. People, he said among other things, apparently want the law to serve as a "father figure." Through it all, Frank showed a remarkable shallowness--a partisanship unleavened by any apparent awareness of the history of the Rule of Law going back to the Greeks or of the reasons that those who wish to limit the state through law have given for their views.

Of course, this is what Smith and Beard were doing, too, with their economic determinism, albeit without the elaborate trappings of pseudo-psychoanalysis. None of them ever considered classical liberal legal philosophy <u>on its merits</u>.

240

This means that they contented themselves with considering only straw men or reductionistically understood motives.

This is revealed in the caricatures that liberal writing has painted of conservative views and personalities. Arthur Schlesinger, Jr., has written, for example, that conservatives saw judges as "the infallible expositors of an unchanging document." This transforms the classical liberal preference for adherence to a body of precedent in Constitutional law into a parody of the Catholic doctrine of papal infallibility. It is hard to imagine that any serious conservative thinker has ever claimed infallibility for judges.

The combination of partisanship and limited understanding has resulted in virtually all conservative judges being belittled in liberal literature as dull and intransigent, while the liberal judges have been praised as brilliant and courageous. For example, Oliver Wendell Holmes, Jr., has come down to us as "the Great Dissenter." The description given of him in the Foundation of the Federal Bar Association's book is "philosophic dissenter." Notice, however, how that same book characterizes the four conservative justices' dissent from the rulings that began to uphold New Deal legislation in 1937: "Stubbornly the 'four horsemen' dissented." 16

The same book speaks of Justice John Marshall Harlan's having written "a fighting dissent." He "won fame as a defender of democracy" and fought "an ardent battle for civil rights." Along with Holmes, he is said to have been "one of the great dissenters." Other liberal justices are praised along the same lines: Chief Justice Warren was a "champion of civil liberties" and Justice Abe Fortas a "champion of individual liberties." Schlesinger describes Justice Harlan Fiske Stone as "tough, articulate [and] passionate." 17

Here, in contrast, is Schlesinger's description of the four conservative justices in the

1930's: Justice Willis Van Devanter was lucid and knowledgeable in person-to-person dealings, but was struck by "an awful paralysis" so far as writing opinions was concerned. Justice James C. McReynolds was a surly anti-Semite who used an undistinguished "scissors and paste" technique in writing opinions. Justice George Sutherland was the most able, but "evidently nothing happened after the eighteen eighties to cause him to doubt" the writings of Thomas Cooley and Herbert Spencer. Justice Pierce Butler was bellicose, "a bruiser, burly and contentious, untiring at his desk, bullying in conference, vigorous and dogmatic in his opinions." In all, compared to a quite sparkling set of liberal justices, they were either intellectually mediocre or personally undesirable, or both.[18]

There would be little reason to note this partisanship if it did not have a broader significance. It is important for anyone reading liberal legal philosophy to realize that the authors are creating their own myth, which is populated by its own heroes and villains. An objective scholar will need to understand that the liberal analysis is far from dispassionate. And someone wanting to decide which of the competing legal philosophies deserves support will essentially have to decide which overall philosophy he favors, since the legal philosophies are merely applications of the larger philosophies. Having made this decision, he will see that the myth that has been formulated by that philosophy is serviceable to the perceptions and values it supports, and will probably find reason enough to favor that myth.

From judicial restraint to judicial activism

Until the New Deal, most liberal social legislation could be expected to come from the states rather than from the federal government. The liberal need tactically was, accordingly, for the Supreme Court to take a "hands off" attitude toward state legislation.

242

This gave rise to what J. Joseph Huthmacher has called "the Brandeisian idea that the states should be afforded the utmost freedom to 'experiment.'" The theme of "let the local majorities experiment" was then picked up by Franklin Delano Roosevelt. Eleanor Roosevelt wrote that "it is quite probable that Franklin derived his concept of the forty-eight states as experimental laboratories from his study of Justice Brandeis' writings and opinions."19

During the 1930's, once Roosevelt was in the presidency, the focal point for activity became the federal government. Until 1937, modern liberals remained basically in the minority on the Supreme Court. In that context, liberalism's most pressing tactical need was to call for "judicial restraint." This position was calculated to take the Court, dominated by conservatives, out of the equation.

The situation changed radically, however, after 1937. The conservative justices rapidly left the Court. It wasn't long before all of the justices were liberals in the pre-1937 sense.

What tactical need was there then for "judicial restraint"? None at all. Liberals had the power to be activists if they wished. What occurred is an oddity that speaks well for the integrity of such a justice as Frankfurter, who continued to preach the doctrine of judicial restraint even after the tactical need for it had vanished. A split developed among the liberal justices. They slowly formed into blocs based, respectively, upon judicial activism and judicial restraint.

The years of the Warren Court, starting in 1953, represented the predominance of the activist bloc. The majority's judicial philosophy during those years was radical: precedent and 160 years of history were not to stand in the way of what was, strangely enough, an elitist imposition of the dogmas of a "popular democracy."

243

The decision in <u>Reynolds</u> <u>v.</u> <u>Sims</u> about the reapportionment of state senates provides a good illustration of this radicalism. Throughout American history, the states (except Nebraska, which has a one-house legislature) had patterned their senates on the United States Senate in the sense that geographical units, not simply population, were given representation. The United States Senate, we recall, was the product of the "Connecticut Compromise" between the large and the small states in the Philadelphia convention. When in the 1960's the Warren Court held that state senates had to be based upon a "one man, one vote" system of equal representation, there could be no pretense of basing the decision upon anything whatsoever in American history. In addition, the Court had to overrule a century-and-a-quarter old doctrine called the "political question doctrine," which had held that any issue about whether a state government was meeting the requirement of having a "republican form of government" was up to Congress, not the Court. Since there was neither history nor precedent to support the Court's decision in <u>Reynolds</u> <u>v.</u> <u>Sims</u>, it was clear that the Court had come quite openly to the philosophy that "the Constitution is what the judges say it is."[20]

And yet, the Warren Court, radical in method, did not go to the outer limits of Constitutional change. Its innovations largely had to do with a number of issues that were essentially peripheral.

It would have been easy, for example, to move major functions that had traditionally been governed by the states to the federal government simply by handing down a series of decisions saying that each area needed a "uniform national rule." (The "concurrent powers doctrine," enunciated by Chief Justice Taney before the Civil War, says that the states can continue to act in an area that is within the purview of the federal government if Congress has not preempted the field and if the Court has not held that a uniform national rule is needed. Since almost all state jurisdiction exists only by virtue of the concur-

244

rent powers doctrine now that the post-1937 Court has held that the federal government has ubiquitous jurisdiction, the survival of the traditional functions of the states depends very much upon the mutual willingness of Congress and the Court to allow them to continue.)

I do not mean to say that the Warren Court was all sound and no fury, but only to indicate that, in content, its record was not as radical as its reputation. As the cutting edge of liberal activism during that period, however, the Warren Court must nevertheless be considered, for good or for bad, to have been a major agent in causing the social turmoil that rocked the country during that period of our history. In turn, the Burger Court, which followed the Warren years, has to be seen as a factor in settling the country down.

When Richard Nixon became president, he announced that he would appoint justices who were committed to "judicial restraint." This was not, in itself, necessarily an effort to reinstate the pre-1937 classical liberal construction of the Constitution. Rather, it could very well mean no more than a reversion to the philosophy that the liberals themselves had espoused prior to 1937, which was the philosophy of judicial restraint that Justice Frankfurter had continued, in fact, to support. Some of President Nixon's appointments were of that nature; some, especially of Justice Rehnquist, were more ideologically conservative. As this is written, Warren Burger is still the Chief Justice, and President Reagan has as yet had only one appointment (of Sandra Day O'Connor) to make. It seems safe to say, however, that even if we were to assume the election of liberal presidents in the forthcoming elections it will take several years for a majority of liberal activists again to dominate the Court.

One would expect liberal thinking to be cast in a defensive posture during the years of conservative predominance on the Court. This will mean a renewed emphasis on judicial restraint, especially if the conservatives see their way clear at some time to assume a more activist posture on behalf of their own preferences. The more serious intellectual questions now remaining to be answered are within conservatism, as it asks itself what conservative justices ought best to do with the now free-floating Constitution they have inherited.[21]

NOTES

1. New Republic, October 14, 1940, p. 531; New Republic, January 30, 1915, p. 4; New Republic, June 3, 1931, p. 56.

2. New Republic, January 9, 1915, p. 8; Rexford G. Tugwell, The Battle for Democracy (New York: Columbia University Press, 1935), p. 94.

3. In 1936, Lloyd Garrison proposed a Constitutional amendment to give the federal government general power to promote the economic welfare; New Republic, January 29, 1936, p. 329. New Republic, January 23, 1915, p. 3; New Republic, August 17, 1918, p. 74; New Republic, February 28, 1949, p. 3.

4. New Republic, July 13, 1921, p. 177; New Republic, February 22, 1922, p. 353; New Republic, February 26, 1930, p. 30.

5. Jerome Frank, Courts on Trial (New York: Atheneum, 1967), p. 311.

6. New Republic, June 12, 1935, p. 117.

7. William M. Beaney and Alpheus Thomas Mason, The Supreme Court in a Free Society (New York: W. W. Norton & Company, Inc., 1968), pp. 232, 310.

8. New Republic, August 17, 1918, p. 73; The Foundation of the Federal Bar Association, Equal Justice Under Law (Washington: National Geographic Society, 1965), pp. 67, 72.

9. Quoted in Jerome Frank, Law and the Modern Mind (Garden City: Anchor Books, 1963), p. 134.

10. Quoted in Foundation of the Federal Bar Association, Equal Justice Under Law, p. 72.

11. Beaney, Mason, The Supreme Court, p. 231; Felix Frankfurter, Mr. Justice Holmes and the Supreme Court (Cambridge: Harvard University Press, 1961), pp. 63, 62; Arthur M. Schlesinger, Jr., The Politics of Upheaval (Boston: Houghton Mifflin Company, 1960), p. 459.

12. Beaney, Mason, The Supreme Court, p. 312.

13. Eric F. Goldman, Rendezvous With Destiny (New York: Vintage Books, 1977), p. 113; Arthur A. Ekirch, Jr., The Decline of American Liberalism (New York: Longmans, Green and Company, 1955), p. 184.

14. Charles Beard's conclusions are quoted in Goldman, Rendezvous With Destiny, p. 117; New Republic, November 27, 1944, p. 696.

15. New Republic, June 7, 1922, p. 36.

16. Foundation of the Federal Bar Association, Equal Justice Under Law, pp. 68, 83.

17. Foundation of the Federal Bar Association, Equal Justice Under Law, pp. 59, 68, 126, 129; Schlesinger, Politics of Upheaval, p. 464.

18. Schlesinger, Politics of Upheaval, pp. 455-457.

19. J. Joseph Huthmacher, Senator Robert F. Wagner and the Rise of Urban Liberalism (New York: Atheneum, 1968), p. 185; Foundation of the Federal Bar Association, Equal Justice Under Law, p. 53.

20. Reynolds v. Sims, 377 U.S. 533.

21. My discussion in this chapter is similar to

that contained in my article "Myths and American Constitutional History: Some Liberal Truisms Revisited" in the Fall, 1978, issue of <u>The Intercollegiate Review</u>, pp. 13-23. My views about what would be best for the future conservative direction of the Court were stated in broad outline in the paper that I delivered to the annual meeting of the Philadelphia Society in April, 1981. That paper is currently unpublished.

LIBERALISM AND THE MODERN CORPORATION

The corporation has been the dominant form of business entity within modern capitalism. That, of course, would be reason enough for it to have received considerable attention from the social philosophies. But there has been an additional reason: the attention has been heightened by the fact that there have been major schools within both socialist and modern liberal thought that have looked upon the large corporation as a stepping-stone to a collectivist economic system.

Because each of the philosophies has been vitally interested in the role of corporations and other economic aggregates, I have had occasion to discuss the issue in my other books in this series. Those discussions are an important backdrop for this chapter. They should be consulted if a reader wants a more complete understanding of the issues raised by the other philosophies. [1]

Already in the present book I have discussed the competing liberal attitudes toward corporations as part of my reviews of the Progressive period and the New Deal. The present chapter, of course, deals with the issue for its own sake, in light of its importance within liberal philosophy. In this discussion, I will try to avoid repeating the earlier material beyond what is necessary to allow the issue to be understood as a whole.[2]

As a part of reviewing the New Nationalist school, we will examine what I call "the Berle-and-Means thesis," which alleges a crisis of legitimacy within the modern corporation. We will see, too, how the New Left, reflecting the attitudes of 19th century decentralist socialism, levelled a powerful attack upon what it called "corporate liberalism" or the "military-industrial-political complex."

The New Nationalist perspective

In order to understand one of the main liberal schools regarding the modern corporation, it is important to know something about the history of socialist thought.

In _Das Kapital_, Karl Marx wrote about how capitalism itself reaches a transitional phase to socialism through the corporate form. As a large number of investors place their capital in a corporation that is managed by others, thereby making a passive investment, the capital, Marx said, becomes "directly endowed with the form of social capital as distinct from private capital, and its undertakings assume the form of social undertakings as distinct from private undertakings." He referred to this as "a necessary transitional phase" that points toward eventual worker control when finally the corporation is converted "into the property of associated producers, as outright social property."[3]

Although Edward Bellamy's theoretical system was somewhat different from Marx's, this point about the corporation was the keystone of Bellamy's expectation that corporate capitalism would evolve into socialism. In _Looking Backward_ (1888), Bellamy projected a future in which business would become so consolidated that it would be run as "one great business corporation." Then the state would become "the one capitalist in the place of all other capitalists, the sole employer, the final monopoly in which all previous and lesser monopolies were swallowed up...The epoch of trusts had ended in The Great Trust." The reader will recall that his book, which is among the most influential in the intellectual history of the United States, was a futuristic description of how a socialist society would come about and could be expected to function. [4]

Bellamy became the leader of a movement known as "Nationalism." In his introduction to the 1960 republication of Bellamy's book, Erich Fromm explained Bellamy's meaning in using this label. Fromm wrote that Bellamy "called this movement 'nationalist,' referring by this word both to the nationalization of all means of production and to the fact that only this form of society could bring about the rich flowering of a nation's life."[5]

We have seen how during the Progressive period a movement arose called "the New Nationalism" out of the interplay between Herbert Croly and Theodore Roosevelt. The principal expression of this position was in Croly's book The Promise of American Life (1909). It was a natural heir to Bellamy's perspective. It too looked forward expectantly to the continuing consolidation of corporate capitalism; it saw that consolidation as the main chance for government to absorb the corporate system into a comprehensive scheme of national policy; and it too held to an ultimate socialist aspiration.

The difference between Bellamy and Croly was the difference between those who were openly socialist and those who, by adopting dissimulation and a generally unacknowledged Fabianism, fashioned that unique ideological animal known as the American liberal. There is no question but that Croly yearned for socialism. His book Progressive Democracy (1915) embraced, as we have seen, the Guild Socialist enthusiasm for worker-control. But Croly was the master dissimulator--a subject upon which I have already given ample detail.

Again it is important to recognize that not all who have followed in the New Nationalist tradition within modern liberalism have been socialists. In my discussion of the New Deal, we saw that there were several sources for the call for consolidated business. These even included important business elements. Such elements have differed from those who are socialists over an essential point: the business sources have generally wanted the consolidation to serve the pur-

251

poses of business; those who have been socialists have wanted the consolidation to be the vehicle for central state planning and for worker control.

Examples of the attitudes of those members of the liberal intellectual culture who have embraced the New Nationalist perspective are easy to find.

An unsigned article in The New Republic in 1925 illustrates the preference for the large corporation over small-unit capitalism: "Can we force a return to the dominance of the small independent baker, grocer, druggist? Would the public benefit if we could?...A splitting up of the large company would destroy the economies. To get anywhere we must turn away from the old trust-busting tradition towards profits taxation, or price regulation, or public ownership, or consumer ownership." (The reader will notice the reference to "consumer ownership," which within socialist thought has been an alternative to worker owner-ship.) This article is consistent with Croly's view in The Promise of American Life, where he said that "the process of industrial organization should be allowed to work itself out. Whenever the smaller competitor of the large corporation is unable to keep his head above water with his own exertions, he should be allowed to drown."[6]

In this context, the stockholder's role would be minimal, becoming that simply of a bondholder receiving interest on the money advanced. (Even this was a concession to the American political realities. In England, the socialist R. H. Tawney was calling for the expropriation, without compen-sation, of the stockholder. Tawney was, by the way, a frequent contributor to The New Republic. In keeping with the dissimulation, he held such views in check in his articles for American publi-cation. Liberal intellectuals were, of course, fully aware of what he was saying in his books.) A 1931 New Republic article called for "public control in the public interest" and went on to say that "in determining 'public interest,' first consideration [should] be given to the workers in

252

the industry, second to the consuming public, and third to the active management. The interest of the investors [should] be recognized only to the extent of a reasonable rate of interest on the actual investment in the enterprise."7

Liberals have for the most part been discrete in their statements about how much the giant corporations are then to be socialized. (As with the dissimulation in general, though, the guard has been let down on a number of occasions, especially although not exclusively during the more radical periods.) A statement by T. K. Quinn in The New Republic in 1961 has been typical: "Powerful, giant, private corporations cannot safely continue to be treated as wholly private institutions...In addition to the establishment of a Price and Wage Board, we should now reconsider such proposals as public representation on the boards of directors of the biggest corporations." TRB chimed in in his weekly column a week later: "Corporations ...are becoming so big and powerful as to warrant a quasi-governmental status with the kind of supervision applied to other federal agencies." In his book The New Industrial State in 1978, John Kenneth Galbraith spoke in these terms: "If the mature corporation is recognized to be part of the penumbra of the state, it will be pressed more strongly to the service of social goals."8

We know from my review of post-World War II liberalism that the more-or-less futile search for identity by liberals during the 1970's and 1980's has entailed renewed interest in the entire range of options that were considered by liberals during the 'Teens and 1920's. There has been considerable ferment for worker control, with the Japanese system of participatory management and life-time worker security serving as at least one of the models in light of the success the Japanese have been having. The literature has repeatedly brought up the idea of government or consumer or worker representatives on corporate boards of directors, and has often referred to the European principle of "co-determination." This reference

253

is a favorable one, since it evokes the example of the European social democracies. We know, of course, that the idea has also been popular within the main totalitarian movements of the 20th century.[9]

A substantial literature has grown up during the past several years based on the idea of "corporate social responsibility." This literature for the most part presupposes a liberal point of view; it calls upon corporations to serve voluntarily as major social service agencies, and to perform a great many functions that do not relate, except indirectly through the good will that may be generated, to the task of creating a return on their stockholders' investments. An academic discipline has sprung up within the schools of business in our universities, and classes in social responsibility have been made a standard part of business curricula. Within schools of accountancy, a subdiscipline of "social accounting" has developed, and seeks ways to measure just how "socially responsible" corporations are. Efforts are made to plug this accountability into government, so that the federal government can monitor and regulate the social-service activities of business.

To the extent such an _ethos_ can be created and the government gotten involved in requiring and monitoring it, the "social responsibility" approach is another of the efforts to absorb corporations into the state. As such, it is fully in line with the New Nationalist tradition.

To the extent, however, that it constitutes an effort to prevail upon business voluntarily, and without oversight, to perform the functions that liberals have wanted the welfare state to perform, it is something that would have been viewed with contempt by most pre-World War II liberals. T. K. Quinn was speaking very much within this tradition when he wrote in 1961 that "America cannot depend upon any fictitious Corporation Conscience or permit the domination of any

254

private power." He called upon the federal
government itself to exercise the functions that
he considered primarily governmental. It is worth
remembering that after the Progressive movement
liberals came to excoriate the idea of "moral do-
goodism." Consistently with socialist theory and
the deterministic perspective of so much social
science, they wanted a system of entitlements.
These would replace charity and "unplanned, unpre-
dictable" voluntary programs. 10

Another concept that has its origins in the
New Nationalist position is the idea of "yardstick" firms. The latter would be governmentally
operated firms that could supposedly provide a
standard of comparison by which to evaluate the
prices, profits, labor policies and consumer service of private firms. Melville J. Ulmer has said
that the idea originated with Walter Durand in The
New Republic on May 26, 1926. In recent years,
John Kenneth Galbraith has been a strong supporter
of the concept. 11

The Berle-and-Means thesis

There is a part of the New Nationalist tradition that should be discussed separately, since it
occupies a distinct place in the literature. This
is the analysis that is attributed to A. A. Berle,
Jr., and Gardiner C. Means, and which they stated
in their famous book The Modern Corporation and
Private Property in 1932.

It has been commonplace in liberal writing
since 1932 to refer back to the Berle-Means book
as though the analysis originated with them. No
doubt a great many of the writers who make these
references are not aware that the analysis that
Berle and Means made was already quite old by the
time they elaborated upon it. But even if this is
true, the focus on Berle and Means is one of the
best examples of liberal dissimulation; it puts a
20th century American liberal source in the place
of the various 19th century socialist authors who

advanced the same ideas well ahead of Berle and Means. Since many American liberals, especially in the 1930's, were fully conversant with socialist writing, including Marx's _Das Kapital_, the conclusion is inescapable that this substitution was essentially dishonest, arising from a desire to be less than candid about the socialist origins of a major liberal analysis. A good portion of this obfuscation can be attributed to Berle and Means themselves. It was hardly an accident that Berle and Means did not footnote to Marx, G. D. H. Cole, Thomas Kirkup and others.

The Berle and Means thesis, as I summarized it in _Socialist Thought_, is that in large business corporations the control is no longer in the hands of the owners, the stockholders. "Control," the thesis says, "may be held by the directors or titular managers who can employ the proxy machinery to become a self-perpetuating body, even though as a group they own but a small fraction of the stock outstanding." This means that the managers are essentially "irresponsible," since they are not effectively accountable to the stockholders. In turn, this is said to falsify one of the basic assumptions upon which a system of private property is based--the assumption of owner control. Berle and Means suggested that this makes the corporation more "quasi-public" than private.[12]

As a solution for this alleged irresponsibility, Berle and Means, in common with New Nationalists in general, called for marrying the modern corporation to the state, making the corporation an instrument of social policy. "Neither the claims of ownership nor those of control can stand against the paramount interests of the community...(T)he 'control' of the great corporations should develop into a purely neutral technocracy, balancing a variety of claims by various groups in the community and assigning to each a portion of the income stream on the basis of public policy." Other than perhaps the statement I have just quoted, there was no clarion call for government

256

ownership; Berle and Means were committed to a dissimulative style and were willing to go only as far as Croly had gone in The Promise of American Life, with broad suggestions in favor of governmental absorption. But the direction in which they pointed was unmistakeably socialist.[13]

At the beginning of this chapter's section on New Nationalism, I quoted a passage from Marx's Das Kapital that contains all of the same ideas (but without the dissimulation). It is worth noting that the British socialist G. D. H. Cole had stated the thesis in his book Labour in the Commonwealth--and had even considered it a "commonplace." He said that "it is, of course, commonplace that the development of capitalism and the growth of joint-stock enterprise have more and more divorced the ultimate ownership from the actual control and management of industry." In addition to seeing the thesis in the writings of Marx and Cole, I have noticed it in Thomas Kirkup's History of Socialism--published in 1909.[14]

The thesis was also common currency in American liberal writing long before Berle and Means. In an 1895 article, Lester Ward quoted statements by J. R. Commons, made at an even earlier time, expressing the analysis. Jerome Frank, ignoring Marx and the other openly socialist authors, traced the thesis back to Thorstein Veblen. Writing in 1938, Frank said that "Veblen was the pioneer thinker. Repeatedly he pointed out the rise of 'absentee ownership' as an inherent and significant aspect of the growth of the giant corporations...Two of his disciples, Berle and Means, recently gave us striking statistical evidence of Veblen's thesis."[15]

The thesis had received considerable attention, indeed, in The New Republic during the 'Teens and 1920's. The first article I have noted was in an issue just three months after the journal began. John Maynard Keynes authored one of the many articles; in 1926 he wrote of "the tendency of big enterprise to socialize itself." He said that "a point arrives in the growth of a big institution...at which the owners of the capital ...are almost entirely dissociated from the management." Berle himself was actively promoting the analysis in an article as early as 1921. [16]

If we seek to evaluate the merits of the analysis, we see immediately that the thesis offers one of the better examples of how an idea can gain almost universal acceptance by containing just enough of the truth to possess an outward plausibility. The thesis is repeated uncritically by a great many authors. This includes the literature that is read in the colleges of business (which, as to their faculties, are not necessarily hothouses of conservatism).

It is foolish, however, for anyone to accept the Berle-and-Means thesis who is otherwise committed to a market economy. The analysis is only partly an observation of fact and is primarily a rationale for the state's absorption of large corporations.

The thesis' plausibility comes from the fact that it is indeed true, in the absence of unusual circumstances, that a widely diffuse body of stockholders, most of whom do not own enough stock to have a substantial interest in company affairs, cannot do otherwise than rubber-stamp the actions of the existing management. Unless there is a major stockholder revolt, the existing management is easily able to gain reelection and the ratification of its policies.

It does not follow, however, that the managements of large corporations are for that reason "loose cannons"--"unaccountable" and "irresponsible." Nor does it follow that one of the basic premises of the theory of private property is falsified by the fact that there is a separation between ownership and control.

The justification, so far as the theory of property is concerned, is in the freely arrived at

258

contractual relationships through which the stock-holders have come to vest control in the management. Classical liberalism, the philosophy most devoted to private property and the market economy, recognizes "freedom of contract" as a central principle. It has no bias against "a separation of ownership and control"--such as occurs in any bailment, lease or (from the settlor's point of view) trust--so long as the relationship is the product of voluntary contract.

It is rather socialist thought that has always had the bias against "absentee ownership." It is a misstatement to say that the modern corporation's separation of ownership and control violates classical liberal suppositions; it would, however, be accurate to say that it violates those of socialism. (I am aware that John Locke, the major classical liberal thinker of the 17th century, justified private property in a way that left unresolved the question of absentee ownership, since his analysis was quite rudimentary within the context of his discussion of rights arising out of "a state of nature." What he would have said about more extended forms of property if he had addressed them is, of course, a matter of conjecture. The classical liberal position is the product of a great deal of thinking that goes well beyond Locke on this point.)

So far as the accountability of corporate management is concerned, it comes in the market-place, not primarily at stockholders' meetings. Business firms rise and fall according to the flow of equity and debt capital. Most certainly there is a "survival of the fittest" among firms--and consequently among the managements that head them. The argument that managers are insulated from this is an argument that in the short term a management team can bleed a company, oblivious to the fact that the firm is losing its place. But managers who take that attitude are making themselves vulnerable to a hostile take-over: outside financiers see that a firm is faring less well than its prospects would seem to justify, and are accord-

259

ingly willing to acquire the firm for its profit-potential; and the stockholders, if they are dissatisfied with the existing management, are anxious to sell.

It is also true that the courts provide some remedy for minority stockholders in cases where the management has been given more to spoliation than to promoting the business's interests. I don't emphasize this, since it never seems to me that litigation is more than a pale substitute for a satisfactory reality. But there is no reason to think that the reality is not essentially satisfactory. The issue of management spoliation hardly receives any attention in public discussion--including among investors of all types--, and this leads me to think it cannot be a genuine problem. Our media have by no means lost their interest in good "muckraking" where it is available, which it would be if that kind of abuse were common.

At any time that such a problem does actually come to exist, those who favor the market system will be well advised to reexamine the institutional-legal framework for corporations to be sure that existing management is still subject to market forces. The defenses against hostile takeovers should never be allowed to become so effective that they insulate bad management from challenges. Adjustments in corporation law to assure this should not be interpreted as attacks upon the corporate system, but as ways to assure its viability.

If corporate managers were mainly looters, such a situation would indicate a major deviation from a classical liberal atmosphere. Individualistic liberalism presupposes a high ethical level. Ethics are to be socially inculcated and enforced through family, school, church and peer group. There has been a significant undermining of this ethical context due to a number of factors: the relativism of modern liberalism; the "do your own thing" libertarianism of the New Left and even of a good many superficial thinkers on the right; and the hedonism that arises out of the mixture of our intellectual shallowness and our affluence. If "corporate looting" ever becomes a significant problem, much of the cause will be attributable to these factors, not to an inherent flaw in the structure of corporate capitalism.

Before we leave the Berle-and-Means thesis, it is worth noting that there have been some important variations of it. Probably the most significant of these are the "New Class" analyses, which assert that in modern life both the state and the large corporation are effectively in the hands of a uniform culture of technical, bureaucraticized intellectuals. This was the theme of John Kenneth Galbraith's The New Industrial State (1978). "The decisive power in modern industrial society is exercised not by capital but by organization, not by the capitalist but by the industrial bureaucrat...There is no name for all who participate in group decision-making or the organization which they form. I propose to call this organization the Technostructure." Needless to say, Galbraith, a leading "liberal" at the same time that he is a self-proclaimed socialist, sees no legitimate "function" that is being served by stockholders in such a setting. [17]

Overt calls for nationalization

While the New Nationalist school has used dissimulation to place at least a thin veil over the socialist content of its proposals, it is significant that liberal writing has on many occasions called for the outright nationalization of major industries in the United States. As early as 1883, Lester Ward looked forward to government operation of "all private enterprises which concern the general public," although he said that first "there must be a gradual maturing of the conditions."[18]

During its first month of publication in

November, 1914, The New Republic called for the eventual government ownership of the railroads, with control in the workers. "The nationalizing of the railroads has a chance of converting them into genuine agencies of the national economic interest." The journal repeated the call in 1923 and 1931. In the 1920's, liberals were enthusiastic about the Plumb Plan "for national ownership of the railroads and operation by a 'tripartite' board representing management, labor and the public."[19]

There has been a long-term campaign for the public ownership of utilities and of hostility toward private utility companies. After the election in 1948, TRB praised President Truman, saying "now we have in the White House a man with the most radical platform in presidential history ...Truman advocates government ownership and operation of transmission lines from government dams right up to the consumers' electric stoves." We recall, of course, the many proposals for "valley authorities," with their vast implications for regionally implemented socialism.[20]

Included, also, in the call for nationalization have been the telephone and telegraph systems. In 1918, The New Republic said that "for a generation the sentiment for government telegraphs has been growing."[21]

Government ownership has been urged for mines and natural resources. In 1923, The New Republic reported the results of a poll showing that "the sentiment of liberals continues overwhelmingly in favor of public ownership of mines...." For many years, the United Mine Workers called for the nationalization of the mines. Robert Marshall advocated government ownership of forests in a 1934 article. In 1946, the editors favored the continued federal ownership "of the rich submerged oil lands off the coasts."[22]

In 1924, The New Republic came out in favor of governmental construction of homes, arguing

262

that private enterprise builds homes only for the wealthy. In 1948, Henry Wallace argued that private home-construction had "failed miserably," and wanted a government program, in cooperation with business, to build 4 1/2 million homes. [23]

In 1928, Paul Blanshard called for municipal ownership of funeral businesses. We recall how the original thinking for the T.V.A. included government ownership of a variety of small businesses. [24]

Among the more significant areas for which nationalization has been urged is banking. In 1933, The New Republic editorialized that "the most desirable form of banking would obviously be a single, nationwide, government-owned and operated enterprise." A year later, the editors said that "The New Republic [has] long [been] an advocate of complete socialization of banking...."[25]

Soon after World War II, however, there was a distinct change in feeling toward nationalization among European socialists and consequently among American liberals. The Socialist International downplayed it at the time of the International's rebirth in 1951. In 1959, the German Social Democrats abandoned nationalization, except with regard to energy. The experience in England when the Atlee government tried nationalization after World War II was almost immediately unfavorable. In addition, the resurgence of 19th Century-style decentralist socialist thinking within the Left after the events of 1956 caused a movement away from "state socialism," with which nationalization is necessarily identified. [26]

The New Freedom's perspective

The "New Freedom," a name associated with Louis Brandeis and Woodrow Wilson, denotes a school of thought that contrasts with New Nationalism in its views about big business. This school has not favored the existence of immense corporations. It has not seen big business as a stepping-stone to socialism, and has not generally seen significant economies of scale in large enterprises. What the New Freedom has favored has been a "regulated competition," through which government plays an active role in assuring the existence of truly competitive markets. It has favored the nationalization of an industry where such competition cannot be maintained, and it has called upon the state to perform the many functions of the welfare state.

The combination of these ingredients was present, as an example, in a book by Paul Douglas, later a United States Senator, in 1935. Broadus Mitchell's review said that Douglas "urges breaking up as many monopolies as possible...Where this policy fails...ownership will have to be socialized."[27]

Woodrow Wilson is, along with Brandeis, considered the original champion of the position, but a reading of his 1912 campaign speeches shows him to have been given to platitudes that were far from clear in content. His performance as president was quite mixed on this issue.

We have seen how Franklin Delano Roosevelt began strongly in favor of the New Nationalism, and then, although perhaps remaining a New Nationalist at heart, switched to a not-very-resolute New Freedomite position in what is called the "Second New Deal."

There has been considerable activity in favor of New Freedom-style measures since World War II, perhaps reflecting a natural liberal preference for limiting the role of big business if it does not appear feasible at a given time to place large corporations under the wing of government.

In 1945, Alvin Hansen proposed changing the patent law to make "available all inventions and new processes to any user upon payment of a reasonable royalty." In 1946, Senator James Murray of Montana proposed a plan in Congress for stronger anti-trust enforcement--with the alternative being public control. In the late 1940's and early 1950's, Senator Estes Kefauver headed a committee in the Senate that called for stricter anti-merger rules. Kefauver, too, called for the licensing of patents. In 1950, The New Republic advocated the regulation of prices and wages where a large corporation's dissolution is not technically feasible. [28]

In 1960, Paul H. Douglas and Howard Shuman asked rhetorically: "Why...should not the giant industries be split up into almost as many companies as there are production units?" In 1972, Peter Barnes reported that Senator Harris had introduced legislation to break up corporations in concentrated industries. During the presidential campaign that year, Senator McGovern came out for a war against mergers. John M. Blair's book Economic Concentration (1972) advocated "breaking up GM, GE and the others into their constituent parts," according to Bernard D. Nossiter. [29]

A New Republic article in 1974 reported that "Senator Philip Hart (D. Mich.), chairman of the antitrust subcommittee, is pushing for legislation that, for the first time, would make market dominance a basis for breaking up large firms in such oligopolistic industries as autos, steel, aluminum, chemicals, drugs, electrical machinery, computers, communications equipment and energy." [30]

In 1978, Morton Kondracke told his readers that "[Senator] Edward Kennedy favors...a break-up of the big oil companies," along with "deregulation and increased competition." The following year, Lester Thurow reported that Kennedy offered a bill to bar conglomerate mergers where the companies had assets or annual sales exceeding two billion dollars. [31]

In 1982, Mark Green, in his book Winning Back America, called for statutorily established criteria about size: "Whenever a firm, or up to four

265

firms, controls 50 percent of a market, it would have to be decentralized into smaller units unless they could argue by a preponderance of the evidence that economies of scale required their size." Green also called for progressively higher income tax rates for corporations, depending upon their size and market share.[32]

Before I close this chapter, it is worthwhile to point out that conservative thought includes its own division between supporters and opponents of vast corporate size. Many classical liberals argue that growth to any size is a matter of right, and that in any case the problem of bigness has been exaggerated. They argue that market processes, in the absence of governmental favoritism for some economic groups over others, will produce a healthy situation.

Other classical liberals, however, believe that the health of the market and of a free society is best served by limits upon size, and argue that the legal framework of a free society can rightfully state such limits. I count myself among this latter group, since I believe that a market system, to function at its best, requires more of a "framework" of laws and institutions than many market enthusiasts are willing to admit. I would point to the fact that corporate size has given the Left some of its best ammunition against the market, and for many has provided a potential vehicle for collectivization.

NOTES

1. See Dwight D. Murphey, Burkean Conservatism and Classical Liberalism (Washington: University Press of America, 1982), pp. 426-428; Dwight D. Murphey, Socialist Thought (Washington: University Press of America, 1983), pp. 279-281.

2. The earlier discussions in the present book are at pages 63-65 and 81-86.

3. Karl Marx, Das Kapital, Vol. 3, Chap. 27; the passage is quoted in Maurice Cornforth, The Open Philosophy and the Open Society (New York: International Publishers, 1968), p. 191.

4. Edward Bellamy, Looking Backward (New York: Signet Classic, 1960), pp. 53, 54.

5. Bellamy, Looking Backward, p. xvi.

6. New Republic, October 21, 1925, p. 214; Herbert Croly, The Promise of American Life (New York: The Macmillan Company, 1914), p. 358.

7. New Republic, March 25, 1931, p. 144.

8. New Republic, April 3, 1961, p. 10; New Republic, April 10, 1961, p. 2; John Kenneth Galbraith, The New Industrial State (Boston: Houghton Mifflin Company, 3rd ed., 1978), p. 408.

9. As to worker control, see Mark Green, Winning Back America (Toronto: Bantam Books, 1982), pp. 42, 43, 52, and New Republic, November 25, 1981, p. 29. As to co-determination, see New Republic, November 24, 1973, p. 17, and Green, Winning Back America, pp. 44-45.

10. New Republic, June 5, 1961, p. 12.

11. New Republic, January 5, 1974, p. 14; New Republic, September 8, 1973, p. 29.

12. A. A. Berle, Jr., and Gardiner C. Means, The Modern Corporation and Private Property (New York: The Macmillan Company, 1956), p. 5.

13. Berle and Means, Modern Corporation, p. 356.

14. G. D. H. Cole, Labour in the Commonwealth (London: Headley Bros. Publishers, Ltd., no date given), p. 107; Thomas Kirkup, History of Socialism (New York: The Macmillan Company, 1909), p. 356.

15. Lester Ward, Lester Ward and the Welfare State, Henry Steele Commager, editor (Indianapolis: The Bobbs-Merrill Company, Inc., 1967), p. 186; Jerome Frank, Save America First (New York: Harper & Brothers Publishers, 3rd ed., 1938), p. 282.

16. New Republic, January 30, 1915, p. 8; New Republic, February 6, 1915, p. 7; New Republic, July 14, 1920, p. 198; New Republic, August 4, 1920, p. 280; New Republic, September 29, 1920, p. 112; New Republic, September 7, 1921, p. 37.

17. Galbraith, New Industrial State, pp. xv, 74, 409.

18. Ward, Lester Ward, p. 55.

19. New Republic, November 21, 1914, p. 12; New Republic, February 7, 1923, p. 266; New Republic, July 25, 1923, p. 238; New Republic, June 10, 1931, p. 85.

20. New Republic, November 28, 1914, p. 29; New Republic, November 15, 1948, p. 3.

21. New Republic, July 6, 1918, p. 275.

22. New Republic, July 11, 1923, p. 164; New Republic, February 6, 1924, p. 268; New Republic, June 27, 1934, p. 176; New Republic, September 23, 1946, p. 374.

23. New Republic, March 5, 1924, p. 41; New Republic, March 1, 1948, p. 10.

24. New Republic, August 22, 1928, p. 17.

25. New Republic, March 15, 1933, p. 118; New Republic, September 5, 1934, p. 89.

26. New Republic, August 6, 1951, p. 10; New Republic, November 30, 1959, p. 8.

27. New Republic, August 28, 1935, p. 81.

28. New Republic, January 1, 1945, p. 11; New Republic, January 21, 1946, p. 75; New Republic, January 13, 1947, p. 30; Estes Kefauver, In a Few Hands: Monopoly Power in America (New York: Pantheon Books, 1965); New Republic, January 16, 1950, p. 9.

29. New Republic, September 26, 1960, p. 18; New Republic, January 22, 1972, p. 19; New Republic, June 24, 1972, p. 23; New Republic, December 9, 1972, p. 26.

30. New Republic, July 6, 1974, p. 17.

31. New Republic, September 23, 1978, p. 12; New Republic, April 28, 1979, p. 10.

32. Green, Winning Back America, pp. 47, 49.

11

THE PROCESS OF POLITICIZATION

After all that we have seen about modern liberalism's relationship to socialist aspirations, it would hardly seem necessary to include a chapter on "the process of politicization."

A discussion of "politicization" will have the advantage, however, of talking about liberalism in the form in which it has been most directly perceived by the American public. Since dissimulation has obscured liberalism's socialist core, the public has seen liberalism primarily as a movement that has pressed insistently for what we might call the "de-privatization" of most human problems. A great many aspects of the human condition--problems that in the past and within the perspective of classical liberalism have been seen as private, to be solved or suffered by the individuals themselves--have been redefined as public in nature, to be addressed by a combination of social science and the state. As seen in this light, liberalism has constituted an on-going process of absorption of the private into the public.

Such a process relates directly to liberalism's underlying socialist premises and to the gradualistic Fabian method. We will not fully understand it, though, if that is all we notice about it. We must appreciate the dimension that brings together social science, the state, and the rationalism of intellectuals who wish to impose order on the subjects they study. The New Republic was seeing liberalism in this light when in 1920 it spoke of "liberalism [as] the offspring of the coalition between science and humanism." When this mixture is combined with a willingness to use the state as something of a "social church," the result is what Hubert Humphrey referred to as "the humanitarian state." 1

271

Through most of the 20th century this process has produced some major secular trends in the political sphere: the size and power of the state have increased enormously; this power has become centralized as liberalism has sought to focus it in the national government; and much of the newly-found power has come to reside in the hands of the "expert" in the many independent agencies and the bureaucracy.

There are two points that should be mentioned before we begin our discussion of this process.

The ideology of the Left calls into being an alliance of the intellectuals with the "have nots," and invokes the power of the state, of a movement, or of a collective of one sort or another on behalf of this alliance. This in itself accounts for much of what I have just described. And yet there is more. Reformers such as Dorothea Lynde Dix campaigned for state-supported asylums for the insane before the Civil War. Could this be attributed to "an alliance with the have-nots"? Maybe very indirectly, as an offshoot of the mental set that resulted from the alliance that was in fact coming into existence; but certainly there was no evident political value to the intellectual from an alliance with the insane. Such a movement points to the other factors that we will explore in this chapter.

The second point is that both the Left and modern liberalism have had an anti-statist dimension. This is a dimension that has certainly not predominated; but it is one that should be kept in mind if we are not to oversimplify. Much 19th century socialist thought talked in terms of decentralized collectivism: communes, mutual associations, cooperatives, and the like. We have seen that this was important to the Guild Socialist movement in England and to the "industrial democracy" vogue within American liberalism around the time of World War I. Another major source was the anti-modern, anti-scientific, anti-rational Romantic movement that was so powerful in Europe

272

after the disillusionment with the French Revolution. This was to become a central inspiration to the New Left, a diverse phenomenon which included significant elements repudiating both rationality and the "rational state" that springs out of the desire to "rationalize society."

Intellectual, social mindscape underlying the absorption

There is a passage in Lester Ward's _Applied Sociology_ (1906) that is one of the best examples I have seen of the mentality that has mixed science, a planning-type rationalism, and the state in a process that absorbs all of life into it.

Ward wrote that "legislation will consist in a series of exhaustive experiments on the part of true scientific sociologists and sociological inventors working on the problems of social physics from the practical point of view. It will undertake to solve not only questions of general interest to the state,...but questions of social improvement, the amelioration of the condition of all the people, the removal of whatever privations may still remain, and the adoption of means to the positive increase of the social welfare, _in short the organization of human happiness...._" (Emphasis added)[2]

This is precisely what Ivan R. Dee had in mind in 1973 when he wrote that "politically such men as Chase, Soule, Alfred Bingham and Adolf Berle longed for a coherent social order, a rational community that would be 'liberal in strategy, socialist in ultimate aims.'" Dee added that "this is why the seeming confusion of the [Franklin] Roosevelt administration bothered many intellectuals."[3]

It is also what Kimball Young had in mind when he described John Dewey's main thesis, which he said was that "when we learn to observe, corre-

273

late and deduce laws of social phenomena, we shall be able to construct a consciously controlled society." 4

One nuance of all of this was that the image of a thoroughly planned society led the intellectual culture, as we have seen, to a powerful infatuation with the Soviet Union. For many, the infatuation persisted for as long as thirty years. In 1957, Gus Tyler wrote that "for many years—almost up to the present—it was widely believed that, whatever the faults of the Soviet Union, it was dedicated to true internationalism, national autonomy and cultural equality...Then too there is the captivating illusion popular for a time among Western progressives that intelligence and human engineering had come into their own with the Five Year Plan." 5

This infatuation was shattered eventually by a number of events, but the one that most shocked the scientific-rationalist mentality that I am now discussing was the Lysenko affair. In 1949, Julian Huxley wrote in The New Republic that "the U.S.S.R. has officially rejected some of the essentials of scientific method itself." The Soviets, holding to a view that science reflects "the class struggle" and that there are therefore such things as "bourgeois science" and "proletarian science," suppressed Mendelian genetic theory for several years after World War II. During that period, the theory formulated by Trofim D. Lysenko that an organism passes environmentally-acquired properties on to the next generation was given official Soviet sanction. To scientists around the world, this seemed an unpardonable intervention by dogmatic ideology into the scientific realm, comparable to some of the worst actions of the medieval Church. 6

Another nuance that we should note is that the mentality makes certain assumptions about human nature. These are assumptions that are not universally accepted. We see the contrast when we compare the views, say, of Ralph Waldo Emerson and

274

Bruce Bliven. In early 1915, Percy H. Boynton wrote in The New Republic that Emerson had held back from the pre-Civil War reform movements because he felt "that in considering man as a plastic thing they were all in error." Bliven, on the other hand, wrote in 1931 that: "If anyone observes that 'you can't change human nature,' the only intelligent answer is...'Yes, you can so.' Human nature is one of the most malleable things in the world." The Bliven viewpoint is consistent with Ward's and Dewey's, as well as with that of such a thinker as B. F. Skinner, who in Beyond Freedom and Dignity postulates a system in which human beings are totally the subjects of deterministic manipulation.[7]

Identification of private conditions as scientific, political problems

The essence of what I have called "the 'deprivatization'" was expressed by C. Wright Mills when he wrote that "it is the political task of the social scientist--as of any liberal educator--continually to translate personal troubles into public issues."[8]

This has been a process that has been at the heart of American liberalism. We recall how Senator Edward Kennedy once made a trip to Alaska and in effect discovered the plight of the Eskimos, for the solution of which he then urged a federal program. He was actively engaged in "translating personal troubles into public issues." To a classical liberal, the "plight" of the Eskimo would seem to follow from their choosing to live within the Arctic Circle; he would see it as an unenviable condition--but not as a subject for political solution.

Examples could be cited endlessly, since the Ward, Dewey, Mills rationale envisions the broadest possible embrace of the human condition. I have marked a passage in which Walter Mondale has commented on the plight of rural migrants: "They move all over. They belong nowhere. They don't vote. Often their children don't even go to a school. It's a disgrace...These people just go on being exploited." I would direct the reader's attention to the last point, the reference to "exploitation." The idea that millions of people are trapped and exploited, and that the state serves a liberating function as the vehicle for overcoming the exploitation, is one of the key concepts in the ideology of left-wing socialism, such as we see it, say, in the writings of Ferdinand Lassalle. (I say "left-wing" socialism because rightist forms of socialism tend to seek collectivism on other premises, such as a tribalistic appeal to a nation or a race rather than to the "have-nots" as such.) Since much of what we are discussing is a seamless web, the interconnection between exploitation theory and the process of politicization cannot be surprising.[9]

The discovery of "problems" often reflects a utopian mentality that drops the historical context. The process is then oblivious to the fact that instead of becoming worse, the particular condition has often been improving. Action is called for to solve "problems" that have been fading out rather than increasing. Probably the most important example of this has to do with the condition of blacks immediately before the Civil Rights movement began. Anyone listening to the rhetoric of the movement would not have known that there had been a substantial improvement in that condition. Another example was the legal prohibition of child labor. Such a prohibition only became thinkable--and politically possible--when affluence had risen to a level at which families could afford not to have their children work. The whole movement to abolish child labor was necessarily a "tag-end" movement, coming as the "problem" was already disappearing.

Edward C. Banfield has cited the "school dropout problem" as an example. "At the turn of the century," he says, "when almost everyone was a 'dropout,' the term and the 'problem' did not

276

exist. It was not until the 1960's, when for the first time a majority of boys and girls were graduating from high school and practically all had at least some high school training, that the 'dropout problem' became acute."10

Various intellectual tools have been fashioned by modern social science to serve the combined needs of rationalistic empiricism and politicization. It is not coincidental that statistics developed as a discipline in response to the planning requirements of the German state during the Cameralist period. L. L. Bernard and Jessie Bernard tell us in their Origins of American Sociology that "statistical work was early developed in Europe, and especially in Germany in the seventeenth and eighteenth centuries, due to their strong emphasis upon state administration. The Cameralists found quantitative measurement and recording indispensable to efficient administration...."11

Daniel Patrick Moynihan has written about the United States that "the national government began compiling economic statistics that were to make economic planning feasible years before such planning became politically acceptable." He goes on to say that "the truth of John Kenneth Galbraith's observation remains: statisticians are key actors in the process of social change...." Galbraith, he says, attributed this to the fact that "it is often only when it becomes possible to measure a problem that it also becomes possible to arouse any political interest in solving it." I would add that the process is more subtle than this last comment suggests: before there is even a perceived need to "arouse the public," a human condition must come to be seen as a collective "problem." Statistics, bringing together many otherwise isolated cases into a perceivable aggregate, are at the heart of that transmutation.12

Other techniques that have been developed both as modes of analysis and as planning tools have been input-output analysis and its descendant, linear programming. Jacob Oser tells us that "input-output analysis would have been irrelevant in the days of atomistic competition and laissez faire." He cites its uses in a modern corporate setting, but adds that it "is probably more useful in a socialist economy than in one based primarily on private enterprise." We are told by Heinz Kohler that linear programming "is a lineal descendant of input-output analysis" and "was developed in 1939 by Kantorovich in the USSR."[13]

The split within the intellectual culture over social science

Much of American social science has possessed a distinctly liberal content, both because of the worldview its practitioners have held and because of the process I have just described. This is true generally despite the fact that many social scientists have taken quite seriously the teachings of Max Weber to the effect that sociology should be value-neutral. Philip M. Hauser has made a telling point in this regard. He says that "my training in sociology at the University of Chicago during the late twenties and early thirties led me to accept the Weberian model of sociology. That sociology was a science, not a vehicle for social action, was a tenet of faith on the part of the faculty...." He adds, however: "Yet, ...it was clear that many members of the faculty...were making major contributions to action programs...I reconciled the apparent contradictions...by accepting the proposition that the sociologist could play multiple roles...."[14]

I do not mean to overlook the fact that a number of social scientists have been one form or another of conservative. These would not wish to be included within my general description. But they will almost certainly agree with the description I am giving of the impact of social science in general.

Even though most American social science has been related to liberalism and to the de-privatization, there has been a wide difference in the way members of the Left have perceived it. This is a difference that almost certainly tells us more about each of those making the critique than it does about social science itself. Those who have been well attuned to the Fabian process and have been willing to bear with the reverses that liberalism has suffered will have had no difficulty seeing the main bulk of social science as an ally. Those, on the other hand, who have been more impatient, as the more overtly alienated and socialist have been wont to be, will have found the "scientific neutrality" and gradual politicization almost intolerably slow. One would expect them to denounce American social science as having been insufficiently socialist.

Many liberals have praised social science's contribution to liberalism. Herbert Croly wrote expectantly of "the idea of a social science which would be useful in supplying a technique of social progress." In 1926, The New Republic was effusive about the development of social work as a profession: "The forward rank of social workers is creating a new technique, a new philosophy, and a new spirit which, if it succeeds in winning the day, will transform old-style philanthropy into a genuine social therapeutics." I recall how George Soule made himself one of the main protagonists for "national planning," to which "professionally qualified experts...putting together the statistics" were essential.[15]

There has, however, been a steady drumbeat of criticism by those who have wanted an overt expression of "values," heavily socialist in orientation, rather than a "scientifically neutral" approach. We are mistaken if we think that such criticism arose mainly during the years of the New Left. It has been in evidence for many years; the New Left merely continued an existing critique.

In 1931, Benjamin Ginsburg had this to say in

a review in <u>The New Republic</u> of a book about social science: "One begins to wonder whether there is not also present a motive of social conservatism, a motive which uses social science as a sort of Penelope's web to put off the demands of the suitors for social reform." He criticized a "policy of providing millions for research and not one cent for philosophy." 16

It is interesting that, from a conservative point of view, I have had the same criticism to make of the positivist fashion that is insisted upon in high school debate competition. The national debate topic has almost invariably centered on one socialistic proposal or another. Students tell me that they are discouraged from arguing on the basis of social and political values, and that they must confine their points to matters of cost, administrative feasibility, and the like. In that context, the positivism is a way of doing without <u>conservative</u> values. It may seem strange that leftist critics would complain of a lack of socialist values in the broader realm of social science. To understand it, we need to keep in mind their impatience with dissimulation and gradualism. It is a matter of the perspective that the observer brings to the critique.

John Dewey himself was dissatisfied with the non-socialist preoccupations that he saw in the social science of his day. In 1931, he wrote bitingly about "the present zeal for 'fact finding.'...For the most part, the data...are not social facts at all. For their connection with any system of human purposes and consequences, their bearing as means and as results upon human action, are left out of the picture." He wanted social science to be much more consciously geared toward "social planning and control."17

In a <u>New Republic</u> article in 1933, George E. Novack was, from a Marxist point of view, severely critical of the mathematical economics of Walras, Jevons, Marshall and Clark. He said that this economic theory was too abstract, having "only the remotest connection with the real capitalist world of class societies and imperialist states, over-production and recurrent crises...." The "unack-nowledged premise," he said, is "that there was nothing fundamentally wrong or unjust about the operation of the price system...." In 1938, Max Lerner authored a review of a book by Robert S. Lynd about the social sciences. Lerner complained about "American social scientists keeping their placid tenor amid disaster," and spoke of "the fairly patent fact that the 'detachment' and 'ob-jectivity' that they have exacted of themselves have been excuses for keeping quiet...devices for saving their skins." [18]

In 1957, Merle King posed the question "What of social scientists?" In answer, he said that, "confusing form for content, they assume that resort to the forms of the calculating machine, the questionnaire, the interview, and the quanti-fied formula indeed will enable them to travel toward the future with the natural scientists and engineers." To King, their "visions [were] blocked by a massive wall of technology, science, mathematics and expertness." He wanted more "vision" and less technique.[19]

The New Left, which was beginning at about that time, continued this theme. Years later, Morris Dickstein looked back and said "I can re-member the impact that C. Wright Mills' work had on us as undergraduates in the late '50's. He seemed like the one bold spirit in the gray, gray crew of American social science." Mills' position was summarized by Staughton Lynd in 1962: "C. Wright Mills has called modern American social science 'an elaborate method of insuring that no one learns too much about man and society.' Mills argues that the great tradition of George, Bellamy and Veblen has disgraced itself by turgid defini-tion-splitting on the one hand, and the statisti-cal exegesis of trivia on the other."[20]

Edward Chase joined in the criticism in 1968 when he wrote about "academic economists who insulate themselves from troublesome doubts about fundamentals by their absorption in econometrics and data manipulation." In 1975, Martin Duberman referred to "the sharp challenge of recent years to the claims of 'value-free,' 'objective' social science."21

A substantial part of the New Left's criticism took on a different tone from that which we have just traced back to the 1930's. The "counter-cultural" side of the New Left was not mainly criticizing the lack of an effectively socialist social science; instead, drawing deeply from sources in the early 19th century's Romantic revolt against modernity and the Enlightenment, it was in profound opposition to the very existence of science, technology and rationalism. In 1968, Martin Duberman said of "today's student radicals" that "their disgust with traditional procedures is grounded in a growing distrust of rationality itself." Duberman saw this favorably, saying that it meant that the activists wanted men "to become something more than minds."22

Jerry Rubin said it most graphically: "Abstract thinking is the way professors avoid facing their own social impotence. Our generation is in rebellion against abstract intellectualism and critical thinking. We admire the Viet Kong guerrilla, the Black Panther, the stoned hippie, not the abstract intellectual vegetable."23

A more thoughtful, literary expression of the same perspective came from Theodore Roszak in Where the Wasteland Ends. Roszak said that from "the Romantic movement...we inherit a stubborn counter cultural resistance to the pre-eminence of science." He argued for a return to a magical, mystical way of seeing the world, and said that "it is the culture of science from which we must liberate ourselves." He spoke of "urban-industrial society [as] having hopelessly lost touch with life lived on a simpler, more 'primitive' level, and [as being] convinced beyond question of the omnipotence of technical intelligence." Roszak concluded that "we should undertake to repeal urban-industrialism as the world's dominant style of life" and substitute an "anarchist brotherhood and sisterhood" that would be "shot through with mystical sensibility."[24]

During the radical resurgence of the 1960's, the proponents of "behavioral science" were spurred to a point at which they were bidding to become the _avant garde_ of academic radicalism. This was especially in evidence in the mid-western College of Business in which I was teaching. The movement was reflected in Reed Whitemore's observation in late 1969 that "social and behavioral scientists are ambitious and expansionist. They see their revolution coming." [25]

As the New Left faded rapidly after the tumultuous events of the spring of 1970, American radicalism retreated into various forms. One of the more important of these has been the rise of academic Marxism, which prefers to call itself "radicalism". As early as April, 1969, Martin Duberman was able to speak of "a new generation of radical academics." An organization called U.R.P.E. (for "the Union of Radical Political Economy") has published a prolific literature.[26]

Before I leave this subject, I should interject that some of the criticism of social science has been of a sort that would have been present even in the absence of ideological motivations. Various commentators within liberalism have been fully aware of the pseudo-scientific quality of much of the work that is done, and of the stifling neo-Scholasticism and credentialism that is imposed. Thus, Benjamin Stolberg could write in 1922 that "the truth is that to compare actual to social science,...without an acute sense of poetic license is to commit one of the gravest of fallacies." Under the unfortunately partisan title _Social Sciences as Sorcery_, Stanislav Andreski has written an elaborate and thoughtful dissection of the trivia that so commonly clogs the social sciences as we have come to know them during, say,

283

the middle half of the 20th century. Here is a representative statement from his critique: "What is particularly dismaying is that not only does the flood of publications reveal an abundance of pompous bluff and a paucity of new ideas, but even the old and valuable insights which we have inherited from our illustrious ancestors are being drowned in a torrent of meaningless verbiage and useless technicalities." [27]

Irving Kristol has told how the statistical method has been abused and has become a vehicle for ideology rather than of science: "That the concept of poverty should be continually and vigilantly redefined so that 20 percent of the population is always 'poor' is a function of ideology, not sociology." He points out that this reflects the attitudes of people who are "considerably more interested in the perpetuation of a critical attitude toward liberal-capitalist society than in any particular set of objective accomplishments." [28]

The rise of the social-scientific professional

What I have described has become an institutionalized part of American society. Beginning with the formation of the distinct branches of social science in the late 19th century, every part of social science and of social work has become the domain of its own profession and bureaucracy. Referring to "the young economists who in 1885 founded" the American Economics Association, The New Republic in 1915 commented that "it is to these innovators...that we owe the fact that today the specialized economist...is at work for the state, the industrial corporation and the trade union." The journal saw clearly the implications for liberalism: "Social work will be a vocational school where the community learns constructive collectivism." [29]

No doubt this institutionalization can be seen as "in aid of democracy." That it can also become an elitist threat to it became apparent

284

quite early. In 1915, a __New Republic__ article called, for example, for teachers to share power over the schools with the elected Boards of Education. It is an easy matter to see the professional as more qualified than outsiders representing an amorphous and "not specially qualified" public. In the United States, we have insisted that military professionals remain subordinate to civilian authority; a similar subordination of domestic "experts" to elected representatives is not nearly so easy to recognize as a democratic imperative, or to delineate once it has been recognized.[30]

Despite the institutionalization, which suggests that the processes of "social therapeutics" have become regularized, the divisions within the American Left and within the groups that have composed its alliance have been such that the road has not been one of smooth acceptance. The radical Left has upon occasion attacked social workers as representatives of the bourgeois establishment. As early as 1917, for example, Rebecca West was complaining that in England "the welfare worker is a failure...The welfare workers are drawn almost as exclusively as the philanthropic workers from the middle classes. Labor regards this with a resentment that is entirely reasonable."[31]

Even those who have received the ministrations of social work, as so many blacks have, have been bitter critics. Reporting on the Watts ghetto shortly after its 1965 riot, Lewis Yablonsky wrote that "there was a uniform attitude that people trying to do social work in the neighborhood who lived outside were 'fools,' to be exploited as much as possible." In his "autobiography," Malcolm X said that "if ever a state social agency destroyed a family, it destroyed ours...They had looked at us as numbers and as a case in their book, not as human beings." There is, of course, a lesson in this: harmony does not inevitably exist between a professionalized Welfare State and its beneficiaries.[32]

285

Effects of the de-privatization
on American political life

It is in its political effects that the process I have described has been most obvious to the American people.

The ideology that has sought the centralization of functions in the national government has had a distinct aversion to local or private or market solutions to the problems it has perceived. In this, it has differed sharply from classical liberalism, which sought solutions precisely in those areas.

If a classical liberal, for example, were to look at the history of labor-management relations and were to hope for improvements in the condition of labor as it existed in the 19th century, he would welcome the development of job-related amenities by private employers. In contrast, here is the reaction that The New Republic expressed in 1915 to any improvement that came from a private employer: "The despot becomes benevolent. Hospitals, swimming pools, Y.M.C.A.'s, 'profit sharing,' are bestowed, evidently in complete oblivion of the fact that there would be little manhood in men who accepted these benefits at the price of submission."[33]

A classical liberal approves of private education as an expression of freedom and as a decentralization of power over the public's thinking. Here, though, is what another 1915 editorial in The New Republic had to say: "Universities, whether supported by the state or privately, are becoming too vitally institutions for public service to be much longer directed on the plan of a private corporation...Irresponsible control by a board of amateur notables is no longer adequate for the effective scientific and sociological laboratories for the community that universities are becoming."[34]

Before Medicare was established, an

286

alternative that was preferred by conservatives was the Kerr-Mills Act of 1960, under which the federal government would subsidize a state-initiated insurance plan, operated through a private insurance company, for elderly persons in medical need. Eric Goldman tells us that "proponents of Medicare responded in unveiled disgust." They preferred a compulsory, federal program.35

During most of the 20th century, this preference has caused liberals to take a dim view of state and local government. The exceptions have come during the periods, such as the 1920's, in which liberal action has been blocked at the federal level. The more usual view was stated by William Orton when he wrote that "mobilization [for social purposes] is frustrated by the existence of forty-eight separate political and legal jurisdictions...American liberalism...must undoubtedly look increasingly toward the federal power, the only power that is adequate to the largest problems." With this as the premise, it is no wonder that The New Republic was able to call in 1935 for "a new form of government that will...abolish the present states..., substituting flexible regional divisions." This was consistent with Herbert Croly's views years earlier. Charles Forcey has summarized those views this way: "Since the states were largely artificial political units with no real relation to industry, Croly suggested that they be deprived of virtually all control over economic matters. To the towns and the cities would be given the control or ownership of local utilities, while the rest of the economy would be regulated by a much strengthened government in Washington." In Progressive Democracy, Croly had written that "the state governments will be needed and valued, not as independent and coordinate centres of authority, but as parts of an essentially national system."36

Nor are these views that were held only by liberals in Croly's generation. In 1966, Walter Heller described the "federalism" that he favored:

"States and localities...will continue to be the service centers through which important national purposes are achieved." This subordination of the states to federal policy has become quite pronounced, and continues even under the Reagan administration (which, for example, has used strings attached to federal spending as a way to force the states to change their laws about the age at which young people can drink beer).[37]

Why has modern liberalism favored centralization? For a combination of reasons. First, the influence of the intellectual culture can most effectively be brought to bear at the national level. Second, as some of the commentators themselves have stated, the type of planning liberalism has wanted does not lend itself to geographical limitations coinciding with state boundaries. Third, there has over a long period of time been a progressive weakening of local loyalties, and of the romance of providing local political leadership, due to such objective factors as increased transciency, broadened communication, and the like. Fourth, the quality of local and state leadership has for over a century been notoriously low, a fact that reflects perhaps more than anything else the unwillingness of most people even in a democracy, wrapped up as they are in their daily lives, to devote any time (or contribute any money) to politics.

In addition to liberalism's movement away from the local and state units of government, liberal thought has had as one of its premises the assumption that little or nothing will get done without "planning." Senator Hubert Humphrey was thus able to look out upon the world, armed with statistics about current numbers of graduates, and say that "the cold fact is that the number of engineering graduates is declining--as are Ph.D.'s in education and government. We cannot permit this to continue." To Humphrey, there was no "invisible hand" that leads to the automatic flow of resources in response to the free choices made by many individuals. This is one of the profound

288

differences between Humphrey's brand of liberalism and that of the classical liberals, such as Adam Smith and David Ricardo. Those who see chaos in the marketplace of free choices are bound to seek order in other ways.[38]

Another example can be seen in the statement Senator Edward Kennedy made on June 17, 1971. "Between now and the year 2000," he said, "the population of America will increase by nearly 100 million people...The increased population is the equivalent of building 200 new cities with populations of 500,000 or 100 new cities with populations of 1 million. In fact, the development of such new cities, using advanced new technologies and systems analysis, may be the most important challenge we face...." This passage illustrates not only the absence of a "vitalist perspective" within modern liberalism, but also the mentality of planning and of a collectivistically applied social science.[39]

The result of all of this has been that modern liberalism has, at least until its post-New Left disillusionment, called for an ever-expanding role for government. I compare this to "blowing air into the balloon." Many of the specific programs have been of a "foot-in-the-door" nature, carrying an intent that they be expanded once they are started. In 1964, TRB spoke of "the steady expansion of government," and said that "there is no doubt in my own mind that this expansion ought to go on, and will go on." A description of the specific programs could fill several volumes.[40]

Before the collapse of liberal morale in the 1970's and '80's, there was an assumption of irreversibility--that a governmental function, once embraced, would not, indeed could not, be abandoned. Thus, Henry Fairlie could say in 1966 that "departments like Health, Education and Welfare are developing a character which will survive changes in the political climate." He described at least one of the factors that would press for permanence and growth when he said that "the lever

289

of federal funds, once it is given to a bureaucracy, is unlikely to be left unused for very long." Another factor of perhaps equal importance has been that each program has developed its own constituency--and voting bloc. This has placed a premium on opportunistic politicians, and has made political competition increasingly difficult for those not given to the opportunism of a "spend and elect" politics. [41]

It is a mistake to think that federal power has been manifested even primarily through direct legislation. Ubiquitous webs of influence and control have come into being.

Of course, legislation has played a part. But there has been a universe, so to speak, of regulation coming out of the massive independent agencies, to which vast realms of power have been delegated. In 1915 The New Republic exulted about the Federal Trade Commission Act that "a Democratic Congress has actually delegated the broadest kind of personal discretion to a commission of 'experts'" and that "the Act achieves a very happy but a most amazing delegation of legislative function." [42]

In addition, intricate control has been exercised through strings attached to spending. "Affirmative action" programs have probably been the foremost example of this. Every firm that has had government contracts of a certain size has had to have an "affirmative action plan" for the recruitment of minority employees. It has been required that part of the firm's plan be that the businesses with which the firm deals must also have a plan. The principal lever for the enforcement of all of this has been the threat of cutting off government funds and contracts.

Another avenue has been through abjuring all pretense of neutrality in taxation. The tax system has existed only partly to raise the hundreds of billions of dollars that have been needed to fund governmental programs; it has equally been

adapted to "social intervention," by which countless activities are encouraged and many others
discouraged.

The Jacksonians before the Civil War had
argued strenuously against the use of the tariff
for other than the raising of revenue, and feared
the "consolidation" that would result from unrestrained federal spending. But the high-tariff
parties during American history always favored the
use of taxation for interventionist, not simply
revenue-raising, purposes. This was one of the
leading issues throughout the 19th century.

Then, relating to a more modern context, we
are told by Felix Frankfurter that "Theodore Roosevelt was the first President avowedly to use the
taxing power as a direct agency of social policy."
Robert LaFollette, another of the major figures of
the Progressive era, said in his <u>Autobiography</u>
that "I argued openly that the Constitution
authorized the federal government to use the
taxing power, that there was no limit to that
power for police purposes...." In 1935 <u>The New
Republic</u> advocated an interventionist system of
taxation when it called for "a thorough-going
program of social reform through taxation."[43]

The <u>loss</u> <u>of</u> <u>confidence</u>: <u>critical</u>
reevaluation after 1965

As a result of the divisions that occurred
within the American Left during the 1960's, a fact
of considerable significance was reported by James
MacGregor Burns in March, 1968: "For the first
time in decades the power of the Presidency is
undergoing critical reevaluation by American liberals...Liberal political scientists are reconsi-
dering the need for institutional checks and
balances against the man in the White House."[44]

The old magic was gone. Implicit faith was
no longer reposed in the presidency, as Burns'
statement shows--or in any of the rest of the

massive federal enterprise. Many of the factions on the Left began seeing the gigantic apparatus as evil or incompetent, or both. There was a turn inward, as during the 1920's, and toward proposals for decentralized collectivism, such as worker control.

Lee Benson picked up a common New Left theme when he wrote that "1968 showed that the fatal weakness of modern bureaucracies is precisely their inability to satisfy humanist needs." A New Republic editorial in 1970 reported that "black America's confidence in the national government has rapidly, dangerously diminished." In 1972, TRB told his readers that "there is an under-current of disassociation, a feeling almost of despair that it really won't matter much. This lack of confidence in the capacity of government to solve problems is rather terrifying." The New Republic's editors in 1974 stated the problem this way: "[The] national Democratic party has a tradi-tion of benevolent big government. But how sure can our 1976 candidate be that an extension of the New Deal, the New Frontier, the Great Society, will produce more well-being for more people or a federal bureaucracy that's more responsive and benevolent?" [45]

Although there has been some clinging to the old faith, as when the editors said in 1979 that "we still have the faith...that the government can play an aggressive role in improving the national welfare," expressions of doubt continued in the 1980's. In a New Republic review in 1980, Ira Glasser wrote that "since Progressive reformers themselves meant only to help, they saw the ex-panded power of the state as unambiguously good ...The fact is that the Progressive reformers were wrong in their basic assumptions." In May, 1980, attempting to explain why Senator Edward Kennedy "is simply out of his time," Henry Fairlie said "there seems at last to be an end to the belief in the ability of quick if not deep or penetrating minds--seducible or purchasable or both--to iden-tify real problems and their possible political

292

resolution." Then in December, 1984, following Senator Walter Mondale's defeat by President Reagan the month before, a New Republic editorial declared that "the old liberal confidences...now lie shattered...We will have to admit [that] there may be some problems that can't be solved, even with...a hefty bit of cash." "American liberalism," the editors said, "is in crisis."

NOTES

1. New Republic, June 30, 1920, p. 139; Hubert H. Humphrey, The Cause is Mankind (New York: MacFadden Books, 1965), p. 21.

2. Lester Ward, Lester Ward and the Welfare State, Henry Steele Commager, ed. (Indianapolis: The Bobbs-Merrill Company, Inc., 1967), p. 368.

3. New Republic, July 28, 1973, p. 32.

4. Harry Elmer Barnes, ed., The History and Prospects of the Social Sciences (New York: Alfred A. Knopf, 1925), p. 185.

5. New Republic, November 4, 1957, pp. 12, 14.

6. New Republic, December 5, 1949, p. 11.

7. New Republic, January 30, 1915, pp. 16-18; New Republic, December 23, 1931, p. 151.

8. Louis A. Zurcher, Jr., and Charles M. Bonjean, ed.s, Planned Social Intervention (London: Chandler Publishing Company, 1970), p. 14.

9. New Republic, December 25, 1971, p. 22 (Senator Mondale is quoted by Robert Coles).

10. Edward C. Banfield, The Unheavenly City (Boston: Little, Brown and Company, 1970), p. 20.

11. L. L. Bernard and Jessie Bernard, Origins of American Sociology (New York: Thomas Y. Crowell,

1943), p. 807.

12. Zurcher and Bonjean, Planned Social Intervention, p. 43.

13. Jacob Oser, The Evolution of Economic Thought (New York: Harcourt, Brace & World, Inc., 2nd ed., 1970), pp. 298, 299; Heinz Kohler, Welfare and Planning: An Analysis of Capitalism Versus Socialism (New York: John Wiley & Sons, Inc., 1966), p. 106.

14. Zurcher and Bonjean, Planned Social Intervention, p. 27.

15. New Republic, June 18, 1918, p. 168; New Republic, June 2, 1926, p. 48; New Republic, March 4, 1931, p. 62.

16. New Republic, March 11, 1931, p. 104.

17. New Republic, July 29, 1931, p. 276.

18. New Republic, July 19, 1933, p. 258; New Republic, July 5, 1939, p. 257.

19. New Republic, April 8, 1957, p. 15.

20. New Republic, January 29, 1977, p. 36; New Republic, March 12, 1962, p. 30.

21. New Republic, February 24, 1968, p. 37; New Republic, March 8, 1975, p. 23.

22. New Republic, June 2, 1968, p. 27.

23. Jerry Rubin, Do It! (New York: Simon and Schuster, 1970), p. 213.

24. Theodore Roszak, Where the Wasteland Ends (Garden City: Doubleday & Company, Inc., 1972), pp. xxv, 37, 73, 414, 425, 428.

25. New Republic, December 20, 1969, p. 21.

26. New Republic, April 19, 1969, p. 30.

27. New Republic, December 13, 1922, p. 75; Stanislav Andreski, Social Sciences as Sorcery (London: Andre Deutsch Limited, 1972), p. 11.

28. Irving Kristol, Two Cheers for Capitalism (New York: Mentor Book, 1978), p. 202.

29. New Republic, January 2, 1915, p. 9; New Republic, August 28, 1915, p. 108.

30. New Republic, April 3, 1915, p. 229.

31. New Republic, October 13, 1917, pp. 298-300.

32. New Republic, January 1, 1966, p. 10; Alex Haley and Malcolm X, The Autobiography of Malcolm X (New York: Grove Press, 1965), pp. 21, 22.

33. New Republic, January 30, 1915, p. 6.

34. New Republic, July 17, 1915, pp. 269, 270.

35. Eric F. Goldman, The Tragedy of Lyndon Johnson (New York: Dell Publishing Co., Inc., 1969), p. 341.

36. New Republic, January 29, 1930, p. 267; New Republic, June 12, 1935, p. 117; Charles Forcey, The Crossroads of Liberalism (New York: Oxford University Press, 1961), p. 33; Oser, Evolution of Economic Thought, p. 37.

37. Walter W. Heller, New Dimensions of Political Economy (New York: W. W. Norton & Company, Inc., 1967), p. 123.

38. Humphrey, The Cause is Mankind, p. 40.

39. Thomas P. Collins and Louis M. Savary, ed.s, A People of Compassion: The Concerns of Edward Kennedy (New York: The Regina Press, 1972), p. 82.

40. New Republic, October 31, 1964, p. 12.

41. New Republic, January 1, 1966, p. 19.

42. New Republic, January 9, 1915, p. 8.

43. Howard Zinn, New Deal Thought (Indianapolis: The Bobbs-Merrill Company, Inc., 1966), p. 359; Robert M. LaFollette, LaFollette's Autobiography (Madison: The University of Wisconsin Press, 1968), p. 53; New Republic, January 30, 1935, p. 319.

44. New Republic, March 16, 1968, p. 25.

45. New Republic, January 18, 1969, p. 20; New Republic, July 18, 1970, p. 8; New Republic, January 1, 1972, p. 6; New Republic, June 29, 1974, p. 6.

46. New Republic, January 20, 1979, p. 13; New Republic, March 8, 1980, pp. 36-37; New Republic, May 31, 1980, pp. 18, 19; New Republic, December 10, 1984, p. 12; New Republic, December 10, 1984, p. 9.

12

THE NEW LEFT I

A storm of considerable violence swept over American life in the second half of the 1960's and the first years of the Seventies. For those within the alienated Left, it was a thrillingly exhilarating time of uninhibited militancy and mass support that for most ended in fragmentation, exhaustion and despair. For many liberals, less militant, it began hopefully as the expression of several good causes, but became a time of soul searching and anguish that left most of the old certainties profoundly shaken.

For Americans of conservative values, it was a frightening time, a time during which a chasm seemed to open up to reveal all of the barbarism that lurks so close to the surface even in advanced civilization. It was a time of the unthinkable, and of general complicity in the unthinkable. They came to see how tenuous was the hold that the American people of the mid-20th century, shallowly rooted and lacking in an intellectual culture appropriate to a free society, had upon fundamental values. The threat to those values no longer came so much from the ever-expanding power of government as from cultural solvents that dissolved the bonds of loyalty and trust that hold a free society together. To such Americans, it was a scarring time, one that left nothing, ever again, quite as it was before.

This was a decade during which paradoxically, in a high tide of moral catharsis, millions joined hands communally to damn everyone else and the society as a whole. The movie "Network" told it all: millions throwing open their windows and shouting, in unison with all the others, "I'm madder than hell, and I won't take it any more."

Three different but intertwined revolutions

297

were raging at once: what we might for convenience call the Red, the Black and the Green. A resurgent radicalism from the far Left made up the Red; the splintering factions of the Civil Rights movement made up the Black; and the Green was formed of the startling mixture of moralism, ascetic renunciation, hedonism and anarcho-communism that made up the "counter-culture."

From the description I have given, it might be thought that this great spasm was just an American phenomenon. To think so would be a serious mistake. The Red and the Green revolutions can hardly be understood without an appreciation of their continuity with forces that had long been at work within the world Left and of the corresponding movements that were occurring contemporaneously in Western Europe and the Third World. The term "New Left" is sometimes used to refer only to what I am calling the "Red" revolution, but both it and the counter-culture of the Green revolution constituted together a major resurgence of alienation from the far Left as it existed in the years immediately following the death and disgrace of Stalin.

We can fit the pieces together from the elements that have already been relevant to our discussion of American liberalism. The revolutionary ferment during these years was not something _sui generis_. It was one of the manifestations of the complex mixture that we must fathom if we are to "understand the modern predicament."

We have seen how for a century and a half the world intellectual culture had stood outside the predominant commercial, bourgeois civilization. Intellectuals who supported the _ancien regime_ formulated an elaborate philosophical defense of medieval values and set them off against the "Philistine" civilization that had supplanted the old order. Other intellectuals used the same revulsion to create the world Left. As an alienated sub-culture, the intelligentsia then sought allies among all disaffected or unassimilated groups. Socialist projects of many kinds, fragmented but united in their bitter hatred of "bourgeois" civilization, came into being. The Romantic movement itself gave rise to an atavistic renunciation of Reason and of modernity, and contributed immensely to the illiberal clamor that Julien Benda described so well in his <u>Les Trahison des les Clercs</u>. These were the forces that pulsed out of Europe, half-overwhelming the classical liberal vision that had itself led, and continued to offer, a revolution in favor of democracy and individual freedom.

These gigantic forces provide the backdrop for what I call the "inherent presence" of both the radical Left and the counter-culture (itself a part of the radical Left) within all advanced Western societies during the 19th and 20th centuries. If ever it has seemed that they have been absent, the absence has been an illusion, a failure to see what at times is a quiescent core of alienation, militancy and withdrawal. That core will remain present until the alienation of intellectuals withers and ceases to be a major fact in our culture--an event so momentous that we will rightly be able to say that we will have passed into a new period of history.

An appropriate but inherently unfavorable analogy comes to mind. Those who favor the Left won't like it; others will find it graphically descriptive. It has to do with the similarity between this "inherent presence" of radical militance and of the counter-culture to the herpes virus, which never leaves the host individual, but lives unnoticed at the juncture of a nerve and the spinal cord until, under the right circumstances created by weakened body resistance or some other catalyst, the virus moves down the nerve to erupt violently upon the surface of the skin. During periods when the sores are not in evidence, it is a mistake to think the virus is gone. It has simply retreated up the nerve to the spinal cord.

This movement of attack and withdrawal is itself analogous to something I have referred to as part of the psychology of the American Left, including modern liberalism. There is an alternation that consists of a period of yearning-for-activity, followed by one of intense movement and agitation, which in turn is followed by a time of disillusionment, fatigue and withdrawal.

We have seen how this cycle has repeated itself through a century and a half of American alienation, reflecting the psychology of the intellectual. If we treat the yearning as the beginning of a cycle, we can say that the American Left ran through an entire cycle between the years 1956 and 1975.

There is perhaps no better example of the yearning with which it began than the passages that Arthur Schlesinger, Jr., wrote in The New Republic in June and July, 1956. In June, he said that "I feel that an injection of anarcho-syndicalist revolt--dissent for dissent's sake--would ...be enormously helpful in our increasingly homogenized culture. The attack against the Establishment has been going on for some time in Britain. We have our own Establishment, and it needs to be attacked too." Then in July he added that "of the varieties of intellectuals, the sort America most needs at this moment is precisely the opposite of Time's Man of Affirmation...One begins to feel that in the cloying atmosphere of 1956 any assertion of individuality, no matter how crude or vulgar, tends to be liberating...We need more people who don't give a damn and can awaken responses in us." [1]

It is improbable that Schlesinger could even remotely foretell how "crude and vulgar" the militancy of the 1960's would become, but we can see in his statements--in 1956!--the deep psychological impulse that moved the Left toward its great spasm of activity, both in the form of a renewal of a radical critique and of the counter-culture. It is especially significant that this yearning-for-activity was voiced by a leading liberal, not

300

simply by someone who had long been a part of the far Left.

We can infer still another important fact from Schlesinger's 1956 statements. It is that the spasm was not itself a product of the "catalysts"--the confrontations of the Civil Rights movement, the movement against the Vietnam War, the concern over the "environment"--to which it is so often ascribed. From Schlesinger's comments and from other evidence that we will review, we will see that the movement was well under way within the world Left, and in the United States, before those catalysts came on the scene. What the catalysts did do was eventually to provide vehicles for mass support. They lent "warm bodies" to a force that found its core in the alternating cycle through which the alienated intellectual culture was passing.

"Inherent presence": the radical Left

One of the oddest statements I have seen by a serious thinker is Michael Harrington's observation in 1969 that "this radical generation is virgin-born and has no ideological parents." Although it is true that many of the militants of the New Left were not well read, in countless ways they were the inheritors of the preceding century-and-a-half's legacy of alienation and socialism.[2]

According to Malcolm Cowley in 1977, "several leaders of campus rebellions were the sons or daughters of old-time radicals." Irving Howe informs us that during the 1950's "those who left the [Communist] party or its supporting organizations because they feared government attack were often people who kept, semi-privately, their earlier convictions." He tells how the catalysts called them back to activity: "As soon as some ferment began in the civil rights movement and the peace groups, these people were present, ready and eager."[3]

301

It is no coincidence that the rhetoric of the Henry Wallace third-party presidential campaign in 1948 had the same tone and content as the New Left's rhetoric a decade later. We recall how deep the generalized distrust was that the New Left created toward American institutions. Here is what Vincent Sheean reported in November, 1948: "It is in the radical tradition...to charge venality...But the Wallace campaign has generalized the technique into a wholesale insemination of distrust which...would make our processes of government invariably suspect to a considerable minority of our young people." It is a fair inference that this "considerable minority" played no small role in the New Left, which, after all, began to emerge within less than a decade after the Wallace campaign. One such person was Staughton Lynd, who according to Jack Newfield went from being "a national youth leader in the Henry Wallace campaign of 1948" to someone "whom The New York Times Magazine correctly termed 'elder statesman and doyen theoretician of the new Left.'"4

The core of radical thinkers who in the late 1950's germinated the American New Left were, in fact, already active together in the mid-1940's. Dwight MacDonald, who was still around to sign a 1930's-style Manifesto supporting the "Chicago Eight" after the violent confrontation between the Yippies and the Chicago police at the time of the 1968 Democratic convention, started the radical journal Politics in 1944. C. Wright Mills and Paul Goodman, the two who were most prominent in creating the American New Left in the second half of the Fifties, were among the first to contribute articles to MacDonald's journal.5

One of the leading hotspots of New Left activity in the 1960's was at the university at Berkeley. For most Americans, those events erupted, as it were, from a vacuum. But here is what Andrew Kopkind told the readers of The New Republic in 1966: "For ten years a loose community of radicals has been growing in the San Francisco Bay area... Starting with the remnants of the old base carved

302

out by Jack London, then by Harry Bridges and the
Longshoreman's Union, the newer radicals began
their careers demonstrating against the Un-American Activities Committee, then the Caryl Chessman
protest and the formation of a student political
organization called SLATE at Berkeley in 1957; the
civil rights sit-ins in San Francisco followed,
then the Free Speech Movement, and the VDC" (the
Vietnam Day Committee). 6

     The anti-Vietnam War movement during the
1960's had important antecedents in the radical
"peace movement" that had been militant during the
1930's and 1940's. One part of the "peace movement" had long been from the radical Left; another
part had consisted of the various "peace churches"
(which, even though they should be carefully distinguished from the Left as such, have often
reacted to the Cold War environment since World
War II by identifying closely with the radical
Left in its defense of revolutionary movements in
such places as El Salvador and Nicaragua).

     Before World War I, European and American
socialists had made "peace" a major part of their
program, based on their thinking that the proletariat's interests were international and that pro-
letarians would have no reason to fight on anyone's side in what would necessarily be a struggle
among governments representing the bourgeoisie.

     During the interregnum between the world
wars, leftist thought was heavily "neutralist." It
remained so until events in the second half of the
1930's dragged most leftists into the conflict
with Hitler. In his book Rebels Against War: The
American Peace Movement, 1941-1960, Lawrence S.
Wittner says that in 1935 60,000 college students
took part "in a 'strike' against war." Many of
them took the "Oxford oath," which swore an "absolute refusal to serve in the armed forces." (The
taking of this oath reminds us that there was a
comparable radical peace movement in England,
showing, as so many things do, the international
flavor of these movements.) 7

Some of those who were most closely identified with the "peace movement" never did support
the war against Hitler. David Dellinger, later a
leading activist within the New Left and one of
the Chicago Eight defendants in 1968, remained a
committed pacifist even during World War II.
Wittner says that in 1943 "in the Newark slums an
ex-divinity student and Socialist, Dave Dellinger,
and a handful of other revolutionary pacifists
organized the People's Peace Now Committee to
press for an immediate end to the war."8

Thousands of Conscientious Objectors were in-
carcerated in camps and prisons during World War
II. According to Wittner, "prison life provided a
vital fund of experience that pacifists drew upon
in postwar struggles," especially in developing
"non-violent methods of protest." Wittner says
"the steam went out of radical pacifism" between
1948 and 1956, but that "a small band of isolated
pacifists" spent those years formulating theory:
they "subjected America's role in the international power struggle to a critical reexamina-
tion."9

Then in 1956 the journal _Liberation_ was
founded "by a small group of radical pacifists."
It articulated several themes that were to become
important to the New Left: "utopianism, anarchism,
non-violent revolution, civil rights, the Third
Camp, and...peace." Wittner says that "beginning
in 1957 the American peace movement underwent a
revival." In 1963, an advertisement for _Libera-
tion_ claimed that the journal had been "the most
referred to spokesman for the nonviolent movement
in all its aspects--in civil rights, in the peace
movement, in labor." 10

All of this fed inexorably into the anti-
Vietnam War movement when it began in the mid-
1960's. So that we appreciate the continuity, we
should notice that in 1963, which was before America's involvement in the Vietnam War had heated
up, an advertisement in _The New Republic_ for the
War Resisters League included the circular "peace

symbol" that became so well known to Americans later in the decade. Another <u>New Republic</u> advertisement, this time for S.D.S. (Students for a Democratic Society), which was arguably the central New Left organization, said in 1965 that the S.D.S. was working to "create an independent, radical peace movement."11

Thus far, I have told enough to suggest the continuity that existed between American radicalism in the 1930's and 1940's and the later beginnings of the New Left. Considerably more detail could be given, but my purpose is to explain the continuity of the ideas rather than to become encyclopedic about the people and events.

Another dimension providing continuity with the world Left was the international one. Some of the important aspects of this dimension will become apparent when in the next section we review the "inherent presence" of a counter-culture within Western radicalism.

Other vitally important international linkages arose from the trends that emerged within the Left after World War II. In 1956, Nikita Krushchev denounced Stalin in his famous "secret address" to the 20th Soviet Party Congress. This was combined with the repression of the "Polish October" in 1956 and with the crushing of the Hungarian Revolution by Soviet tanks in late 1956. For many, these events sealed the long decline of Soviet influence within the world intellectual movement. As we have seen, there had been many earlier shocks: the purge trials; the persecution and murder of Trotsky; the Hitler-Stalin Pact; the Soviet aggressions against Poland, Finland, Latvia, Estonia and Lithuania; the Lysenko affair; and the development under Tito of a form of Communism that was not totally dominated by the Soviet Union. The split between the U.S.S.R. and Communist China was to provide another.

Although the U.S.S.R. remained a continuing source of orthodox Marxism-Leninism (except perhaps in the eyes of the Chinese), these events splintered Marxist thinking in the West. One of the important effects was the rise of what has become known as "humanistic Marxism." Signs of it began in the late 1930's. It stresses Marx's early writings and focuses on such concepts as "reification" and the "alienation" of the worker from his work. This brand of Marxism was given a boost by Erich Fromm when he republished Marx's early essays in 1961. It has been a significant part of Western Marxist thought during the 1970's and 1980's.

More important to the New Left, however, was the rise of charismatic, Romantic revolutionaries in the Third World. Although these figures--such as Fidel, Che, Mao and Ho--were mostly tied to the Soviet Union, they appeared energetic, untainted and fresh. It was from their inspiration that, as Mark Rudd wrote in 1969, "we learned...the great truth stated by Chairman Mao Tse-Tung, 'Dare to struggle, dare to win.'" Irving Howe has concluded that "most of the 'new leftists' have identified...with the harder, more violent, more dictatorial segments of the Communist world."[12]

When the split occurred between Communist China and the Soviet Union, many revolutionaries in the Third World became associated with the Chinese, while others retained their tie with the Soviet Union. This became one of the sources of ideological fragmentation that contributed to the eventual collapse of the New Left.

C. Wright Mills was one of those who felt a strong affinity for the Soviet bloc. Irving Howe says that Mills travelled to Europe in 1957 and came back "impressed by the industrial achievements of the communist nations." Mills "wanted to see a new alignment of 'the left,' sort of an informal Popular Front that would include intellectuals who were to one or another extent sympathetic to the Communist bloc."[13]

The international origins of the New Left

thus reflected the continued vitality of the world Left after the Second World War despite all of the "shocks" that had rocked the earlier faith in the Soviet experiment. Even though the democratic socialist movements in Europe moved away from Marxism, this did not imply an evaporation of the radical Left.

"Inherent presence": Antecedents of the "counter-culture"

Another side of the Left has been the "counter-culture." By discussing it separately in order to show the many antecedents of the counter-culture of the 1960's, I do not mean to suggest that it has been something separate from the Left. The pre-World War I crowd in Greenwich Village, for example, was intensely committed to radical theory and action at the same time that it was wrapped up in a "culture of radicalism" that involved a lifestyle that was distinctly counter to "bourgeois" values.

Even though the committed theorist-activist and the denizens of the counter-culture have both been parts of the Left, and have sometimes even been the same people, there has been a long-standing tension between these two styles. The disciplined leftist often scorns what he sees as the dissipation of the energies of those who express their alienation by "opting out." If he is a Marxist of one kind or another, as virtually all are, he has a theory of revolutionary development that tells him what forces will be most conducive to success. This usually assigns no place to the mere bohemian.

Throughout history, there have been sub-cultures of withdrawal. As conditions worsened with the impending collapse of the Roman Empire, most ancient philosophies preached withdrawal as the way to escape. The asceticism of the early Christians provides many examples of individuals who renounced not only the existing civilization,

307

but worldly life itself. The doctrines of Augustine, which remained most influential within Christianity for eight centuries, preached withdrawal. Monastic life was a prominent part of the Middle Ages.

The stage was set for a similar pattern when in the early 19th century European thought moved sharply into a renunciation of modernity and of the existing culture. Theodore Roszak's New Leftist <u>Where</u> <u>the</u> <u>Wasteland</u> <u>Ends</u> is a foolish but extremely literate explanation of the tie that existed between this "revolt against Reason" and the counter-culture of the 1960's.

Not only did Romanticism give rise to an impulse toward withdrawal (which we will see manifested in the German Youth Movement when we discuss it next); it provided much of the intellectual rationale that was continued by the American counter-culture of the 1960's. An example is evident in what Leo Stein said about John Ruskin in 1919 on the 100th anniversary of Ruskin's birth. "He soon came to see," Stein said, "that the bitterest enemy to beauty in life was the factory system and the modern industrial organization." As Roszak said, "Romanticism is...a critical counterpoint to the imperial advance of science." He spoke of "their challenge to science and industrialism" and "their loathing for system, abstraction, routine, in their passion for free self-fulfillment." The sophisticated denunciations of modern life that came so freely to the lips of those within the "hippie culture" of the Sixties were not formulated out of thin air by nineteen and twenty year olds; they were ideas that had been articulated in a vast literature a century before. [14]

Some of the earliest manifestations of a counter-culture were the various "utopian communities" of the 19th century. But perhaps the first open counter-culture as we think of it was in Greenwich Village prior to World War I. Lewis Coser tells us that "young men and women...began flocking to Greenwich Village about 1910" with an "implied commitment to a lifestyle." "Bohemia," Coser says, "attempts to create countersymbols and a special and distinct culture of rebellion. The Village provided a refuge from middle class philistinism and permitted the widest experimentation in dress, sexual mores, and life styles generally...For a few years the Village embodied the full flowering of an intellectual, artistic, political, and emotional counterculture that gave sustenance and support to the assault against the dominant values of nineteenth-century America." 15

This continued during the years of disillusionment after World War I. William Harlan Hale told the readers of The New Republic in 1931 that "carried on the wave of post-war revolt in thought and morals, the students of the early twenties were the last word in radicalism...Everyone remembers...the baggy trousers, the collegiate semi-bohemianism." In 1923, H. M. Kallen had told of "rebellious youth," of which he said that it "has no alternative ideal to present. Its spirit is discontent; its cry: There is no good in the institutions of modern life." 16

In Exile's Return, Malcolm Cowley summarized the ideas that moved the counter-culture of the early 1920's. The similarity to the ideologically anarchic, hedonistic "flower children" of the 1960's is apparent: "...the system of ideas... could roughly be summarized as follows: 1. If... children are encouraged to...blossom freely like flowers, then the world will be saved by this new, free generation. 2. The idea of self-expression ...3. The idea of paganism.--The body is a temple ...to be adorned for the ritual of love...5. The idea of liberty.--Every law, convention or rule of art that prevents self-expression or the full enjoyment of the moment should be shattered and abolished...6. The idea of female equality." 17

This was the time of the "Lost Generation" and of the flight to Europe. The spirit of that time continued, for some, into the 1930's. A product of that continuation that was later to become important as a source of the New Left was Henry Miller's The Tropic of Cancer, published in 1934. Edmund Wilson said that this book was ignored by the activist radicals of the 1930's as representing "the decadent expatriate culture."[18]

In the late 1930's, as catastrophe after catastrophe shook the Left, Malcolm Cowley wrote that "I notice that many writers are drawing back--either into ultra-radical idleness or else into an assortment of mysticisms, cynicisms and revolutions of the pure word." George Soule reported a similar phenomenon in 1946.[19]

Thus we see that my phrase "inherent presence" is aptly applied to the counter-culture. At varying levels, anti-bourgeois withdrawal has been a permanent part of the Left in the 20th century. When later I describe the Beatniks of the 1950's and the Hippies of the 1960's, the description will not be of something startlingly new, but of an "ultra-radical idleness," to use Cowley's expression, that has been one of the principal styles of alienation.

An ominous forerunner: The German Youth Movement before and after World War I

I remember what an electric effect it had upon the national meeting of the Philadelphia Society in 1968 when a speaker read the following passage from Ludwig von Mises' Bureaucracy--which had been published in 1944! It was as though Mises had been describing the youth culture of the New Left. Mises' language makes his own revulsion clear, an attitude shared by the conservatives who heard the passage:

In the decade preceding the First World War Germany...witnessed the appearance of a phenomenon hitherto unheard of: the youth movement...In bombastic words they announced the gospel of a golden age. All preceding generations, they emphasized, were simply idiotic; their incapacity has converted the earth into a hell...Henceforth the brilliant youths will rule. They will destroy everything that is old and useless,...they will substitute new real and substantial values and ideologies for the antiquated and false ones of capitalist and bourgeois civilization ...We are the deadly foes of the rotten bourgeois and Philistines....

The chiefs of the youth movement were mentally unbalanced neurotics. Many of them were affected by a morbid sexuality, they were either profligate or homosexual...The only trace they left were some books and poems preaching sexual perversity.[20]

I have described the German Youth Movement in <u>Understanding the Modern Predicament</u>, and will repeat only enough here to lay the foundation for a comparison with the New Left. There are excellent books by Howard Becker and Walter Laqueur describing the Youth Movement in detail.

Here is some of the discussion from my earlier book: "The Movement's first phase was that of the <u>Wandervogel</u> between 1896 and 1919. The second was the Bund...which continued from 1919 until the Movement was absorbed into the Hitler Youth in 1933...Alienation from the bourgeoisie was the consistent thread. Laqueur says that 'the <u>Wandervogel</u> chose the other form of protest against society--romanticism. Their return to nature was romantic, as were their attempts to get away from a materialistic civilization, their stress on the simple life, their rediscovery of old folk songs'...Becker says...that 'German youth of Karl Fischer's day loathed and hated the world of their elders.' (I would, of course, have us ask how it happened that so many young people were suddenly independent philosophers having so great a sensibility to higher and finer values. Instead of reaching this subtle and extensive analysis themselves, they were no doubt picking up the entire body of values and social critique from the alienated intellectual generation that preceded them....)" 21

A difference between all of this and the later New Left was that the totalitarian ideologies that the Youth Movement's members proclaimed were drawn from a wide variety of left- and right-wing socialisms, whereas the New Left drew exclusively from the many factions of the far Left. We recall that in Germany after Hegel, movements of Leftwing Hegelians championed ideas of class struggle and that movements of Rightwing Hegelians championed ideas of racial struggle. Both were equally antithetical to the bourgeoisie and to liberalism in the classical sense. Both were in evidence in the German Youth Movement.

In 1969, Michael Miles reported in The New Republic that "cultural historians have compared it [the New Left] to the Russian nihilists; social historians compare it to the Nazi paramilitary organizations of the 1920s. 'There is, they say, the same obsession with direct action, the myth of violence, the revolutionary claims without substance.' This is a comparison that could also include the Youth Movement. (It is relevant that both Hitler and Mussolini's movements were initially youth movements, and shared the characteristics I have described.) 22

In a New Republic book review in 1970, David Bromwich argued that "to people who have known campus radicalism first hand the found parallels between Nazi youth and SDS enrages will be the least convincing part of the book." From this we see that the similarity is not agreed to by all. My own opinion, however, is that both the New Left and the German Youth Movement, with their respective counter-cultures, were the product of the same forces at work within modern Western civilization. If we "distinguish away" vital similarities, we refuse to learn from experience. 23

312

1. New Republic, June 4, 1956, p. 20; New Republic, July 16, 1956, p. 17.

2. New Republic, February 8, 1969, p. 30.

3. New Republic, August 20, 1977, p. 37; Irving Howe, Steady Work: Essays in the Politics of Democratic Radicalism, 1953-1966 (New York: Harcourt, Brace & World, Inc., 1966), p. 48.

4. New Republic, November 1, 1948, p. 19; Jack Newfield, A Prophetic Minority (New York: The New American Library, Inc., 1966), pp. 194, 195.

5. New Republic, August 9, 1969, p. 5; Lawrence S. Wittner, Rebels Against War: The American Peace Movement, 1941-1960 (New York: Columbia University Press, 1969), p. 94.

6. New Republic, June 4, 1966, p. 17.

7. Wittner, Rebels Against War, p. 7.

8. Wittner, Rebels Against War, p. 56.

9. Wittner, Rebels Against War, pp. 92, 228.

10. Wittner, Rebels Against War, pp. 237, 240; New Republic, August 31, 1963, p. 36.

11. New Republic, September 28, 1963, p. 22; New Republic, October 30, 1965, p. 2.

12. Carl Oglesby, ed., The New Left Reader (New York: Grove Press, Inc., 1969), p. 312; Irving Howe, Steady Work, p. 73.

13. Irving Howe, Steady Work, p. 247.

14. New Republic, February 8, 1919, p. 52; Theodore Roszak, Where the Wasteland Ends (Garden City: Doubleday & Company, Inc., 1972), pp. 278-9.

15. Lewis A. Coser, Men of Ideas: A Sociologist's View (New York: The Free Press, 1965), pp. 111, 113.

16. New Republic, May 13, 1951, p. 348; New Republic, January 10, 1923, p. 168.

17. Malcolm Cowley, Exile's Return (New York: W. W. Norton & Company, Inc., 1934), pp. 69-70.

18. New Republic, March 9, 1938, p. 140.

19. New Republic, November 9, 1938, p. 23; New Republic, August 5, 1946, p. 146.

20. Ludwig von Mises, Bureaucracy (New Haven: Yale University Press, 1946), pp. 94-5.

21. Howard Becker, German Youth: Bond or Free (New York: Oxford University Press, 1946); Walter Z. Laqueur, Young Germany (New York: Basic Books Publishing Co., Inc., 1962); for my quotations from my earlier discussion, see Dwight D. Murphey, Understanding the Modern Predicament (Washington: University Press of America, 1982), Chapter 16.

22. New Republic, April 12, 1969, p. 17.

23. New Republic, September 26, 1970, p. 26.

13

THE NEW LEFT II

The Green revolution: the counter-culture

On November 16, 1952, *Time* magazine carried an article "This is the Beat Generation," describing the forerunners of what would become known as the Beats or Beatniks. Jack Newfield later told of "an underground subsociety that developed about 1953, was mythicized by the Beat novelists and poets, and quickly spawned colonies."[1]

It has been said that the "Beats" did not take on a distinct identity until after the appearance of Jack Kerouac's novel On the Road, which is referred to as "the Bible of the Beat Generation." Its considerable influence should not be taken as a sign of any particular merit--to someone outside its ethos it is a rather undistinguished telling of the story of a drifter; but the extent of its influence does point to the receptivity in the 1950's of a certain type of literary individual who was ready, as so many had been in the past, to respond to a message of withdrawal.[2]

Despite the importance that is assigned to Kerouac, we should augment this with an understanding that the movement was international in scope and reflected the contributions of several authors and influences. In what follows, we will simultaneously discuss Beat culture and these sources.

In his The Beat Generation, Bruce Cook has described contributions by William Carlos Williams, Gary Snyder, Allen Ginsberg, John Clellon Holmes, Kenneth Rexroth, Diane diPrima (who he says wrote a "scandalous, semipornographic little book, Memoirs of a Beatnik"), Gregory Corso, and William S. Burroughs.

Jack Newfield has said that "the Beat Generation was partly a small literary faction... Kerouac, who according to critic Seymour Krim 'single-handedly created the Beat Generation,' was the leader. The more gifted followers included Allen Ginsberg, the Jewish-radical-mystical-homosexual from Paterson, New Jersey." Newfield describes "the Beats' mysticism, anarchy, anti-intellectualism, sexual and drug experimentation, hostility to middle-class values, and idealization of the Negro and of voluntary poverty."[3]

One of the more famous works within the movement was Ginsberg's poem Howl. Bruce Cook informs us that it was "written during a long weekend spent in his room under the influence of various drugs--peyote for visions, amphetamine to speed up, and dexedrine to keep going." He tells us that Ginsberg's mother had emigrated from Russia and "became involved in radical politics and eventually a member of the Communist party." Cook calls Ginsberg "the Beat Generation's Walt Whitman."[4]

The reference to Ginsberg's mother simply reenforces our awareness of the tie that all of this had to earlier radicalism. Cook interviewed Gary Snyder, and quoted him as saying: "Formative influences?...well, that's kind of funny. I guess my grandfather, the one up in Washington, was pretty important. He was a Wobbly, dues-paying member of the Industrial Workers of the World ...The old I.W.W. mythology became very important to me as I grew up in the Northwest."[5]

When he interviewed Kenneth Rexroth, Cook "asked if he felt the western radical tradition was important to the development of the Beat thing...'Oh, sure. No doubt about it. It goes back to Jack London and the I.W.W....there was a lot of native radical feeling out here...good old-fashioned anarchist-pacifist...There were a lot of things happening back then...for instance, all the Conscientious Objectors...San Francisco was within hitchhiking distance of half the C.O. camps in

America." [6]

Cook considers it "an accident of time" that a movement similar to the Beats was occurring in England, which he describes as "a group of young English writers—which their press had dubbed the Angry Young Men." He sees no real relation between these and the Beats. He also gives short shrift to the fact that, as he says, "there were Dutch Beats, Turkish Beats, French Beats, and German Beats." But I consider Cook's conclusion a serious mistake; these phenomena were by no means disassociated, especially if we see them as part of a common heritage of anti-bourgeois alienation. Referring in 1959 to "today's 'lost generation' in England," Edmund Wilson was right, it seems to me, when he said that "our 'beat' generation here more or less corresponds to them. These anti-social writers are typical of the world in its present state." [7]

We see the ideological similarity from Wilson's comment that "the appearance of this phrase 'the Establishment' in England is very significant." Oddly, he added that "I don't think that in this country we could talk about anything equivalent." It wasn't long before reference to "the Establishment" was a standard part of the New Left's rhetoric in the United States. [8]

Wilson then spoke of "Jean Genet, the French writer, who carries the anti-social attitude farther than any of the rest." It would be a serious mistake to overlook the contribution of alienated French authors, especially Genet and Camus.

The French philosopher Jean Paul Sartre believed Genet's "masterpiece" to be "Our Lady of the Flowers." Stanley Kauffmann would later look back and call Genet "a genius of homosexuality, who has also been a prostitute and a professional criminal (ten convictions for theft)." Robert Brustein said of Genet that his "most important ideological influence, aside from de Sade, is the tradition of French pornography." "For Genet...

317

all functions are the manufacture of fakery and sham, and the artifice of the brothel is identical with the make-believe of the world. If the whorehouse is a mirror of society, society, in turn, reflects the whorehouse." To this, Victor Lange has added that Sartre valued Genet's work because "he regards his notorious life of crime and homosexuality as a significant and entirely legitimate form of anti-bourgeois action."9

As the counter-culture continued to develop in this country, Paul Goodman was another of the leading influences. (I will mention C. Wright Mills in another connection.) His works included <u>Growing Up Absurd</u>, consisting of articles that he authored between 1956 and 1960, and his later <u>Utopian Essays</u> and <u>Seeds of Liberation</u>. In <u>Growing Up Absurd</u>, Goodman wrote that "the Beat Generation has contrived a pattern of culture that [turns] against the standard culture." He said that "characteristics of the present-day poor are essential in Beat culture. As, contrariwise, are the organizational characteristics of being hip and convinced that society is a Rat Race. But finally, there are essential traits...[that comprise] the essential morality...One striking trait is nonconformism and tolerance in sexual and racial questions and behavior." Speaking of the Beats' language, he said that "the paucity of its vocabulary and syntax is for the Beats essentially expressive of withdrawal from the standard civilization and its learning." He went on to say that "they have the theory that to be affectless, not to care, is the ultimate rebellion."10

As we proceed into the 1960's, there was so much writing of this sort that it becomes arbitrary to select just a few for comment. With that qualification in mind, I will nevertheless point to Joseph Heller's <u>Catch 22</u>, about which Robert Brustein wrote in a review in 1961 that "through the agency of grotesque comedy, Heller has found a way to confront the humbug, hypocrisy, cruelty, and sheer stupidity of mass society." Brustein said the book "is one of those sublime expressions

318

of anarchic individualism...Heller has come upon a new morality based on an old ideal, the morality of refusal."[11]

A vast literature developed over the ensuing fifteen years. The literature that was primarily oriented toward the counter-culture came to include such works as Theodore Roszak's The Making of the Counter-culture and Where the Wasteland Ends; Ken Kesey's Sometimes a Great Notion; Charles Reich's The Greening of America; Norman Mailer's The White Negro; Abbie Hoffman's Revolution for the Hell of It; Norman O. Brown's Life Against Death and Love's Body; Anthony Burgess' A Clockwork Orange; and Timothy Leary's High Priest and The Politics of Ecstasy. Among the journals, The Realist is generally considered to have been the most representative counter-cultural vehicle. There were hundreds, if not thousands, of "underground" newspapers and journals.

The ideology of the Red revolution

The denizens of the Left take seriously the differences that for a century and a half have raged within the Left over such matters as method, ultimate social model, historical rationale, and which coalitions to form. To those involved in the New Left, the distinction between what can be described as the "soft" or "Green" Left of the counter-culture and the "hard" or "Red" Left of those who preferred greater discipline and organization seemed very real. Anyone who is not "of the Left," however, will be justified in seeing these as intramural disputes among people whose ideas and emotions were in most respects similar. Even though I am separating "the ideology of the Red revolution" into a different section from the counter-culture, the reader should not conclude that the two were sharply different in their thinking.[12]

Although I would have us keep in mind the common ground that existed among these factions, a

319

student of the subject needs to know that there were a number of specific viewpoints. There was no universally recognized version of "New Left" thought. I will not attempt a review of the versions put forward by the many factions, since the fine details of the doctrinal disputes on the Left are not important to the analysis I am making. A good reference for such a review is Kenneth and Patricia Dolbeare's American Ideologies.

Newfield says that in the late 1950's "a New Left began slowly to take root, nourished by the pacifist and socialist British New Left of the Aldermaston marches and the New Left Review; by the Beasts' private disaffection from and rage at the Rat Race; by the Cuban revolution; and by the writings of such men as C. Wright Mills, Albert Camus, and Paul Goodman." Peter Clecak, in his Radical Paradoxes: Dilemmas of the American Left, 1945-1970, attributed the New Left's thinking to four "plain Marxists"--C. Wright Mills, Paul Baran, Paul Sweezy and Herbert Marcuse.[13]

In early 1958, Frederick L. Schuman reported in The New Republic that "C. Wright Mills sees the U.S. and the U.S.S.R. as both 'overdeveloped' and 'superior' nations dedicated to 'technological prowess' and the blind worship of 'the science Machine." This was one of the first references to Mills in that journal. Mills' famous "Letter to the New Left" appeared in England's New Left Review (which had begun publication in January, 1960) in the fall of 1960. The importance of Mills to the New Left was underscored by Ronald Berman in 1968 when he wrote that "Mills' 'On the New Left,'...on the subject of ideology at least, has become the Das Kapital of the present radicalism." Mills was the sociologist who more than any other writer gave form to the New Left's attack on the Establishment as involving a "military-industrial-(and political)" triad.[14]

Phillip Abbott Luce, who was one of the leaders of the Chinese-oriented Progressive Labor faction of the New Left until his break from it in February, 1965, wrote that "by the fall of 1958...most of the young radicals that I knew were searching for a program of initiating a New Left in America." He pointed to the beginning of the Marxist journal Studies on the Left in 1959 as having "expressed the views of the emerging New Left." He has added that C. Wright Mills was "one of the first American political mentors of the new era." 15

I earlier quoted Arthur Schlesinger, Jr.'s, statements--penned in 1956!--expressing his yearning for a new radical movement. In my reading of The New Republic, I found that the first statement of a comprehensive New Left position in that journal appeared in the issue of October 20, 1958. Philip Green showed the new passion there when he spoke of the "stirrings of critical thought" about "the ugly botch we call our 'way of life.'" He denounced "the damned Organization...the system," and said that "our society...is materialistic, technology-worshipping...Our vaunted stability is composed partly of war preparedness, and partly of anti-social waste...[The] citizenry is becoming progressively unenlightened, an object of cynical manipulation...."16

It is important to focus on these early statements because they show us, as I have commented before, that the alienation and ideology of the New Left came into existence well before America's involvement in the Vietnam War and even before the radicalization that occurred through the confrontations of the Civil Rights movement. Only the mass support was added later.

These developments are consistent with the opinion expressed by Irving Howe that it was not the new "humanistic Marxism"--which was burgeoning in eastern Europe and among some intellectuals in the West--that mainly influenced the New Left's Red revolution. I earlier quoted Howe's comment that "most of the 'new leftists "have identified ...with the harder, more violent, more dictatorial

321

segments of the Communist world." Thus, in 1966 Christopher Lasch could say that "the New Left in general more and more identifies itself with Castro, Guevara, Regis Debray, and Ho Chi Minh." And he pointed out that the "black power" ideology, which spearheaded the more militant part of the Black revolution, had come to represent more than just "a revival of Afro-American nationalism," transcending issues based solely on race to become a part of the "romantic anarchism" of the New Left. [17]

This is reflected in The New Left Reader, which was published by the Grove Press in 1969 and consisted of articles going back to 1958. Included were pieces by C. Wright Mills, Herbert Marcuse, Frantz Fanon, Fidel Castro, Malcolm X, Huey Newton, Rudi Dutschke, Daniel and Gabriel Cohn-Bendit, and Mark Rudd. Such a compilation shows not only the "hard" nature of the leftism involved; it also shows the international nature of the "Red" side of the New Left. This corresponds to the international dimensions of the counter-culture, which I discussed earlier. Dutschke was a leader of the German New Left; the Cohn-Bendits, one of whom was "Danny the Red," were part of the French; and Frantz Fanon focused on the example of the Algerian revolution.

Herbert Marcuse was a professor of philosophy at the University of California in San Diego. His thinking was heavily steeped in Marxism, although there was also a substantial admixture of Bakunin, Rousseau and Fourier. Orthodox Communists denounced him as "petit-bourgeois" and considered him a "revisionist." Marcuse has been referred to as the intellectual mentor of Angela Davis. [18]

The thesis of Marcuse's book One Dimensional Man is that modern industrial, capitalist civilization is suffocating the human potential by obliterating values that are not part of its system. In An Essay on Liberation, Marcuse argued that modern society has lost touch with the original, socialist nature of man. (Here we see Rousseau's very considerable shadow.) He argued that the workers within capitalism, who traditionally have been the principal revolutionary hope for orthodox Marxists, have been lulled to sleep by a manipulative affluence. "The masses themselves are forces of conservatism and stabilization." Since they would no longer be the source of an anti-capitalist revolution, he looked hopefully to "the young middle-class intelligentsia" and to "the ghetto populations" as catalysts for revolution among a newly sensitized majority. "The political consciousness exists among the nonconformist young intelligentsia; and the vital need for change is the very life of the ghetto population." He saw that "at present in the United States, the black population appears as the 'most natural' force of rebellion." "The Cuban revolution and the Viet Cong have demonstrated: it can be done; there is a morality, a humanity, a will, and a faith which can resist...capitalist expansion."[19]

Although Marcuse saw great value in the counter-culture's reorientation of consciousness, he was no friend to "the wild ones and the noncommitted, the escapists...." It is because of this that I am discussing him as having been on the Red, not the Green, side of the New Left.[20]

The revolutionary nature of his message is clear from what I have just quoted. His totalitarian nature was especially evident in his essay "Repressive Tolerance." He argued that the very "tolerance" that democratic society encourages has been one of the manipulative factors that have lulled the masses to sleep. He called for a "liberating tolerance" that would encourage all views from the Left and suppress all conservative views. "Liberating tolerance would mean intolerance against movements from the Right, and toleration of movements from the Left."[21]

Despite Marcuse's affinity for the Fidel Castro's and Ho Chi Minh's of the Soviet bloc, there were certain elements in his thinking that

justified placing him within a "new" Left. He
could speak in post-Stalinist terms of "the
repressive Stalinist development of socialism."
And he could say that "the new radicalism
militates against the centralized bureaucratic
communist as well as against the semi-democratic
liberal organization. There is a strong element
of spontaneity, even anarchism, in this rebellion
...Therefore the aversion against preestablished
Leaders, apparatchiks of all sorts, politicians no
matter how leftist." [22]

Nevertheless, the word "new" was appropriate
only to those whose memories were short. The
revival of "romantic anarchism" was in most ways a
harking back to the wilder varieties of 19th
century socialist thought. When at last the
Soviet Union had lost its role as the focus for
emulation, Bakunin and Fourier stood ready to fill
the void.

A time of intense activity

I will not attempt an exhaustive review of
the events of the 1960's, but will give only
enough of the detail, drawn primarily from my
notes from The New Republic, to paint a picture of
those tumultuous years and to highlight any
important observations about the content:

  . In August, 1960, an article by David Eva-
nier spoke of "the sit-ins of the Negro students
in the South, followed by the heroic demonstrations against the Un-American Activities Committee
in San Francisco."[23]

  . Advertisements appeared in The New
Republic in November, 1960, for the S.D.S. journal
Venture; in April, 1962, for the "radical journal"
Studies on the Left; in September, 1963, for Lib-
eration; in January, 1964, for the counter-cul-
tural journal The Realist; and in July, 1964, for
The Psychedelic Review.

• Andrew Kopkind reported that the League for Industrial Democracy was sponsoring the Students for a Democratic Society (S.D.S.). "In the summer of 1962, the new SDS students met near Port Huron, Michigan, and approved a statement of ideas and principles. The 'Port Huron Statement' is the seminal document of the new left--or 'the movement.'" He told of the rapid spread of S.D.S. chapters and the beginning, in early 1964, of "SDS projects in a number of Northern cities" to organize among poor whites. Tom Hayden had drafted the Port Huron Statement, and then became an organizer in Newark. In April, 1965, the S.D.S. sponsored the "March on Washington to End the War in Vietnam." 24

• In July, 1963, Reese Cleghorn wrote that "today the banner taken to jail [in connection with the Civil Rights movement] is usually that of the Student Non-Violent Coordinating Committee [SNCC]...born of the 1960 college student sit-ins, cut free by its young leaders' decision not to accept direction from older organizations or Dr. King...." Two years later, Andrew Kopkind described SNCC as "the most radical civil rights group...It is anarchic rather than monolithic." He reported that SNCC had no desire to work within the Democratic party, wishing rather "to demolish it." 25

• At the Democratic National Convention in August, 1964, the Mississippi Freedom Democrats demanding seating in place of the regular-party delegation, and then, in the words of Andrew Kopkind, "rejected a compromise that would have given them 'tokenism.'" Despite the Johnson administration's success in securing the enactment of civil rights legislation, the conflict at the 1964 convention was looked back upon later by black militants as indicating their inability to trust, and to work with, "white liberals."26

• In early 1965, an editorial told of the Berkeley sit-in that occurred in December, 1964, at which 800 students were arrested after occupy-

325

ing the administration building on the campus. In
an article, Robert Brustein said that "these two
revolutions--the Negro and Sexual (or Homosexual)
--are currently supplying the major dialogues of
our time." [It is a sign of the enormous variety
within this radical resurgence that I have not
previously seen fit to emphasize the "homosexual
revolution," as such.]27

. An editorial in April, 1965, reported that
"among styles of protest [the teach-in against the
war in Vietnam] is all the rage this month" on the
campuses at Michigan, Berkeley, and the like.28

. An advertisement in June, 1965, told about
Saul Alinsky's efforts to build "FIGHT, a militant
Negro organization," in Rochester. Alinsky was
the author of the 1946 book Reveille for Radicals,
which advocated organizing "conflict groups." "A
war," he had said, "is not an intellectual debate,
and in the war against social evils there are no
rules of fair play." James Ridgeway wrote in 1965
that "Alinsky would not be in Rochester were it
not for the Council of Churches...various denomi-
nations had put up the first part of a total of
$100,000...."29

. In December, 1965, Kopkind described the
November "March on Washington" by 30,000 anti-war
activists. "The weekend was an informal first
Party Congress of the 'New Left.'" Instead of
reporting strength, however, he told of fragmentation and lack of purpose. "There was a mood of
uncommon pessimism...The students find they have
no workable program for effecting the changes
...The frustration is particularly apparent in the
tension between the radicals and the liberals."
Speaking of the march's National Coordinating
Committee, he said that it was a "recreation of
the sectarianism of the left of the 'thirties...
There were the Trotskyists--all 28 flavors...the
Stalinists...the Maoists...the Russian revision-
ists...the Castroites....Many had allegiance to
Students for a Democratic Society."30

    • The New Republic's first alienated "eco-
logy" editorial (although it did not use the term,
which had not yet caught on) appeared in the issue
for June 25, 1966. By the end of the decade, and
especially during the winter of 1969-1970, "the
environment" became the focus for an hysterical
attack on American life. The Environmental
Handbook, rushed to print in time for the massive
"Earth Day" protests that took place on April 22,
1970, spoke in doomed tones, saying "time is running out." In the Foreword, Garrett De Bell
italicized his warning that "a year is about one-
fifth of the time we have left if we are going to
preserve any kind of quality in our world." Don
Marquis said "america [sic.]...is dying because of
the greed and money lust of a thousand little
kings who slashed the timber all to hell and would
not be controlled." Another author spoke of
"smashing the worms of capitalism and totalitarianism." In The New Republic, Wayne Davis rung
his hands: "...as the curtain gets ready to fall
on man's civilization." It was too late to save
ourselves, he argued, unless we give up capitalism. "Let no one make the mistake of thinking we
can save ourselves by 'cleaning up the environment.'" Only governmental ownership of land and
resources would offer any hope.[31]

It is worth observing that to the true devotees of the Red revolution, the ecology craze
seemed a serious digression. Instead of indicating strength, it was a harbinger of loss of
purpose and of fragmentation.

    • In July, 1966, an editorial commented that
"in the space of three years, ghetto riots have
become part of America's summer scene." The Watts
conflagration was in 1965. In 1966, there were
"riots" (if mass burning can be encompassed by
such a word) in Chicago, Cicero and Harlem. In
1967: Newark, Detroit, Minneapolis, Plainfield
(New Jersey), Hartford, Kansas City (Missouri),
Waterloo, and Cambridge (Maryland). And these
are simply the riots that preceded the
assassination of Martin Luther King, Jr., in

April, 1968.[32]

.   Phillip Abbott Luce had been among the
many "radical youth" who had gone to Cuba for
inspiration after Castro's victory there. He
called Cuba "the Mecca of the early New Left."
Even though the emphasis later shifted to the
Vietnamese and Chinese Communists, it is worth
noticing that, according to an unnamed reviewer in
The New Republic, "in late November of 1969 216
young Americans, black and brown and white, left
for Cuba by way of Mexico; and in February of 1970
687 more left--followed later that year by another
group of 409."[33]

.   The project called "Vietnam Summer," with
a peace group hiring 2,000 full-time field workers, took place at Cambridge in the summer of
1967. It was patterned after the 1964 Freedom
Summer. There had been a flow of activity from
the militant Civil Rights movement to the anti-
Vietnam War movement.[34]

.   One of the wilder spectacles of the period
occurred in 1967 with "the New Politics Convention." In an extensive report to The New Republic, James Ridgeway told how the convention was
attended by black nationalists, members of the
W.E.B. DuBois Clubs (the Communist youth organization), the Communist Party, peace activists,
"people from SDS, various community workers,
southern student organizers, and a large contin-
gent who had come from the Vietnam Summer project." Ridgeway observed that "the Communists
...were out in the open for the first time in
years," but added that "they were the most conservative element present." [35]

Just how the convention was held is a question, judging from Ridgeway's report. The black
militants, he says, tried to get the blacks to
leave; others formed a "white radical caucus,
split off from the blacks; and "some jews [who]
had financially supported the convention...walked
out." It is interesting that Martin Luther King,

Jr., the apostle of "non-violence," gave the key-note address. Ridgeway mitigates this, so far as King is concerned, by pointing out that the speech was "such a bore to the delegates."[36]

Ridgeway viewed the convention with despair. "For some of us who have held out hope for the future of the radical reconstruction of America, our despair was...in quite suddenly realizing that neither the new nor the old left takes America seriously...It is indeed the worst of times, and the National Conference of New Politics destroyed what was left of our hope and we are alone."[37]

. In early 1968, Michael Miles reported that the S.D.S. had adopted Marxism, together with a non-exclusionary policy toward the Communists. Thus the New Left was reversing the position taken by American liberals through the Americans for Democratic Action in 1947 and 1948. The A.D.A. had stood for the refusal of liberals to "cooperate with" Communists. In my chapter on "Liberalism and a World in Revolution," " we will see how critically important that issue has been throughout the world.[38]

. In April, 1968, Daniel Zolo reported that "a violent students' revolt began about seven months ago in all major Italian universities," based on "non-orthodox Marxists" who looked to Che Guevara. Then in June of the same year, Robert Greenstein told of the student revolt in West Germany, led by Rudy Dutschke and based on the doctrines of Marcuse, Mao, Ho Chi Minh, Che Guevara and Rosa Luxembourg. An article by Peter Brooks in July, 1968, told of the May revolt by French students, which expressed "the tradition of 'creative anarchy,'"[39]

. In May, 1968, Dotson Rader and Craig Anderson gave an account of the rebellion at Columbia University. They said that a "small group of students, led by Tom Hayden,...had stormed Math Hall on Thursday night and secured it for the liberation." The "students" remained in

329

the building, "building barricades, pulling up the tiles...." On Tuesday, April 23, "approximately a hundred radical students, lead by Mark Rudd, chairman of SDS, had marched on Morningside Park." Eventually, "plainclothes police forcibly entered Low Library, using their night sticks to break through the crowd of professors who had blockaded the entrance...SDS had won a clubbed and outraged faculty to its side."[40]

The Columbia revolt is analytically significant for at least six reasons. First, it shows that the militant "student" activity was not spontaneous, nor a response to provocation by police. Rader and Anderson reported that "months before, at an SDS conference in Maryland, the decision had been reached to take physical control of a major American university this spring." Second, it shows that the "issues" that were taken so seriously by the media and by academia were mere sham: "The...issues were pretexts. The point of the game was power. In the broadest sense, to the most radical members of the SDS Steering Committee, Columbia itself was not the issue."

Third, the fact that professors were blockading the building demonstrates the role of militant leftist faculty during those years. Fourth, in the comment about SDS's having "won an outraged faculty to its side" (necessarily those who were not already militant, such as the ones doing the blockading), we see the process of "radicalization" which was deliberately created by the confrontation and which no doubt served as one of its main purposes.

This relates, fifth, to a structural fact about modern society that is quite important in understanding the 1960's: that the intelligentsia, being attached to the Left, was prepared to articulate a high moralistic defense of the militants and an equally moralistic attack upon the police, the national guard, or any other representatives of the established order. Thus we see that, despite everything they have told us, Rader and An-

330

derson were able, incredibly, to reach the conclusion that "<u>police</u> violence was <u>unprovoked</u> and unlimited" (emphasis added). At the same time, the predominant society, having very little by way of an intellectual culture to speak for it, could rally no moral defense of itself and no articulation of a rationale on its own behalf. This led, in large measure, to the majority society's paralysis and moral equivocation.

My sixth point relates directly to this. It is that the processes of orderly society were bared as being much more tenuous than we are accustomed to imagine. The social cements are not to be taken for granted; they can readily disappear. To those who value a free society, this is perhaps the most frightening single fact demonstrated by the New Left.

. Similar episodes, with similar responses, occurred at many other places, including Harvard in early 1969. After black militants took guns into Willard Straight Hall at Cornell, the editors of The New Republic made the typical moral inversion: "The black students at Cornell, or at least some of them, had their reasons for thinking they might need to defend themselves against violent attack."[41]

This voices a perspective that has been inherent in the Left's view of the world for more than a century. The masses, exploited, are no more than exercising their dignity as human beings by rising up; it is the bourgeoisie, in putting down the revolution, that commits the violence.

. The Columbia, Harvard and Cornell episodes served as a paradigm for the confrontation between the militants and the police in Chicago at the time of the 1968 Democratic National Convention. Except for a few admissions here and there, the intellectual culture has insisted to the American people that "Chicago" represented the beating of "kids" by the "brutal Chicago police." Several prominent "liberals"--including Michael Harrington, Jules Feiffer, Nat Hentoff, Christopher Jencks and Norman Mailer--signed a 1930's-type manifesto that appeared as an advertisement in The New Republic on August 9, 1969. It defended the "Chicago Eight" defendants and said that "both the mass media and the government's own Walker Report made it clear that the principal responsibility for acts of violence that occurred in Chicago last August lay with the Chicago authorities."[42]

Here, though, is how James Ridgeway, The New Republic's own correspondent, described the events in Chicago right after they occurred: "The strategy was to confront the Chicago police, and thereby demonstrate that America was a police state...The radicals talked enthusiastically about little acts of violence...to provoke the police and manipulate the liberal McCarthy youth into their ranks. In effect, the idea was to simulate a little guerrilla war...Chicago smelled of revolution." This was consistent with Jerry Rubin's boasts in Do It!, where he said that "Sunday night a police car drove through Lincoln Park. From every direction the yippie's own brand of rock music started: the rhythm of rocks rending cop-car metal and shattering windshields. The Battle of Czechago was on."[43]

. During the second half of the 1960's, the various revolutions going on simultaneously under the New Left banner were torn by fragmentation and eventually by disillusionment and fatigue. During the summer of 1970 following the incident at Kent State in May, 1970, various fragments of the Red revolution went underground and formed the basis for the bombings and kidnappings of the 1970's. A great many of the militants, and especially those involved in the counter-culture, withdrew into mystic fads and cults. Others "went straight," and this included, with some, going into electoral politics.

I will discuss the collapse of the New Left in the next section, since it deserves detailed attention for its own sake.

. Also during the second half of the 1960's, there had been some major developments within the Black revolution. The goal of "integration," which had received the imprimatur of the United States Supreme Court in <u>Brown</u> v. <u>Board</u> <u>of</u> <u>Education</u> in 1954, came under attack from the more militant blacks themselves. An article in <u>The</u> <u>New</u> <u>Republic</u> in late 1966 was able to speak, for example, of "the myth that integrationist measures are bringing better housing to the Negro poor." In January, 1967, Kopkind reported Stokely Carmichael's views about the Great Society's "War on Poverty": "The war on poverty may give some black people some of the things they need, but to Carmichael it keeps them under white manipulation ...What galls SNCC people most is the way white radicals seem to have treated SNCC as a kind of psycho-therapy, as a way to work out problems of alienation and boredom." This points to a double split that was occurring: between integrationist blacks and separatist blacks; and between whites and blacks within the Civil Rights movement. "What is happening now," Kopkind said, "is that many of those whites feel hopelessly rejected by their Negro friends." Simon Lazarus would later speak of "the sharp turn toward separatism and violence taken by SNCC in 1967." He mentioned "SNCC's scorn for moderates like Martin Luther King--on the ground that the latter direct their appeals to whites rather than blacks."44

. One last development that I will mention is that there had been a direct flow of energy from the early Civil Rights movement to the anti-Vietnam War movement. Kopkind told in 1965 how many of those who had participated in the anti-war March on Washington that year had earlier taken part in the 1963 civil rights March on Washington and had been at Selma. This is consistent with Barry Kalb's observation in 1969 about one of the women in S.D.S.: she was "a veteran of the Southern Christian Leadership Conference, SNCC, the Mississippi Freedom Democratic Party, the National Mobilization Committee to End the War in Vietnam, and SDS." Ronald Berman quoted Mario Savio as

333

having said that "last summer I went to
Mississippi to join the struggle there for civil
rights. This fall I am engaged in another phase
of the same struggle, this time in Berkeley."[45]

The collapse of the New Left

To an outsider, it appeared as though the New
Left collapsed suddenly and dramatically between
the end of the academic year in May, 1970, and the
beginning of the fall semester. Great spasms of
activity had accompanied the events of the spring,
which had included the observance of Earth Day on
April 22, the demonstrations that followed the
United States armed forces' invasion of the North
Vietnamese sanctuaries in Cambodia, and the outcry
that followed the National Guardmen's opening fire
at Kent State University. Radicals urged renewed
vigor in the fall, including a shutting down of
all universities; but the movement, strangely
enough, had lost all its impetus. The masses were
gone. Slowly the realization set in that a major
change had occurred. What remained were the bombings and kidnappings by those who "went underground," the flight of many thousands into mysticism and the occult, the turning of others to
electoral politics, and the rise of "women's liberation" as the principal issue on the Left during
the 1970's.[46]

The suddenness of this collapse was something
of an illusion. The truth is that the New Left
had been dissolving internally for perhaps as long
as five years, although it would be arbitrary to
assign a beginning date. As we review the causes
of the collapse, we will see that many of them had
been underway since the mid-1960's. The New Left
was, to borrow a Marxist phrase, collapsing "from
its own contradictions." (It would be a mistake,
of course, to assume that the New Left fully "had
its act together" at any one time and then began
to collapse from there. Because of this, there is
some artificiality in thinking in terms of a
collapse. We do, however, seek an understanding

334

of the New Left's downward, rather than upward, trajectory, and of its eventual demise.)

There were at least nine causes, and almost certainly more, that contributed to the eventual evaporation of the New Left. Needless to say, several are related.

1. The militants' fatigue. Michael Unseem conducted interviews among the militants and found that by early 1969 one-fourth had dropped out. Some, he said, told him that they were "suffering from general exhaustion."47

The phenomenon of "tired radicals" corresponds to a like phenomenon during the 1920's, after the intense effort of the Progressive years. After recounting the effort of those years, George Soule said in 1931 that "the effect of all this upon us differed according to the individual. Some became 'tired radicals' and surrendered by going out for conventional success." According to L. Otis Graham, Jr., a symposium in 1926 on "Where are the Pre-War Radicals?" cited "the high personal cost..., costs both financial and professional" as a cause of their disappearance.48

2. The intellectuals' cycle: a time for withdrawal. This is a theme that I discussed earlier, tracing it back as far as Emerson's generation. We see the withdrawal part of the cycle taking effect in Charles Kerr's April, 1970, statement that "Robert Brustein would have young radicals lower their voices and settle down to a 'revolution of the spirit.'" Brustein, in so urging, would be following in the footsteps of Herbert Croly in the 1920's.49

3. The public's fatigue. In its very first editorial in its opening issue in November, 1914, The New Republic attributed the loss by Progressive candidates in the 1914 elections to the fatigue the public felt toward political agitation. Can we doubt that the public who laughed at the antics of a Bruce and a Rubin in the 1960's would

335

come to feel a similar fatigue after several years of New Left agitation? The operative human factors stay much the same from one episode to another.[50]

4. The displacement of moderates. Like slapstick as a mode of entertainment, in which the old devices cease after a while to be startling, the New Left had to keep increasing its militance and its shock techniques to hold the attention of its audience (especially since the young, in an age of television, had become accustomed to rapidly changing images). And, too, those who were caught up in it were propelled to more and more extreme conduct. Jerry Rubin says that "By 1970 there was tremendous pressure on all activists to translate their radical talk into action--shoot a gun or plant a bomb." The "going underground" with terroristic activity by the end of the 1960's was a predictable product of these forces.[51]

The effect, however, was slowly to lose the support of the "moderates" and those who shrunk from violence. Rubin writes that "most of us were not ready for an armed confrontation with the state. I felt that I was being set up for martyrdom by death or jail." In addition to militants like Rubin, there were the people who had "supported the goals of the New Left" while only mildly "faulting the means." Some were moderates out of wisdom, some out of the timorousness that had so long set American liberals apart from the remainder of the Left.[52]

Thus Robert Greenstein reported in June, 1968, that the German movement under Rudi Dutschke was incurring "the alienation of liberals (such as Gunter Grass), who dislike the authoritarian style." Recalling a scene reminiscent of the Nazis, Greenstein said "the end of the Vietnam Congress...is a case in point...SNCC representative Dale Smith jumped on a table and raised a clenched right hand. Virtually every one of the 3,000 German students rose from his seat. Three thousand right fists shot up and down together, as students chanted in unison with Smith, 'Burn, baby, burn.'" 53

5. <u>Sectarianism; sterile factional in-fighting.</u> The fragmentation within the Left has been a source of great weakness for over a century. Although for a while it added to the range of New Left expression, it was certainly a major factor in the eventual collapse.

Andrew Kopkind told in 1965 about the debate over "how far radicals can go in accepting liberal forms of action," thus revealing a split between the moderates and the revolutionaries. In 1969, it was reported that many within the New Left sympathized "with the Arabs as part of the romanticized third world," and a year later Reed Whittemore commented that "the Middle East struggle...is dividing the left ideologically." When we realize how much of the traditional Left has been Jewish, we know how significant a division this represented. The foreseeable split between the disciplined Left and the undisciplined romantic anarchist also developed. Michael Miles wrote in early 1969 that "at Berkeley...there is an open split between radicalism with a rational analysis and program and 'militancy' empty of political content." Other disputes simply reflected old sectarian differences: Barry Kalb reported in July, 1969, that "The National Office group of the SDS last week informed the [Peking-oriented] Progressive laborites that they were no longer members of the family. Each party thereupon elected a slate of officers; each called itself 'the real SDS'." Looking back several years later, <u>The New Republic</u> added an additional split to the list: "Black leadership in this country has been splintered and quiescent since the assassination of Martin Luther King, Jr." 54

6. <u>Lack of revolutionary commitment on the part of the rank-and-file.</u> We see the seeds of a major problem for the New Left in the comment by the editors of <u>The New Republic</u> in 1967 that "the overwhelming majority of the 150,000 Americans who

337

took part in antiwar demonstrations in New York and San Francisco on April 15 almost certainly knew nothing, and probably care less, about what went on behind the organizational scenes." The New Left was, for a time, able to draw large crowds, but these did not consist of committed cadre. They could be, and were, there one day-- and not the next.[55]

The same point was made about the black side of the New Left in The Nation. In a 1972 article entitled "Where Did Their Revolution Go?," the author wrote that "the explanation would be that there simply never was a 'black revolution.' There was militancy...but never much of a genuine revolutionary conviction on the part of most black students." [56]

This lack of commitment could be due to a number of causes, but we might conjecture that perhaps Sombart's "schoals of apple pie and ice cream" were coming back to haunt the New Left.

7. The annual loss of continuity among college students. The New Left of the second half of the 1960's was largely centered within the universities. The annual graduation of approximately one-fourth of the students, including always those who were older, makes continuity in any effort difficult. This should not obscure the fact, of course, that the New Left did have an inner core of full-time militants, such as the ubiquitous Tom Hayden.

I have seen no study concerning it, but I have wondered whether it may be that the younger brothers and sisters of the students of the late 1960's were perhaps reacting negatively to the antics of their older syblings, so that when they arrived at college they were not so inclined to continue the agitation. This would be an interesting area for empirical study.

8. Removal of the catalysts. The alienated core of the Left gains wide public support when it

exploits issues that can bring in others who deeply feel their own interests at stake. Both the "black" and the "red" revolutions involved "catalysts" of this sort. In each case, the catalyst gradually disappeared. Despite the calls by black militants for more, the civil rights legislation enacted under the Johnson administration, including especially the Voting Rights Act of 1965, went far toward satisfying the needs that moderate blacks had perceived. (The New Left denounced such a removal of a catalyst as "cooptation," ascribing it to a manipulative cleverness on the part of the Establishment.)

The mass movement faded, too, as the Vietnam War ceased being an issue. As early as June, 1968, Richard Anthony and Phil Semas told _The New Republic_'s readers that "SDS support...[has been] drifting away in response to the McCarthy candidacy and the Paris peace talks." In February, 1970, before the final spasm of that spring, the editors reported that "the young who once shouted, 'Hey, hey, LBJ, how many kids did you kill today' are now talking about ecology...The explanation for this thinning of resistance is Mr. Nixon's 'Plan for Peace.'"[57]

9. _A rallying of the forces loyal to the existing society_. Eventually signs began to develop of an articulated defense of American society. After Kent State, Andrew Greeley wrote that "it doesn't take those patriotic parades of 'hard hats' to demonstrate that there is immense dissatisfaction in the country with 'radical protest'" Then Greeley noted something that to him seemed quite incredible: "The outrage in academia notwithstanding, it appears that more than half of the American people blame the Kent State killings on the students themselves!"[58]

NOTES

1. Jack Newfield, _A Prophetic Minority_ (New York: New American Library, Inc., 1966), p. 45.

2.   New Republic, November 8, 1980, p. 24.

3.   Newfield, Prophetic Minority, pp. 44, 45, 47.

4.   Bruce Cook, The Beat Generation (New York: Charles Scribner's Sons, 1971), pp. 64, 113, 28.

5.   Cook, The Beat Generation, p. 32.

6.   Cook, The Beat Generation, pp. 32, 59-60.

7.   Cook, The Beat Generation, pp. 21, 155; New Republic, March 30, 1959, p. 14.

8.   New Republic, March 30, 1959, p. 14.

9.   New Republic, November 23, 1963, p. 23; New Republic, May 3, 1975; New Republic, March 28, 1960, p. 21.

10. Paul Goodman, Growing Up Absurd (New York: Random House, 1956), pp. 64, 65, 175, 281.

11. New Republic, November 13, 1961, p. 12.

12. In my discussion here, I am using the word "Green" in the sense Charles Reich used it in The Greening of America to denote the counter-culture, and not directly in the sense that the term is used by the "Green" faction (an anti-nuclear movement) in Europe in the 1980's. It is perhaps unnecessary to explain that the word "Red" as I am using it in these chapters on the New Left is intended more broadly than just to denote the Communist Party or even pro-Soviet groups.

13. Newfield, Prophetic Minority, p. 21; for a review of Clecak's book, see New Republic, January 5, 1974, p. 29.

14. New Republic, February 3, 1958, p. 15.

15. Phillip Abbott Luce, The New Left (New York: David McKay Company, Inc., 1966), pp. 51, 47, 54.

16. New Republic, October 20, 1958, pp. 19, 20.

17. Irving Howe, Steady Work: Essays in the Politics of Democratic Radicalism, 1953-1966 (New York: Harcourt, Brace & World, Inc., 1966), p. 73; Christopher Lasch, The Agony of the American Left (New York: Vintage Books, 1969), pp. 130, 131.

18. New Republic, December 24, 1977, p. 36.

19. Herbert Marcuse, An Essay on Liberation (Boston: Beacon Press, 1969), p. 80, 51, 58, 81.

20. Marcuse, Essay on Liberation, p. 60.

21. Herbert Marcuse, essay entitled "Repressive Tolerance" in A Critique of Pure Tolerance (Boston: Beacon Press), pp. 90, 109.

22. Marcuse, Essay on Liberation, pp. 85, 89.

23. New Republic, August 8, 1960, p. 13.

24. New Republic, June 19, 1965, pp. 15-19.

25. New Republic, July 20, 1963, p. 15; New Republic, April 10, 1965, pp. 13, 14.

26. New Republic, December 11, 1965, p. 17.

27. New Republic, March 27, 1965, pp. 6, 26.

28. New Republic, April 17, 1965, p. 9.

29. Saul D. Alinsky, Reveille for Radicals (Chicago: University of Chicago Press, 1946), pp. 153, 154; New Republic, June 26, 1965, p. 16.

30. New Republic, December 11, 1965, p. 15.

31. Garrett De Bell, ed., The Environmental Handbook (New York: Ballantine Books, 1970), pp. xiv, vii, 2; New Republic, January 10, 1970, p. 15.

32. New Republic, July 30, 1966, p. 5.

33. See <u>Venceremos Brigade: Young Americans Sharing the Life and Work of Revolutionary Cuba</u>, no individual author given; Luce, <u>The New Left</u>, p. 60; New Republic, July 10, 1971, p. 28.

34. New Republic, May 27, 1967, p. 5.

35. New Republic, September 16, 1967, pp. 9-11.

36. New Republic, September 16, 1967, pp. 9-11.

37. New Republic, September 16, 1967, p. 12.

38. New Republic, February 3, 1968, pp. 25, 22.

39. New Republic, April 27, 1968, pp. 16, 17; New Republic, June 8, 1968, pp. 18-20; New Republic, July 6, 1968, p. 25.

40. New Republic, May 11, 1968, pp. 9-11.

41. New Republic, May 3, 1969, p. 5.

42. New Republic, August 9, 1969, p. 5.

43. New Republic, September 7, 1968, p. 11; Jerry Rubin, <u>Do It!</u> (New York: Simon and Schuster, 1970), p. 170.

44. New Republic, December 17, 1966, p. 20; New Republic, January 7, 1967, p. 18; New Republic, January 13, 1968, pp. 28, 32.

45. New Republic, December 11, 1965, p. 18; New Republic, July 5, 1969, p. 12; Ronald Berman, <u>America in the Sixties: An Intellectual History</u> (New York: The Free Press, 1968), p. 161.

46. Regarding the desire to shut down all universities, see New Republic, September 12, 1970, p. 19.

47. Michael Unseem, <u>Conscription, Protest, and Social Conflict</u> (New York: John Wiley & Sons, 1973), pp. 276-277.

48. New Republic, January 21, 1931; L. Otis Graham, Jr., _An Encore for Reform: The Old Progressives and the New Deal_ (New York: Oxford University Press, 1967), pp. 162-163.

49. New Republic, April 25, 1970, p. 29.

50. New Republic, November 7, 1914, p. 4.

51. Jerry Rubin, _Growing (Up) at 37_ (New York: Warner Books, 1976), p. 93.

52. Rubin, _Growing (Up) at 37_, p. 93.

53. New Republic, June 8, 1968, p. 20.

54. New Republic, December 11, 1965, p. 17; New Republic, February 15, 1969, p. 9; New Republic, March 21, 1970, p. 32; New Republic, April 12, 1969, p. 18; New Republic, July 5, 1969, p. 11; New Republic, September 17, 1977, p. 6.

55. New Republic, April 29, 1967, p. 3.

56. The Nation, Vol. 215, p. 272.

57. New Republic, June 29, 1968, p. 13; New Republic, February 14, 1970, p. 1.

58. New Republic, June 27, 1970, p. 14.

14

THE NEW LEFT III

The New Left's methods

One of the issues that have fragmented the Left for a century and a half has had to do with what methods are to be considered both justifiable and effective in bringing about social change. It is not surprising to find that a variety of methods were used by the different factions of the New Left. Those that we will consider will be the Dadaist method; the "non-violent" method that was derived from Thoreau and Gandhi; and violence. We have already seen a fourth method: protest by withdrawal.

1. Most Americans are not aware that the "comical" method that was used so effectively, especially among the young, by many New Left militants has had a long history within the Left. I will refer to it as "the Dadaist method."

Before I trace its origins, we should first see how it was used by the New Left. The following examples, even though they will only cite specific instances, represent an extensively used style. They should be sufficient to illustrate both the method and the intentions behind it:

• A New Republic article in 1964 reported that Lenny Bruce "turned up in court looking like a bearded rabbi in the garb of the concentration camp." 1

• The Free Speech Movement at Berkeley asserted a right to use obscene language, which in turn became useful for its shock value and its symbolic shattering of what the Left likes to call "bourgeois" norms. Stanley Kauffmann reported in 1968 that the Canadian Broadcasting Corporation refused to carry an item "because it contains--

often--the words 'fuck' and 'bullshit.'" [It is relevant to my later discussion of the complicity of liberalism with the New Left that Kauffmann went on to say--in The New Republic--that "I hope that at least some members of the CBC felt that this decision was a fucking disgrace."] [2]

. In early November, 1970, David Sanford reported from Kent State University that "last Saturday the Yippies staged a carnival on the famous Kent commons to raise bail money. They sold commie pinko bubblegum for a penny, fished for fake dope, threw painted rocks at paper pigs, and built a 10-foot penis out of papier-mache." [3]

. The entire "movement" was seen as part of an on-going "happening" of "guerrilla theater." It consisted not only of startling behavior, but of a complete cultural identification. The outspoken Jerry Rubin stated the rationale: "We were a religion, a family, a culture, with our own music, our own dress, our own human relationships, our own stimulants, our own media...Long hair is communication...We longhairs recognize each other as brothers in the street...Man was born to let his hair grow long and to smell like a man...We even smell our armpits once in a while." He showed how much of this was acting for effect when he said that "an event happens when it goes on TV and becomes myth...The presence of a camera transforms a demonstration." [4]

In his 1934 book Exile's Return, Malcolm Cowley traced the development of the Dadaist technique. "Tristan Tzara says that Dada was born in 1916...He wrote the Dada Manifesto in March, 1918...All over Europe Dadaist groups had sprung into being, and everywhere they spread the same pattern of childishness and audacity...But the history of Dada was in reality much longer. Its existence was rendered possible by a succession of literary schools beginning before the middle of the nineteenth century." It was then that Cowley quoted Edmund Wilson about the episode in which the French writer Flaubert had made love to a

346

prostitute in front of his friends "without removing his hat or taking the cigar from his mouth." Flaubert's purpose, Wilson had said, was to "announce a furious contempt for everything held sacred by society." 5

Kenneth Coutts-Smith's book _Dada_ gives the history of the post-World War I Dadaist movement. "The most obvious aspect of Dada...was a savage anarchism, a deliberate programme designed to undermine the moral and social assumptions of existing middle class society." Among many examples, he cited a 1920 art exhibit in which patrons entered through a public lavatory and were then confronted "by a young girl dressed as for her first communion who suddenly began to recite obscene verses." 6

Oddly enough, the precedents in America in- clude Huey Long. A 1935 _New Republic_ editorial commenting on Long's assassination said that he "used the manners of a clown to achieve his ends ...He concealed his furious energies and hatreds beneath...an act of deliberate buffoonery." We have already seen the influence that the I.W.W. (the Wobblies) had as a source of the New Left. It is pertinent that in 1948 in _The New Republic_ Wallace Stegner described Joe Hill, a "folk hero" of the Wobblies, as having had "the poet's knack of self-dramatization. His whole conduct during his trial was dramatic...." During my discussion of the origins of the counter-culture, we have seen the importance of Jean Genet's influence. Those of us who recall the tumultuous "revolution- ary theater" of the 1960's will know what Robert Brustein had in mind when he spoke of "the boiling 'total theater' of Artaud."7

All of this lent itself to an ideological characteristic of the New Left about which I have not yet commented. I have in mind the role that exaggeration played in the ideology--a super- inflation of every American defect.

Marcuse, for example, was capable of describing American society as one "which compels the vast majority of the population to 'earn' their living in stupid, inhuman, and unnecessary jobs; ...which is infested with violence and repression while demanding obedience and compliance from the victims of violence and repression...." Robert Theobald said in 1968 that "we have something like six to nine months to make visible the beginning of a change...If trends continue to develop as they are presently developing, we will move into a fascist police state in this country." Also in 1968, William Barrow reported in The New Republic that "the so-called 'militants' long ago gave up expecting anything other than efforts at genocide from the white majority." And the journal's own Robert Brustein, in 1964 before he eventually turned against the more extreme elements of the New Left, had described the United States this way: "What has been the most characteristic pattern of American history? The commission of some crime, paid for with a hundred years of remorse." 8

As a result of its method, its alienation and its ideology, the New Left, with a great deal of liberal complicity, built a fantasy-world which it then projected onto American society. The amazing thing is that it was all granted a prima facie plausibility at the time by the media, by academia, and by public acquiescence. Those who opposed it had few avenues of expression.

2.   The Civil Rights movement made extensive use of the technique of "non-violent protest." The same method was later used in the anti-Vietnam War movement in the sit-ins and lie-ins.

There is obviously a broad continuum of possible activity within what might be called non-violent protest. It can range from the normal processes of speaking-up in a free society to the mass seizure of public and private property. When it is carried to the extent of mass action that involves the seizure of property and the building of intense emotions within large numbers of peo-

348

ple, it is properly considered a revolutionary technique, This is, in fact, precisely what David Dellinger considered it, as we see from the title of his book Revolutionary Nonviolence.

This militant, revolutionary form of non-violence has a long history. It is usually attributed to Gandhi, although Gandhi is said to have drawn inspiration from the United States' own Henry David Thoreau, who wrote an "Essay on Civil Disobedience." Sorel's "General Strike," in which all of a country's workers would go on strike simultaneously, was certainly in the tradition. The United Auto Workers' sit-down seizure of the General Motors plant in Flint, Michigan, in 1936 is another example.

I have already discussed "non-violence" in detail in my chapter on liberalism's attitudes toward methods of social change. (See Chapter 8, pages 215-221.)

I made the point there that the advocates of non-violence are often willing to create the setting in which violence is bound to occur. In the context of the New Left, we can see that the seizure of university administration buildings, sometimes by people with weapons, is "non-violent" only if we are willing to accept the sophistry, which we heard voiced in connection with the Columbia seizure, that it is the police who, by responding on behalf of the larger society, commit the violence.

The hypocrisy of so much of the "non-violent" movement is seen when we consider, too, that Dellinger's book Revolutionary Nonviolence was published in 1970--after the bombings had started and after a large number of American cities had experienced riots and mass burning. To extend one of Oliver Wendell Holmes, Jr.'s, analogies, this is like continuing to shout "Fire!" even after the crowd has started to stampede in a theater. Thus Tom Hayden told how activists planned a "demonstration" the day after the Newark riot. [9]

The term "non-violence" is, I think, widely misunderstood by many who praise it as a method. The term seems to suggest that the method is a mild one that is consistent with the framework of a free and orderly society. When "non-violence" is used on behalf of revolution against a free (albeit imperfect) society, however, and involves substantial coercion, violation of law, denial of public and private property rights, and a building of mass emotions to a point at which it is foreseeable that violence will result, it is a technique that should be seen in a very different light. It then bears the same relationship to violence that gross negligence (defined in law as "the doing of something highly dangerous without caring") bears to intentional harm.

3. On March 28, 1970, The New Republic reported six bombings, of which three "were unmistakably revolutionary." A month later, Robert Brustein told how "recently, three young people blew themselves up on W. 11th St. with bombs, said to be intended for Columbia University." Brustein, who by that time had become an opponent of the extremists, spoke of "the atrocities being prepared by Americans in the name of 'revolutionary idealism'" [although, to show that he wasn't letting such thoughts go too far, he was careful to point out that the atrocities were no more than on a par with "atrocities" being committed by Americans in Vietnam].[10]

In September, 1970, Stephen Solomon reported an "18-month wave of fire-bombings" at the University of Wisconsin. This had culminated in the now-infamous terrorist attack in which "an explosives-laden truck destroyed [a] building, [and] killed a young physics scholar." In the same issue, Albert A. Eisele wrote from Minnesota that there was "a deep insecurity and even fear about violence." "This was sickeningly brought home when dynamite bombs smashed the federal office building...and a downtown department store." Significantly, he pointed out that Senator Hubert Humphrey called on "true liberals" to "condemn criminality."11

Fortunately for Americans, the violence ebbed away during the 1970's instead of building. Terrorism, including truck-bombings, has become common in Europe and the middle-East during the 1980's, largely from the same types of leftist guerrilla organizations--such as the Red Brigades in Italy--that were beginning to form in the United States. A significant portion of this terrorism has come from Soviet client-states, such as Syria and Lybia. This informs us that it is a technique that is not unique to the Bakuninist-style Left but is also one of the weapons in the arsenal of the Soviet bloc. Although terrorism is also used by individuals and groups outside the Left, and is thus a commentary on the general level of civilization in the way that Jose Ortega y Gasset considered so important, it is a mistake to think that much of it is not related to aliena-tion and Leftist ideology. We saw this in 1970 when Eldridge Cleaver, in a book published by McGraw-Hill, declared that "we have to fight a revolutionary struggle for the violent overthrow of the United States government and the total destruction of the racist, capitalist...power structure."12

Liberalism's relationship to the New Left

One of the factors that killed the New Left was that eventually even a good many American liberal intellectuals turned against it. Certain individuals and parts of the "liberal coalition" had been against it all along.

And yet, one of the more important facts that we must note in our analysis of the New Left, especially in this book about liberal thought, is the liberal intellectual culture's complicity with it. (The word "complicity" is not value-free and is not intended to be.)

The New Left received vitally important in-

351

stitutional support from liberal sources. It is likely that without this support the movement would have been severely limited.

Dell Publishing Company and McGraw-Hill published the book Conversation with Eldridge Cleaver from which I just quoted Cleaver's revolutionary comment. Ballantine Books published The Environmental Handbook. Simon and Schuster published Jerry Rubin's Do It!, and Warner Communications Company published his Growing (Up) at 37. Beacon Press published Herbert Marcuse's An Essay on Liberation. Doubleday & Company, Inc., published Theodore Roszak's The Making of the Counter Culture. The Left may argue that these are just examples of "capitalist publishers' being so venal that they are willing to profit from the attack on their own system," but a Marxist interpretation of that sort would be only partly true. It was the intellectual culture even more than the investors of capital in publishing companies that determined what was published--and that then provided much of the readership, and consequently the market, for such books to make them financially feasible.

We have seen how the Council of Churches put up $100,000 in Rochester to support Saul Alinsky's activities there. Jerry Rubin boasted about how much financial support he was receiving from what was probably university "forum board committees" as well as student government associations: "After some of my speeches on campus, the students would close down the school with a strike, or blow up the ROTC building, or riot. Meanwhile, I was being paid $500 to $1,000 from the official student organization for giving the speech." I myself resigned from the Wichita State University Forum Board Committee in protest over its funding of an on-campus showing of revolutionary films featuring Angela Davis. In July, 1968, Paul Marx told the readers of The New Republic that many of the "community action organizations" established by the Johnson administration as part of its War on Poverty "have on their payrolls radicals who advocate tearing down the whole society."13

352

But even more important was the moral support given by the liberal intellectual culture. This is readily seen in the pages of The New Republic. Following the seizure of the chief administration building on the Berkeley campus in December, 1964, The New Republic ran an editorial applauding the students. In July, 1965, D. W. Brogam reported in a review of Michael Harrington's The Accidental Century that "Mr. Harrington is afraid not that we will be faced with a revolutionary situation, but that we won't, that the unemployed...will be... docile." After The New Republic ran a series of "personal statements" by "young radicals" in late 1965, Harrington commented that "whatever their shortcomings, the New Leftists hold out the hope for a renewal of American social criticism and action." In January, 1967, Stanley Kauffmann wrote that "a good deal of the Young Generation's behavior is admirable and promising, much of it is at least comprehensible, and most of it is preferable to the torpor that prevailed in the Eisenhower years." 14

The first strong denunciation in The New Republic appeared in an editorial on August 5, 1967, which said that "'Burn this town down' is the shout of the angry, exalted young Brown Shirt ...it leads to madness." Thereafter, we might expect to have seen a consistent opposition by the editors to at least the more extreme part of the New Left. This is especially so since the editors clearly perceived the danger; in July, 1968, they said that "as in the pre-Civil War period, the American political system may not be able to withstand the strains put upon it. One can foresee the possibility that our major parties may again be incapable of containing violent pressures from below, that the government elected in November may be impotent and our internal conflicts irreconcilable." 15

Despite this awareness, it was just two months later, in September, 1968, that Kauffmann made his statement about a decision by the Canadian Broadcasting System being a "fucking dis-

353

grace," a use of language that must certainly have been intended to show his, and <u>The</u> <u>New</u> <u>Republic</u>'s, "solidarity" with the very movement the editors saw threatening civil war. In the following issue, an article by Marcus Raskin bitterly denounced Democratic liberalism as having "transformed the society into an authoritarian one which stood on the legs of the labor bosses, the large corporations, the military and the city bosses."[16]

In April, 1969, an editorial described the seizure of University Hall at Harvard. It followed the usual line of blaming the police for the ensuing violence, saying that they "went beserk." A few pages later, an author wrote that "even when they strike out in apparently un-American directions--tribal living and doped mysticism ...--they do so in the pioneer spirit of discovery." Then a couple of weeks later the editors supplied their apologia for "the decision of black militants at Cornell to bring guns into Willard Straight Hall," saying, as we saw earlier, that they "had their reasons for thinking they might need to defend themselves...."[17]

Even after the editors began to denounce the revolutionary movement with somewhat more genuine feeling, as they did finally in November, 1969, when they said that "those who preach or practice violence in this country are nihilists and fools," they were willing to run an advertisement for <u>Ramparts</u> in April, 1970, that said that "the students at Santa Barbara who burned down the Bank of America probably did more to save the environment than all of the Teach-Ins and Survival Fairs put together." And in 1972 the editors were appalled that "there is persuasive evidence that the FBI undertook a massive surveillance program to keep tabs on most of the dissident political groups...." They thought it reprehensible that the main society should protect itself, even by surveillance, against an impending civil war.[18]

The relationship of the intellectual culture to the New Left, as illustrated by these examples

354

(and by countless others that could be given from many sources and from the memories of those who lived through the period), was similar to its relationship to the Communist Left during the 1930's. There was during both periods just enough ambivalence to allow liberal intellectuals to keep a foot planted at least shakily in the American context. But both decades provide windows into the depths of the alienation and of the liberal intellectual culture's identification even with totalitarian forms of socialist thought. Jane Fonda's trip to Hanoi while American forces were fighting in Vietnam was more than the isolated action of an opinionated but talented actress; it symbolizes how profound the complicity became. This is magnified by the fact that even today most liberals do not acknowledge it as complicity.

The host culture

We cannot fully understand the New Left, however, without fathoming the weakness of the main culture. A medical analogy is appropriate: If the antibodies had been strong enough, the disease would never have become virulent.

The series of books of which this one is the final volume has largely been an effort to explain that weakness. I have elaborated upon both the peculiar nature of modern intellectual culture and upon the essential "infancy" and "immaturity" of humanity even during the modern age. As I grow older, I see nothing to contradict the analysis I made of that immaturity in Understanding the Modern Predicament. (I would remind the reader, of course, that I hold to a mixed, rather than to an Augustinian or Hobbesian negative, view of human nature.)

One of the more important weaknesses of American society during the period was, of course, the continuing failure of a "bourgeois" culture to generate a sufficient intellectual culture to both (a) give its fundamental values a voice and (b) provide it with the constructive criticism that it will always need. It is this void that created the "silent majority." Tens of millions of people had no bent toward, nor means of, articulating ideas in support of American society during the years of the onslaught.

This gave rise, in turn, to several additional phenomena: One was the fact that, hearing only the exaggerated drumbeat of the Left, a great many average Americans, including especially the young, grew spongy in their commitment to values that have been of the utmost importance to the classical liberal underlay that has sustained American freedom. Another was the mechanism I have already mentioned: that the New Left could count on an articulated moralistic response from the media and academia even for the worst outrages, while the representatives of the main society would be subject to derision. Much of the activity of the New Left would have fallen totally flat without this mechanism.

A third effect was the impact on American foreign policy and the conduct of the war in Vietnam. Fifty-five thousand young Americans died in a war for which the true purpose, which was anti-Communist, was not articulated even by American presidents until it was almost over. It was the division internally within the United States, and not the prowess of the North Vietnamese on the battlefield, that caused the United States to lose the war. (I say "lose the war" advisedly. The delay from 1945 to 1975 that the French and American resistance caused in Communist expansion almost certainly prevented a victory by Communism throughout Southeast Asia. It was during that period that the Indonesians overthrew a Communist-dominated regime, and the delay gave Thailand many years of respite. Unfortunately, the "dominoes" did fall in Laos and Cambodia, leading to a holocaust that in terms of percentage of the population outdid the enormities of Hitler, Stalin and Mao. When liberals even today point out how "the dominoes didn't fall" after the collapse of South

Vietnam, thereby proving how right they were in their condemnation of the war as an unnecessary intervention on America's part, they are guilty of the most unspeakable moral obtuseness, since they are wilfully ignoring this holocaust.)

In addition to the failure of "bourgeois" society to generate an intellectual culture appropriate to itself, we must look to the spiritual-intellectual weakness of the average person in American society. (A book could be written, of course, about the splendid qualities of this same average person, since weakness is only part of the story. But it is weakness that is relevant to an analysis of problems.)

The counter-culture in particular drew upon the hedonism, the moral shallowness and the lack of roots in 20th century America. It was a strange mixture, this combination of drugs and sex, overweening moral sensibility and outrage, and pretentious mouthing of Leftist cliches and slogans. These were people to whom it meant nothing that the raised clenched fist had been a Communist symbol in countless parts of the world for a half a century, or that the slogan "All power to the people" was a direct picking up of the Leninist slogan "All power to the soviets." It turned out that shallow hedonists make bad revolutionaries. What is very little acknowledged today is that they also make bad citizens of a free society.

This is the mentality that has lent itself to the many fads of ideology. Nothing has been able to stand in their way, thus verifying Alexis de Tocqueville's observation a century and a half ago that there is nothing quite so omnipresent and suffocating as majority opinion in a democracy. The fads have been both large and small, and have usually been formed of a mixture of fatuous ideology and hedonistic self-interest. While a fad is "in" there is no truth that can be put up against it; everything outside it is outmoded and, worse, a sign of bigotry. (It is now considered "sex-

357

ist"--a newly coined word--to use the pronoun "he"
in a general way to designate a person of unspeci-
fied sex.) It is no wonder that Ben Wattenberg
could exclaim in 1970: "Crisis. Crisis. Crisis.
That so very much of this is preposterous...should
come as no real surprise to those who follow the
fads of crisis in America."[19]

The spring of 1970, when Wattenberg made his
remark, was no doubt one of the worst periods for
it. But in general we can say that we breathe a
neurotic atmosphere. Public discourse is reduced
to what will fit the fixation of the moment, and
the media so penetrate our lives with all of this
that the content of private existence is profoundly discolored. What is worse, the great positive
values of high civilization are all but forgotten
in the ubiquitous wash of mediocre music, mediocre
theater, mediocre television, mediocre writing,
incomprehensible art. Technique is everywhere
valued, but without aesthetic judgment. The intellectual culture's anti-bourgeois values come
together with the public's disregard for taste to
produce, what?--the zoot-suiter of the 1940's, the
beads and bell-bottoms of the 1960's, the shaved
temples of the punk-rockers of the 1980's, and a
public that smiles indulgently upon it all.

Our affluence makes possible an ever-increas-
ing quantity of everything, and productions of all
kinds are done on a scale that would have been
dazzling to earlier generations. Fortunately, a
lot of good work, and even some great and memor-
able work, is done as part of the sheer volume.
It would be an amazing fact that would itself
require explanation if so many millions of people,
trained so highly in technique, were not to allow
some real sensibility to shine through a certain
fraction of the time. And, too, there are individuals who separate themselves from the flood. It
is not, however, the good or the great work that
sets the tone of contemporary culture.

This vacuity translates, too, into a willingness of Americans to allow themselves to be "used"

by movements that they do not bother to understand. Irving Howe spoke of "a kind of complicity
[that is] set up between the outraged and/or
amused urban middle class and the rebels of
sensation." This lays the foundation for
political and social instability such as we saw
during the 1960's and could see again.[20]

Continuing residuals and effects
of the New Left

Virtually all of the factors I have discussed
are present, some of them at a muted level, today.
The great question is what is happening within the
intellectual culture. The alienation still burns
within a good many, especially among the academic
Marxists, but in the 1980's the overall tone has
been quieter, more accepting, than it has been at
any time during my lifetime. (It is a mistake to
think the intellectual culture was quiescent in
the 1950's. It wasn't; it burned with alienation
while I was on the Colorado University campus
between 1951 and 1954.)

The slashing attacks upon the "Establishment"
and upon "interest-group liberalism" by the New
Left, together with the "do your own thing" combination of hedonism and anarchist ideology, set the
stage, paradoxically enough, for liberalism's loss
of faith in itself, for the questioning of the
assumption that a government program is the solution for all problems, and for the success of
conservatism in the 1980's (a success that was
probably delayed by Watergate). What no amount of
conservative warning and exhortation could accomplish, the New Left brought about in a flood. It
would be too much to say that the Reagan administration is a "residual" of the New Left, but it is
certainly one of the "effects."

The main "residuals" we see today are cultural. There has been an evangelical Christian
movement against pornography, say, but it has
barely been able to dent the public's apparent

359

desire to acquiesce in, and even to encourage, the cultural slide. Dress and entertainment still show the influences of the 1960's.

There have been conservative authors who purport to see a great conservative intellectual resurgence. If there is one, I (writing in 1986) do not see it, other than marginally. And the failure of conservatism, most particularly in the form of a renewed classical liberalism, to light a fire in the minds especially of the young means that the problematic nature of "bourgeois civilization" remains uncorrected. Without intellectual ferment on behalf of the values of the main society, the Reagan presidency is almost certainly bound to be an interregnum based upon circumstance and a remarkable personality. Where we are going is an open question formed out of the weakness of both the Left and the Right and the indifference of a practical, life-absorbed people, a people that is rapidly changing in its composition. This is a theme upon which I have touched before, but which deserves reiteration.

NOTES

1. New Republic, September 12, 1964, p. 13.

2. New Republic, September 21, 1968, p. 42.

3. New Republic, November 7, 1970, p. 17.

4. Jerry Rubin, Do It! (New York: Simon and Schuster, 1970), pp. 55, 93, 97, 107.

5. Malcolm Cowley, Exile's Return: a Narrative of Ideas (New York: W. W. Norton & Company, Inc., 1934), pp. 148, 151.

6. Kenneth Coutts-Smith, Dada (New York: E. P. Dutton and Co., Inc., 1970), pp. 22, 116-117.

7. New Republic, September 18, 1935, p. 146; New Republic, January 5, 1948, p. 24; New Republic,

January 22, 1966, p. 24.

8. Herbert Marcuse, _An Essay on Liberation_ (Boston: Beacon Press, 1969), p. 62; Robert Theobald, _An Alternative Future for America_ (Chicago: Swallow Press, 1968), pp. 47, 48; New Republic, April 20, 1968, p. 13; New Republic, October 31, 1964, p. 85.

9. Tom Hayden, _Rebellion in Newark_ (New York: Random House, 1967), pp. 24-25.

10. New Republic, March 28, 1970, p. 5; New Republic, April 25, 1970, p. 30.

11. New Republic, September 19, 1970, pp. 12, 19.

12. Lee Lockwood, _Conversation with Eldridge Cleaver/Algiers_ (New York: Delta Books, 1970), p. 54.

13. Jerry Rubin, _Growing (Up) at 37_ (New York: Warner Books, 1976), p. 90; New Republic, July 6, 1968, p. 31.

14. New Republic, March 27, 1965, p. 6; New Republic, July 24, 1965, p. 26; New Republic, February 19, 1966, p. 20; New Republic, January 28, 1967, p. 26.

15. New Republic, August 5, 1967, p. 6; New Republic, July 27, 1968.

16. New Republic, September 21, 1968, p. 42; New Republic, September 28, 1968, p. 17.

17. New Republic, April 26, 1969, pp. 6, 21; New Republic, May 3, 1969, p. 5.

18. New Republic, November 15, 1969, p. 9; New Republic, April 18, 1970, p. 5; New Republic, January 29, 1972, p. 11.

19. New Republic, April 4, 1970, p. 18.

20.   Irving Howe, <u>Steady Work: Essays in the Politics of Democratic Radicalism, 1953-1966</u> (New York: Harcourt, Brace & World, Inc., 1966), p. 59.

15

LIBERALISM AND INTERNATIONAL AFFAIRS

In our discussion of liberalism's orientation toward international affairs, it will be necessary once again to differentiate between the thinking of the liberal intellectual culture and the positions taken by liberal presidents. Here, as elsewhere, liberal politicians have stayed much closer to majority opinion. Liberal thought, as such, has been considerably further to the left.

So far as the intellectual culture is concerned, it would be surprising if its outlook on world affairs had not been formed from the same elements as its ideology in general. The liberal intellectual culture has been as far to the left in its attitudes toward foreign policy as it has been toward other things.

It is true that there has been an anti-Communist wing to liberalism. In the July, 1947, issue of <u>Foreign Affairs</u> George F. Kennan enunciated the doctrine of containment. This is the doctrine that has lain behind the policy of most liberal presidents and politicians during the Cold War. Organized labor, one of the elements in the liberal coalition, has for the most part been adamantly anti-Communist. Senator Henry Jackson, who had strong ties to organized labor, can be cited as one of a number of liberal leaders who have been strongly anti-Communist. We remember, too, that the Americans for Democratic Action was established right after World War II as a vehicle for liberals who did not want to collaborate with Communists.

The main thrust of the liberal intellectual culture, however, has been something quite different--and much further to the left. This main thrust of "liberal thought" is what I will examine in this chapter. It would be a serious mistake to

363

think that such a focus will center on something that has been irrelevant to practical policy. The international outlook injected by left-liberal thought has had telling effects. Since well before the end of World War II, it has introduced a paralyzing intellectual and moral ambivalence into American thinking and policy. We come to understand the importance of that ambivalence when we consider that, during all of that time, historic circumstances have called upon precisely the United States to serve as the world leader against the spread of Communism.

The extreme leftward orientation of liberal thought regarding international affairs has an unfortunate consequence so far as a dispassionate discussion is concerned. A direct statement, all in one place, of the liberal intellectual culture's positions will almost certainly be shocking to most Americans. It will even be shocking to liberals themselves; consistently with the dissimulation that is so basic to their posture, liberals instinctively prefer (and have come to expect) that such views be expressed so transparently only in liberalism's "in-house" literature. To defer to that preference, however, would keep us from completing our study of liberal thought. As I discuss the liberal attitudes, I will be careful to illustrate each of them amply from the writings of prominent liberal authors so that the reader can form a judgment from those sources, rather than simply from any imputation I might make.

Because the formative influences have been the same, we can expect to find the main contours to be:

. That liberal thought has held to a fundamentally Left-oriented point of view toward the world at large, but without any longer seeing the Soviet Union as a champion. This has included an ever-recurring tolerance toward Communist regimes (including even the Soviet Union). Exceptions will have occurred if in a given case a regime has done something quite recent to outrage liberals or

364

to make that tolerance more than ordinarily impolitic.

. That the outlook has reflected the divisions that have plagued the Left. In foreign affairs this will have appeared mainly in the tension between the traditions of pacifism-neutrality, on the one hand, and of Progressive-style, idealistic internationalism, on the other.

. That liberal thought has exhibited a readiness, so far as Europe and the Third World are concerned, to see value in democratic socialism, in "non-alignment" and "neutralism," and even in Communist regimes when they fit into the pattern of "pluralistic Communism." (The latter refers to the pattern that emerged with Tito in Yugoslavia and with the Chinese after their split with Moscow.)

. That the thinking has included a variety of alienations: toward the residuals of Western influence as they have appeared in the form of the last vestiges of 19th-century colonialism; toward non-Communist and non-socialist regimes whenever they have seemed especially vulnerable to criticism; and, perhaps most important of all, toward American policy whenever that policy has reflected, as it so often has, an anti-Communist purpose.

Several conceptual elements

1. Perhaps the most important conceptual element in the main thrust of liberal thought about international affairs since World War II has been its conviction that for one reason or another Communism is not a significant problem. Although "Russian nationalism" acting under the rubric of Communism has been seen as bothersome and as something that should be countered, Communism as an expansionist totalitarian ideology has been seen as more of a phantom of conservatives' imaginations.

365

This premise lay behind many of the statements about Vietnam. In 1971, Senator Frank Church said that "the threat of Communism in the third world is exaggerated...for many countries radical revolution is the only real hope...." Two years earlier, The New Republic had quoted Walter Lippmann as saying that a Communist South Vietnam "won't make very much of a difference." In 1972, the editors wrote that "no considerations of national interest or moral imperative required the United States to designate the Vietcong and Hanoi as an enemy and to move militarily against them." A short time before the collapse of South Vietnam in 1975, TRB was able to write that "if Congress cuts off aid hostilities probably will stop. Communists will win. How bad is that?"[1]

We know, of course, the overwhelmingly favorable liberal perception of the Soviet Union that existed during the three decades following the Bolshevik Revolution, a perception that suffered some very real shocks in the late 1930's but that was substantially rehabilitated during World War II. The Cold War that followed put a damper on that enthusiasm, and there was an anti-Communist side to liberal thought that was manifested in the Americans for Democratic Action. But the enthusiasm continued, for those further left, under Henry Wallace's leadership. In December, 1946--at the highpoint of Stalin's Gulags!--the extent of Wallace's self-deception was revealed by his statement that "today democracy is a universal ambition. The Soviet government no longer prides itself on the Dictatorship of the Proletariat." In March, 1947, he argued that "the Soviet Union has made no warlike moves. The real world crisis is the crisis of millions of people left homeless, hungry...."[2]

The persistence of this illusion among a great many liberals, predicated upon one pretext or another, is shown by Louis J. Halle's observation in 1960 that "the simple geographic image of the expanding Communist 'empire'...is too simple. (Is it one 'empire'? Does it include Yugoslavia?

...China?)." In 1973, Stanley Karnow said about the 1950's and early 1960's that "Eisenhower and Kennedy were battling against monolithic communism long after the Sino-Soviet dispute proved that the international Red menace was a myth" (emphasis added). In May, 1977, President Jimmy Carter declared that "we are now free of that inordinate fear of Communism which once led us to embrace any dictator" (emphasis added).[3]

2. One of the consequences of this illusion has been the double standard that has existed in liberal attitudes toward Nazism and fascism, which were correctly perceived as despicable and expansionist, and Communism.

In order to refresh ourselves about the early background, we should compare the attitudes toward the two systems in such a year as 1933. The reader will recall that this was the year in which in Soviet Russia variously estimated millions of kulaks were deliberately starved to overcome their opposition to the collectivization of agriculture. The New Republic ignored the slaughter. Within a few months after that dreadful winter of 1932-33, however, it was moved to condemn "Hitler's anti-Jewish campaign, which is on the whole the most uncivilized episode in modern history." The condemnation of Hitler was, of course, justified even though Hitler's anti-Jewish efforts were just in their beginning phase; but the selective perception, which has shielded Communism from being similarly condemned, must be understood as a central fact about the liberal intellectual culture's view of the world.[4]

I have several times commented that the 1930's "provides us a 'window' into liberal thinking." This continues to be true here. A candid explanation of the double standard, which will be helpful in understanding attitudes expressed throughout the fifty years that have followed, was provided in a New Republic editorial in 1935. The editors said that "those who are more tolerant of the Soviet Union than of Nazi Germany or Fascist

367

Italy are so because they sympathize with the main objectives and the chief policies of the workers' republic...To attempt to establish a classless society...is quite a different thing from enforcing industrial autocracy based on private ownership of the means of production." This explanation was given in response to a letter from William Henry Chamberlin in which he had demanded to know: "What is the background for the double standard of morals that not a few American and British radicals have consciously or unconsciously set up, one for Russia, one for the rest of the world?"5

The editors had more to say about this in late 1936: "Those individuals go seriously astray who announce that they are opposed to the dictatorships both of fascism and communism. The fascist dictatorship is an end in itself; the dictatorship of the proletariat is a means to a very different end." They spoke of Communism's being only in its "transition stage." A year later, Matthew Josephson added that "to liken the labor dictatorship of Stalin to the more opportunistic dictatorships of Mussolini or Hitler reveals a crudeness of judgment...."6

In 1943, a New Republic editorial praised the editors of Time magazine for an article about the Soviet Union. "The editors do not let what happened to the kulaks overbalance the fact that Russia solved one of her gravest problems by collectivizing agriculture." Again we see the concatenation of an extreme insensitivity toward Stalin's crimes and condemnation of Hitler's; a few months later, an editorial said that "the greatest tragedy of modern times is the murder of Jews and other victims by Hitler."7

In 1946, as we emerged into the postwar era, Joseph and Stewart Alsop wrote that "only a fool could fail to recognize the difference between the fascist system and the Soviet system, which though brutal in method, is entirely civilized in its basic concepts."8

368

In 1949, E. H. Carr wrote in The New Republic that Stalin's "own contribution to collectivization was the courage, determination and ruthlessness with which the policy was carried out and without which it could not have succeeded." It is hard to imagine similar virtues--about the formulation of policies that led to the deaths of millions of people!--being attributed to Adolf Hitler.[9]

In 1956, Eric Bentley wrote that "Bertolt Brecht...was a Communist, and I am anti-Communist ...yet I had the experience of being his political enemy and his personal friend...." As part of this analysis, we should ask ourselves whether a similar relationship would have been tolerable for Bentley if Brecht had been a Nazi. Again, it reflects the double standard. [10]

In 1961, after Patrice Lumumba's assassination, a New Republic editorial said that "Lumumba...was a very human African national whose association with the Soviet Union was pragmatic rather than ideological." Most certainly we can recall no similar rationalization justifying Vidkun Quisling's collaboration with Nazism in Norway. [11]

In 1963, Graham Greene reported that "the huge crowd that gathered before the monument to Marti to hear Castro's three-hour speech on July 26 was not the regimented or hypnotized crowd that used to greet Hitler."[12]

This attitude must certainly have lain behind The New Republic's editorial in 1967 that argued that "fortunately, Mr. [Lyndon] Johnson is willing not to let his Vietnam obsession get in the way of better relations and increased trade with Russia, even though Russia is helping arm people we're fighting."[13]

3. It helps us understand liberal positions on international affairs to realize that the result of this abstracting-away of the problem of Communism has been that liberal thought has tended

369

<u>to interpret the world in pre-World War I terms</u>. Instead of a world beset by an expansionist totalitarian ideology, it has been a world of contending nation-states, of national suspicions and jealousies, of arms races arising out of nothing more substantial than provincialism and jingoistic posturing. The solutions that have recommended themselves for such a world have been obvious: more cultural exchanges, more mechanisms for "improving understanding," the expectation that an international organization such as the United Nations should be able to serve as a truly meaningful instrument for peace, the pursuit of arms limitation treaties, and the like.

All of these would make real sense if the pre-World War I syndrome were indeed the central problem. If, however, expansionist totalitarianism has been the overriding source of difficulty, creating a "protracted conflict" that has been fought, in effect, on a worldwide scale at a number of different levels, these things will have trivialized and misdirected the response to it. Constantly to urge "detente" and "improved understanding" with regard to a system that all the while is subverting every vulnerable society that is not already within the circle of its totalitarian ideology is to act on illusion, not reality.

4. As we have seen in our discussion of the origins of the New Left, a radical peace movement has long been in existence, fed partly by the Left and partly by the "peace churches." This has stressed pacifism and neutrality. I would make the point that this peace movement is, at its core, something very different from the messianic "Progressive-style" liberalism that will favor foreign intervention if it approves of the particular cause.

For most purposes, these positions have overlapped during the Cold War, since neither has wanted America to be the leader of an adamant anti-Communism. Both pacifists and the liberals who have simply held the illusions that I have just recounted have shared a deep antipathy toward the United States' supporting the forces opposed to Communism in such places as, for example, El Salvador, Nicaragua and Grenada.

The distinction between the two lines of thinking was strikingly manifested, however, in connection with the response to the Nazi threat in the late 1930's. This has been the subject of James J. Martin's two-volume _American Liberalism and World Politics, 1931-1941_. I will illustrate it simply by taking the example of _The New Republic_'s stance toward Brazil in 1938 and 1939 when Brazil was threatened with a Nazi take-over. Consideration was being given by American policymakers to an intervention to prevent that from happening.

The Left was acutely aware of the despicable nature of Nazism and of its dangers to other peoples. It harbored no illusion about it comparable to that which it has held about Communism. If we were to go on the hypothesis that illusion has been the main obstacle to a willingness to support anti-totalitarian action, we might expect that the liberal intellectual culture would have supported an anti-Nazi intervention in Brazil. An intervention would have been consistent with the views of non-pacifist liberals, as we see from the fact that in 1915, before it became pacifist, _The New Republic_ called for American intervention in Mexico because of internal conditions there. 14

By 1938, however, _The New Republic_ had adhered to a pacifist-neutralist position for several years. The point I would make here is that _The New Republic_ remained consistent with that stance even in the face of _Nazi_ expansion. The editors opposed an anti-Nazi intervention in Brazil. Their argument included some of the same points that have since been used against anti-Communist interventions: that a large power such as the United States should not "dictate to" a less powerful nation, whose independence would thereby be compromised; and that no aid should even be extended, in this case even to anti-Nazi governments, until "they have shown that the aid will actually benefit the people."[15]

We know from this episode, and most especially from substantial other evidence, that the pacifist-neutralist tradition has been powerful within liberal thinking. It would be a mistake to think that the illusion about Communism has been the only source of liberal thought's apparent weakness in the face of Communism. The ideological sources are more complex than that.

5.   This mix of ingredients has led liberal thought to welcome the prospect of a world in which most of the nations would be either democratic socialist (and neutral toward what liberal thinkers see as primarily a struggle between two contending superpowers) or "independently Communist."   Conservatives would consider such a world a disaster both in a military and a value-oriented sense.   But what to conservatives is unthinkable has to liberal thought been a fully acceptable solution to the world's post-World War II plight.

That liberal thought would welcome the spread of democratic socialism became clear quite early. In September, 1945, a New Republic editorial said that "the scene is being set for a great experiment in democratic socialism, perhaps covering all of Europe, alongside the differently oriented Soviet experiment."   In 1947, Michael Straight wrote that "a great democratic, socialist force in the world today could isolate Soviet nationalism and American reaction.   It could expand into a world society, bringing peace."   In 1957, an editorial was critical of an anti-socialist policy underlying American aid to India.   In 1961, TRB wrote that "we bow down to the sacredness of private property and yet almost certainly an adequate revolution in Latin America must stand private property on its head."[16]

Liberal thought has at the same time seen great value in the "pluralization" of Communism,

372

by which I mean the existence of movements and regimes that are not strictly subject to Moscow's direction. It has even been argued that the establishment of a Communist regime, such as in Angola, can be a good thing, provided it is "independent." In January, 1950, the editors of The New Republic urged the American people to "distinguish between Communist-type revolutions and Kremlin-directed revolutions."[17]

In 1968, TRB wrote that "the theory was that there was a global communist conspiracy--but this evaporated when Moscow and Peking split." In 1977, Hans J. Morgenthau referred to "the polycentric character of Communism" and said that "the real issue...is not whether a certain government professes and practices Communism, but to what extent a government's foreign policy supports the foreign policies of the Soviet Union or of other governments hostile to the United States."[18]

This was the thinking pursued by Zbigniew Brzezinski, who became the principal architect of President Jimmy Carter's foreign policy. In 1962, Brzezinski argued that containment and liberation "have ceased to be relevant. Both were based on the premise that there is a united Soviet bloc." He called for a policy of "differentiated amity and hostility [to] consolidate differences within the Communist world." During the Carter presidency, Stanley Hoffmann wrote that "Brzezinski saw the world as far too diverse and complex to be managed by a Kissingerian balance-of-power system." This was the worldview that explains Andrew Young's actions as ambassador to the United Nations during the Carter administration.[19]

The third aspect of this has been liberalism's readiness to see vast portions of the globe declare their "neutrality." So much of the world has been included within this that, if the liberal intellectual culture's wishes had been fulfilled, the United States would very largely have come to stand alone, stripped of allies. (To a disconcerting degree, that is where the United States does find itself in the mid-1980's.)

In 1950, Michael Straight argued that "if Nehru could help to bring China out of the Soviet orbit and into an Asiatic bloc, the neutrality of Asia might not be too high a price to pay...." In 1957, the editors wrote that "what is needed, basically, is...a new Asian policy, one that does not assume that 'neutralism' helps Communism." In 1958, they said that "the main reason for our loss of influence in the Middle East and Asia was the attempt to extend the alliance system to areas whose peoples did not feel threatened by Russia-- the Baghdad pact and SEATO, followed by an inter- pretation of the Eisenhower Doctrine as something on which the Middle Eastern states had to declare 'for' or 'against.'" 20

In 1958 there was discussion of George F. Kennan's "disengagement" proposal, under which the Soviet Union would withdraw its forces from East- ern Europe and the United States would withdraw militarily from Western Europe. The New Republic supported the proposal, calling for a Europe that would be both neutral and free of nuclear arms. Consistently with its policy of serving as an intellectual clearing house for liberalism, which means that some articles have been run that have been at odds with the journal's editorial posi- tions, The New Republic included an article by Eugene V. Rostow in March, 1959, that pointed out that "such a policy would shift the balance of power against us appallingly." 21

In his book on Walter Lippmann, Hari N. Dam says that "in June 1960, Lippmann wrote an article urging a reappraisal of the policy of containment initiated under the Truman Doctrine...In view of the nuclear parity between the two [super]powers, the most prudent policy would be to promote neutrality among the peripheral states." 22

Shortly after John F. Kennedy's inauguration, a 1961 editorial said that "Mr. Kennedy is espous- ing a new U.S. doctrine around which a new non-

Communist coalition can be formed--the integrity of neutralism." Later that year, Denis Warner wrote that "there is nothing wrong with neutrality; it is no longer considered 'immoral.'"23

Meanwhile, the Soviet Union had itself been seeking to advance the movement toward "non-alignment." In 1967, Ernst Halperin wrote that "in 1956 Khrushchev sought to legitimize his new policy of encouraging 'non-alignment.'" He even went so far as to say that Khrushchev had considered Castro's victory in Cuba a "bitter setback" to Khrushchev's larger strategy of seeking the neutralization of all of South America. 24

In 1962, The New Republic called for a settlement of the Vietnam War on the basis of a neutralized South Vietnam. Incredibly, this took the form in September, 1963, of a call for "uniting the country" under Ho Chi Minh's rule, at which time "he could become another Tito" [i.e., independent Communist]. 25

All of this was advocated despite the fact that "non-alignment" very soon came to bear about the same relationship to Soviet Communism as "fellow-travelling" did during the 1930's. In 1961, Walter Z. Laqueur and Alfred Sherman gave the following description of a meeting of the "non-aligned" countries held in (the Communist city of) Belgrade: "For many American well-wishers of the newly independent countries of Africa and Asia, the meeting of the 'non-aligned' in Belgrade came as a shock...Tito's stand at the conference, which was the most obdurately anti-Western on all questions, should serve as a reminder that Yugoslavia is a Communist state...The Cuban performance lent further weight to the belief that for all practical purposes the country's leaders at present are wholly identified with the Communist bloc and that their adherence to the flexible principle of non-alignment is a matter of temporary expedience."26

A New Republic editorial in 1958 described

375

Nasser's ostensible "neutrality" in Egypt: "We are neutralist but we fervently hope that the Soviet bloc will defeat the imperialist West...We are not Communists; we only want to establish a popular democratic society on the pattern of Mao's China." Another editorial, this time in 1971, described the scene as "cheers and dancing in the aisles of the General Assembly" when finally Communist China was given a seat and the Republic of China was ousted. [27]

All the while, both Moscow and Peking were taking advantage of the moral and intellectual weakness by treating Asia, Africa and Latin America as a "soft underbelly" for Communist subversion. Moscow worked to build up its traditional bases for revolution among the workers, seeking to tie its worldwide network to Soviet foreign policy; Peking provided nurture for those who sought "revolution now." In 1962, the New Republic reported that "in the last few years the Chinese have trained thousands of Spanish and Portuguese agents who have traveled all over Latin America." In 1967, Bjorn Kumm spoke of "North Vietnam, where the hard core Bolivian guerrillas were sent for training...." Kumm said that "it is known that [Che] Guevara appeared at a secret meeting in Prague in early May 1965...[with] a group of Bolivians who were later to become the nucleus of the guerrilla force." We know, of course, that Guevara was eventually killed fighting as a guerrilla leader in Bolivia. [28]

6. An important part of all of this has received attention in conservative circles during the mid-1980's. It is that one of the premises of the worldview that I have been discussing is that there is a moral equivalency between the Soviet Union and the United States.

In light of all that I have covered, it should perhaps be considered an improvement, from the United States' point of view, even to be considered morally equivalent to the Soviet Union. There were many years during which the world intellectual culture gave the Soviet Union the better of it.

Nevertheless, the fact that "moral equivalency" can even be entertained as a notion now that the world has seen the deflation of the Soviet dream demonstrates how skewed the perception is. That after the purges, the Gulags, the crushing of Hungary and Czechoslovakia and Afghanistan, and after the many additional "shocks" that have rocked world opinion about Communism it is still possible for the Soviet Union to have any moral stature at all is perhaps the best example I know of of what Ayn Rand called "moral counterfeiting." It is just another manifestation of the attitudes that I have been tracing in this chapter. At the same time, to place the United States on a moral par with the Soviet Union, even at what is for the Soviet Union an inflated level, is a function of the abiding hatred that lies at the heart of the world Left.

The concept of "moral equivalency" is one that is used to disarm any anti-Communist action or attitude. In 1960, TRB wrote that "we can't abide the thought of Cuba going Communist; doesn't that help give us an idea of the way Red China feels about Capitalist Quemoy and Matsu and Formosa?" Then in 1961, TRB wrote that "the U.S. has been complaining of the Soviets' recent airlift into Laos, a country into which we ourselves dumped a third of a million dollars, nearly all military." The editors added to the theme a couple of months later: "The President is correct when he says that the Communists 'send arms...to every troubled area.' But it is only part of the truth. For this is what the United States has been doing since the start of the Cold War...." In 1970, the editors argued that "as long as this country keeps 400,000 or even 200,000 troops in South Vietnam...it cannot convincingly claim that the Russians have no right to put 8,000 or even 12,000 troops in Egypt." [29]

7. It perhaps goes without saying that these

377

attitudes have led to bitter criticism of all anti-Communist efforts. It is a mistake to think that the criticism arises mainly out of the circumstances of a given case. Jean Kirkpatrick had an electric effect with her speech to the 1984 Republican National Convention in which she denounced those "who always blame America first." She was putting her finger on one of the many aspects of the ideological syndrome I am describing. I hardly need to illustrate the continuing condemnation of anti-Communist and American actions, since virtually everything that I have quoted has such criticism at least implicit within it.

8. An extremely important part of all of this has been the manner in which liberal thought has reacted to revolutionary situations throughout the world. Because of its importance and magnitude, this will be the subject of the next chapter.

9. There are a number of corollary issues, each significant in itself. One of these has to do with the often-mentioned "principle of non-intervention." Another has to do with what the attitude of American foreign policy should be toward non-Communist governments that are for one reason or another undesirable. (The questions of democracy and of "respect for 'human rights'" are rarely raised about Communist governments, so it is non-Communist governments that, interestingly enough, constitute the "universe of discouse" here.) A third pertains to what is derisively called "the domino theory."

Most liberal thought gravitated in the late 1930's to a position favoring the Allies' eventual war against Hitler; and we have seen that The New Republic favored intervention in other countries on moral or humanitarian grounds prior to 1920. But, with these as the main exceptions, the overwhelming refrain within liberal thought has been that there is no right to intervene in another country for any reason internal to that country.

378

The international nature of the Communist problem
has not been thought to make an overwise "internal" issue an "external" one.

A few examples of how the "principle of non-
intervention" has been applied will suffice: A New
Republic editorial in 1927 criticized American
domination of Nicaragua and the Phillipines,
speaking of "American imperialism." In 1929, the
editors were displeased that "the Monroe Doctrine
has come to mean the 'right' of the United States
to police the western hemisphere." Many years
later, in 1961, TRB wrote that "the State Department ejaculated—'Communism in this hemisphere is
not negotiable.' What virtue! What stupidity!
It means that we deny the sovereignty of Latin
nations to choose their government." In 1965, the
editors argued that "sending 25,000 American servicemen to the Dominican Republic violated the
O.A.S. charter." In 1978, TRB called the DeCon-
cini reservation to the Panama Canal treaty "arro-
gant" for "asserting the U.S. right to intervene
after the year 2,000 to keep the canal open." In
1980, an editorial said that Americans should
apologize to the Iranians for having interfered in
Iran's affairs "to shore up a despotic regime."
The involvement of the Central Intelligence Agency
in the overthrow of Salvador Allende in Chile to
prevent the Communization that he was openly
carrying out has been roundly condemned within
liberal circles. The Reagan administration's
invasion of Grenada after the Communist take-over
there has been condemned. These examples are
merely a few of many that could be cited.[30]

It would be misleading, however, to conclude
that this represents a genuinely held principle of
"non-intervention," except for liberals who are
actually a part of the pacifist-neutralist tradition. We have already seen how in 1915 The New
Republic criticized Woodrow Wilson's "hands-off"
policy toward Mexico's turbulent internal situation. At that time, the editors argued that "an
unalterable rule of non-intervention ignores the
truth...that no country can in the long run be

allowed to behave as it pleases without regard to the interests and standards of other nations." Later that same year, in connection with the Turks' massacre of the Armenians, they held that "the dogma that all governments are sovereign and that intervention is never justified...is of course an impossible doctrine...."[31]

I believe it has mainly been hypocrisy, rather than a well-reasoned return to the principles that The New Repubic stated in what I have just quoted, that has underlain liberalism's long-standing attack upon apartheid in South Africa and the attack by the Carter Administration on "human rights abuses" by non-Communist governments in several countries. Unless racial discrimination can be considered "external" in a way that Communism cannot, there would seem to be no basis, consistently with the pure principle of non-intervention that the liberal intellectual culture has espoused for so long, for the article by Ian Robertson and Phillip Whitten in an April, 1968, issue of The New Republic entitled "The Olympics: Keep South Africa Out!" In 1980, Bernard-Henri Levy wrote passionately that "the time has come to reestablish in the world, in its most desolate corner, the principles of an entirely different internationalism: the internationalism of human rights and of help for the tortured." At least so far as non-Communist governments were concerned, but only as to them, the principle of non-intervention had been repudiated.[32]

What this shows us, as so many things do, is that, except with a few purists, principles such as "non-intervention" have been instruments of ideological convenience. I would be the last to suggest that hypocrisy is a vice exclusively of American liberalism; but we are foolish if we do not take into account the extent to which liberal thought has applied double standards in a great many areas.

"Non-intervention" is closely related to the second of the three areas that I am presently discussing. This is the question of how the United States and the world community should react to "undesirable" regimes. We will see that here too there has been enormous inconsistency.

Immediately after Mao completed his conquest of the Chinese mainland in late 1949, The New Republic called for the United States to win back the "friendship of the Chinese people" by extending diplomatic recognition to the newly-created People's Republic of China and by engaging in trade. Again in 1958, and at various other times as well, the editors called for recognition of Red China and its admission to the United Nations. Obviously these attitudes were calculated not to take into account the holocaust that occurred under Mao (in which, according to Time magazine's report after Mao's death, a variously estimated 10 to 60 million Chinese were put to death following the Communist takeover) or the lack of democracy under his regime. The principle of ignoring such matters had been enunciated years before when The New Republic had written that "we have opposed this policy of making diplomatic recognition the equivalent of moral approval...."33

This should be compared with Harold L. Ickes' position in 1949 that "Franco's Spain should not be admitted to the United Nations or the North Atlantic Pact unless it genuinely adheres to democratic principles." Over the years, liberal thought has invoked a similar moral sensibility with regard to Nationalist China, Rhodesia, South Africa, the Shah of Iran, the regime of the Greek colonels, the Pinochet government in post-Allende Chile, the Marcos regime in the Phillipines, and several others. It amounts, of course, to a selective morality; but our purpose right now is to see how it raises havoc with the principle, often asserted, that moral considerations should not affect America's willingness to recognize, to trade with, and otherwise to share a world with a given regime.34

A thread of consistency did appear back in

1933 when The New Republic argued for the recognition of Hitler's regime, at which time it pointed out that the journal had always held that moral considerations should not stand in the way of recognizing Soviet Russia. We have already noted how The New Republic did hold consistently to a pacifist-neutralist position in 1938 with regard to taking action against Nazis in Brazil, so we know that consistency is possible. But whether the position taken about recognition of Hitler in 1933 represented a true consistency, or merely a tactical one in light of the journal's passionate affinity for Soviet Russia at that time and desire for American recognition of its government, is a matter of conjecture. It would have been too directly self-contradictory to have embraced opposing rationales in so brief a period.

The third point among those I am now discussing has to do with the shifting positions on what liberals have come to call "the domino theory."

Liberal rhetoric has often spoken of "the domino theory" in its criticisms of the Vietnam War, both during the war and since, and also in connection with the threats posed by Communism in South and Central America. The concern that a Communist victory in one place will create a threat to adjacent areas has been caused to sound far-fetched, a remote conjecture. This is accomplished by demoting the concern to the status of a "theory." An example occurred in 1970 when Salvador Allende took office in Chile with an openly announced program of Communizing the country. A New Republic editorial said that "the White House ...put forward a new Latin-style domino theory, according to which Peru, Bolivia and Argentina... might be the next three countries to fall."[35]

Oddly, this rhetoric is accepted at face value in a great deal of public discussion, despite the fact that the concern that the "domino theory" reflects is a valid one. In several connections in which there has not been an ideological reason to denigrate the concern, liberal

382

thought has itself used the point, taking its validity for granted. In 1937, a New Republic editorial about Spain observed that "if Franco wins, the war-willing powers will be immensely encouraged for their next aggression." In 1967, the editors asked the readers to "imagine the world as it would have been had Israel lost on the battlefield or remained passive...The Middle East would have become an exclusive Soviet preserve." In 1980, an editorial said about the Soviet invasion of Afghanistan that it was not "by itself, that important. The danger is that for destabilizing--or actually attacking--neighboring areas that are important, specifically Pakistan and Iran." (Interestingly, the so-called "domino theory" was applied in these last two instances even to Communist expansion. I have never seen an explanation within liberal writing of why the "theory" is thought to make perfectly good sense in certain circumstances, but in others, such as in Southeast Asia and Central America, to reflect the most obvious stupidity.)[36]

Consequences of the worldview

In the next chapter, which deals with "Liberalism and a World in Revolution," I shall discuss the consequences of the liberal worldview as they have been felt in a number of different countries. In the present chapter, I will mention only certain consequences that will not fit into that discussion. Needless to say, a brief space will not allow an attempt to be exhaustive.

The consequences of the self-deception can be seen in America's failure to fight World War II with political objectives in mind. We "won the war" but "lost the peace" in a way that can only be characterized as a disaster for millions of people and for the free world. Garet Garrett pointed to a startling fact: "When the Yalta Agreement was signed [in February, 1945] the number of people in the Communist world was hardly more than 200 million. Five years later it was

800 million...."[37]

Our illusions about the nature of Stalin's dictatorship were such that we forcibly returned a reported two million Russians to the Soviet Union at the end of the war. A review in The New Republic in 1978 said that "Nikolai Tolstoy's The Secret Betrayal may well be the most authoritative accounting of the monstrous repatriation to the Soviet Union of more than two million Russians living (mostly imprisoned) in the countries liberated by the western allies at the end of World War II."[38]

In Volume I of The Gulag Archipelago, Aleksandr Solzhenitsyn, who spent years in Stalin's labor camps, commented bitterly about this and other associated events: "In their own countries Roosevelt and Churchill are honored as embodiments of statesmanlike wisdom. To us, in our Russian prison conversations, their consistent shortsightedness and stupidity stood out as astonishingly obvious. How could they, in their decline from 1941 to 1945, fail to secure any guarantees whatever of the independence of Eastern Europe? How could they give away broad regions of Saxony and Thuringia in exchange for the preposterous toy of a four-zone Berlin, their own future Achilles' heel? And what was the military or political sense in their surrendering to destruction at Stalin's hands hundreds of thousands of armed Soviet citizens determined not to surrender? They say it was the price they paid for Stalin's agreeing to enter the war against Japan. With the atom bomb already in their hands, they paid Stalin for not refusing to occupy Manchuria, for strengthening Mao Tse-tung in China, and for giving Kim Il Sung control of half Korea!"[39]

Some small part of the personal tragedy caused by this Allied policy, which so strongly found its origins in liberalism's illusions about the Soviet Union, came home forcefully to me on November 14, 1976, as I read the Sunday paper. The Wichita Eagle-Beacon carried a feature story

384

about a World War II prisoner-of-war camp near Concordia, Kansas. The article quoted a Yugoslavian who had become a prisoner there after he had been impressed into the German Wehrmacht: "Later, I was sent to a camp in Nebraska and then to another for Yugoslavs in North Carolina. There were some Russian soldiers there who had fought on the side of the Germans, and the United States had no choice but to send them back. Rather than go back to be shot, most of them committed suicide."

Solzhenitsyn tells how the entire army of Russian soldiers under General Vlasov who had defected from Stalin and had been fighting against the Red Army were tricked into thinking they were surrendering to the English when in fact they were being turned over to the Red Army.[40]

During World War II, Heinz H. F. Eulau wrote prolifically for The New Republic favoring a post-war domination of Eastern Europe by the Soviet Union. In April, 1944, he wrote that "Soviet influence in future Balkan politics is natural... Those who raise the cry of 'Soviet imperialism' fail to understand that the overwhelming majority of the common people in the Balkans do not fear Soviet influence." In August, 1944, he wrote that "Poland will be in close alliance with the USSR and form an integral part of the security system which the Soviet Union is building up in Eastern Europe under her hegemony." A month later, Jerome Davis told the journal's readers that "the Soviet Union wants to work with the rest of the world. In the postwar world she doesn't want to foist communism off on other nations...." In April, 1945, a contributor with the initials E. L. P. spoke of "the Anglo-American Russia-haters [who] bewail the allegedly undemocratic lot of the Eastern European countries under the Soviet heel...." In July of that same year, the New Republic's editors said that "the Russia-hating American press has long argued that once anybody got into the clutches of Soviet Russia, he was never again permitted to escape. For the record, let it be noted that this seems to be false so far as it

385

concerns the Poles."[41]

The lack of geopolitical strategy within the Roosevelt administration reflected this outlook. A _New Republic_ editorial in June, 1945, told the story: "While Roosevelt was alive he acted as mediator between two stubborn men, Churchill and Stalin...who clashed...notably as to whether the Anglo-American invasion of Europe should be in the Balkans, as Churchill wished, through territory which the Russians regard as their sphere of influence, or through France." It was Stalin, not Churchill, who, with Roosevelt's decisive vote, won this argument. The decision in favor of Operation Overlord, the invasion of Normandy, consigned Eastern Europe to Soviet domination, since it was the occupation by the Red Army, even more than any decision made at Yalta, that determined the fate of those countries.[42]

In a book in 1957, Rexford Tugwell discussed the decision to invade Normandy rather than to attack through Eastern Europe: "The Americans were still wary of Churchill,...being fearful that he would soon begin, as usual, to find reasons for postponement...He did now suggest that going north to meet the Russian...drive somewhere in the Balkans would be a way of preventing future trouble in Europe." Tugwell said that "Marshall and Hopkins were his [Churchill's] active counters. Their acceptance of Russia as an ally was much more sincere than that of the British...."[43]

W. W. Rostow told about yet another facet of this strategic struggle in a book in 1960. He said that "the United States did not support Churchill's efforts in 1945 to seek Anglo-American victory in the race for Berlin and Prague or encourage his notion that Western troops withdraw to the occupation areas in Germany only when the Yalta provisions concerning the method of forming the Eastern European governments were actually carried out."[44]

With regard to this same point, Senator

Robert A. Taft observed that "our troops could have reached Berlin before the Russians if they had not been called back. We withdrew from Dresden and Leipsig, which we had already occupied. General Patton would have been in Prague the next day, but he was called back so that Czechoslovakia could surrender to Russian generals, and his own book shows that he was not pleased with the recall."45

After Eastern Europe was lost, The New Republic began the slow process (which in the next chapter we will see became part of an often-repeated cycle) of regretting it--although at first with a heavy doze of rationalization. In November, 1945, the editors reported that "the Soviet government has exercised terrific pressure on the countries liberated by the Red Army--Rumania, Bulgaria, Yugoslavia, Hungary, Czechoslovakia, Poland and Austria--...It has used techniques of political control which are objectionable to democratic nations." But the editors asked, "Can it be blamed?...If we would share the [atomic] bomb with them..., our opposition to Russian-controlled governments in Eastern Europe might carry real weight." Even in late 1947, the best face was being put on things. The New Republic ran an article by Owen Lattimore, later of China fame, that said that "it may be that the Czecho-slovakian Communists, heartily backed by the Soviet Communists, are giving a thorough trial run to a policy of suggesting, to the nation's neigh-bors, that socialism and eventual communism can be reached by an easy transition, with prosperity all along the way and without massacre or coercion."46

NOTES

1. New Republic, November 13, 1971, p. 13; New Republic, September 27, 1969, p. 8; New Republic, May 13, 1972, p. 8; New Republic, February 1, 1975, p. 2.

2. New Republic, December 16, 1946, p. 789; New

Republic, March 24, 1947, p. 12.

3.   New Republic, February 29, 1960, p. 14; New
Republic, September 8, 1973, p. 18; New Republic,
June 4, 1977, p. 8.

4.   New Republic, June 7, 1933, p. 84.

5.   New Republic, February 27, 1935, pp. 61, 77.

6.   New Republic, December 9, 1936, p. 160; New
Republic, December 1, 1937, p. 107.

7.   New Republic, April 5, 1943, p. 428; New
Republic, February 7, 1944, p. 164.

8.   New Republic, September 16, 1946, p. 322.

9.   New Republic, November 28, 1949, p. 21.

10.   New Republic, August 27, 1956, p. 19.

11.   New Republic, February 20, 1961, p. 6.

12.   New Republic, November 2, 1963, p. 17.

13.   New Republic, April 22, 1967, p. 4.

14.   New Republic, January 23, 1915, p. 7; see
also New Republic, October 9, 1915, p. 245, regarding the massacre of the Armenians by the
Turks.

15.   New Republic, February 9, 1938, p. 4; New
Republic, December 7, 1938, p. 127; New Republic,
November 22, 1939, p. 137.

16.   New Republic, September 3, 1945, p. 272; New
Republic, December 29, 1947, p. 9; New Republic,
September 23, 1957, p. 4; New Republic, May 8,
1961, p. 2.

17.   New Republic, January 23, 1950, p. 6.

18.   New Republic, January 20, 1968, p. 6; New

Republic, January 22, 1977, p. 54.

19. New Republic, March 26, 1962, pp. 13, 14; New Republic, July 29, 1978, p. 20.

20. New Republic, November 20, 1950, p. 14; New Republic, June 24, 1957, p. 8; New Republic, June 2, 1958, p. 4.

21. New Republic, January 6, 1958, p. 3; New Republic, March 2, 1959, p. 23.

22. Hari N. Dam, The Intellectual Odyssey of Walter Lippmann (New York: Gordon Press, 1973), pp. 152-153.

23. New Republic, April 3, 1961, p. 3; New Republic, September 25, 1961, p. 13.

24. New Republic, November 27, 1961, p. 11.

25. New Republic, March 12, 1962, p. 4; New Republic, December 15, 1962, p. 5; New Republic, September 14, 1963, p. 5.

26. New Republic, September 25, 1961, p. 9.

27. New Republic, March 10, 1958, p. 4; New Republic, November 6, 1971, p. 9.

28. New Republic, January 29, 1962, p. 6; New Republic, November 11, 1967, p. 15.

29. New Republic, August 29, 1960, p. 2; New Republic, April 3, 1961, p. 2; New Republic, June 5, 1961, p. 4; New Republic, August 1, 1970, p. 5.

30. New Republic, January 12, 1927, p. 203; New Republic, January 30, 1929, p. 286; New Republic, May 8, 1961, p. 2; New Republic, May 15, 1965, p. 1; New Republic, April 22, 1978, p. 2; New Republic, March 8, 1980, p. 6.

31. New Republic, January 23, 1915, p. 7; New Republic, October 9, 1915, p. 245.

32. New Republic, April 13, 1968, p. 12.

33. New Republic, September 26, 1949, p. 6; New Republic, June 16, 1958, p. 4; New Republic, June 21, 1933, p. 138.

34. New Republic, May 30, 1949, p. 15.

35. New Republic, November 7, 1970, p. 9.

36. New Republic, January 13, 1937, p. 315; New Republic, June 17, 1967, p. 1; New Republic, January 26, 1980, p. 8.

37. Garet Garrett, The American Story (Chicago: Henry Regnery Company, 1955), p. 349.

38. New Republic, December 1, 1978, p. 51.

39. Aleksandr I. Solzhenitsyn, The Gulag Archipe-lago (New York: Harper & Row, 1974), Thomas P. Whitney, trans., Vol. I, pp. 259-260.

40. Solzhenitsyn, Gulag, Vol. I, p. 259.

41. New Republic, April 3, 1944, p. 462; New Republic, August 7, 1944, p. 157; New Republic, September 4, 1944, p. 277; New Republic, April 25, 1945, p. 555; New Republic, July 16, 1945, p. 59.

42. New Republic, June 4, 1945, p. 771.

43. Rexford G. Tugwell, The Democratic Roosevelt (Garden City: Doubleday & Company, Inc., 1957), pp. 621-622.

44. W. W. Rostow, The United States in the World Arena (New York: Harper & Brothers, 1960), p. 184.

45. Senator Robert A. Taft, A Foreign Policy for Americans (Garden City: Doubleday & Company, Inc., 1951), p. 54.

46. New Republic, November 5, 1945, p. 589; New Republic, September 22, 1947, p. 7.

16

LIBERALISM AND A WORLD IN REVOLUTION

It has been a source of enormous tragedy for the world that since 1917 liberal thought has, with regard to one country after another that has come under attack from Communist revolution, followed a discernible pattern that has started with illusion and ended with an admission of horror. The cycle has been repeated many times, since the ultimate recognition of that horror has not prevented the illusion that begins the cycle from being present again and again with regard to later Communist revolutions in other countries.

In this chapter we will review the positions of the liberal intellectual culture before, during and after the revolutionary challenges to Russia, Spain, Western Europe, Greece, China, Taiwan, Korea, Guatemala, Cuba, Guinea, the Dominican Republic, Vietnam, Chile, Rhodesia, Nicaragua, El Salvador, South Africa and Grenada. In several cases, we will be able to see the playing out of the entire pattern. In others, such as where the revolution did not succeed or is still in progress, the situation will have lent itself to the presence of only part of the cycle.

By limiting my discussion to the countries and areas named, I do not mean to suggest that there have not been others. My primary concern, as it has been throughout this book, is to analyze and illustrate the ideological elements rather than to write an exhaustive history.

Stages in the cycle of liberal response

Without caring to reach a round number for its own sake, I have identified ten related but separate components of the liberal intellectual culture's response to leftist revolutions as they have occurred throughout the world:

1. Most especially since World War II, the world Left, including the American liberal intellectual culture, has held many non-Communist countries in what we might call "simmering contempt." Accordingly, it would not be accurate to say that liberal thought has ever fully accepted the status quo within them. But it is significant that with others, at least until a revolution has gotten underway, the existing society and its government have been accepted, despite their imperfections, as normal parts of the world community.

Chiang Kai-shek and his government in China offer a good example. In August, 1943, a New Republic editorial praised Chiang as both a man of action and a thinker. "The meliorism of Thorstein Veblen and J. A. Hobson he finds in harmony," the editorial said, "with the best present tendencies in Chinese thought."[1]

2. After the revolutionary challenge has begun, the liberal attitude toward the country has escalated into a dramatic condemnation. The existing regime has then been painted in the darkest colors. Those who have been identified with the government and who have opposed the revolution have been pictured as corrupt oligarchs whose repressions and violations of human rights have made them representatives of unmitigated evil.

If we pursue the Chinese example a step further, we see that in May, 1944, just a few months after the praise I have just quoted, The New Republic's TRB was beginning to talk about "the anti-democratic movement in China...the heavy censorship...the disregard of the tragedy of the poor" and another article was speaking of "the autocratic, one-party rule of [Chiang's] Kuomintang." We know now that these were the opening volleys in what was to become a decades-long campaign of vilification that painted Chiang and the Kuomintang as reactionary and that continued until long after Chiang and his army had retreated to

392

Taiwan.[2]

3.   In casting the existing government in this light, liberal thought has abandoned the cultural relativity that it has used in so many other connections. The regime has been judged not in the context of its own society, with its unique history and conditions, but by an ideal standard.

Even more importantly, the regime has been judged without regard to the fact that it has at the time been actively embroiled in combatting riots, anarchy and organized revolution under what have inevitably been wartime conditions.

With regard to China the effects of many years of war and inflation upon the Chiang Kai-shek government were ignored. In a perceptive comment, Freda Utley has observed that "to ascribe the defeat of the Chinese National Government to its 'corrupt and reactionary' character is to beg the question. What is required is an examination of the causes which led to the frustration of the great national renaissance led by the Kuomintang in the 1920's and 1930's...It was useless to expect that an economically backward country, exhausted from an eight-year war with Japan and currently involved in an undercover war with Russia, could, almost overnight, set up a 'democratic' government. Add to these drawbacks the fact that China had no past experience of representative government."[3]

South Vietnam provides another example. The distortions imposed upon the society by the systematic assassination of thousands of village chiefs and other leaders were never considered. In June, 1961, President Kennedy spoke of 4,000 civilian officials who had been assassinated in the preceding twelve months. The statistics about the dead might briefly be recited, but then the successors of the dead leaders were themselves condemned as venal and unrepresentative. In the same month that Kennedy told of the assassinations, an article in The New Republic accused the South Viet-

393

namese government of "lies and fakery," of being "undemocratic" and of using "connivance and force to prolong its life." The unspoken assumption was that such a bleeding was of no consequence and that the government should be judged just as though it had never happened.[4]

In each case, the existing governments have been judged according to criteria that Americans would apply to, say, an American presidential administration. This has subsumed, as well, a country not torn by internecine hatreds. No doubt such a standard has been used with considerable cynicism by the intellectual culture, which is hardly so naive in other connections. Such a standard has been a natural one in the 20th century American context. It has been able to play upon the simple-mindedness and provincialism of millions of Americans. There have been many, some of them on the edge of the intellectual culture and others simply members of the public at large, who have prided themselves upon keeping their minds fully attuned (without so much as a moment's genuine thought) to the twists and turns of fashionable opinion. In countless ways, people of this sort have made themselves the instruments of propaganda and ideological bias.

4. At the same time as a country's existing regime has been condemned, the leftist revolutionaries have been lavishly praised. The Communist and totalitarian nature of the revolution has almost invariably been denied. The "national liberation front" has been pictured as democratic, led by men who have represented a people in revolt against intolerable conditions. By this process Mao has become an "agrarian reformer" and Fidel a romantic swashbuckler. While the revolution is seen as an explosion resulting from the indignation of exploited masses, the central role of the intelligentsia and of trained Marxist-Leninist cadre within it is given scant attention.

5. A point that should be considered separately, for emphasis if for no other reason, is

394

that in most cases the precise nature of the revolutionary movement has been obscured by the fact that the "social democratic" Left throughout the world has been willing (beginning with Russia in 1917) to join in a United Front with the Communist Left. This coalition of the various segments of the Left is what has made it possible to say that "only a part of the revolution consists of Communists" and to treat as mere speculation the concerns of anti-Communists about whether the Communists will control the revolution after it succeeds.

The ambiguity created by this collaboration has been one of the more important facts about the world since World War II. It has meant that in one revolutionary situation after another public opinion within the free world has been unable clearly to identify its enemy. The effect has been devastating. The support of the social democratic Left has not only helped the revolutionary movements materially and politically; it has contributed immensely to a semi-paralysis on the part of the non-Communist world.

. The collaboration has been the factor that more than any other has laid the foundation for the moral and intellectual uncertainty that the free world, and especially the American public and the Congress of the United States, has experienced about resisting Communist expansion. This has resulted in serious internal division, such as exists as this is written about American policy toward the Sandinista regime in Nicaragua.

. The result has been the lack of an articulated anti-Communist rationale for American policy in such a place as Vietnam. In March, 1967, TRB wrote that "we are not there to prevent South Vietnam going Communist. ('We do not seek to impose our political beliefs upon South Vietnam,' says the President [Lyndon Johnson] categorically.)...What are we there for, then? Mr. Johnson tells us. It is terribly simple. It is to give 'a concrete demonstration that aggression across international frontiers is no longer an acceptable means of political change." We see in this passage that President Johnson was choosing to rationalize the war in terms of a post-World War I "Kellogg-Briand" type of thinking, in which the problem was seen as one of aggressive nation-states attacking one another. Johnson was playing to the Left and to the ambiguity within American public opinion, deliberately avoiding an anti-Communist rationale.[5]

    . These factors in turn have led to an irresolute response to Communist revolutionary attacks upon the free world.

    . Although Americans find it most comfortable to brush the fact under a rug and to pull back mentally into the shelter of their own lives, the fact remains that since 1939 there has been a loss of hundreds of millions of people to Communist domination. One country after another has succumbed to one-party Marxist-Leninist dictatorship. Our mental defenses are such that it seems almost ungracious to recall their names: Estonia, Latvia, Lithuania, Poland, Hungary, Czechoslovakia, Yugoslavia, Rumania, Albania, China, North Korea, North Vietnam, South Vietnam, Laos, Cambodia, Angola, Mozambigue, Ethiopia, Rhodesia (if Mugabe succeeds in consolidating his rule), Cuba, Nicaragua, Afghanistan....and others. But of course these are not just names; they are whole peoples who now live under a totalitarian system.

    . There has been an increasingly discernible isolation of the United States within a world that, to the extent it is not Communist, has become ever-more hostile and "neutral." The French refusal to allow American warplanes to fly over its territory to make the retaliatory raid on Libya in 1986 is symptomatic of this shift. The change reflects more than just the decisions of politicians. It manifests their awareness of opinion within their respective countries.

Because of the things I have just mentioned,

we should recall the division that occurred within American liberalism at the end of World War II. At that time, the Americans for Democratic Action (ADA) was formed primarily to represent liberals who opposed "working together" in the same organizations with Communists. The Progressive Citizens of America (PCA), which formed the basis for Henry Wallace's presidential candidacy in 1948, represented those further to the Left. Its supporters included Communists and those who were willing to continue the old United Front coalition that had been so important in the 1930's.

This seems simply a footnote in American history, but in fact the principle that it involved should long have been considered, for the reasons I have just mentioned, one of the single most crucial issues in the world since World War II. Unfortunately, most (although not all) of the world's "social democratic" Left has taken the position of the PCA. And even more fatefully, the American liberal intellectual culture has encouraged it in this. The principle of non-collaboration has largely been lost sight of since the debate over it in the late 1940's. As we saw in our discussion of the New Left, the principle was abandoned in the 1960's. Further, we saw in our discussion of liberal attitudes toward world affairs that liberal thought has encouraged the collaborationist posture of the so-called "non-aligned" factions throughout the world. The failure to insist upon a moral imperative of non-collaboration has, because of its consequences, marked the intellectual bankruptcy of American liberalism and of the social democratic Left in the world arena.

6.   The sixth component in the cycle has been an active opposition to the giving of any support to the existing government in its struggle against the revolution.

This opposition has been rationalized in a number of ways: the denial of the "domino theory" has allowed liberals to argue that the loss of the particular country will have no further ramifications, so that any intervention by the United States is not really justified by our national interest. The concept that the revolutions have "just been civil wars between the existing government and factions that are actually nationalist, and to whom Marxism-Leninism is simply a facade" has had the same effect. And the perception of the unworthiness and corruption of the existing government has meant that support, if given, would seem both wasted and morally reprehensible.

We have seen this opposition to support wherever the existing regime has sought American or Western backing. Countries to which this has applied have included, among others, Russia (with regard to Western assistance to anti-Communist forces in the post-1917 civil war in which Lenin succeeded in consolidating his power), Greece, China, Korea (before the North Korean invasion), Taiwan, Quemoy and Matsu, Vietnam, Guatemala, the Dominican Republic, and El Salvador. In addition, the liberal intellectual culture has opposed any effort to overthrow a Communist regime once it has been in place. We can call to mind the severe condemnation of such efforts in Cuba and Nicaragua, where they have not yet succeeded, and in Chile and Grenada, where they have.

7. Once the Communist revolution has taken the particular country, liberal thought has urged a friendly posture toward the revolutionary regime. The hope has been expressed that the revolution will either (a) prove itself not truly to have been Communist, or (b) be tamed by the conciliatory gestures and thereby become one of the "independent Communist" regimes within a pluralistic rather than a monolithic Communist system.

8. Closely related to this seventh point has been the consequent blaming of the United States for the hostility that has followed between it and the Communist regime. The hostility, the argument says, is the product of the American government's

not having been conciliatory enough.

We recall how the United States was blamed for not having cultivated Ho Chi Minh as a Vietnamese "nationalist" after World War II. According to this argument, the American government was responsible for the Communist nature of Ho's regime. (The fact that Ho was a Moscow-trained revolutionary and that Walter Briggs pointed out in a 1948 issue of The New Republic that he was "fanatically loyal to Moscow" was considered irrelevant to this line of reasoning, which was not based upon evidence but upon ideologically induced sophistry.)[6]

Along the same lines, Samuel Shapiro wrote in The New Republic after Fidel Castro's victory in Cuba that it was Eisenhower's hostile policy that had driven a not-too-reluctant Castro "into the arms of Nikita Krushchev." We have heard a similar argument about the Sandinistas in Nicaragua, despite the Carter administration's extensive efforts to cultivate a friendly relationship both before and after they took power. Such a conciliatory policy was followed until the Reagan administration decided to stop most American aid because of the Sandinista government's supplying of arms to the leftist guerrillas in El Salvador.[7]

9. Finally, at the end of the cycle, there has been a belated recognition that in fact the Communists have used the revolution to impose a dictatorship and oppressive conditions.

We have seen that it took many years for this realization to sink in with regard to Soviet Russia, which is where the cycle probably played itself out over the longest time. Usually it is much quicker. A year and a half after the victory by Mao in China in late 1949 a New Republic editorial told for the first time about "the Chinese Communist terror campaign," and finally in 1955 Robert C. North told the readers that "from the day of its establishment the Chinese Communist government has functioned as a police state patterned after the Soviet model."[8]

Not long after Castro's victory in Cuba, George Sherman wrote that "I came away from Cuba profoundly disturbed...by the growth of totalitarian organization." And after the Sandinista takeover in Nicaragua, we eventually saw the New Republic article in October, 1983, entitled: "Darkening Nicaragua: Still not Totalitarian, but the Drift is Disturbing."[9]

10. A tenth point to make about the cycle is one that I mentioned at the very beginning of this chapter: that the ultimate realization of the Communist nature of the revolution and of the totalitarianism that it has imposed has not prevented the cycle from being replayed, with the beginning illusion fully intact, when the next country comes under attack. It is as though the illusion is so strong that it cannot be dispelled by experience. Only the horror itself dispells it, and only for the particular case.

The Chinese experience, for example, was no help to liberals in understanding the assault upon Cuba or Vietnam. And neither of these was any help in understanding Chile or Nicaragua.

After a country is lost to Communist brutality, there is no introspection within liberal literature, no self-examination in which an admission of error is made.

As this is written, fashionable opinion throughout the world is clamoring to pull down the South African government. No responsibility whatsoever is being shown about what will take its place. The fact that one bloody dictatorship after another, Marxist or simply personal, has been fashioned throughout Africa out of the ruins of a departed Western influence counts for nothing. The system of apartheid is seen simply as an unmitigated evil. American celebrities and young people, without having taken the least effort to study the history of South Africa and to

400

understand the extreme difficulty of its multi-racial situation, demonstrate outside the South African embassy in Washington, wear white armbands at college graduation ceremonies, and congratulate themselves on the humanity of their position. If history teaches any lessons at all, it is that these same people will in a few years, without any introspection into the role they themselves played, throw themselves into a generous effort for humanitarian aid to alleviate "starvation in South Africa," just as they have recently for Ethiopia. (It is significant that during all of the clamor for aid to the millions starving in Ethiopia, almost no attention was given to the fact that there was a Communist government there. Even in that instance, the ideological insistence upon not learning from experience was in evidence.)

Several revolutions: Specific examples of the liberal cycle

The various elements of the cycle have appeared in connection with a series of countries:

Russia. In 1918, after Lenin had overthrown the democratic socialist Kerensky regime that had supplanted the Czarist government, H. N. Brailsford urged the West to desist from any attack upon the Bolsheviks. His rationale was that if the Bolsheviks were assured of the safety of socialism within Russia, they would have no need to become aggressive. The New Republic's editorials opposed the Western nations' "indefensible and mischievous policy of military intervention" against Lenin's regime. [10]

An article by John Chamberlain in 1939 put part of the blame on Western nations for Stalin's collectivization of agriculture, which included the liquidation of the kulaks. "In 1927," he said, "just before embarking on the first Five Year Plan, the Bolsheviks hoped to get capital from the Western nations. But the capital was not forthcoming...The gosplanners were forced to divert most of the available Russian manpower, [with] nothing much to pass on to the farmer for his grain." This, he said, led to events that culminated in the decision to collectivize. Such an argument corresponds to the phase in the cycle in which the abuses of the Communist regime are said to be due to the non-Communist world's not having been sufficiently supportive. [11]

We know, of course, that the world intellectual community's perception of the Soviet Union eventually soured, which corresponds with the end of the cycle. Representative of this was the reference in The New Republic in July, 1948, to "the vast forced labor system" within the U.S.S.R. (Even though the souring did occur, it is worth noticing that this was probably the journal's first mention of the Gulags and that there was no complete article devoted to them at any time.)

Spain. In March, 1936, a New Republic editorial reported that a United Front coalition was in power in Spain, consisting of "Left Republicans, Socialists, Communists and Anarcho-Syndicalists." Throughout the Spanish Civil War, the journal supported the Left without objecting to the collaboration of the democratic socialist factions with the Communists and the anarcho-syndicalists. [12]

Opprobrium was heaped upon Franco's side, while the Left was praised. The New Republic's statement that "if Franco wins, the war-willing powers will be immensely encouraged for their next aggression" saw fascist expansion as a bad thing, for example. But the editors treated Communist expansion as a different matter. The editors chose to overlook the implications of Leon Trotsky's prediction, which had been reported in The New Republic itself in 1931, "that Spain would be 'next'" for the Communists.

Western Europe; France. In a discussion of the "underground resistance [against the Nazis] in

Europe," a <u>New Republic</u> article by a "J.H." in 1942 praised the Communists who were active in the resistance. In keeping with the phase in the cycle in which liberal thought has obscured the nature of the revolutionaries, he denied the seriousness of their Communist faith: "The Soviet Union and the Communist Parties in Europe are not preaching Communism or social revolution. But they are advocating anti-fascist revolution and the restoration of democratic government and human rights and liberties...." In February, 1944, a <u>New Republic</u> editorial reported a rumor that the State Department was opposing arming the French underground "because some of its members are Communists." "If this charge is true," the editors said, "it represents a genuine low mark in stupidity."[13]

To appreciate the importance of this tolerance toward Western European Communists and of the willingness to see them armed, we need only note the <u>New Republic</u>'s own observation, made in 1950, that "the loss of Western Europe [would be] irreparable for the Free World." The comment was made in a context of rationalizing the acceptability of losing Asia, but we can draw from it the awareness, however belated, of how crucial it was that Western Europe not be seized by the Communists at the end of World War II. This recognition is assignable to the "realization" phase.[14]

<u>Greece</u>. Writing in <u>The New Republic</u> in March, 1947, Henry Wallace set forth an argument based on the same phase that we just saw with regard to Western European Communists, of again obscuring the nature of the threat posed by the revolutionaries. He argued that the Greek Communists "are largely Communists because of their extreme misery and have little ideological knowledge of what communism is."

An editorial incorporated two aspects of the cycle. It opposed the Truman Doctrine's assistance to Greece in its fight against the Communist

403

insurgency, and damned the non-Communist regime as composed of "the survivors of an old and wretched order--the royalist officeholders pledged to King George II of Greece." Freda Kirchwey in The Nation added her own contribution to the phase that condemns the non-Communist government. She argued in 1948 that the Truman Doctrine had been a "failure" because it had kept in power "a cruel, corrupt oligarchy that survives on terror."[15]

By 1952, though, The New Republic had entered into the "realization" phase (although it was helped in this by its break with Henry Wallace). An article by Thomas R. Phillips then pointed out that "control of Greece would have extended Soviet influence into the Eastern Mediterranean and would have isolated Turkey, the Middle East and the Suez Canal." [16]

China. In 1931, Malcolm Cowley reported favorably about the Chinese Communists and added that "Communism has captured a generation of Chinese intellectuals." The same year, William Prohme told The New Republic's readers that "several thousand villages are under this Soviet rule," which he said was a good thing because "non-resident landlords no longer exploit the endless labors of the farmers." In 1936, an editorial argued that the Chinese Communists were free of Russian control, citing a report by Edgar Snow that "he found no Russian Communists whatever with the army." [17]

As we have seen, however, the campaign to blacken the name of Chiang Kai-shek did not begin until near the end of World War II. The New Republic made Richard Watts, Jr., its leading author on China, and in numerous articles he condemned the Chinese Nationalists and praised the Communists. In May, 1945, he reported something "upon which all the American visitors to Yenan [the Communist headquarters] during the summer and fall of 1944 seemed to agree...that these so-called Communists were concerned, not with collectivizing China, but with building a progressive,

democratic, non-feudal, unified nation." He argued that "their current aims and tendencies are
in the direction of agrarian democracy rather than
collectivization." Such passages illustrate
again, of course, the early phase during which the
Communist nature of the revolution is denied or
sugared over. At the same time, those opposing
the Communists were steeped in evil; in the article immediately following the one I have just
quoted from by Watts, Agnes Smedley told the
readers of The New Republic about "Kuomintang
concentration camps" and speculated: "How many men
and women have been done to death in these camps
or in the dark cells of Kuomintang prisons, mankind will never know." 18

The next phase--or rather one that ran along
concomitantly--was to oppose American support for
the anti-Communist side. A New Republic editorial
in August, 1945, said that "it is to be hoped that
American policy...will not uphold Chungking
against the Communists as another 'bulwark against
Communism.'" In a long series of convoluted developments, this was accepted by the Truman administration as its policy, as we see from the fact
that in July, 1947, an editorial reported that
"about a year ago, the State Department, bolstered
by [George] Marshall's concurrent opinion, decided
that Chiang's government was hopeless as an instrument for counteracting Communism in Asia. It
decided to fulfill the promises made after V-J
Day, but to make no new commitments of aid." 19

Immediately after Mao's victory, an exultant
headline for a book review by Edgar Snow declared
that "In China the People Decided." But, as we
have seen from Robert C. North's 1955 comment
about "a police state patterned after the Soviet
model," the "realization" phase eventually set in.

This awareness did not lead to introspection
over liberalism's role, however, or to an admission of error. Thus, a New Republic editorial in
1975 was able to say that "the U.S. made a mistake
in Vietnam that it had averted in China. Thanks

to the wisdom of Gen. George Marshall...the U.S. turned away from the Chinese civil war and left Chiang to his fate."20

Formosa/Taiwan. Following Mao's victory on the mainland of China, a New Republic editorial predicted "that Formosa will fall to the Communists by a combination of popular revolt and transfer of allegiance by its naval and air-force commanders." In August, 1950, the journal criticized General Douglas MacArthur for establishing a liaison with Chiang on Formosa and voiced its opposition to American involvement in the defense of the island. TRB at the same time called it "the ultimate cost of McCarthyism" that "Truman paid the GOP price for Congressional unity [by having] included Formosa in our defense program." But then, after the "realization phase" set in with regard to Communist China, an article by Clarence Decker said that Formosa was "a beacon of hope to the Communist-oppressed Chinese on the continent."21

South Korea. Again at the time of the fall of the Chinese mainland to Mao, a New Republic editorial in October, 1949, remarked passingly that "Korea...soon will pass under Communist control." In her The China Story, Freda Utley told how "Syngman Rhee's [non-Communist] government, like Chiang Kai-shek's, was called reactionary, tyrannical, corrupt and undemocratic...In Korea, as in China, willingness to collaborate with Communists was regarded as the hallmark of a democrat...The 1949 United Nations commission on Korea regretfully reported that the South Korean government had been 'uncooperative.' The evidence...was its refusal to 'participate in official discussions with the [Communist] North looking to unification." She related how in the July 17, 1949, issue of the New York Compass Owen Lattimore wrote that "the thing to do is to let South Korea fall, but not to let it look as though we pushed it. Hence the recommendation of a parting gift of 150 million dollars."22

406

In the meantime, the ideologically induced illusions of the Truman administration were setting the stage for the North Korean invasion of the south, which we know occurred on June 25, 1950. In 1947, General Albert C. Wedemeyer's report had sought to dispel any illusion. He told of the Soviet Union's building up of North Korean forces. Wedemeyer wrote that "the Soviet-equipped and trained North Korean Peoples' army of 125,000 is vastly superior to the United States organized constabulary of 16,000 Koreans, equipped with Japanese small arms. The North Korean Peoples' army constitutes a potential military threat to South Korea, since there is a strong probability that the Soviets will withdraw their occupation forces and thus induce our own withdrawal."[23]

It is one of the great tragedies of the period that Wedemeyer's warning went unheeded. Chesly Manly has written that, "as predicted by General Wedemeyer, the Soviet government, on September 18, 1948, informed the United States that the withdrawal of its occupation forces from North Korea would be completed by the end of December, 1948. In the General Assembly, the Russians were demanding withdrawal of the American forces from South Korea. The United States soon complied. On June 29, 1949, the U.N. commission reported that it had verified the withdrawal of American occupation forces."[24]

This withdrawal in the face of Communist military superiority was coupled with still another failure. Freda Utley wrote that "not only was the American Army withdrawn from Korea in the summer of 1949, the military aid voted for Korea by Congress in 1949 was not delivered."[25]

Most of this has never been known, or has long since been forgotten, by most Americans. The next step, however, has been frequently commented upon. It was that Secretary of State Dean Acheson declared in January, 1950, that our defense perimeter included Japan, Okinawa and the Phillipines. "We thus made it clear," Senator Robert A. Taft

407

wrote later, "that we would not defend South Korea if attacked." But of course Acheson's statement was merely an important capstone to a policy that in substance had already been carried out. [26]

Senator Taft showed his understanding of the link between liberal illusion and American policy when he said that "the Korean war and the problems which arise from it are the final result of the continuous sympathy toward communism which inspired American policy." [27]

Guatemala. The Eisenhower administration intervened to prevent a Communist consolidation in Guatemala. The critique in The New Republic was voiced by David L. Graham when he wrote that "to a man, Guatemalans and Latin Americans remember the Liberation as a violent, American-engineered overthrow of a legal government." [28]

Cuba. In Cuba, as in China, the entire cycle ran its course. In February, 1958, before Fidel Castro's victory, Daniel N. Friedenberg attacked the non-Communist president, Fulgencio Batista, in The New Republic as "a thug called an anti-Communist." An editorial in the same journal in January, 1959, repeated what we have come to see is a common theme: "Batista's regular army was not only venal, but incompetent and cowardly." [29]

American policy responded to such liberal criticisms in the usual way. A New Republic editorial in April, 1958, reported that "two weeks ago the [State] Department imposed an embargo on further shipment of arms to Batista (as well as on arms to the rebels)." The editors added that "it might soon be incumbent upon us to put pressure on Batista to give way and get out...." David Morris looked back in 1968 and said that "it took an arms embargo and a complete break between the United States and Batista to give Castro sufficient momentum to overcome the established regime...The United States in 1958 was ambivalent toward Castro, and large segments of the liberal policy-making establishment (e.g., CIA) supported him." [30]

408

The concomitant sugar-coating of the Communist revolutionary movement is nowhere better evidenced than the same editorial in April, 1958. It said that "to hint that Castro is a 'revolutionary' in any Marxist sense, or is the enemy of the United States and a friend of the Russians is silly." In January, 1959, the editors spoke of "the absence of any evidence of significant Communist penetration of the Castro movement." Even though they were speaking of an absence of evidence, they explained away some that was quite material: they argued that "neither Castro's brother Raoul nor his Argentine adventurer-lieutenant Che Guevara--often described as pro-Soviet --are powerful enough (or pro-Communist enough) for alarm."[31]

Herbert Matthews of _The New York Times_ played a central role in this sugar-coating. William L. O'Neill writes that "when...Matthews met Castro in the Sierra Maestra on February 17, 1957, he described Fidel as nationalistic, socialistic, anti-American, and noncommunist." O'Neill adds about Castro that "in 1959 he repeatedly denied being a communist, in 1960 he no longer bothered. Later he announced that not only was he now a communist but always had been."[32]

After Castro's victory, there was the usual period of rosy expectation, followed by the slow acknowledgment that his regime was indeed Communist. We recall that Castro soon began a large number of executions. In early 1960, Robert Taber came to his defense in _The Nation_: "The question remains whether it would have been possible to implement the program which has given the Cuban masses their first glimpse of hope...by less arbitrary, more conventional methods. One concludes, however reluctantly, no." But _The New Republic_'s editors showed the beginning tremors: "Cuba's leaders have unquestionably given grounds for uneasiness...." Nevertheless, they were still able to say that "Castro's is a nationalist revolution...." By October, 1960, Daniel Friedenberg was telling the readers that "I am not saying that

409

Fidel Castro is a Communist, but that in every way he supports Soviet imperialism." Finally, a month later, The New Republic's Gerald W. Johnson was ready to declare that "Communism has crossed the Atlantic and now squats 90 miles off-shore."[33]

Next the argument was raised by Samuel Shapiro in The New Republic that it was Eisenhower's unfriendly disposition that had forced Castro into the Soviet orbit. The solution, Shapiro argued, was to be conciliatory, not anti-Communist: "The only sensible course open to us is one of patience [and] forebearance...." It was predictable that The New Republic would be bitterly critical of the Bay of Pigs invasion's attempted overthrow of the Castro government. Indeed, it was the ambivalence of the Kennedy administration, manifested by the last-minute withdrawal of American air support, that assured the failure of that invasion.[34]

Guinea. In June, 1960, Robert C. Good provided an interesting speciman of the liberal illusion in a New Republic article entitled "Is Guinea Communist?" After reciting:

. that "virtually every ministry [of the government] has some Czech advisers;"

. that the Soviet Union had made the government a $35 million loan;

. that "Communist China will soon start a large demonstration scheme in rice culture;"

. that "more than fifty percent of Guinea's trade is now committed to the East;"

. that "Guinea increasingly is sending its students to the East to pick up generous scholarships offered by Communist governments;"

. that "Guinea's leaders have been schooled in left-wing labor groups. They are Marxian socialists;" and

410

. that "Guinea seeks a centralized society, a monolithic party, a state-directed economy;"

Good said that "despite all this, my conclusion is
that Guinea has not 'gone Communist.'"35

Dominican Republic. In May, 1965, a New
Republic editorial spoke sceptically of "its [the
Johnson administation's] claim that Communists had
'infiltrated' the Dominican revolt and were
rapidly rising to the top." The editors' conclusion was that "sending 25,000 American servicemen
to the Dominican Republic violated the OAS charter." 36

Vietnam It is to be expected that the cycle
went full circle as to Vietnam.

The initial acceptance of the existing regime
appeared somewhat obliquely in a comment by Joseph
Buttinger in The New Republic in 1955 that "the
French have tried to get rid of Premier Ngo Dinh
Diem because they cannot use him for their policy
of appeasement."37

From at least 1957 on, however, The New
Republic followed the pattern of painting the
blackest possible picture of the successive non-
Communist governments. The journal rampaged
against Diem, even calling for and then justifying
his assassination; but neither did it then see any
good in the later governments. This was compounded by the usual failure to feel any empathy
toward a society bled and forced into counter-
measures by terrorism and guerrilla attack.

An article by David Hotham in 1957 criticized
the widespread arrests "and imprisonment without
evidence and without trial of persons suspected of
being Communists or 'enemies of the State." In
January, 1961, Denis Warner wrote that under Diem
"democratic institutions, such as free elections,
have been turned into a farce. Imprisonment is
the punishment for criticism." It was in June,
1961, that TRB told of President Kennedy's report

411

of the 4,000 assassinations of South Vietnamese leaders within the preceding twelve months; and it was in the same month that Adrian Jaffe and Milton C. Taylor complained of the lack of democracy and the use of the secret police by the South Vietnamese government. In December, 1961, Frank C. Child wrote that "South Vietnam is a police state with...secret police harrassment, arbitrary arrest and police brutality...." [Childs did not reflect upon what any society, including our own, would resort to to protect itself if there had been the killing, even within the one-year period cited, of 4,000 of, say, its cities' mayors and aldermen.]38

In August, 1983, a New Republic article by Erich Wulff implored that "Vietnam will fall into chaos if Diem does not resign, and soon." Then in October, Ho Thong Minh wrote that "the current situation renders imperative the overthrow of the Diem regime; for this the Vietnamese Army will be the ineluctable instrument." This was followed in short order, of course, by Diem's actual assassination; and on November 16, 1963, a New Republic editorial praised the assassination, saying that "the coup...obliges us to admit that there are two kinds of military putsches: 'bad' ones which have not received Presidential encouragement; 'good' ones which enjoy such sanction. The effect of that on would-be military dictators from Togo to Honduras will bear watching." Ironically, John F. Kennedy's own assassination occurred within a few days.39

The New Republic pressed on. Without any introspection, an editorial in September, 1966, said that "ever since the Kennedy administration permitted Diem to be assassinated in 1963, successive governments in Saigon have been too weak to dare to contemplate negotiations." Then the condemnations of the new government began. In September, 1967, an editorial referred to the Thieu-Ky regime as a "puppet military government." In 1970, the editors spoke of "the fiction that the Thieu regime is the only one which could and should represent the people of the South, and that its survival is a sacred trust."40

Meanwhile, the revolutionary movement was given the usual sugar-coating. Since Ho was clearly a Communist it used other pretexts than a full denial. In the early 1950's, The New Republic said that "Ho has become a hard-core Communist." But in 1965, the editors were calling the war a mere "civil war." In 1969, Walter Lippmann made his statement that if the Communists won "it will be...more or less like Yugoslavia is Communist, relatively speaking, and it won't make very much of a difference." Senator Fulbright argued that the war was "a civil conflict in which Communism is and always has been secondary to the drive for national independence."'41

As in other countries, this perspective led many liberals to oppose American aid to the non-Communist side. In 1950, even at the time when The New Republic was acknowledging the hard-core Communism of Ho Chi Minh, the editors argued that aid to Ho's opponent, Bao Dai, would be "going back to a policy that has been a disastrous failure before." Later in 1950, the editors were saying that "further losses in Asia...will be costly but not irreparable. Only the loss of Western Europe is irreparable for the Free World." In 1957, David Hotham opposed all military aid and made an argument that would seem especially strained to today's public opinion, that the West's nuclear umbrella was the primary factor with which to restrain North Vietnamese aggression. 42

It is little known in the United States that a major turning-point of the Vietnam War was brought about through very much the same mechanism that led to the North Korean attack upon South Korea. President Lyndon Johnson, reflecting liberal attitudes and playing presidential-election politics, announced in the 1964 campaign that the United States would stand back. Acting upon this premise, Ho Chi Minh changed the nature of the Vietnam War by sending his own regular army troops

413

into the South. The war on that side had until then been fought by the Viet Cong, the Communist guerrilla force in the South. Here is Dave Richard Palmer's analysis from his Summons of the Trumpet: A History of the Vietnam War from a Military Man's Viewpoint: "That very August [of 1964],...President Johnson had announced publicly that he would not consider bombing North Vietnam or 'committing American boys to fighting a war that I think ought to be fought by the boys of Asia to help protect their own land.' Just as the North Koreans, listening to American pronouncements in 1950, had become convinced that the United States would not make a stand for Korea, so was North Vietnam convinced fourteen years later that America would not fight for Vietnam." Palmer says that "by committing its regular forces... Hanoi dramatically altered the entire thrust and scope of the conflict. It was a key command decision. Indeed, it may well have been the key command decision of the war." 43

The tragedy reached its culmination in 1974 and early 1975. In November, 1974, Fred Branfman reported that "Congress cut military aid to Vietnam from $1.6 billion requested to $700 million appropriated, economic aid from $750 million to under $450 million...." In February, 1975, TRB exulted that "if Congress cuts off aid hostilities probably will stop, Communists will win. How bad is that?" Gareth Porter told how Theiu was complaining that the Paris Accords, which left regular North Vietnamese forces in the South, threatened the existence of the South Vietnamese government. We all know the rest of the story: the South, together with Laos and Cambodia, fell to the Communists in the spring of 1975. North Vietnamese tanks entered Saigon as helicopters evacuated the last Americans from the rooftop of the embassy. 44

During the years since that terrible spring, frequent reference has been made to "the lessons of Vietnam." These lessons have necessarily varied with the commentator. As we will see from

414

liberal attitudes toward leftist revolutionary challenges arising since Vietnam to such countries as Nicaragua and El Salvador, the lessons, as understood by most liberals, have not called for introspection about the cycle that we have been examining. Instead, liberals have merely understood the lessons to confirm how right they have been in holding the views that make up the cycle.

Chile: The first reference I noticed about Salvador Allende in The New Republic was in an editorial in 1964. It expressed the characteristic view that blames the supposed intransigence of the United States for any leftist's becoming a revolutionary. "Will Dr. Allende, if he wins," the editorial asked, "be turned into another Castro by U.S. stiffness?" 45

In 1967, Joseph A. Page referred to Allende and spoke of "an exaggerated spectre of Communism." He told of "...FRAP, the name given to a coalition of the Socialist and Communist Parties." His discussion shows us not only the typical sugar-coating, but also the role that a United Front of socialists and Communists plays in creating an arguable ambiguity. 46

In August, 1970, Georgie Anne Geyer told The New Republic's readers that "when asked whether he would create a 'popular democracy' and a one-party socialist state, he said that the election is 'not an electoral fight but the definitive battle,' that there would be a 'change of regime and of system'" (emphasis added). An editorial in November said that "an unabashed Marxist is inaugurated this week as President of Chile." Despite this awareness and what Allende himself had said about creating a one-party state, the editorial put things in the best possible light: "Allende is too aware of the limits of the possible in Chile to attempt imposing a rigid totalitarian structure on pluralistic Chile." William R. Long added that "only the most excitable anti-Marxists believe that Allende wants to establish a dictatorship of the proletariat, at least in the first years of his term."[47]

Allende himself continued to show his intentions. In May, 1971, he praised Castro and told how he looked forward to revolution throughout Latin America: "The Cuban revolution is a national revolution, but it is also a revolution of the whole of Latin America. It has shown the way for the liberation of all our peoples." Nevertheless, The New Republic never acknowledged the danger. In September, 1973, after Allende was killed in the coup that toppled his regime, an editorial commiserated that "the fact that Allende was toppled by a military junta is a tragedy for Chile..." He wasn't really for Communism, just socialism: "Allende's program was to put Chile on the road to socialism." (Perhaps for sake of analysis we ought for a moment to assume the correctness of this view that "only" socialism was involved. It has been hard to imagine The New Republic declaring it a tragedy for any regime that is not on the Left to be overthrown, in Chile or anywhere else, that declared itself intent upon creating a "one-party state.")[48]

Since 1973, it has been commonplace within liberal writing to declare Allende's anti-Communist successors "repressive and incompetent" and to blame the United States for assisting in Allende's overthrow. The "realization" phase about the horrors of a Communist regime has never been reached. His failure to complete his consolidation of power meant that the usual demonstration that comes from hard reality never had a chance to command an acknowledgment from them.[49]

Rhodesia: The cases of Rhodesia and South Africa are somewhat different from the others. The white-minority rule over blacks has made it much more plausible to condemn the existing regimes. Nevertheless, the same cycle of illusion and irresponsibility has been in evidence. The very real question, raised by the experience of several other African nations, of whether a black government, even though it would represent a majority,

416

would be able to maintain adequate standards of civilization—for blacks as well as for whites—has not seemed relevant in arriving at the condemnation of the "white minority." The main object has been the destruction of the white regime, without regard to whether chaos or dictatorship might arise from the ashes.

Worldwide pressure was for several years brought to bear on Ian Smith to turn power over to a black majority. Milton Viorst told in 1975 how "it's been almost a decade since Rhodesia...declared its independence of Great Britain...Since then, it has lived in diplomatic isolation, and under the shadow of the United Nations economic embargo." A New Republic editorial used language in 1978 that it has rarely, if ever, applied to the world's worst butchers: "There is probably no way to exaggerate the malignancy of Smith's 13-year rule of Rhodesia. His regime was created in the name of white supremacy." 50

The pressure succeeded eventually in bringing a new constitution under which the erstwhile guerrilla leader Robert Mugabe became the prime minister. An Associated Press dispatch on July 7, 1985, reported that "Prime Minister Robert Mugabe, more powerful than ever after a landslide election victory, vowed Saturday to create a one-party state in the next five years" (emphasis added). It went on to say that the country was "dividing ...on clearly tribal lines."

Nicaragua: For several years, following the usual pattern, liberal writers attacked the anti-Communist Somozan government. "The United States," The New Republic said in 1978, tracing this country's support of non-Communist regimes over several decades, "is deeply implicated in the suppression of the Nicaraguan people."51

The same editorial sugar-coated the Sandinista revolutionary challenge, citing, as has so often been the case, the ambiguity of the revolutionary situation: "Certainly there are hardened

417

Communists among the leaders of the Sandinista guerrillas, but it is not a foregone conclusion that they would rule Nicaragua if Somoza decided to leave the country."[52]

The characteristic result followed in the wake of this illusion. "The Carter administration," the editorial said, "has stopped military aid to Somoza and in July the Senate wisely ended U.S. training of the Somoza National Guard. Economic aid continues...." [53]

After the Sandinistas won, the Carter administration tried the expedient that liberal thought has so long favored: to secure the independence, if not the good will, of the revolutionary regime by showing every possible sign of friendship. Shirley Christian reported in 1981 that "the United States is trying to balance the Cuban influence and the less obvious Soviet presence with a large aid program." It didn't work. She went on to say that "a substantial portion of it [the aid program] was suspended recently by the Reagan administration...over the issue of arms supplies to Salvadoran guerrillas." In 1983, Robert W. Tucker told how "the Carter Administration went to some lengths to show its goodwill and desire for normal relationships. The government of Managua responded in a manner that was bound to put it on a collision course with Washington, and did so well before the present [the Reagan] administration came to office." [54]

We saw earlier how the eventual "realization" set in. In October, 1983, The New Republic published Ronald Radosh's article entitled "Darkening Nicaragua: Still not Totalitarian, but the Drift is Disturbing." [55]

But there has nevertheless been the usual opposition to efforts to displace the Communist regime. In April, 1983, Morton Kondracke wrote in The New Republic that "the United States is risking disaster--another Bay of Pigs and possibly worse--by giving aid to rightist guerrillas bent

418

on overthrowing the government of Nicaragua."[56]

El Salvador: Contrary to the pattern, The New Republic has not itself undertaken to sugar-coat the nature of the guerrillas in El Salvador, although at the height of revolutionary activity it painted a black picture of the non-Communist alternative.   In November, 1982, the editors conjectured that "the people of El Salvador may be caught between a Fascist rock and a Communist hard place."[57]

The liberal pattern of denial was present, however, as we see from Robert W. Tucker's reference in late 1983 to "a growing number of administration critics" whose "common point of departure is that we have no valid and certainly no vital interest in opposing the emergence of radical governments in Central America." Tucker himself suggested the sharing of power with the guerrillas. After the election of Napoleon Duarte as a centrist and moderately leftist president, the liberal media have largely been silent about El Salvador. It is notable, though, that the Reagan administration has continued to feel the pressure of divided American opinion, which we can infer from the fact that there has been no increase in the miniscule number of American military advisors there. [58]

The prospects for Central America's ability in the future to attempt to solve its many problems free of Communist penetration are today clouded by obstacles that are a typical part of the syndrome we have been examining:

One of these is the tolerance by the world Left toward "some" Communism. European and Latin American socialists have supported the revolutionary movements in Central America. The Mexican government, far from being stalwartly anti-Communist to prevent a revolutionary attack on Mexico itself, has long followed a policy of appeasing Castro and his revolutionary spinoffs.

419

Another is the division and consequent lack of will within American public opinion and in Congress. To a very large degree we are rendered impotent by the liberal illusion. And there is an additional factor: After the experience of the 1960's, the United States, which we want to keep in mind is the main anti-Communist power in the world, is in effect held hostage by the implicit threat, which cannot be very far from anyone's mind, that if it takes strong anti-Communist action it will become subject to the same sort of internal anarchy that it faced during the 1960's.

South Africa: The system of racial separation in South Africa called apartheid has come to be universally condemned during the 1970's and 1980's. In the mid-1980's, this condemnation is being driven to the point at which, whether the purpose is admitted or not, revolution is quite clearly being encouraged to overthrow the white Afrikaner government.

This condemnation marks the acceptance of a principle that has certainly not been universally agreed to until recently and which is of dubious merit. It is one that will almost certainly be held to hypocritically by many who proclaim it. What I am referring to, of course, is the principle that there can be no racial separation within a society without that being per se unjust. (I am aware that criticism is made of the particular incidents of the racial separation in South Africa, such as the proportion of the land set aside for blacks. But I feel certain that those who are pressing the condemnation would agree that they mean to condemn the principle of apartheid, not just the form it presently takes.)

It was not all that many years ago--in 1961-- that Harry Oppenheimer was able to write in The New Republic that "it would be quite wrong to think of their apartheid philosophy, in theory anyhow, as either willfully stupid or immoral." He pointed out that "partition has, after all, been applied as a last resort in quite a few parts

of the world." The difficulties he saw in South
African apartheid were not moral, but practical.
For Oppenheimer to express such views today would
brand him a moral leper. [59]

The general position that Oppenheimer was
expressing was also stated by Leonard Fein in The
New Republic in 1977, not in connection with South
Africa but in relation to Jewish opposition to
racial and sexual "affirmative action" in the
United States. "Jews know that there is such a
thing as group culture," he said, "and that the
culture of the group--for better, for worse--makes
the goal of integration as it is sometimes understood a totalitarian goal." And yet, an editorial
in an issue a month later was prepared to say that
"South Africa is in danger of placing itself outside as an entire society, by defining the human
race in terms that everyone else now rejects."[60]

The great moral clamor now being raised
against South Africa seems to me to include substantial ingredients from the cycle of illusion
that we have been examining in this chapter. It
is a matter of alienation and ideology rather than
of reliance upon a sound and long-established
moral principle.

This is not to say that I consider the
Afrikaners blameless. Their mistake, it seems to
me, was to think that they could "have their cake
and eat it, too." They have welcomed the presence
internally of an ever-growing black population for
the labor that it provides, while they have also
hoped to maintain a white society based upon a
European model. In the long run, these are incompatible. An analogy would be the mistake European
countries made in thinking that they could establish colonies, as the English did in America, and
keep them wedded to the mother country after they
had grown and matured. There are realities that,
once they have developed, have ineluctable consequences.

It is worthwhile to be aware that "mistakes"

about such things usually never come to a head for decision at any one time so that responsibility for them can be assigned to specific leaders. They creep up as part of an historical development. I do not know enough about South African conditions in 1948 to have an opinion about whether that year could have been an effective "time of decision." The Afrikaners, descended from the Dutch, were assuming power and were then instituting the system of apartheid. Whether it would have been a viable option to have worked to limit the black population over the long run is not altogether clear. Culturally, the Afrikaners have long thought of physical labor as beneath them. It is possible that there would have been no constituency politically for limiting the growth of the black population. And if that path was not open, history and their own characteristics had locked them into the problem that they now face.

The questions that constructive people should be asking about South Africa today are: Would blacks themselves be better off, in terms of freedom or of material well-being, if the Republic of South Africa were destroyed by revolution? and, if the answer to that question is in the negative, What are the evolutionary changes that should be encouraged within South Africa to create an accommodation that is acceptable to all of the diverse racial groups? It is relatively certain, however, that anyone pursuing this moderate course, which is essentially that which the Reagan administration has wanted to follow, would be excoriated by those who are now chanting, in effect, for the destruction of South Africa.

Grenada: In 1983, during the Reagan administration, the United States invaded the Caribbean island of Grenada after one Marxist government had been supplanted in a coup by another, more militant, Marxist faction. American medical students on the island were rescued, preventing a possible situation comparable to the holding of American hostages in Iran during the Carter administration. After an interregnum of a few months, the island was made an elective democracy.

In keeping with the accommodation that American politicians have thought it necessary to make to the liberal illusions, even the Reagan administration did not think it possible, at least initially, to justify the invasion in anti-Communist terms. Instead, it based its rationale on the danger to the American students. This reason was by no means far-fetched, but it was almost certainly not the principal motive.

Typically, the liberal intellectual culture took the dimmest view of the American intervention, although the success and popularity of the invasion within the country at large put a damper upon the condemnations. The tone of <u>The New Republic</u>'s reaction is indicated by the following passage from an editorial: "The United States invaded Grenada to rescue Americans...It is a mere excuse. There is no evidence that American nationals, many of them medical students in St. George's, were in any peril." We are interested in the tone, but we should recall that we have seen the claim of "no evidence" before, such as with regard to Cuba about whether Castro was a Communist. The editorial is correct in saying that the rescue of the students was not the main motive; but that there was "no evidence" that the students were in danger makes little sense. The American people had vivid memories of the Iranian hostage episode.61

Conclusion

My analysis of the liberal cycle relating to Communist revolutionary attacks upon one after another of the non-Communist nations of the world is not meant to suggest that there would have been simple solutions in those countries if only the liberal illusions had not been so pervalent. Even the greatest clarity would not have done away with the Communist thrust. Nor would it have cured the weakness of what has come to be known as the Third

World.

Nevertheless, a great many of those peoples would almost certainly have avoided subjugation to Communism. It is worth asking how much the weaknesses within pre-Communist Vietnam would have contributed to Communist victory if China, the colossus to the north, had not already fallen to the Communists? How great would the threat to El Salvador be if Cuba and then Nicaragua had not succumbed? Each successive revolution has not occurred in a vacuum, but with the support of an expanding Communist world.

NOTES

1. New Republic, August 30, 1943, p. 269.

2. New Republic, May 8, 1944, p. 628; New Republic, May 29, 1944, p. 729.

3. Freda Utley, The China Story (Chicago: Henry Regnery Company, 1951), pp. 55, 58.

4. New Republic, June 5, 1961, p. 2; New Republic, June 19, 1961, pp. 17, 20.

5. New Republic, March 25, 1967, p. 4.

6. New Republic, December 13, 1948, p. 16.

7. New Republic, February 6, 1961, p. 16; New Republic, October 24, 1983, p. 26; New Republic, July 18, 1981, p. 19.

8. New Republic, May 21, 1951, p. 7; New Republic, July 4, 1955, p. 20.

9. New Republic, October 24, 1960, p. 15; New Republic, October 24, 1983, p. 7.

10. New Republic, March 9, 1918, pp. 167-170; New Republic, April 6, 1918, p. 280; New Republic,

February 8, 1919, p. 38.

11. New Republic, September 6, 1939, p. 123.

12. New Republic, March 25, 1936, p. 182.

13. New Republic, September 14, 1942, p. 311; New Republic, February 7, 1944, p. 163.

14. New Republic, December 18, 1950, p. 7.

15. New Republic, March 17, 1947, p. 12; New Republic, March 24, 1947, p. 6; The Nation, Vol. 166, p. 341.

16. New Republic, January 21, 1952, p. 15.

17. New Republic, July 8, 1931, p. 205; New Republic, August 12, 1931, p. 334; New Republic, December 30, 1936, p. 256.

18. New Republic, May 28, 1945, pp. 735, 747.

19. New Republic, August 27, 1945, p. 236; New Republic, July 21, 1947, p. 14.

20. New Republic, November 7, 1949, p. 18; New Republic, April 19, 1975, p. 7.

21. New Republic, December 12, 1949, p. 6; New Republic, August 21, 1950, p. 5; New Republic, August 14, 1950, p. 3; New Republic, January 12, 1953, p. 14.

22. New Republic, October 31, 1949, p. 6; Utley, The China Story, pp. 87-90.

23. Chesly Manly, The Twenty-Year Revolution from Roosevelt to Eisenhower (Chicago: Henry Regnery, 1954), pp. 174, 175.

24. Manly, Twenty-Year Revolution, p. 176.

25. Utley, The China Story, pp. 89, 90.

26. Senator Robert A. Taft, A Foreign Policy for Americans (Garden City: Doubleday & Company, Inc., 1951), p. 59.

27. Taft, A Foreign Policy, p. 60.

28. New Republic, September 16, 1957, p. 9.

29. New Republic, January 26, 1959, p. 5.

30. New Republic, February 17, 1958, p. 14; New Republic, April 14, 1958, p. 4; New Republic, November 16, 1968, p. 28.

31. New Republic, April 14, 1958, p. 4.

32. William L. O'Neill, Coming Apart: An Informal History of America in the 1960's (Chicago: Quadrangle Books, 1971), pp. 36, 38.

33. The Nation, Vol. 190, p. 63; New Republic, May 30, 1960, p. 8; New Republic, October 10, 1960, p. 11; New Republic, November 21, 1960, p. 10.

34. New Republic, February 6, 1961, p. 16; New Republic, April 17, 1961, p. 3.

35. New Republic, June 13, 1960, p. 11.

36. New Republic, May 15, 1961, pp. 1, 6.

37. New Republic, February 28, 1955, p. 9.

38. New Republic, November 25, 1957, p. 14; New Republic, January 30, 1961, p. 8; New Republic, June 5, 1961, p. 2; New Republic, June 19, 1961, p. 17; New Republic, December 4, 1961, p. 14.

39. New Republic, August 31, 1963, p. 14; New Republic, October 12, 1963, p. 19; New Republic, November 16, 1963, p. 3.

40. New Republic, September 17, 1966, p. 5; New Republic, September 2, 1967, p. 7; New Republic,

May 2, 1970, p. 7.

41. New Republic, April 24, 1950, p. 6; New Republic, December 18, 1965, p. 6; New Republic, September 27, 1969, p. 8; New Republic, December 20, 1969, p. 6.

42. New Republic, February 13, 1950, p. 9; New Republic, December 18, 1950, p. 7; New Republic, November 25, 1957, p. 14.

43. Dave Richard Palmer, Summons of the Trumpet: A History of the Vietnam War from a Military Man's Viewpoint (New York: Ballantine Books, 1978), pp. 90, 80.

44. New Republic, November 23, 1974, p. 11; New Republic, February 1, 1975, p. 2; New Republic, February 8, 1975, p. 19.

45. New Republic, April 11, 1964, p. 6.

46. New Republic, December 23, 1967, p. 30.

47. New Republic, August 29, 1970, p. 10; New Republic, November 7, 1970, p. 9; New Republic, November 28, 1970, p. 8.

48. New Republic, May 22, 1971, p. 30; New Republic, September 22, 1973, p. 7.

49. New Republic, January 17, 1976, p. 20.

50. New Republic, March 29, 1975, p. 10; New Republic, October 28, 1978, p. 6.

51. New Republic, September 16, 1978, p. 5.

52. New Republic, September 16, 1978, p. 5.

53. New Republic, September 16, 1978, p. 5.

54. New Republic, July 18, 1981, p. 19; New Republic, October 24, 1983, p. 26.

55. New Republic, October 24, 1983, p. 7.

56. New Republic, April 25, 1983, p. 8.

57. New Republic, November 22, 1982, p. 9.

58. New Republic, October 24, 1983, pp. 24, 31.

59. New Republic, February 20, 1961, p. 17.

60. New Republic, October 15, 1977, p. 17; New Republic, November 12, 1977, p. 6.

61. New Republic, November 21, 1983, p. 8.

17

LIBERALISM AND ANTI-COMMUNISM

Civilization has during the twentieth century been threatened by two major totalitarian ideologies. One of these was defeated rather quickly in a World War and is remembered with universal loathing. The other, despite suffering a great many "shocks," mostly self-inflicted, that have shattered the faith that millions once reposed in it, has not been defeated. For almost seventy years it has continued its expansion vis a vis the non-Communist world. Although this expansion has not kept pace with its own expectations and has involved some fragmentation, it has in historic terms been very rapid.

In light of this challenge, it is to have been expected that all of the non-Communist world would have come together in a common cause against a common enemy. Nothing would have been more natural or more justifiable. According to this expectation, the non-Communist governments and peoples, despite the diversity that would otherwise have separated them, will have had one thing at least in common: their mutual antagonism to Communism as a totalitarian ideology.

A recognition of the validity and importance of anti-Communism is essential to the analysis I am about to make. A study of the relationship of modern liberalism to anti-Communism is significant only to the extent that anti-Communism is important. And to anyone who equally opposes brutal totalitarian systems of all types, an antagonism to Communism is every bit as important, and as valid, as an opposition to Nazism was in the 1930's and 1940's. It is both a civilizational necessity and a moral imperative.

From the review we have made of the history of liberal thought, we would have to say that between 1917, the year of the Bolshevik Revolution, and approximately 1947, a period of thirty years, the main thrust of modern liberal thought, certainly as it was evidenced in The New Republic and The Nation, was not anti-Communist at all. Nor was it tolerant of those who were. The liberal intellectual culture during those years overwhelmingly attacked any sort of anti-Communist as a "Red baiter."

There were inevitably many individual exceptions, although during those years they did not influence substantially the tone and content of liberal discourse. We know, too, that in the late 1930's and early 1940's the Soviet purges, the persecution of Trotsky, the Hitler-Stalin Pact, the joint Nazi-Soviet attack on Poland, and the Soviet invasions of Finland and of Estonia, Latvia and Lithuania sent many former Communists and fellow-travelers reeling. Some then became strongly and permanently anti-Communist. Although somewhat shaken, the main body of the liberal intellectual culture found it possible, however, to renew its emotional bond with the Soviet Union when World War II rehabilitated the Soviet image.

It is one thing, of course, to speak of the liberal intellectual culture; it is another to refer to the many other constituent elements of the "Democratic" or "liberal" coalitions, which were themselves identified with liberalism as a political movement. My subject in this book is liberal "thought," and hence my focus is upon the intellectual culture, not upon all aspects of the broad political movement. The generalization I have made about the intellectual culture does not describe, for example, the great majority of Democrats. No one, for example, took more abuse for precisely their anti-Communism than the successive Democratic Congressmen, including such a man as Martin Dies of Texas, who for several years headed the House Committee on Un-American Activities.

Since World War II, the picture with regard to the intellectual culture has been considerably more complex. There have been a great many more liberal thinkers who have felt a distinct separation from Communism. I have in mind such a figure as Sidney Hook, who though a declared socialist has also been an articulate enemy of Communism. The Americans for Democratic Action was founded immediately following the war for the express purpose of opposing any further United Front with Communists. (We have seen, however, that this principle was abandoned during the period of the New Left in the 1960's. And we have also seen that non-Communist leftists in several of the revolutions around the world have received liberal sympathy despite a failure to maintain a distinct separation from Communists.)

What I seek, however, is a generalization about the main thrust of the liberal intellectual culture since World War II. The history of the period shows that that culture has argued for what it has called a "more intelligent" form of anti-Communism. We saw in the chapter on "Liberalism and International Affairs" that it has argued that Communism can be tamed and preempted only by a world composed predominantly of neutralist and of either democratic-socialist or independently Communist states. This is a worldview that has placed the liberal intellectual culture in a sympathetic relationship with all parts of the world Left except a narrowly defined Soviet bloc. Since much of the world socialist movement has been willing to collaborate with Communists and since the true "independence" of any given Communist regime has always been problematic, the "anti-Communism" of the liberal intellectual culture since World War II has been obscured by the ambiguity within the world Left itself.

At the same time, any form of anti-Communism that has not embraced the world Left has seemed to the liberal intellectual culture to be misguided and even vicious. Liberals have argued that any "reactionary" form of anti-Communism would be counter-productive, in that it would only alienate the Fidel Castro's and Indira Gandhi's of the

431

world--which is to say, the "independent Communists" and "neutralists." Moreover, it has felt
that such an anti-Communism would be worse than
Communism itself. We have already examined the
attitudes that downplay the problem of Communism
and that treat it as virtually non-existent. To
anyone holding such a perspective, the real problems in the world come from the many non-Communist regimes that are "venal, corrupt and repressive," or that are at the very least "unjust."
The result is that the emotions of the liberal
intellectual culture have become most heated not
toward Communism, but toward anti-Communists and
toward a good many non-Communist governments.

If, then, we compare the 1917-1947 period
with the four decades that have followed, we find
something quite significant: (a) that both periods
have shared a consistent anti-anti-Communism; and
(b) that so far as its own position vis a vis
Communism is concerned, the liberal intellectual
culture has during the more recent period moved
only incrementally to the right. It has remained
on the far Left, disassociating itself only from
what has become most disreputable.

The attitudes of the intellectual culture
have had a profound impact upon the other elements
of the liberal coalition. Most liberal political
leaders, such as Adlai Stevenson, Hubert Humphrey
and Henry Jackson, have shared the country's
general anti-Communism. And yet this fact should
not obscure the effect that the ambivalence that
has been interjected by the intellectual culture
has had upon American politicians in general, and
especially upon liberal politicians. Even though
the United States has occupied an historic role as
the principal defender of the free world against
Communism, the "anti-Communism" that has been
manifested through its government and through
liberalism as a political and popular movement has
during most of the post-World War II period been
apologetic and half-hearted. We saw tragic evidence of that fact with regard to one world situation after another in my examination of "Liberal-

ism and a World in Revolution."

Specific aspects of the relation to anti-Communism

1. The playing down of the problem of Communism, while virtually all anti-Communists are subjected to unrestrained attack.

An attitude that has run through the literature for many years is that Communism has not been a significant problem, but has been an exaggerated "Red bogey" that has been conjured up by those who are hysterical and overreactive. This downplaying of the problem of Communism has been accompanied by an attack upon almost all efforts of an anti-Communist nature.

This attack has been so continuing and widespread that we would be wise to realize that it has had very little to do with the alleged clumsiness or insensitivity of any particular expression of anti-Communism. This is true even though in each instance the attack has taken the form of a criticism of the specific form of anti-Communism. It is a mistake to think that the liberal intellectual culture has objected only to types of anti-Communism that have actually been "unfair" or "unfounded" or "abusive." The attack has been so general that every form of anti-Communist effort has been subjected to it. In what follows, I certainly won't try to cite the instances exhaustively, but I hope to give enough examples to illustrate the long-term, impersonal nature of the liberal intellectual culture's anti-anti-Communist position. The examples will also show that the attack on anti-Communists has been equally violent during the periods both before and after World War II--with the exception that there have been fewer such attacks since the mid-1950's precisely for the reason that anti-Communism itself has largely been silenced.

. As I begin my review, my notes from The

New Republic lead me to an article in 1928 that denounced "professional patriots," who were said to have had "anti-Russian prejudices." In 1929, an editorial chided school authorities for opposing the formation of a Young Pioneer [Communist] group in a high school.[1]

. In May, 1930, an editorial spoke of "the good old Red bogey" and called anti-Communism "witch-hunting." Later that year, an article by Conrad Seiler entitled "The Redmongers Go West" attacked the committee headed by Congressman Hamilton Fish that was investigating Communist activities in Los Angeles.[2]

. In early 1933, at the very time that thousands of Communist Party members were pouring into Ukrainian villages to enforce Stalin's decision to starve several million peasants to death there, an unsigned review in The New Republic was attacking a book by Dr. William I. Robinson for its "truculent" criticisms of the U.S.S.R.[3]

. In 1935, a New Republic editorial argued about the trial of eighteen radicals in Sacramento under a criminal syndicalism statute that "the real crime of these eighteen defendants is not being Communists--which they are--but fighting for decent wages and working conditions." An article by Ethel Thornbury in June of that year called a Wisconsin state senate committee "witch hunters" for investigating Communism at the University of Wisconsin. Then in August, the editors wrote about "Red baiting in the A.F. of L.," arguing that Communists should not be excluded from unions.[4]

. In 1937, an editorial spoke of "a Red-baiting session of Fordham University Alumni." In 1938, the editors wrote that "witch-hunting has no place in the progressive labor movement."[5]

. In 1939, the editors urged readers to send money to The New Masses. They said that "a real fight for the freedom of the press is going on

434

down at the offices of The New Masses, the only national Communist weekly...Well-to-do America is letting The New Masses starve, by not advertising in it, not buying it and not mentioning it." 6

. Also in 1939, an editorial charged that "the Dies Committee has been trying to smear the American Youth Congress as a Communist group." [Notwithstanding their charge of "smear," an editorial in July, 1940, reported that "the convention of the Youth Congress was dominated by Communists as previous ones have been."]7

. In 1941, Bruce Bliven reviewed Eugene Lyons' The Red Decade, attacking Lyons for his "heavy-handed ruthlessness...His fanaticism like theirs, only turned inside out."8

. In 1942, the editors wrote of "the irresponsibility of the Dies Committee" and said "Go away, Mr. Dies; go away." 9

. In 1943, they complained that "Robert Morss Lovett has at last resigned his post in the Virgin Islands," saying that "Dr. Lovett has been hounded from office by a small group of witch-hunters in Congress...They falsely charge him with being a Communist." Significantly, they added: "Even if the charge were true...."10

. In 1944, an editorial said that Congressman "Dies has never understood the principles of fair play...We hope...that Congress will put his committee [in]...the ash can."11

. In 1945, a New Republic review attacked a book by William Henry Chamberlin, which the review said "largely devotes itself to belaboring Soviet Russia." A review by Harvey J. Bresler said that Alexander Barmine "claims a special competence for his hatchet-job on the Soviet Union by virtue of his career as Red Army officer, industrial leader and diplomat."12

. In 1946, F. L. Schuman wrote this about

435

Victor Kravchenko's I Chose Freedom: "Take one Soviet renegade. Mix with several professional Russophobes. Stir well...The latest spicy dish from the Red-baiters' kitchen purports to be an autobiography of Victor Kravchenko, industrial engineer and Red Army captain, who fled...on April 4, 1944."[13]

. In 1947, an editorial called it "anti-Red hysteria" when Secretary of State George Marshall fired ten State Department employees. That same year, Bruce Bliven wrote of "many liberals and progressives everywhere terrorized into silence, with witch hunts...." Henry Wallace wrote that "the American imperialists who masquerade as defenders of American democracy against the Red menace...are interested in extending...the area of human exploitation."[14]

. After Congressman Martin Dies retired, Henry Wallace attacked his successors in 1947, speaking of "the intimidating tactics of Thomas, Rankin and the House Un-American Activities Committee."[15]

. In 1948, Daniel S. Gillmor said that 125 government employees were fired between 1942 and 1947 for disloyalty. This, he argued, was a case of "guilt by association." A week later, an editorial charged the Truman administration with "guilt by association" when Attorney General Tom Clark listed thirty-two organizations as subversive. Also in 1948, a New Republic editorial charged the New York City Board of Education with "bigotry and hysteria" for "attempting to bar from the teaching profession in New York known Communists or suspected Communists."[16]

2. The defeat of Senator Joseph McCarthy.

It should be noted that everything that I have just cited occurred before Senator Joseph McCarthy began his anti-Communist crusade in February, 1950. Everything that was eventually said about Senator McCarthy had already been charged

436

against countless other anti-Communists.

This record necessarily places Senator McCarthy's career and character in a different light than his current infamy dictates. In light of the record we have just traced, we know that Senator McCarthy would have been painted in the blackest terms regardless of the merits of his case or the validity of the methods he used in pursuing it. In 1938, J. B. Matthews published <u>Odyssey</u> <u>of</u> <u>a</u> <u>Fellow</u> <u>Traveler</u> in which he told of his own movement to anti-Communism after for several years having been one of the leading figures in Communist "front" organizations. What he said <u>in</u> <u>1938</u> fully fits Senator McCarthy's case twelve years later: "Any critic of Communism who hopes to escape the charge of red-baiting by holding his criticisms rigidly within the bounds of fact and good temper is simply deluding himself ...Any criticism of communists is, <u>per</u> <u>se</u>, red-baiting."

This is a caution that is important for any scholar today who wishes to make an objective evaluation of Senator McCarthy's anti-Communist crusade. Such a person will need consciously to set aside all preconceptions based on the Senator's present reputation. From my own study, I believe that four major conclusions will follow from an objective analysis:

• First, that, contrary to opinion today, Senator McCarthy's "methods" were, with only minor exceptions, legitimate, and were the same as those that liberals themselves had long favored in the investigation of other subjects.

• Second, that his personal style had both good and bad aspects about it. He was an articulate, militant slugger, consistently with his background as an ex-Marine and former prize fighter. His appearance and demeanor were gruff (which is something that was played upon unmercifully by the cartoonist Herblock, who never failed to picture him with a heavy five-o'clock shadow).

437

These elements are objectionable to people who especially value gentility--which is, after all, properly to be valued. On the other hand, he required every bit of his prize-fighter temperament if he were energetically to champion the anti-Communist cause. Such an effort would need to challenge the illusions that the Left harbored about Communism--a superhuman task. And it would need to articulate anti-Communism as a moral issue, so that Communism would come to be seen in the same light as Nazism. In doing these things, McCarthy was going against an enormous force. It meant facing all of the abuse that the liberal intellectual culture would inevitably muster. The abuse eventually dispirited and killed him. But until it did, he fought a harder fight than anyone had before, or has since.

. Third, that the cause that he championed was of the utmost validity and importance. When Senator McCarthy raised the issue of Communism as a moral imperative and insisted that it was not to be evaded through illusion or a desire to enjoy the comfort of a false moderation born out of blindness and insensitivity, he spoke for hundreds of millions who no longer had a voice to speak for themselves. His enemies, on the other hand, arose from two main sources. The first consisted of those who clung to or who wished not to acknowledge the illusions of the Left. The second were of a breed that has been quite common in twentieth century America: the millions who congratulated themselves on their sophistication while finding it personally and politically comfortable to evade moral judgments about Communism.

The five years immediately prior to 1950 had seen 600 million new victims fall under Communist dictatorship. Stalin was still in power and, shielded by a veil of silence from the world intellectual culture, held millions enslaved in his concentration camps--the Gulags that Aleksandr Solzhenitsyn was to tell us about years later after he had himself served in the camps for several years. These facts are essential for an

438

adequate perspective of Senator McCarthy's crusade. It is important, too, that we recognize something that I have never seen commented upon before: that the terrible years of the New Left, which were soon to follow, demonstated the enormous power of Leftist subversion in the United States itself. With these facts in mind, we can conclude that, whatever we may think about Senator McCarthy's lack of gentility, he was vastly superior to his detractors both in insight and moral sensibility.

This is especially true in light of the hypocrisy of such a man as Michael Straight, who during the entire McCarthy episode was the editor of The New Republic. During those years in which his journal continually lashed Senator McCarthy for unjustifiably "smearing" liberals with a Communist label, Straight knew the secret that was not to become public knowledge until 1981--that Straight had for several years been a member of the Communist espionage ring that included Guy Burgess and Anthony Blunt. Straight's own confession of the relationship came in his book After Long Silence, published in 1983. He said there that his last meeting with Burgess was in 1949-- long after the Hitler-Stalin Pact and just months before Senator McCarthy began his attacks on Communism. His book is full of self-serving rationalization, but he nevertheless saw his way clear to make one statement that is fully pertinent to my discussion of the McCarthy era. He wrote that "my fear and sense of guilt were secret, shared by no one. At the same time, as editor of The New Republic, I had to share my thoughts and my feelings week after week on the allegations of espionage that were surfacing and on the larger issues they raised." [17]

. Fourth, that it is impossible to credit the notion that Senator McCarthy was an insincere, self-serving demagogue. The only way that we can interpret his actions as fundamentally self-serving is if we presume that he was pathologically masochistic. He knew that he had the support of many Americans. He also knew that everything he said or did would bring down upon him an avalanche of vituperation. In an evaluation of his personal characteristics, he must be credited with enormous courage and with a willingness to subject himself to unremitting attack. It will serve as a litmus test for the detachment and courage of future historians to see what they say about his character.

3. McCarthy's defeat was a major victory for the Left and marked the silencing of articulate anti-Communism.

When Senator McCarthy was discredited all possibility of an articulate anti-Communism was crushed with him. The silencing of anti-Communism has been the greatest victory the American Left has enjoyed. Since the mid-1950's, anyone who has viewed Communism as a moral issue has been considered a bigot per se, not just by the intellectual culture but by the society at large. The result is that public figures have not been willing to cast the issues in that light. This is why Presidents Johnson and Nixon did not see their way clear to articulate an anti-Communist rationale for the Vietnam War. It is why Jane Fonda is still a popular actress in the United States despite her trip to Hanoi while American soldiers were dying a few miles to the south. It is the reason the liberation of Grenada had to be justified on other grounds than anti-Communism—even by the Reagan administration.

Not only was anti-Communism silenced as a conscious force; the attack upon it, which was waged for several decades and which came to a head in the defeat of Senator McCarthy, served yet another vitally important function for American liberalism. It obliterated American consciousness of the intimate connection that had existed between the liberal intellectual culture and Soviet Communism during the three decades prior to 1947, a connection that, if it had been fully comprehended in the context of the Cold War

440

following World War II, would have been thoroughly discreditable to liberalism.

Liberal authors had for many years charged that conservatives raised the issue of Communism in order to taint liberalism with it. TRB expressed a common theme in 1939 when he wrote that "the danger in the tactics of the Red hunt remains, as always, that the smear will be spread to anyone with the least progressive or liberal leanings." [18]

Interestingly, there is more to this than meets the eye:

In the first place, the charge that conservatives sought indiscriminately to smear liberalism with a Communist taint imputes something to conservatives that was far from their actual intent. Most of the time, conservatives bent over backwards to qualify what they said. They took great pains precisely to distinguish between Communism and liberalism. They did this both because they were aware of what they themselves thought was a vital difference and because they knew that they would be severely criticized if they did not make the distinction.

The second aspect is somewhat startling. It is that, in light of the record of the liberal intellectual culture between 1917 and 1947, conservatives _would_ _have_ _been_ _more_ _accurate_ if, instead of avoiding the imputation of a connection between Communism and liberal thought, they had spoken quite candidly about just how great and widespread the infatuation had been. "Liberalism" as a domestic agenda in American politics had clearly been distinguishable from Communism, but the attitudes of the liberal intellectual culture certainly had not been.

Conservatives' own anxiety not to overstep acceptable bounds caused them for the most part to join in a vitally significant obfuscation of ideological reality. One of the illusions under which the American people have lived for many years has

441

been a failure to have any conscious, articulated understanding of just how far left the liberal intellectual culture has been. That culture was pro-Communist before 1947, and has been, as we have seen, only slightly to the right of Soviet Communism during the four decades since. It has been a fact of the utmost significance that on a great many foreign policy issues there has been something of a perpetual "fifth column" within the United States. This has caused a seriously divided public opinion and has half-paralyzed the United States' response to Communist expansion. And yet, as true and as important as these conclusions are, they have been "off limits" in our political discourse. The result, as in so many other areas, is an insufficient understanding of reality.

4. Anti-anti-Communism has reflected the liberal critique of American culture.

From the perspective of the liberal intellectual culture, anti-Communism has been a manifestation of the very same "petty bourgeois" social ingredients that liberal social critics have so long deplored as coming from "ignoramuses" and "Babbitts." To understand this fully, the reader will do well to review the earlier chapter on "Liberalism and American Culture."

The continuing attack upon anti-Communists and eventually upon "McCarthyism" was an extension of the attack upon American culture that had been waged in the generation of Harold Stearns and Randolph Bourne. This stands out clearly in TRB's comment in May, 1950, that "'McCarthyism' really represents the revolt of the 'frustrated primitives' against the 'intellectuals' in the complexities of foreign affairs...."[19]

5. The continuation of the anti-anti-Communist posture since 1954.

Since the defeat of Senator McCarthy, there has been much less articulate anti-Communism for

442

the Left to oppose. But the pressure against any active anti-Communism has remained the same in the few instances that have arisen:

. In 1956, The New Republic's Gerald W. Johnson praised Arthur Miller for having "refused to betray his friends" by identifying who had attended Communist meetings with him in 1947.[20]

The reader needs to understand the significance of the fact that this had to do with meetings in 1947. That was a decade after the Soviet purges and eight years after the Hitler-Stalin Pact. It should be realized that only the really "hard" people retained a direct affiliation with Communism after the late 1930's. In the passage I have quoted, Johnson was treating Communist meetings in 1947 as though they were interchangeable with what liberalism has generally argued was the "excusable naivete and idealism of the pre-purge and pre-Pact period." In doing so, he showed that he was ready empathetically to defend the Communist Left even when there was no such "excuse."

. In August, 1957, a New Republic editorial commemorated the thirtieth anniversary of the executions of Sacco and Vanzetti. It said that "almost no one believes any more that Sacco and Vanzetti were guilty." It said that "they were victims in part of the anti-radical hysteria after World War I."[21]

. In 1961, TRB wrote that "the witch-hunters are riding again: Eastland's Internal Security Committee demands the names of all members of the 'Fair Play for Cuba Committee.'" [Two years later, Lee Harvey Oswald, a member of the Fair Play for Cuba Committee, assassinated John F. Kennedy.][22]

. In 1966, TRB wrote that "the House Un-American Activities Committee is out to smear the whole [New Leftist] protest movement with a red brush. Philip Abbot Luce...is the Golden Boy of changecoats."[23]

6. A double standard about investigations.

Liberal writing has condemned all Congressional and state legislative investigations of Communism over a span of many decades. This stands in stark contrast to the support that liberals have given to Congressional investigations into the Teapot Dome scandal, the munitions industry in 1935, the use of labor spies, the utility industry, and the Watergate scandal.

We have seen how in 1930 Congressman Hamilton Fish was called a "Redmonger" for investigating Communist activity in Los Angeles. In January, 1931, The New Republic accused his committee of "witch hunting activities." In 1934, an editorial charged that "California is engaging in an anti-Red campaign worthy of the worst days of Palmerism just after the great war." We have seen, too, how the Dies Committee was attacked in the late 1930's for its "Red-baiting" and its "slandering all sorts of innocent citizens without the slightest respect for truth or the ordinary amenities." Then in the late 1940's the House Committee on Un-American Activities was attacked for its "intimidating tactics" and for "depriving men of their good names." In 1948, a New Republic editorial referred to "the Hiss-Chambers circus," which it considered "gaudy." This was followed in the early 1950's by the hostility poured onto Senator Joseph McCarthy. Later, TRB called Senator James Eastland a "witch-hunter" for inquiring into the Fair Play for Cuba Committee. And in 1966, TRB charged that "HUAC is out to smear the whole protest movement...."24

All of this is to be compared with The New Republic's attitude toward investigations into other subjects.

An unsigned article in 1924 about the Teapot Dome investigation said that "the most shocking aspect...is the attitude displayed toward the revelations by a large part of the press. All

444

their indignation is saved for the mistakes and
frailties of the investigators...." An editorial
a month later said that "we wish Judge Gary or
anyone else would give us the name of a single
honest man whose reputation has been ruined by any
of the current investigations...We admit that the
work of the Senate Committee has not been in all
points perfect; Washington is not the place in
which to expect either perfection or an utter
absence of political partisanship."[25]

In early 1935, The New Republic declared that
"no Senatorial committee has ever performed a more
useful public work than the one investigating the
munitions business." In 1937, an editorial
attacked those who opposed a Congressional
investigation into the use of labor spies.[26]

Arthur Schlesinger, Jr., has told about
Senator (later Supreme Court Justice) Black's
investigation of utility companies in 1936. "The
methods employed by Black...underwent much
criticism then and later. Certainly his was no
model of fair and impartial investigation. He was
criticized most for his use of subpoenas duces
tecum--dragnet subpoenas...In response, Black
contended persuasively that he was 'proceeding in
exactly the same line of policy and under the same
type of proceedings' that had characterized every
investigating committee since 1792...Nor did Black
often permit his witnesses to amplify their
answers when they deemed 'yes' or 'no' inadequate
or misleading." Schlesinger defended Black, arguing that an important distinction is that he
inquired into actions, not into "opinions."[27]

7. Liberal intellectuals who repudiated the far
Left.

A large number of prominent intellectuals who
during the 1920's and 1930's were, in common with
the liberal intellectual culture generally, deeply
immersed in the Soviet infatuation moved rightward
on an individual basis, becoming staunchly anti-
Communist. Many of these eventually became the

intellectual core of the group that, led by William F. Buckley, Jr. (who of course had never been on the Left), founded National Review magazine. In the next section, we will see that liberal writing has been severely critical of the great majority of those who repudiated Communism and who then articulated an anti-Communist position.

John Dos Passos. In 1931, Granville Hicks wrote that "Dos Passos is a radical" and referred to "his communistic theories." Dos Passos enjoyed a close association with The New Republic until 1934. He told of his later repudiation of Communism in his book The Fourteenth Chronicle. A major factor in his change was the execution of a friend by the Communists during the Spanish Civil War.[28]

J. B. Matthews. Arthur Schlesinger, Jr., tells us that Matthews was the first chairman of the American League against War and Fascism, which Schlesinger calls "probably the most successful of the Communist fronts." Matthews wrote in his book Odyssey of a Fellow Traveler that he had been introduced to radicalism through the Social Gospel and had become a member of the Socialist Party before becoming a full-fledged "fellow traveler" in 1932 after returning from his fifth visit to the Soviet Union. In the mid-1930's, however, he moved sharply away from Communism. Matthews became a prolific anti-Communist writer, and served also as an investigator for the House Committee on Un-American Activities.[29]

William Henry Chamberlin. Chamberlin's father was a socialist, and he himself grew up favoring a "mild anarchism." He lived in Soviet Russia for twelve years, where he served as the Moscow correspondent for the Christian Science Monitor and married a Russian girl. He served as assistant book editor under Heywood Broun, and wrote under the pseudonym "A. C. Freeman." While he was in Soviet Russia, his opinions gradually evolved from pro- to anti-Soviet. They reached a breaking point with "the horrors of the First Five

446

Year Plan." In 1937, he authored a book <u>Collec-</u><u>tivism: A False Utopia</u>. Chamberlin eventually embraced Burkean conservative thinking.

Eliseo Vivas. An advertisement in <u>The New</u>
<u>Republic</u> in 1937 for <u>The Marxist Quarterly</u> listed
an article by Vivas on "The Class Nature of
Science." Vivas later became a leader within
American conservative thought.

Eugene Lyons. Lyons grew up in extreme
poverty on the east side of New York City. He was
the editor of the <u>Soviet Russia Pictorial</u> and
worked for the Soviet news agency TASS for four
years. After his break with Communism, he wrote
<u>The Red Decade</u> and throughout the rest of his life
was a leader among anti-Communist intellectuals.

Max Eastman. Eastman was editor of <u>The</u>
<u>Masses</u> and <u>The Liberator</u> during the years between
1913 and 1922. He then went to Europe for five
years. During a trip to Soviet Russia, he became
a follower of Leon Trotsky. He later wrote that
"it was in 1933 that my resolute faith in the
Soviet system began really to break down." In
1941, he even repudiated socialism. He authored
<u>Reflections on the Failure of Socialism</u> and was an
important member of the <u>National Review</u> group.

James Burnham. Burnham was active as a
radical from 1932 to 1940. In 1939, he was one of
the signers of the League for Cultural Freedom and
Socialism's statement calling upon people not to
abandon the ideals of revolutionary socialism. He
was at one time the editor of <u>The New Interna-</u>
<u>tional</u>, the chief theoretical journal of the Trot-
skyists. His break with Marxism came in 1940.
Until 1953, he was on the board of editors of <u>The</u>
<u>Partisan Review</u>. He resigned from that journal in
1953 to defend Senator Joseph McCarthy. Burnham
then wrote for <u>National Review</u> for twenty years.

Freda Utley. In 1940, Richard Rovere wrote
that Utley "is a British economist who during the
twenties became a Communist and, with her Russian

447

husband, went to live in Moscow. She lost her dream...when she found life there a nightmare and the Soviet economy a planned chaos. She left Russia in 1936, when the OGPU jailed her husband for a wisecrack made in Japan years earlier." Utley wrote The Dream We Lost, in which she denounced Stalinism, and The China Story about the fall of China to Mao.[30]

Frank Meyer. After having been a Communist organizer at Oxford and at the University of Chicago, Meyer began to lose his Communist faith after reading Friedrich Hayek's The Road to Serfdom. Meyer became a prominent member of the National Review circle, and is known for his advocacy of the "fusionist" position that would bring together Burkean conservatism and classical liberalism.

Willmoore Kendall. Kendall was a Trotskyist in the early 1930's, and sided with the Trotskyists in the Spanish Civil War, at which time he was the UPI correspondent in Madrid. His thinking evolved from a strong anti-Stalinism to anti-Communism. He continued on the Left until at least 1946, but in 1955 became an editor of National Review.

Whittaker Chambers. His conversion from Communism has been described in his book Witness, where he says that the culmination of a long process of breaking from Communism came when he "heard screams in Moscow." Chambers left the party in the early months of 1938. He was later the principal witness against Alger Hiss, developed strong religious conviction, and became an important member of the National Review circle.

William S. Schlamm. Born in Austria, Schlamm was a Communist as a teenager, but became anti-Stalinist when he was 25. During the 1930's, he considered himself a "non-Marxian socialist." He was an early editor of National Review.

Irving Kristol. At one time a Trotskyist,

448

Kristol became a co-founder of Encounter, a liberal anti-Communist journal. He has been a leading member of the neo-conservative movement in the 1970's and '80's, and is the author of Two Cheers for Capitalism.

Will Herberg. Norman Podhoretz tells us that Herberg was at one time a Lovestoneite (i.e., a follower of a splinter Communist group after its ouster from the Communist Party). Herberg, too, became eventually a prominent member of the National Review circle.

Louis Fischer. Fischer was during the 1930's one of The New Republic's and The Nation's most prolific apologists for Soviet Russia. He resided in Moscow between 1922 and 1938. In a book in 1935, he told how he traveled through the Ukraine in October, 1932, witnessing the famine; but he argued that the famine was the peasants' fault and that Stalin was justified in taking as much as sixty percent of their crop to make urban industrialization possible. Fischer was the author of a 1957 book, however, called Russia Revisited: A New Look at Russia and Her Satellites in which he concluded that "Communism has failed."[31]

Philip Abbott Luce. Luce was a leader in the Progressive Labor Party faction of the New Left until early 1965, when he broke with it after finding that it crushed the individuality of its members. His book The New Left is an excellent insider's account of radicalism in the late 1950's and first half of the 1960's.

It is pertinent to our analysis of liberalism, although not to our present discussion of liberalism's relation to former Communists, to point out that several other thinkers who became prominent within American conservatism had at one time been on the liberal side. Among those who my notes show moved to the Right in varying degrees, but without having been involved with Communism, were Henry Hazlitt, Al Smith, Walter Lippmann, Amos Pinchot, John T. Flynn, and Richard

Weaver.

8. The reaction of the liberal intellectual culture to those who repudiated the far Left.

Consistently with the far-Left nature of the liberal intellectual culture and its attitude toward anti-Communism generally, liberal thought has looked upon the great majority of those who abandoned Communism with suspicion and contempt. The attitude was expressed in 1946 by Max Lerner when he spoke of "the paranoid anti-Russian hysteria of former Communist believers grown disillusioned...." In 1953, Reinhold Niebuhr favorably compared those who left Communism but who did not speak up about it with those who became articulate anti-Communists: "It is ironic that men who extricated themselves with the least hurt to their spirit are now declared suspect by our vigilantes because they have not proved their repentance by adhesion to some dogma of the Right or by imitating its hysteria." In like fashion, Hannah Arendt made a distinction between "former Communists" and "ex-Communists." She said that the "former Communists" were those that did not have a "neurotic compulsion." [32]

These general attitudes have been reflected in bitter commentary about the specific individuals who became openly anti-Communist:

About Eugene Lyons, a New Republic editorial in late 1939 (after the Hitler-Stalin Pact and the joint attack by Germany and the Soviet Union on Poland) sneered that "Lyons...has served up another dish of Red-bait." Two years later, Bruce Bliven wrote a review of Lyon's The Red Decade in which Bliven attacked Lyons for "heavy-handed ruthlessness" and "fanaticism." [33]

About Willy Schlamm, a 1945 article by Richard Watts, Jr., who for several years was The New Republic's main author in support of the Chinese Communists, said that Schlamm "was one of the leftist of the left-wing boys until he saw the light and went in for the usual violent flight from Moscow."[34]

About Louis Fischer, Harvey J. Bresler wrote in 1946 that "Fischer's detailed indictment of Russia [is] but old wine in a new bottle." Richard Watts, Jr., spoke in 1947 of Fischer's "violent revulsion from Moscow."[35]

About James Burnham, George Soule wrote in 1947 that "he may be regarded as a sample of those who, having been too close for comfort to extreme left factions, have swung violently...[to] the fanatical anti-Communist line."[36]

About Lee Pressman, a New Republic editorial in 1950 said that "Pressman is the latest to renounce Communism, this time over Korea; somehow we can never get very enthusiastic over these repentant sinners."[37]

About Philip Abbott Luce, TRB argued in 1966 that "Luce...is the Golden Boy of changecoats."[38]

About Whittaker Chambers, John Kenneth Galbraith wrote in 1970 that "when I came to accept Hiss's guilt,...I never got around to forgiving Whittaker Chambers...Hiss hadn't made it to the Establishment but Chambers was all the way in as a patriot." Galbraith said, however, that he later grew to respect Chambers. The passage I have quoted is valuable in its demonstration of how much the intellectuals' alienation from the mainstream of America contributed to their unwillingness to accept those who repudiated Communism.[39]

9. Alienation and "the loyalty issue."

Until in the mid-1950's liberalism succeeded in its drive to silence anti-Communism, one of the most heatedly debated public questions in the United States was the "loyalty issue." Conservatives were profoundly suspicious of the loyalty of those on the Left, and sought, among other things, to prevent the employment of those who were of

451

doubtful loyalty by the United States government.

In light of all that we have covered, it ought to be apparent that this issue reflected something quite different from the "paranoia" to which liberal writing has generally ascribed it. The problem of disloyalty had its origins in two associated phenomena: the intense alienation of the liberal intellectual culture from the predominant American culture; and the very close affinity that a great many within the intellectual culture felt toward the Soviet Union over a span of three decades.

The relationship of the loyalty issue to alienation appeared clearly in a 1917 essay by Randolph Bourne. The essay described a fictional young intellectual who was in many ways similar to the character Benjamin in the 1960's movie "The Graduate." Bourne described him as in "a rather constant mood of futility." I would have us note the following passage, which relates directly to the attitudes that have constituted the root cause of the "loyalty issue": "With his groping philosophy of life, patriotism has merely died as a concept of significance for him. It is to him merely the emotion that fills the herd when it imagines itself engaged in massed defence or massed attack. Having no such images, he has no feeling of patriotism." [40]

Another passage, this time by Edmund Wilson, also illustrates the relationships extremely well. Looking back in 1952, Wilson told how "the writers and artists of my generation" had reacted to the Great Depression:

"The next month the slump began, and...a darkness seemed to descend. Yet, to the writers and artists of my generation who had grown up in the Big Business era and had always resented its barbarism, its crowding-out of everything they cared about, these years were not depressing but stimulating. One couldn't help being exhilerated at the sudden unexpected collapse of that stupid

452

gigantic fraud. It gave us a new sense of freedom; and it gave us a new sense of power to find ourselves still carrying on while the bankers, for a change, were taking a beating...[W]e wondered about the survival of republican American institutions; and we became more and more impressed by the achievements of the Soviet Union, which could boast that its industrial and financial problems were carefully studied by the government, and that it was able to avert such crises."41

It is fitting that I should conclude this series of books about the modern predicament, which have occupied me these past 21 years, with this quote from Wilson. It captures the essence of the alienation of the intellectual and of the immense consequences that have flowed from it.

NOTES

1. New Republic, February 22, 1928, pp. 2, 3; New Republic, November 20, 1929, p. 360.

2. New Republic, May 14, 1930, p. 336; New Republic, November 12, 1930, p. 346.

3. New Republic, March 8, 1933, p. 112.

4. New Republic, January 30, 1935, p. 315; New Republic, June 19, 1935, p. 158; New Republic, August 14, 1935, p. 6.

5. New Republic, April 7, 1937, p. 251; New Republic, January 26, 1938, p. 324.

6. New Republic, May 10, 1939, p. 4.

7. New Republic, December 13, 1939, p. 215; New Republic, July 15, 1940, p. 69.

8. New Republic, October 6, 1941, p. 433.

9. New Republic, September 7, 1942, p. 268.

10. New Republic, March 27, 1944, p. 397.

11. New Republic, May 22, 1944, p. 695.

12. New Republic, February 26, 1945, p. 309; New Republic, August 20, 1945, p. 228.

13. New Republic, May 6, 1946, p. 667.

14. New Republic, July 14, 1947, p. 8; New Republic, November 3, 1947, p. 19; New Republic, December 29, 1947, p. 11.

15. New Republic, September 1, 1947, p. 14.

16. New Republic, May 31, 1948, p. 17; New Republic, June 7, 1948, p. 5; New Republic, July 12, 1948, p. 8.

17. Michael Straight, After Long Silence (New York: W. W. Norton Company, 1983), p. 231.

18. New Republic, December 6, 1939, p. 189.

19. New Republic, May 22, 1950, p. 4.

20. New Republic, August 6, 1956, p. 10; see also New Republic, May 27, 1957, p. 8.

21. New Republic, August 27, 1957, p. 7.

22. New Republic, May 22, 1961, p. 2.

23. New Republic, August 27, 1966, p. 4.

24. New Republic, November 12, 1930, p. 346; New Republic, January 28, 1931, p. 283; New Republic, August 1, 1934, p. 305; New Republic, December 14, 1938, p. 160; New Republic, September 1, 1947, p. 14; New Republic, December 8, 1947, p. 10; New Republic, December 13, 1948, p. 5; New Republic, May 22, 1961, p. 2; New Republic, August 27, 1966, p. 4.

25. New Republic, April 2, 1924, p. 134; New

Republic, May 7, 1924, p. 269.

26. New Republic, January 16, 1935, p. 259; New Republic, February 10, 1937, p. 2.

27. Arthur M. Schlesinger, Jr., The Politics of Upheaval (Boston: Houghton Mifflin Company, 1960), pp. 320-321, 323.

28. New Republic, June 24, 1931, p. 157.

29. Schlesinger, Politics of Upheaval, pp. 199, 198.

30. New Republic, September 23, 1940, p. 424.

31. Louis Fischer, Soviet Journey (Westport: Greenwood Press, 1973), first published in 1935.

32. New Republic, September 16, 1946, p. 324; New Republic, October 12, 1953, p. 14; New Republic, November 9, 1953, p. 16.

33. New Republic, December 20, 1939, p. 219; New Republic, October 6, 1941, p. 433.

34. New Republic, December 3, 1945, p. 742.

35. New Republic, September 30, 1946, p. 419; New Republic, December 29, 1947, p. 29.

36. New Republic, March 24, 1947, p. 32.

37. New Republic, September 11, 1950, p. 4.

38. New Republic, August 27, 1966, p. 4.

39. New Republic, March 28, 1970, p. 17.

40. Quoted in Henry May (ed.), The Discontent of the Intellectuals: A Problem of the Twenties (Chicago: Rand McNally & Company, 1963), at p. 17.

41. Edmund Wilson, The Shores of Light (New York: Farrar, Straus, 1952), pp. 498-499.

INDEX

322
"Black Revolution,"
333, 338
Blair, John M., 265
Blanshard, Paul, 263
Bliven, Bruce, 78, 89,
93, 165, 174, 275,
435, 436, 450
Blunt, Anthony, 167
Bonjean, Charles M.,
110, 293
Bourne, Randolph, 56,
184, 203, 452
Boynton, Percy H., 275
Brailsford, H. N., 74,
79, 401
Brandeis, Louis, 64-65,
69, 84
Branfman, Fred, 414
Brannan Plan, 105
Brazil, Nazi threat to,
371
Brecht, Bertolt, 369
Bresler, Harvey J.,
435, 451
Bridges, Harry, 303
Briggs, Walter, 399
Brogam, D. W., 353
Bromwich, David, 312
Brooks, Peter, 329
Broun, Heywood, 446
Brown, Norman O., 319
Bruce, Lenny, 345
Brustein, Robert, 317,
318, 326, 335, 347,
348, 350
Brzezinski, Zbigniew,
373
Buenker, John D., 69,
108
Burger, Warren, 245
Burgess, Anthony, 319
Burgess, Guy, 167
Burkean conservatism,
13, 191-193

Burnham, James, 447, 451
Burns, James MacGregor,
124, 137, 291
Burroughs, William S.,
315
Buttinger, Joseph, 411

Care, Norman S., 123
Carlyle, Thomas, 185
Carmichael, Stokely, 333
Carr, E. H., 369
Carter Administration,
134-136, 380, 418
Carter, Jimmy, 29, 122,
146, 189
Chafee, Zechariah, 240
Chamberlain, John, 63,
91, 95, 200, 401
Chamberlin, William
Henry, 94, 368, 435,
446-447
Chambers, Whittaker, 448,
451
Chase, Edward, 281
Chavez, Cesar, 217
Chicago confrontation,
1968, 331-332
Child, Frank C., 412
Chile, 379, 382, 415-416
China, 393, 399, 404-406
Christian, Shirley, 418
Church, Frank, 366
Churchill, Winston, 384
"Civil Liberties," 212-
215
Civil Rights, conserva-
tive view on, 217-218
Civil Rights movement,
32-36, 102, 117, 129,
130, 144
Civil War, post-, period,
18-19, 52-56
Civil War, pre-, period,
45-52
Clark, Tom, 436

464

465